OXFORD HISTORICAL M

GOTHS AND ROMANS
332–489

P. J. HEATHER

CLARENDON PRESS · OXFORD

Oxford University Press, Walton Street, Oxford OX2 6DP

Oxford New York
Athens Auckland Bangkok Bombay
Calcutta Cape Town Dar es Salaam Delhi
Florence Hong Kong Istanbul Karachi
Kuala Lumpur Madras Madrid Melbourne
Mexico City Nairobi Paris Singapore
Taipei Tokyo Toronto
and associated companies in
Berlin Ibadan

Oxford is a trade mark of Oxford University Press

Published in the United States by
Oxford University Press Inc., New York

First published 1991
First issued as an Oxford University Press paperback 1994

British Library Cataloguing in Publication Data
Data available

Library of Congress Cataloging in Publication Data
Heather, P. J. (Peter J.)
Goths and Romans, 332–489/by P. J. Heather.
p.   cm.—(Oxford historical monographs)
Includes bibliographical references and index.
1. Goths.   2. Migration of nations.   3. Rome—History—Empire.
284–476.   I. Title.   II. Series.
D137.H43   1991
936–dc20   91–12261
ISBN 0-19-820234-2
ISBN 0-19-820535-X(p.b.)

3 5 7 9 10 8 6 4 2

Printed in Great Britain
on acid-free paper by
Biddles Ltd.
Guildford and King's Lynn

TO
MY MOTHER

PREFACE

This monograph is a direct descendant of my doctoral thesis, 'The Goths and the Balkans AD 350–500'. Much of the action, especially of Parts II and III, is still set in the Balkans, but the change of title reflects a genuine shift of emphasis. The provincial communities of the Balkans, in my original conception, were to be a major topic for consideration, and there is indeed more than sufficient material available to explore the ways in which their reactions to immigrant tribal groups, and particularly the Goths, differed from those of emperors and their advisers based in Constantinople and Ravenna. My studies have been hijacked over the years, however, by the Goths themselves. This had already happened to a considerable extent by the time I completed the thesis, and when I eventually decided—with much regret—that there was simply no room in this book to deal properly with the Balkan provincials, and hence to omit them, it was the final acknowledgement of a long-standing change of direction.

The Goths are not, of course, a neglected subject. A fine tradition of German scholarship stretches back over a hundred years or more, and Schmidt's *Die Ostgermanen* remains quite indispensable. For the Anglo-Saxon audience, the many works of Edward Thompson have made the subject accessible and proved a constant source of inspiration. There has also been a considerable amount of recent work. In the past few years have appeared the very welcome English translation of H. Wolfram's *History of the Goths*, two major contributions to the history of the Ostrogoths by T. S. Burns, together with a re-evaluation of the career of Alaric by J. H. W. G. Liebeschuetz. What follows owes a tremendous amount to all these scholars.

My main justification for producing yet another book on the Goths, and the main reason why the Balkan provincials lost out to them as my studies progressed, is that I have been led to undertake a thorough reconsideration of the work of Gothic history composed in *c*.550 by one Jordanes, the *De origine actibusque Getarum* or *Getica*. Part I in particular is devoted to this task and develops a number of related lines of argument. Chapter 1 attempts to show that all modern accounts of Gothic history between the third and sixth centuries—from their arrival in what is now the south-western USSR to the foundation of Gothic successor states in western Europe—to a very considerable extent follow an interpretative framework that Jordanes supplies. More contemporary sources suggest, however, that this framework is quite misleading in its account of the history of Gothic political groupings and of the dynasties who ruled them. In particular, the Hunnic invasions (from *c.*370 onwards) emerge as a complete watershed in Gothic history, one social and political order among the Goths being destroyed, and a new one created. In the course of these invasions, a number of Gothic groups moved into the Roman Balkans in two major waves (I use the word deliberately, although it is currently unfashionable), one in the late fourth century, the other in the third quarter of the fifth. The constituent groups of these waves had no history of close political association in the immediate past, but, once inside the Empire, eventually united themselves to create respectively the Visigoths and Ostrogoths who founded successor states to the Roman Empire in western Europe. New dynasties also emerged at this time to lead the new political units.

Chapter 2 attempts to establish why the *Getica* should contain a quite different view of Gothic history, in which both the Visigoths and Ostrogoths are held to have existed before the Hunnic invasions, with Amals and Balthi already at their head. To do this, the chapter considers its sources, the methods of composition employed, and the influences at work upon its author, or perhaps authors. For Jordanes drew on the now lost *Gothic History* of Cassiodorus, and a further, much more mysterious work on the same subject by a certain Ablabius. The *Getica* contains many such twists and turns, and has provoked much scholarly interest. To do justice to both Jordanes and this scholarship, I have not confined myself simply to the question of why its vision of Gothic history should be so misleading, but have attempted to develop an answer in the context of a broader interpretation of the *Getica* as a whole. This is particularly necessary because since Momigliano's compelling study ('Cassiodorus and the Italian Culture of His Time') much of the debate concerning the *Getica*, it seems to me, has focused on just a few passages of the text, and not taken the work as a whole.

Parts II and III investigate the two phases in Gothic history which emerge from Part I as criticial to the reordering of Gothic society. After examining the Goths before the Hunnic invasions, Part II deals with the forty or so years after 376 in which the Visigoths were created, largely in the Balkans, out of a number of Gothic (and some other) groups who united to preserve their independence and integrity in the face of hostile Roman power. Part III deals with the events in the same region *c.*450–90, which saw the creation of the Ostrogoths. The approach followed in both parts is essentially the same, using detailed contemporary sources to explore exactly how and why Gothic groups re-formed themselves in this way. The importance of Roman interference and Gothic responses to it, it is argued, are crucially important to the process, so that the discussion operates within a framework of diplomatic history. The date-limits of this study have been chosen with this in mind. Constantine's treaty with the Goths (332) marks the opening of the first phase of Gotho–Roman relations about which we are at all well informed. The choice of 489 for the lower limit is meant to dampen any expectation in the mind of the reader that I shall deal in any substantial way with the history of the independent Gothic kingdoms after the fall of the western Roman Empire. This monograph is firmly devoted to the prehistory of Visigothic Gaul and Ostrogothic Italy.

The three parts of the study are to a considerable extent self-contained, and can, I hope, be read by themselves. At the same time, the many cross-references underline the fact that they are also closely related; it is the re-evaluation of Jordanes which generates the need for a closer examination of the Balkan phases of Gothic history. The conclusion also attempts to pull together the main threads common to the three parts, and to set them in the context of recent scholarly debate on the nature of the tribal groups that invaded the Roman Empire from the late fourth century onwards. The argument is neither comprehensive nor conclusive at this point, but the re-evaluations of Jordanes and the Balkan phases of Gothic history undertaken here do suggest some lines of thought which differ in significant ways from some of those currently in vogue.

A note on names is more than usually necessary. There were of course no standard transcriptions of Gothic names into Latin and Greek, and the sources present a bewildering number of variants for most names. I have generally used the Latinized forms which will be familiar to most readers and which are enshrined in *PLRE*. For names offering the choice of endings *-mer* or *-mir*, I have adopted the former (*-mer* = 'famous'). I discuss the likely original Gothic names only when some historical point is at issue, and any reader requiring further guidance should consult M. Schönfeld, *Wörterbuch der altgermanischen Personen- und Völkernamen*. Faced with the particular problem of two Theoderics fighting one another in the 470s and 480s, I have been persuaded by wise heads to call the leader of the Thracian Goths by his nickname Strabo, the Squinter. I hope that this will clarify the action. For the sake of any undergraduate readers, I quote most sources in translation. The classicizing historians Eunapius, Olympiodorus, Priscus, and Malchus are quoted in the translation of R. C. Blockley, Ammianus Marcellinus in that of J. C. Rolfe, and Jordanes in that of C. C. Mierow; I have on occasion modified their translations. Other translations either are my own, or are credited at the appropriate point.

My final and deeply pleasurable task is to thank all those from whom I have received help and encouragement in the course of the decade or so in which I have been working, in one way or another, on this project. The trustees of Dumbarton Oaks awarded me a Pre-Doctoral Fellowship for the academic year 1985/6, without which the doctoral thesis on which this study is based would probably not have been completed. Since 1987 I have been extremely fortunate in holding the Robert Henry Murray Fellowship in History at Worcester College, Oxford. I should like to express my gratitude to the trustees of the endowment and to the Fellows of the College for my appointment, and, in particular, to thank the latter for providing a highly stimulating, but at the same time relaxed and enjoyable environment for work. Many thanks too to the staff of the Bodleian and Ashmolean libraries, who are always ready to help.

On a more personal note, I owe an enormous amount to Dr J. D. Howard-Johnston and Dr J. F. Matthews, the supervisors of the thesis on which this monograph is based, who kept both me and it on the rails. James Howard-Johnston also first inspired me to take up research, and John Matthews's sense of humour is so strong that he managed to read it all again as sub-editor for the Oxford Historical Monographs Committee. Many thanks too to

Henry Mayr-Harting for wise advice and for recommending my thesis to the committee for publication. My examiners, Professor J. H. W. G. Liebeschuetz and Mr B. Ward-Perkins, made many pertinent observations and suggestions, which have been gratefully received. Wolf Liebeschuetz also very kindly let me see a typescript of *Barbarians and Bishops* before publication. Many friends have read large parts of what follows, and/or discussed its contents with me to my great benefit. In particular I should like to thank John Hudson, Neil McLynn (whose influence on Part II is much greater than might appear), Bryan Ward-Perkins, Mary Whitby, Michael Whitby, Mark Whittow, and Mark Vessey. Last, but not least, my copy-editor Leofranc Holford-Strevens has saved me from much inelegance and many errors, for all of which I would like to express my gratitude.

This book is dedicated to my kin group by blood and marriage, who are much more harmonious than some of their Gothic counterparts, and particularly to Gail and my soon-to-be offspring (whether she or he).

Worcester College, Oxford

FIGURES

ABBREVIATIONS

AM	Ammianus Marcellinus
Blockley	R. C. Blockley, *The Fragmentary Classicising Historians of the Later Roman Empire: Eunapius, Olympiodorus, Priscus and Malchus*, 2 vols. (Liverpool, 1981, 1983)
Chrysos	E. K. Chrysos, *Τὸ Βυζάντιον καὶ οἱ Γότθοι* (Thessalonica, 1972)
Demougeot	E. Demougeot, *La Formation de l'Europe et les invasions barbares*: i. *Des origines germaniques à l'avènement de Dioclétien* (Paris, 1969); ii. *De l'avènement de Dioclétien (284) à l'occupation germanique de l'Empire romain d'Occident (début du VIᵉ siècle)* (Paris, 1978)
JAH	*Journal of African History*
Jones	A. H. M. Jones, *The Later Roman Empire: A Social, Economic and Administrative Survey*, 3 vols. (Oxford, 1964)
JRAI	*Journal of the Royal Anthropological Institute*
Maenchen-Helfen	O. J. Maenchen-Helfen, *The World of the Huns* (Berkeley, 1973)
Mommsen	Th. Mommsen, edn. of Jordanes (*MGH AA* v. 1; Berlin, 1882)
Paschoud	F. Paschoud, Budé edn. of Zosimus, 3 vols. in 5 (Paris, 1971–89)
RgA	*Reallexikon der germanischen Altertumskunde*, 2nd edn. (Berlin, 1973–)
Schmidt	L. Schmidt, *Geschichte der deutschen Stämme bis zum Ausgang der Völkerwanderung: Die Ostgermanen*, 2nd edn. (Munich, 1933)
SCIV	*Studii şi cercetări de istorie veche şi arheologie*
Stein	E. Stein, *Histoire du Bas-Empire*, ed. and trans. J. R. Palanque, 2 vols. (Paris, 1949, 1959)
Wolfram	H. Wolfram, *History of the Goths* (Berkeley, 1989)

CONTENTS

PART I

JORDANES AND GOTHIC HISTORY

1

RECONSTRUCTING GOTHIC HISTORY

This chapter will attempt briefly to introduce the reader to the broad outlines of the political history of the Goths in the migration period (*c*.350–500), surveying the major surviving sources, both literary and archaeological, and how they have been pieced together in modern historical reconstructions. While much of the detail of our knowledge has been preserved by writers falling within the Graeco-Roman classicizing historical tradition, the much less full and, in matters of detail, often inaccurate account of Gothic history in the *Getica* of Jordanes has nevertheless played a crucial role. Written in the mid-sixth century, it is the only source which purports to provide an overview of Gothic history in our period, and has decisively influenced all modern historians of the Goths. This chapter will attempt first to demonstrate the extent of Jordanes' influence, and then to test the reliability of the *Getica* against what can be gleaned from our other sources.

A. *Sources*

The available sources pose many problems for anyone trying to reconstruct the tribal world of the Goths and its evolution. There probably never was a tradition of Goths' writing history in Gothic, and few documents illustrative of tribal life have survived. Even the Visigothic Law Codes refer largely to the Gallo-Spanish kingdom, which combined both Romans and Goths. Literary Gothic was created by Ulfila and his disciples so that they could translate the Bible, and seems to have been confined largely to the religious sphere. Little now survives apart from a substantial part of the New Testament.[1]

---

[1] On Ulfila, see Streitberg, *Die gotische Bibel*, i, pp. xiii–xxv; cf. Thompson, *Visigoths*, pp. xiii ff. For Ulfila's linguistic achievement, see Friedrichsen, *Gothic Version of the Gospels* and *Gothic Version of the Epistles*.

Archaeological investigation has provided some properly Gothic material to supplement the literary evidence. Gothic material culture can be followed from the first two centuries AD, when the Goths seem to have occupied lands in what is now Poland, to the time that they entered the Roman Empire. This kind of evidence does not greatly assist the kind of study attempted here, concerned with the evolution of the Goths in the face of changing political and strategic circumstances, because broad cultural areas cannot be equated with particular tribal groups. Separate Gothic political units within cultural areas cannot be distinguished, nor can Goths be differentiated from other ethnic groups sharing essentially the same material culture. This is not to deny the value of archaeological insights into cultural influences at work upon the Goths, and the distribution of wealth.[2] As we shall see, however, political events were the main driving force behind changes to the Goths between *c*.350 and 500, and the more precise (if more limited) information provided by Graeco-Roman authors must be our main concern.

Literary works of many kinds refer to the Goths, but a succession of narrative histories have particular importance. Belonging to a tradition reaching back to Herodotus and Thucydides (and hence often labelled classicizing), all had at their core a detailed account of roughly contemporary events, although substantial introductions sometimes covered earlier periods, and they often did not describe the reign of the current emperor.[3] A chain of Graeco-Roman historians from Eunapius to Theophylact Simocatta thus provides us with detailed accounts of different sections of our period, and it is essentially the collective testimony of these historians which makes it possible to study Gothic history in worthwhile detail. This, of course, has its disadvantages. Not only were these authors not themselves Goths, but they can also be hostile towards them, since Gothic migrations often brought severe disruption to the Empire. There are, moreover, gaps in the sequence of histories, and some works survive only in fragments.

---

[2] A good introduction is Todd, *Northern Barbarians*, 55 ff. (esp. 86–9, 90–2). For the early period, see Hachmann, *Goten und Skandinavien*, 221 ff.; cf. Burns, 'Early Gothic Migrations'. See also Ch. 3.

[3] See generally Blockley, vol. i, esp. 86 ff.

One other literary source, Jordanes' *Getica*, allows us at least partial first-hand access to the Gothic tribal world. Drawing on the lost Gothic histories of Ablabius and Cassiodorus, it was put together in Constantinople around AD 550 by a man of Gothic origins. Two features have made it central to modern historical reconstructions. First, it covers the entire sweep of Gothic history. Jordanes traces the Goths' origins back to Scandinavia, and follows their fortunes to the founding of Gothic successor states to the Roman Empire in western Europe, and, in the case of Ostrogothic Italy, even covers its destruction. This is in marked contrast to the discontinuous record of the Goths in the surviving classicizing histories. Second, there is a Gothic origin to some of the *Getica*'s material, which makes it unique among surviving sources. It specifically refers, for instance, to Gothic songs and tales recording Filimer's migration to the Black Sea (4. 28), and the deeds of Gothic heroes (Eterpamara, Hanala, Fritigern, and Vidigoia, 5. 43). The death in battle of King Theoderic I is also said to have stimulated further compositions (41. 214).[4]

The mark of such oral history on the *Getica* seems to go some way beyond this handful of explicit references. Origin-tales for Gepids and Huns come from such a tradition (this is stated specifically for the Huns). In both cases, the names of peoples who were on occasions in conflict with the Goths are derived from Gothic words with derogatory connotations. 'Gepid', according to Jordanes, comes from the Gothic *gepanta* meaning 'slow', since the Gepids lagged behind in the crossing from Scandinavia. The point of this derivation is made explicit (17. 95),

because, as I have said, *gepanta* signifies something slow and stolid, the word Gepid arose as a gratuitous name of reproach. I do not believe this is very far wrong, for they are slow of thought and too sluggish for quick movement of their bodies.

The name of the Huns, likewise, is derived from *Haliurunnae*, a type of witch. The Huns (according to the Goths) were the offspring of these witches and some evil spirits (24. 121–2). The derivations are nonsense, but, at the same time, the very stuff of a

[4] Oral traditions are also referred to at 11. 72 and 14. 79. This material has long been recognized; e.g. Mommsen, pp. xxxvii ff.

chauvinistic oral tradition. A comparable example is provided by Olympiodorus, who records the origin of a similarly derogatory Vandal name for the Goths (fr. 29. 1).[5]

Some sections of narrative may also derive from oral tradition. We hear of King Berig, for instance, who led the Goths' migration from Scandinavia (4. 25), and of King Filimer guiding them into lands above the Black Sea (4. 28). Both are events of the distant past, and Gothic oral history seems the most likely source of these stories. Archaeological evidence also seems to suggest that the move to the Black Sea, at least, was not an organized tribal migration under a single leader, but that many smaller groups moved individually over an extended period.[6] If so, the *Getica*'s stories would resemble those found in modern oral traditions, where important tribal events of the past are often preserved in highly personalized form, pictured as the inspiration of one individual.[7] In similar vein, the *Getica* alleges that warfare between the Goths and Gepids was caused by the greed of the Gepid king Fastida. Underlying tensions and rivalries between two great peoples have thus been simplified and personalized into the deeds of one man. This had the additional benefit of blaming the Gepids for originating a quarrel (17. 97) which lasted into the sixth century, revealing, like the origin-tales, the mark of Gothic chauvinism.

The full range of Gothic oral history cannot be reconstructed from such material. At the very least, however, it would seem to have dealt with the origins of the Goths and their neighbours, Gothic migrations, and great kings of the past.[8] The sense of humour evident even in the fragments preserved by the *Getica* also warns us not to underestimate its inventiveness.

---

[5] Wolfram, 26 implicitly suggests that Olympiodorus' derivation of τροῦλοι (from the price paid by the Goths for Vandal grain in a time of famine) misunderstands the Vandal for 'troll'; it seems to me more likely that Olympiodorus knew what he was talking about.

[6] Hachmann, *Goten und Skandinavien*, pt. IV; cf. Burns, 'Early Gothic Migrations', 195 ff.

[7] e.g. Boston, 'Oral Tradition'; Henige, 'Oral Tradition and Chronology', 375; Miller, 'Listening for the African Past', 18 ff.; Berger, 'Deities, Dynasties'.

[8] For the range of material in modern traditions, see Finnegan, *Oral Literature in Africa*.

B. *Jordanes' Framework for Gothic History*

This uniquely Gothic character of some of its contents has greatly strengthened trust in the *Getica*'s overall account of Gothic history. Herwig Wolfram, author of the most recent history of the Goths, for instance, considers that Jordanes gives us unparalleled insight into the historical traditions preserved by the Amals, the royal clan to which Theoderic the Great belonged. Such traditions cannot, he argues, be used uncritically, but Wolfram believes that the Amals at least had originated in Scandinavia, as Jordanes reports, and accords this 'Amal house tradition' unique value.[9]

Given the nature of our other written sources, the importance of the *Getica* has lain not so much in its factual information, as in the framework it provides for Gothic history. The classicizing Graeco-Roman tradition preserves more detailed information, and its contemporary testimony often shows up errors in the *Getica*'s account of particular events. But this tradition, as we have seen, is not unbroken, and rarely makes specific the relation of different Gothic subunits to what might be termed 'the Gothic people as a whole'. The *Getica*'s general outline of Gothic history has thus come to provide the framework for the more detailed information available in classicizing histories.

For instance, Malchus of Philadelphia and John of Antioch describe in some detail a conflict between the two Gothic groups in the Balkans in the 470s and 480s, both confusingly led by Theoderics: one the son of Thiudimer, the other the son of Triarius. These sources give no sense of the origins of these groups and their conflict, but the *Getica*, while barely mentioning the dispute, provides it with a context. The son of Thiudimer, we are told, belonged to the Amal dynasty who had ruled the 'Ostrogoths' since they moved to lands above the Black Sea, while the son of Triarius was not an Amal (*Getica* 52. 270). The struggle has thus often been characterized as one between the legitimate ruler of the Ostrogoths and a breakaway group relying heavily on Byzantine support. In a similar way, the thread of 'Visigothic' history is

---

[9] Wolfram, *passim*, esp. 5 ff., 13 ff., and 248 for a more guarded comment; cf. Wenskus, *Stammesbildung und Verfassung*, 464. The Gothic origin of material in the *Getica* has long been crucial to its perceived value; cf. Goffart, *Narrators*, 23 ff., esp. 30–1.

followed through Ammianus, Eunapius, and Olympiodorus (the latter preserved in Zosimus and Sozomen). None of these earlier sources ever refers to 'Visigoths' as such, and unity is only given to the sequence of events by the *Getica*. This tells us that the Visigoths who fled south of the Danube in 376 (25. 131), had formed the other half of the Gothic people since their arrival north of the Black Sea (5. 42).

Examples could be multiplied, but the pattern is clear enough. Though certainly with reservations, all modern reconstructions of Gothic history have fitted information from Graeco-Roman historians into a historical framework provided by the *Getica*. This historical framework consists of a broad overview of Gothic tribal subdivisions, and of the dynasties who ruled them.

Of tribal subdivisions, the *Getica* reports that from the time they lived above the Black Sea (namely from the third century onwards), the Goths were divided into two groups, the Ostrogoths, so named because they lived to the east, and the Visigoths living to the west (5. 42, 14. 82). Since these two groups later formed the successor states in western Europe, this report has often been taken at face value to indicate that, from the mid-third century onwards, the Goths had been divided into two basic political units, which had a continuous history. An extra twist has been given to the argument by Ammianus Marcellinus, who records the existence of two Gothic subgroups in the fourth century, but names them Tervingi and Greuthungi. Many have simply supposed that these are simply alternative names for the Visigoths and Ostrogoths mentioned by Jordanes, and it has long been traditional to view the Tervingi as Visigoths, the Greuthungi as Ostrogoths, and to make no further alteration to the picture painted by Jordanes.[10] Such an approach obviously upholds Jordanes' account of Gothic tribal subdivisions in its entirety.

A slight, but noteworthy modification to this view has been adopted by a second strand of opinion, which has taken more note of third-century sources. These seem to show that at that date raids were being undertaken by groups much smaller than those referred to by Jordanes, and it has consequently been argued that the larger groups came into existence only in *c*.300, when the name

---

[10] e.g. Musset, *Germanic Invasions*, 36; Demougeot, ii. 325, 342; Thompson, *Visigoths*, 1–2; Latouche, *Les Grandes Invasions*, 44–5, 64–5; Halphen, *Les Barbares*, 6–7; Lot, *Les Invasions germaniques*, 50; Chrysos, 42.

Tervingi first appears in a Graeco-Roman source.[11] This is only a relatively minor chronological adjustment to Jordanes' account, however, and both these strands of opinion have essentially followed the *Getica* in supposing that there were two basic Gothic subgroups who had a continuous history from well before the Hunnic invasions to the time that they established successor states to the Roman Empire.

Wenskus and Wolfram, by contrast, have departed more substantially from Jordanes' account. They have successfully demonstrated that considerable disruption separates fourth-century Gothic groups from those who founded the successor states; the Tervingi are not simply the Visigoths by another name, nor the Greuthungi the Ostrogoths. The Hunnic invasions are seen as causing great disruption among the Goths, in the course of which some Tervingi became part of the Ostrogoths, and some Greuthungi part of the Visigoths. Both also highlight the degree to which non-Gothic groups were absorbed by the Goths in this period, Wolfram in particular seeing the Goths as a migrating army which anyone who could fight was allowed to join.[12] Yet even these scholars consider that the Goths were permanently divided in two from the third century onwards, and perceive a broad continuity between the two pairs. For Wolfram, the Tervingi and Visigoths are 'ethnically identical' (p. 24), and the two sets of names are alternative designations for the same groups. Tervingi and Greuthungi are the names each gave the other, where Ostrogoth and Visigoth are self-chosen, boastful names (p. 25). Thus even though Ostrogoths and Visigoths are in certain respects new peoples, there is nevertheless much continuity between them and the fourth-century Tervingi and Greuthungi.[13] This view

[11] Tervingi are mentioned in *Pan. Lat.* 11(3). 17. 1 of 291. For this modification to Jordanes, see Schmidt, 197 ff.; cf. Burns, *The Ostrogoths*, 5 ff., 29 ff., who suggests that Tervingi and Greuthungi were the smaller groups around whom the Visigoths and Ostrogoths formed.

[12] Wenskus, *Stammesbildung und Verfassung*, 471 ff. (applying his general conclusions to the Goths); Wolfram, *passim*, esp. 5–12 (an overview), with more detailed discussions at 231 ff. (the Visigoths) and 300 ff. (the Ostrogoths). See also 482 n. 1 and the title of his ch. 5: 'The "New" Ostrogoths'.

[13] Thus Wolfram, 248 considers that Theoderic the Amal's following in the 5th c. was composed of 'the majority of the Greutungian Ostrogoths who had been subjugated (by the Huns) in 375/376'. Wolfram (and Wenskus) would root much of this continuity in the survival of royal dynasties, see below.

again owes much to Jordanes, discussing the disruption caused by
the Huns within the *Getica*'s framework for Gothic history, and it
seems reasonable to conclude that all modern reconstructions of
the history of Gothic tribal subdivisions have broadly accepted the
Getica's account.

The influence of Jordanes is equally marked on modern accounts of the Goths' royal dynasties although the *Getica* is itself
somewhat ambiguous on this subject. At one point, it reports that
when the Goths were settled in their two basic groups above the
Black Sea, they served two ruling families: the Visigoths the
Balthi, and the Ostrogoths the Amals (5. 42). Since these dynasties
also ruled the successor states, it has often been supposed that each
subdivision of the Gothic people had its own ruling family which
maintained its position throughout the migration period, from say
the mid-third to the sixth centuries.[14] The *Getica* also reports,
however, that, before the arrival of the Huns, both Visigoths and
Ostrogoths were ruled by an Amal called Ostrogotha (17. 98).
And, apart from the one statement at 5. 42 which puts the two
dynasties on equal footing, Jordanes consistently presents the
Amals as much more important than the Balthi. This is partly the
result of differing depths of coverage; the Balthi receive few
mentions, whereas a whole passage is devoted to the genealogy of
the Amals (14. 79–81). But the point is also made explicit. The
Balthi are a noble lineage, but secondary to the Amals (29. 146),
and if the fifth-century Visigoths had realized they had an Amal
among them, they would certainly have chosen him to rule them
rather than representatives of the Balthi (33. 174–5). Overall, the
Amals have a special status as *Ansis* or demigods (13. 78).

Because the *Getica* incorporates these quite contradictory views,
a wide range of positions have been adopted by modern scholars
on the question of Amal and Balth. All, however, depend in some
way upon the *Getica*. Some have simply combined the views.
According to Wolfram, for instance, both families established
themselves before the Hunnic invasions, but the Amals always had
the greater prestige, 'demigods' where the Balthi were mere
mortals (pp. 14 ff., 30 ff.). The Amals also had the status of kings
in the fourth century (pp. 85 ff.), whereas the Balthi ruled the
'Tervingian Visigoths' as 'judges', wielding less than monarchical
power, and only transformed themselves into kings in the course of

[14] e.g. Musset, *Germanic Invasions*, 42 ff.

subsequent migrations (pp. 94 ff., 143 ff.). The influence of Jordanes on this view is obvious. The continuous pre-eminence of these two families is also one of the main reasons leading Wenskus and Wolfram to argue that there was some basic continuity in Gothic political organization, even after demonstrating that Tervingi and Greuthungi did not evolve neatly into Visigoths and Ostrogoths.[15]

A second group of opinion has taken the *Getica* at face value for the Amals, accepting that they ruled the Ostrogoths continuously from the third century to the sixth. The Balthi's lesser prestige, however, is taken to mean that they achieved prominence only at a later date. Schmidt, for instance, suggested that Alaric was the first Balth, because many discontinuities can be detected in the leadership of the Visigoths before his rise to power in the 390s.[16] This view received strong implicit support from Thompson, who argued that the Visigoths (= Tervingi) of the fourth century lacked any overall permanent ruler. These arguments can be combined to suggest that the 'Visigoths' had no ruling dynasty before the Balthi, of whom Alaric was the first representative.[17]

Although the *Getica*'s own ambiguities thus leave much room for disagreement, its influence on all of these major reconstructions of Gothic history is clear. Arranging the other sources around Jordanes, scholars have seen total, or, at least, broad continuity in tribal subdivisions from before the arrival of the Huns to the foundation of the successor states. Similarly, there is a consensus that at least one ruling family, the Amals, maintained pre-eminence throughout the period, and some would argue that the Balthi did the same. A source of the mid-sixth century has thus provided a framework for events, which took place between *c*.200–50 (the Gothic settlement in what is now the south-western USSR) and *c*.500 (the foundation of the Italian state). Within this framework, information from the fragmentary, but more detailed

---

[15] Wenskus, *Stammesbildung und Verfassung*, 322–3, 472 ff. is similar, although there is some disagreement on precise points; cf. Wenskus, 'Amaler' and 'Balthen'.

[16] Schmidt, 240 ff.

[17] Thompson, *Visigoths*, 43 ff.; Demougeot, ii. 335–6, 342 ff. A variation supposes that Amal rule over the Ostrogoths arose from competition between smaller-scale leaders of the 3rd c. For Schmidt, 201 ff., 240, the Amals rose to power with Ostrogotha in *c*.300, whereas Burns, *The Ostrogoths*, 35–6 and *History of the Ostrogoths*, 33 ff. chooses Ermenaric in *c*.350.

and contemporary accounts of the classicizing historians has been arranged. When they are examined in detail, however, their cumulative account of Gothic history proves to be incompatible with the framework commonly taken from the *Getica*. Where Jordanes paints a picture of broad continuity, these more contemporary sources suggest both that Gothic subdivisions were entirely redefined in the course of the fourth and fifth centuries, and that entirely new royal dynasties emerged to lead them.

C. *Gothic Tribal Subdivisions, c.350–500*

As we have seen, Ammianus Marcellinus mentions two fourth-century Gothic groups, the Tervingi and Greuthungi. Jordanes' *Getica*, written nearly 200 years later, also suggests that two Gothic tribal units existed at this time, but identifies them as the Visigoths and Ostrogoths, who eventually formed successor states to the Roman Empire. For Jordanes' view of Gothic history to be allowed to stand, the different sets of names must be shown to be alternatives for the same groups, or some direct continuity, at least, must be demonstrated between Tervingi and Greuthungi, and Visigoths and Ostrogoths.

When the history of the Goths in the migration period is reconstructed (in so far as that is possible) from the classicizing histories, a clear pattern emerges. They indicate that the Tervingi and Greuthungi fragmented into a number of smaller groups, some of whom then re-formed along new lines to create the 'Visigoths' and 'Ostrogoths', the latter terms being used to designate the two groups who eventually founded successor states in Spain and Italy. My discussion owes much to Wenskus and Wolfram, who have already demonstrated some of these discontinuities in Gothic political history, but the argument will suggest that the overall extent of this disruption was considerably greater than they envisage. Readers may also be surprised by the degree to which the size of various Gothic groups enters the discussion. The numbers of people participating in the great migrations of the fourth and fifth centuries is a question fraught with difficulties, but, in certain Gothic cases at least, an order of magnitude can be established with a fair degree of probability. These numbers underline the basic point being made, but even without them, it seems clear enough that Gothic political loyalties were completely redefined in the hundred years or so after 370.

Ammianus Marcellinus is the only source to describe in any detail the impact of the Huns upon the Goths in the 370s. From his account, it is clear that the Tervingi split into the two sizeable fragments.

1. Those who fled south of the Danube in 376 to seek asylum in the Roman Empire, led by Alavivus and Fritigern (AM 31. 3. 8 ff.). This group probably consisted of *c.* 10,000 men, suggesting a total, with non-combatants, of about *c.* 50,000 (p. 139).

2. A second group remained outside the Empire under Athanaric. According to Ammianus, the 'majority of the population' fled with Fritigern (31. 3. 8), but Athanaric's group was still powerful enough to drive some Sarmatians out of its new refuge (31. 4. 13), and may have maintained its independence into the 380s.[18] A third or quarter of Athanaric's original following would still have amounted to 3,000–5,000 men.

A similar process seems to have affected the Greuthungi, of whom the following fragments are known,

1. The group originally led by Ermenaric, which moved south of the Danube in 376 under Alatheus and Saphrax (AM 31. 4. 12–13; 5. 3). We have no explicit indication of its size, but it may have been broadly comparable to the 10,000 warriors of the first group of Tervingi (p. 139).

2. Ammianus also mentions a force led by Farnobius, which arrived at the Danube with Alatheus and Saphrax (31. 4. 12). It is unclear whether Farnobius was entirely independent, or whether Ammianus mentions him because this group later suffered a separate fate from the rest of the Greuthungi (31. 9. 3–4).

3. A group of Greuthungi led by Odotheus tries to cross the Danube in 386. The sources are rhetorical, but it was a large force, and its defeat occasioned an imperial triumph.[19]

---

[18] Athanaric was expelled by his remaining followers in *c.* 380 (pp. 337–8), but Achelis, 'Der älteste deutsche Kalender', 318–19 refers to the remains of 26 Gothic martyrs being brought into the Empire between 383 and 392. They had been martyred under Athanaric (Sozomen, *HE* 6. 37. 13–14), so that the remains must have come from some Tervingi left north of the Danube after 376.

[19] Zosimus 4. 35. 1, 38–9 (a doublet); *Cons. Const.*, s.a. 386 (*CM* i. 244); Claudian, *IV cons. Hon.* 626 ff.

In contrast to his account of the Tervingi, Ammianus does not make it explicit that the Huns caused the Greuthungi to fragment in the 370s; his narrative reads as though all the Greuthungi he knew (led before the Hunnic invasions by Ermenaric) fled south of the Danube in 376 (31. 3. 1–3; 4. 12–13; 5. 3). But since another large force of Greuthungi attempted to cross the Danube in 386, then either the Greuthungi must have fragmented in the face of Hunnic attacks, just as the Tervingi had done, or more than one independent group of Greuthungi had existed in south Russia before the Huns arrived. Both possibilities completely undermine the *Getica*'s picture of smooth political continuity.

Moreover, other Gothic groups, some of them quite substantial, came into contact with the Roman Empire in the fifth century,

1.   In 405/6 a pagan Goth, Radagaisus, led an invasion of Italy, seemingly from lands above the Danube. His force may have been multiracial, but the sources suggest that its core, like its commander, was Gothic. The sources preserve some unreliable figures for its total size, but it certainly consisted of over 10,000 warriors (p. 213).

2.   From at least the 460s another Gothic force had close political links with Constantinople and was settled by treaty in Thrace. Led by Theoderic the son of Triarius in the 470s, its military capacity was at least 10,000 men (p. 256).

3.   A Gothic group, led by Valamer and then his nephew Theoderic the Amal, emerged from the wreck of Attila's Hunnic Empire in the 450s and 460s, and again numbered at least 10,000 warriors (p. 248).

4.   A Gothic king Bigelis was killed by the imperial general Ardabur between 466 and 471. His group would not seem to have been large, making little impact in the sources.[20]

5.   Two smaller Gothic groups were established in the Crimea.[21]

The fourth-century origins of these Gothic groups of the fifth and sixth centuries are obscure, but all the Goths known from fourth-

[20] Jordanes, *Romana* 336; other Goths remained under Hunnic domination: Priscus fr. 49.
[21] Tetraxitae: Procopius, *Wars* 8. 4. 9 ff. ('not numerous'); Goths of Dory: id., *Buildings* 3. 7. 13 (3,000 strong).

century sources (with insignificant exceptions[22]) were south of the Danube by *c*.400. The arrival of more Goths from north of the river after this date would indicate, therefore, that other Gothic groups (whether Tervingi, Greuthungi, or something else) must have existed in the fourth century from whom these fifth-century groups were descended. The only other possible explanation is that the intervening years saw a Gothic population explosion, but the chaos and insecurity of the migration period seem to rule this out. Hence three other very substantial groups of Goths (those led by Radagaisus and the two Theoderics), along with other smaller ones, must be added to those already known from Ammianus' account of the break-up of the fourth-century Tervingi and Greuthungi. In sum, either two fourth-century confederations splintered into at least seven major component parts (eight counting fragment 2 of the Tervingi), or more than two independent Gothic groups already existed north of the Black Sea before the Huns attacked. Neither possibility supports Jordanes' picture of direct continuity between two Gothic subdivisions in the fourth century and the Visigoths and Ostrogoths who established the successor states. The point can be reinforced by examining the ways in which these fragments realigned themselves to produce the 'Visigoths' and 'Ostrogoths'.

Between the Tervingi and the Visigoths, there was undoubtedly some continuity. The Tervingi who fled south of the Danube in 376 (fragment 1: *c*. 10,000 men) provided a significant part of the Gothic force which gathered around Alaric and eventually established a kingdom in Gaul and Spain.[23] But Alaric's force also combined major contributions from two other Gothic groups: fragment 1 of the Greuthungi and the survivors of Radagaisus' attack on Italy. These Greuthungi were perhaps indistinguishable from the Tervingi by 395, and certainly by 408 (p. 191). The survivors of Radagaisus' force, previously drafted into the Roman army, joined Alaric in 408 (Zosimus 5. 35. 6). As far as we can tell, therefore, to create the Visigoths approximately 10,000 Tervingi joined with perhaps another 10,000 Greuthungi, and a further

---

[22] Some of Athanaric's Goths (fragment 2 of the Tervingi) remained north of the Danube (n. 18), and part of Odotheus' force (fragment 3 of the Greuthungi) returned north of the river under Gainas, but was not large enough to maintain its independence (Zosimus 5. 21. 6–22.3; *PLRE* i. 380).

[23] Cf. Wenskus, *Stammesbildung und Verfassung*, 475 ff.; Wolfram, ch. 3.

10,000 survivors from the force of Radagaisus. The group's overall size increased to *c*. 40,000 when large numbers of runaway slaves, again probably former followers of Radagaisus, attached themselves to Alaric's command (Zosimus 5. 42. 3). The Visigoths comprised large contingents from three sources of Gothic manpower, and there is no sign that they had previously operated together before the Hunnic invasions.[24]

The Ostrogoths, led to Italy by Theodoric the Amal, were likewise the product of an amalgamation, this time between the forces of the two Theoderics (groups 2 and 3 on p. 14). Again, there is no evidence that they had previously belonged to the same political unit, and, before unification, they even fought one another (Part III, *passim*). Like the Visigoths, the Ostrogoths were the product of a major realignment in Gothic society, and in no way a natural successor to any fourth-century political grouping. Nothing suggests that the forces of the two Theoderics had ever belonged to the Greuthungi, and the Greuthungi who entered the Empire in the fourth century (fragments 1–3 on p. 13) did not contribute to the Ostrogoths.[25]

There is thus no meaningful continuity between Tervingi and Visigoth, and Greuthungi and Ostrogoth.[26] Nor does the process outlined here seem to have been an evolution of one political configuration into another. Only between the Tervingi and the Visigoths do contemporary sources show any overlap in personnel, and even then, the Tervingi provided but a part of the new group. The classicizing historians' accounts suggest that one Gothic political structure was broken apart by the Huns in the late fourth century, and that periods of migration and of living within the Hunnic and Roman Empires produced a complete realignment in

---

[24] Cf. Rosenfeld, 'Ost- und Westgoten', 247–9. Wenskus, *Stammesbildung und Verfassung*, 473–4, 477 and Wolfram, 143 (less explicitly) envisage the Tervingi as the core of Alaric's Visigoths. On Radagaisus and the slaves, see further p. 214.

[25] Wenskus, 'Amaler' (revising *Stammesbildung und Verfassung*, 478 ff.), and Wolfram, 248 ff. argue that although the 'Greuthungian Ostrogoths' fragmented, Theoderic the Amal to a considerable extent reunited them. But there is no evidence that the constituent groups of the Ostrogoths had ever previously operated as a single unit (see below).

[26] The appearance of these names in sources other than Jordanes supports such a conclusion, see App. A.

Gothic society. The Visigoths were composed of previously separate groups who had all fled south of the Danube by the early fifth century, the Ostrogoths united equally separate groups who had remained north of the Danube for a longer period. More contemporary sources, in sum, differ markedly from the framework for Gothic history which has been taken from Jordanes; the twofold division of the Goths was the result of differing responses to the Hunnic invasions, and did not date back to the third or even the fourth centuries.

This suggests, more generally, that the *Getica*'s view of the tribal history of the Goths cannot simply be combined with information from the classicizing Graeco-Roman historians, as has been done in the past. Rather, we must make a conscious choice between contradictory views of Gothic history. Where Jordanes seems to place the origins of the Visigoth–Ostrogoth divide in the south-western USSR of the third century, more contemporary sources suggest that these two groups were the product of realignment taking place after *c*.370. There seems only one possible response to this disagreement. The view built up from more detailed contemporary sources must be preferred to the *Getica*'s later overview. The Hunnic invasions destroyed the political structure of the fourth century, and a new one was defined in the course of the migrations that these invasions stimulated.

Further confirmation that this is indeed the correct way to view Gothic history is provided by Procopius. He is the one classicizing historian of late enough date and sufficiently broad geographical scope to deal with both Gothic successor states, and he provides a very similar view of the origin of Visigoth and Ostrogoth to that reconstructed here. According to Procopius, the 'Visigoths' (Οὐισίγοτθοι) can be defined as those Goths who separated from the others at the time of the first Hunnic invasions in the late fourth century (*Wars* 3. 2. 7 ff.; 8. 5. 5 ff.). The 'Goths' (Γότθοι) who accompanied Theoderic to Italy, by contrast, are those who did not appear south of the Danube until the second half of the fifth century, after the destruction of the Hunnic empire (*Wars* 3. 2. 39–40). Procopius had no doubt that a Visigoth could be distinguished from a Goth (=Ostrogoth) by having crossed the Danube to escape Hunnic domination, and as we have seen, our better sources would suggest that here, at least, he was substantially correct.

Moreover, when Jordanes is reread with this view of Gothic history in mind, the strongest strand within even his work agrees that the Huns were primarily responsible for dividing Visigoths from Ostrogoths. This is demonstrated above all by the tripartite structure of the work. A first section deals with the united Goths (*Getica* 4. 24–24. 130), and there then follow separate sections on the Visigoths (25. 131–47. 245), and the Ostrogoths (48, 246–60. 316). This schema focuses attention on the division of the Goths, and this, in Jordanes' expressed opinion, was caused by Hunnic interference. Before the Hunnic invasions, the Visigoths and Ostrogoths are reported to have served one king (17. 98), and Ermenaric's death at the time of the invasions is the moment the two cease to live side by side (24. 129–130, 48. 246). The *Getica* envisages some kind of division or distinction between them before the Huns arrive, but Ermenaric's death hardens this into separate existence.

This is at first sight surprising. It is, after all, two explicit references in the *Getica* which have made scholars think that Visigoths and Ostrogoths already existed separately in south Russia (5. 42; 14. 82). As with the relative positions of Amal and Balth, however, the *Getica* again incorporates contradictory views. The explanation for this perhaps lies in the fact that Jordanes adds to one of these two references (14. 82), the note that the information came from the mysterious Ablabius. The view that Visigoth and Ostrogoth existed separately before the Huns perhaps originated, therefore, with him, and Jordanes included it even though it implicitly contradicted the underlying drift of his own work.[27] Jordanes clearly had no idea of what had existed before the Huns attacked the Goths; there is no mention of Tervingi or Greuthungi in his account of the Goths in the fourth century. He was aware, however, that, as the classicizing historians demonstrate, the Huns profoundly altered the course of Gothic history.

[27] On Ablabius, see further p. 65. *Getica* 17. 98, stating that Visigoth and Ostrogoth served the one king before the Huns, is something of a compromise; the distinction existed but did not matter.

D. *Gothic Ruling Houses c.350–500*

As we have seen, the *Getica* reports that the Goths owed allegiance to two royal houses, the Amals and Balthi, although it is ambiguous over their exact status. Now that we have examined the transformation of Gothic tribal subdivisions between *c*.350 and 500, the history of these ruling houses can be reconsidered. The classicizing historians are less helpful for this investigation, devoting little space to the lineage of Gothic leaders. It seems clear, all the same, that there was far less family continuity among leaders of the Goths than Jordanes believed.

The Amals

In the *Getica*, the Amals are the supremely royal Gothic family of demigods, whose genealogy is traced into the distant past (14. 79–81: Fig. 1). In words penned for a later Amal, Athalaric, Cassiodorus refers to his determined efforts to uncover the full story of this family (*Variae* 9. 25. 4–5),

[Cassiodorus] set out our lineage from antiquity, gaining by reading a knowledge that even the grey-haired wisdom of our [Gothic] elders scarcely recalled (*lectione discens, quod vix maiorum notitia cana retinebat*). He drew forth from the hiding-place of antiquity long-forgotten kings of the Goths. He brought the Amal family back into view, showing clearly that our ancestors have been royal for seventeen generations.

This is usually, and surely correctly, taken to imply that the *Getica*'s Amal genealogy is largely the work of Cassiodorus, and Jordanes' whole view of the Amals is in tune with these words. As we have seen, Jordanes seems to have thought that they ruled all the Goths before the Hunnic invasions, and half of them afterwards. He does report another tradition in which the Amals only ever ruled half of the Goths, but probably did not share this opinion himself.

Both traditions exaggerate the Amals' standing. It accords with the *Getica*'s view of the past to have Amal kings ruling a united Gothic people before the Hun invasions, and half of them afterwards. But in the fourth century, at least two Gothic confederations (the Tervingi and Greuthungi known to Ammianus) existed, so that, even if the Amals led one of these groups, the *Getica*'s view of Amal pre-eminence is considerably overstated. Nor did the Amals rule all Goths left north of the Danube after the

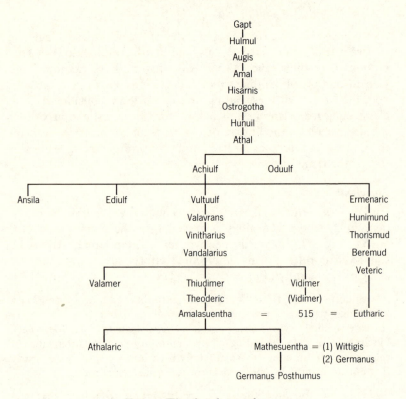

FIG. 1. The Amal genealogy

Hunnic invasions. In *c*.450, Theoderic the son of Triarius, whose line Jordanes explicitly describes as non-Amal (50. 270), led an independent Gothic group which rivalled in power that headed by the three Amal brothers (see further Ch. 7). Similarly, there is no sign that the other Gothic groups of the fifth century—those led by Radagaisus and Bigelis, and the Crimean Goths—had leaders from the Amal family. The Amals enjoyed neither unique pre-eminence over all Goths before the Huns, nor over those remaining north of the Danube after the 370s.

The *Getica* is also misleading over the time-span of Amal rule, which, probably following Cassiodorus, it extends over the entire seventeen generations of the Amal genealogy. There are a number of features of particularly the upper reaches of the genealogy which suggest very strongly that the names are not those of historical kings. Some of them, first of all, seem to belong to mythical figures. Gapt (if a variation of Gaut) is met elsewhere as a semi-divine hero,[28] Hulmul appears in Danish royal genealogies, suggesting that he was a figure common to Germanic folklore,[29] and Hisarnis can be translated 'Man of Iron', which may well indicate that he was a legendary hero.[30] Seventeen generations of kings also separate Romulus from Aeneas in Roman historical tradition, and it has been plausibly argued that Cassiodorus chose this particular figure for the length of Amal rule out of a desire for Gothic history to echo that of the Romans.[31] This implies, of course, that names had to be omitted or included to achieve the required length, and some of these names of rather general significance were probably imported by Cassiodorus to make up the right number.

Second, these upper reaches of the genealogy also recall the kinds of legitimizing genealogy which anthropologists have identified in modern traditional (non-literate) cultures. A suitable genealogy provides a *de facto* king with part of his legal title to rule, so that royal genealogy will often part company with biological fact. If a king is expected to have numerous royal ancestors, they will be found for him.[32] The first eight generations of the Amal genealogy, for instance, consist of an extended chain of father to son succession from Gapt to Amal. Such successions are common in traditional genealogies and king-lists, and always refer (as here) to the earliest period of a dynasty's rule. But father-to-son successions of this kind are extremely rare, and a priori likely to be fictitious. In later, independently documented generations of the dynasty, by comparison, the course of succession did not run anything like so smoothly. Valamer was followed by his brother

---

[28] Moisl, 'Anglo-Saxon Royal Genealogies', 219 ff.

[29] Schönfeld, *Wörterbuch*, 142; cf. Wolfram, 31, 37.

[30] Wolfram, 31.

[31] Wagner, 'Amalergenealogie', 27 ff.; Wolfram, 'Einige Überlegungen', 490 ff.

[32] Cf. Richards, 'Social Mechanisms', 175 ff.; Henige, *Oral Tradition, passim*; or Miller, 'Listening for the African Past', 18–19. For a compelling historical application, see Dumville, 'Kingship, Genealogies', 72 ff.

(Thiudimer), then his brother's son (Theoderic), then his brother's great-grandson (Athalaric), and finally his brother's granddaughter (Amalasuentha) in association with one of her cousins (Theodahad), before the Amals were replaced altogether. In the period *c*.460 to *c*.535, then, only one succession of four was from father to son. The upper reaches of the genealogy would thus seem to echo a common, legitimizing dynastic practice, imposing an ideal pattern of succession on the distant past, which has little to do with the ebb and flow of dynastic rivalries, the fact that fathers may outlive sons, and the statistical improbability that a single line will produce male heirs over many generations.[33]

A third point is that the Amal genealogy includes eponymous heroes: Amal (from whom the dynasty took its name), and Ostrogotha (name-giver to the Ostrogoths). These seem analogous to eponymous heroes found elsewhere, and were probably used to explain why the Amals ruled the Ostrogoths; that is, how the two got their names. Naming groups after the individuals who founded them seemingly was practised among the Goths. Both the Visigoths and Ostrogoths, for instance, were originally named after the leaders who first united them: Alaricoi and Valameriaci respectively.[34] There is a great difference, however, between cases where the person concerned is an independently documented historical figure, and others where suitably named individuals from the distant, undocumented past—such as Amal and Ostrogotha—explain a much later political configuration. In these cases, the process has been reversed; because of the tendency to name groups after leaders, suitable individuals have been found to explain current political groupings.[35] The *Getica*, it should be noted, has nothing to report of Amal, a confirmation that he is fictional. Two wars of Ostrogotha are described, on the basis of which he is usually treated as a real king,[36] but neither in fact supports this conclusion (see p. 36). The existence of Amal and Ostrogotha presupposes that of the Amals and Ostrogoths; placed in the

---

[33] Henige, *Oral Tradition*, 34 ff. and esp. ch. 2; cf. Miller, 'Listening for the African Past', 12 ff. with refs. The Capetians from Hugh Capet to Philip IV provide an (extremely) rare counter-example of ten father-to-son successions.

[34] John of Antioch fr. 206. 2; Malalas, Bonn 460; cf. Wolfram, 26.

[35] On eponyms and other so-called 'spurinyms', see Henige, *Oral Tradition*, 46–8.

[36] e.g. Wolfram, 24, 58 ff., who recognizes that Ostrogotha is eponymous.

genealogy of the Amal rulers of Ostrogothic Italy, the names are unhistorical.

Indeed, such figures come and go as circumstances change. If the Amal dynasty had fallen, Amal and Ostrogotha would surely have been replaced by new and more suitable eponymous heroes. The Bulgars provide a roughly contemporary illustration of such processes. In the sixth century, Utigurs and Kutrigurs explained their circumstances—when they were conscious of a relationship, but lived apart—by the story that a certain man had two sons, Utigur and Kutrigur, from whom the tribes were descended (Procopius, *Wars* 8. 5. 1 ff.). The much wider diffusion of Bulgar groups in the seventh century is reflected in stories of a man, here called Koubrat, who had five sons.[37] Such myths encapsulated contemporary reality and changed with it. Amal and Ostrogotha probably played a similar role among the Italian Goths, and do not show that Amal rule extended into the distant past.

Of the first eight names, then, at least six (Gapt, Hulmul, Amal, Hisarnis, Ostrogotha, and Athal) belong, in all probability, to fictitious kings, and the whole schema of descent from father to son is highly suspicious. On the other hand, Valamer and his brothers are genuine enough, and subsequent generations of the family are independently documented. The time-span of Amal pre-eminence is thus a question of deciding where, between Ostrogotha and Valamer, history begins. Most of the intervening names, however, are quite mysterious; the majority do not appear elsewhere in the *Getica*, let alone in classicizing histories. The question must revolve, therefore, around Ermenaric, the one figure from an earlier part of the genealogy also known to a classicizing historian; he appears as a king of the Greuthungi in Ammianus' narrative of the 370s (31. 3. 1–2). If he and Valamer really were related, Amal pre-eminence could be pushed back to the period before Hunnic invasions.

Ermenaric and his successors to the time of Valamer are dealt with in two separate sections of the *Getica*. The first describes Ermenaric as the ruler of all Scythia and Germany, listing the

---

[37.] Cf. Whitby, *The Emperor Maurice*, 129. This strongly recalls the Gonja cited by Goody, *Literacy in Traditional Societies*, 33–4, where the number of a notional king's sons varied with the number of tribal subunits.

peoples he ruled and recounting some of his victories. It also recalls how he was wounded in an internal political dispute, and how this allowed the Huns to attack his subjects. The king himself then died from a combination of the wound and dread aroused within him by the Huns, who were then led by Balamber (*Getica* 23. 116–24. 130). The second section, opening the *Getica*'s account of the Ostrogoths, describes how Amal rule continued, after Ermenaric's death, under the aegis of the Huns, until Valamer restored Ostrogothic independence. Ermenaric was succeeded by his great-nephew Vinitharius, who broke with the Huns briefly before being killed by Balamber. Rule then passed to Ermenaric's son Hunimund, and subsequently to his son Thorismud. The latter died after two years, and the Goths mourned so deeply that they did not elect another king for forty years; after this, rule passed to Valamer (*Getica* 48. 246–52).

I have examined these two passages elsewhere, and will do no more here than summarize the conclusions. Close scrutiny of the first section suggests strongly that Ermenaric has been fraudulently added to the Amal line from Ammianus. His brief words tell us, first, that Ermenaric ruled 'extensive and rich cantons', second, that he was feared by his neighbours for his warlike deeds, and, third, that he gave himself up to a voluntary death in the face of the Huns (31. 3. 1–2). The *Getica*'s account is much longer, but has been constructed around Ammianus' three pieces of information. Its description of Ermenaric's death imports other material of a highly dubious nature to transform Ammianus' potentially embarrassing account of a Gothic king who preferred to die rather than fight the Huns.[38] Other disparate information, much of it from classical literary sources,[39] similarly fills out Ammianus' account of Ermenaric's dominions and wars, as a result of which the king becomes ruler of all the Scythian and German nations, and hence a Gothic rival for Attila the Hun, who also claimed, the *Getica* tells us, this singular distinction (49. 257). A final literary importation makes Ermenaric die at the age of 110, placing him on a par with biblical patriarchs. None of this extra information has any historical value, so that, of the real Ermenaric, we have only what Ammianus reports. Since he says nothing about Ermenaric

---

[38] Heather, 'Cassiodorus', 110 ff.; cf. Gschwantler, 'Ermanrich', 109 ff.

[39] Heather, 'Cassiodorus', 113 ff.; cf. Korkkanen, *The Peoples of Hermenaric*, 48 ff.

being an Amal, and since the *Getica* starts from Ammianus and adds nothing of value to his account, there is no reason to think that Ermenaric really did belong to the family of Valamer and Theoderic. Further confirmation that this approach is substantially correct is provided by the fact that other borrowings from Ammianus are visible in the *Getica* at precisely the point where it mentions Ermenaric.[40]

The point of this fictional rewriting of Ermenaric emerges from the crucial role he plays in the Amal genealogy. It is the fact that Ermenaric is supposedly the brother of Vultuulf (cf. Fig. 1) which makes Eutharic, whom Theoderic married to his daughter Amalasuentha and designated as his heir for the Italian kingdom when he himself failed to produce a son, into an Amal. Ermenaric has probably been rewritten, therefore, precisely to turn him into a figure of suitable standing for this important role. This in turn makes it likely that it was Cassiodorus who found Ermenaric in a copy of Ammianus. Cassiodorus wrote his *Chronicle*, for instance, for Eutharic, bringing history to a culmination with the latter's consulship in 519, and was later a faithful servant of Eutharic's son, Athalaric, who eventually succeeded Theoderic after Eutharic's untimely death. It would be quite natural, therefore, to find him suitably adjusting the ancestry of Eutharic's line, and the general approach would also be in tune with Cassiodorus' use of written sources to supplement the Goths' deficient memories (*Variae* 9. 25. 4–5, quoted on p. 19).

The second passage, dealing with Ermenaric's successors to the time of Valamer, does nothing to strengthen Amal claims to ancient pre-eminence either. What the *Getica* considers an account of Ermenaric's successors actually describes part of the process by which Valamer first rose to prominence in *c*.450. The author has been confused by an unfamiliar form of Valamer's name (Balam[b]er), and by certain similarities between Ermenaric's successor according to Ammianus, one Vithimeris, and the Vinitharius who appears in this passage as an enemy of Balamber/ Valamer. Equating Vithimeris and Vinitharius allowed him to join

---

[40] Heather, 'Cassiodorus', 111; cf. Mommsen, pp. xxxiii f. *Getica* 24. 127–8 reworks Ammianus' digression on the Huns (31. 2. 2 ff.); its characterization of the Alans (24. 126) parallels AM 31. 2. 21; *Getica* 25. 131 strongly recalls AM 31. 3. 8–4. 1 (not marked by Mommsen); *Getica* 25. 131–26. 138 corresponds to AM 31. 4–5.

together the information about Ermenaric, which he had just taken from Ammianus, and that from different sources about Vinitharius and other Gothic kings. This solved one problem but created others. Events concerning the latter which took place *c*.450 (dated by the participation in them of Valamer) were now thought to have commenced *c*.375, causing considerable chronological problems, which Cassiodorus solved by adding a forty-year interregnum. Stripped of extraneous material, the passage describes a power-struggle between Valamer and Vinitharius, from which Valamer emerged victorious. Both were clearly Gothic rulers, but the fact that Valamer married Vinitharius' granddaughter Vadamerca suggests that Vinitharius was not an Amal. He does appear in the Amal genealogy, but it is a fairly common genealogical manipulation to include defeated rivals in a victor's pedigree. In this case, moreover, the process was probably facilitated by the marriage, since Vinitharius appears in the genealogy as Valamer's grandfather, and the marriage made him (if posthumously) Valamer's 'grandfather-in-law'. Instead of extending Amal rule back into the fourth century, the passage strongly suggests that the Amals first rose to real prominence in *c*.450, when Valamer united several smaller groups under his sway.[41]

A number of other indications confirm this conclusion. The most important is the account of one Gensemund in Cassiodorus, *Variae* 8. 9. 8, addressed to a certain Tuluin. Gensemund was a Gothic hero renowned for his loyalty to the Amals, which he transferred over more than one generation, even though some Goths sought to crown him in his own right. In return for his loyalty, he was adopted by the Amals as son-at-arms, so that he was clearly not an Amal himself. Cassiodorus confirms this important point by contrasting Gensemund with Tuluin in precisely this respect; unlike Gensemund, Tuluin had been made part of the Amal family by marriage. Gensemund thus demonstrates that other families had at some point been able to supply kings for those Goths whom the Amals later came to dominate. If, as seems likely, Gensemund can be equated with the Gesimund who appears in the *Getica*, we can be more precise about his position in Gothic society. Jordanes describes how Gesimund, son of Hunimund, led his own Goths in support of Balamber/Valamer's war

---

[41] Heather, 'Cassiodorus', 120 ff.; cf. p. 240.

against Vinitharius (48. 248). He thus commanded his own military force, which is presumably what made him a potential Gothic king. Hunimund himself, and another son, Thorismud, are also said to have been Gothic kings (*Getica* 48. 250), so that Gensemund/Gesimund would seem to have belonged to an alternative, non-Amal ruling line, which, unlike Vinitharius', eventually accepted Amal hegemony peacefully.[42]

Between the collapse of the Hunnic Empire and the move of these Goths to Italy (*c.*450–90), Valamer's name was also closely associated with this group. One source styles them the 'Valameriaci', a personalization which seems to stress the role he played in their creation, just as the Visigoths were originally called the 'Alaricoi' (see above). Theoderic the Amal is also consistently described as 'the son of Valamer', when he was really the son of Valamer's brother. The title appears so widely in such well-informed sources as Malchus of Philadelphia,[43] that it surely originated somehow with Theoderic himself. He was perhaps stressing that he was Valamer's successor, suggesting again that the latter's name had a particular mystique.

A glance, finally, at events which unfolded in Ostrogothic Italy after Theoderic's death is very suggestive of the true standing of the Amals among the Goths. While Gothic supremacy there was secure, the Amals retained their followers' loyalties, despite a far from ideal line of succession: the minor Athalaric, followed by his mother and the treacherous Theodahad. As soon as Belisarius threatened the Goths' position, however, their nobles acted decisively. They murdered Theodahad, and in his place elected Wittigis, who had previously won renown in battle. He married Theoderic's granddaughter Matasuentha, but Procopius explicitly states that Wittigis was elected for his military ability (*Wars* 5. 11. 1–9). This is confirmed by his own propaganda (penned by Cassiodorus), which stressed that he belonged to Theoderic's line only because his deeds were of similar stature, and which made no mention of the marriage (*Variae* 10. 31). The Goths thus suffered few qualms in deposing the last representative of what the *Getica*

---

[42] Heather, 'Cassiodorus', 121–2.

[43] Theophanes AM 5977 (130–1 de Boor); Anon. Val. 9. 42, 12. 58; Marcellinus Comes s.a. 482 (*CM* ii. 92); John of Antioch fr. 211. 4; Malchus of Philadelphia frr. 15, 18. 1–4, 20; Damascius in Photius, *Bibliotheca* 242.

supposes to have been a family of demigods who had ruled them since time immemorial. After Wittigis leaders were chosen without reference to the Amal family; Ildibad and Totila were elected by the Gothic nobility, neither having Amal connections (Procopius, *Wars* 6. 30. 4–17; 7. 2. 10–13).

In sum, the *Getica*'s claims for the unique pre-eminence of the Amal family cannot be maintained in either of Jordanes' versions. The family did not rule all Goths before the Hunnic invasions, and there is no sign that its members ruled even half the Goths afterwards. Ermenaric's addition to the Amal line is a late fiction, and the non-Amal line of Triarius led a powerful group in the mid-fifth century. The Amals probably first rose to prominence *c*.450, when, surviving competition from other dynasties, Valamer united a powerful force around himself. This was based not on historic pre-eminence, but on practical leadership ability. When later Amals failed to secure their followers' position in Italy, the line was quickly ousted. The Amals must have been a powerful family in *c*.450 even to have participated in the leadership struggles, but they were not demigods with unique prestige.

The Balthi

As we have seen, there is some doubt about when Jordanes thought the Balthi established themselves. On the one hand, he states that they ruled the 'Visigoths' before and after the Hunnic invasions (5. 42), but elsewhere restricts their rule to the later period (17. 98). The Visigothic grouping was itself only created in the reign of Alaric (395–410), and to understand the Balthi, the history of the leaders of its constituent groups must be traced as far as the emergence of a ruling dynasty for the Visigoths. The subject will receive full coverage below, and only the conclusions need be presented here.

Three pre-existing Gothic groups contributed to the Visigoths: the Tervingi and Greuthungi who crossed the Danube in 376, and the fifth-century Goths led by Radagaisus. Any enquiry is hampered by our sources' lack of interest in the lineage of Gothic leaders, but enough breaks can be documented to guarantee that it is meaningless to speak of continuity between the leaders of these three constituent groups, and the dynasty which eventually ruled

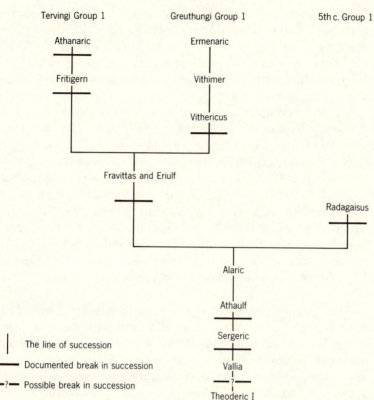

Tervingi Group 1   Greuthungi Group 1   5th c. Group 1

Athanaric

Fritigern

Ermenaric

Vithimer

Vithericus

Fravittas and Eriulf

Radagaisus

Alaric

Athaulf

Sergeric

Vallia

Theoderic I

| The line of succession
—— Documented break in succession
—?— Possible break in succession

FIG. 2. The emergence of a Visigothic ruling dynasty

the Visigothic kingdom (Fig. 2). To start with, none of the leaders under whom the three crossed the frontier maintained his control in the first shock of contact with the Roman Empire. Radagaisus, most obviously, was executed outside Florence on 23 August 406.[44] When the other two crossed the Danube in 376, the Tervingi were led by Fritigern and the Greuthungi by Alatheus and Saphrax, acting as regents for Vithericus. These leaders are mentioned during the subsequent war, but disappear before the peace agreement of 382. The peace even seems to have prohibited

[44] *Addit. ad Prosp. Haun.*, s.a. 405 (*CM* i. 299).

the Goths from electing an overall leader, and nothing suggests
that any of them founded a dynasty (p. 173). In any case,
Fritigern's leadership of the Tervingi was itself a break with
established loyalties, since he had ousted Athanaric, whose family
had probably ruled the Tervingi throughout the fourth century
(AM 31. 3. 4–8).

Within the Empire, another generation of leaders equally failed
to found dynasties (this does not apply to Radagaisus' group,
whose survivors joined Alaric without re-forming as an independent political unit). From those who had crossed the Danube in
376 emerged Fravittas and Eriulf some time before 392. Champions of alternative policies, they were also rivals attempting to fill
the leadership vacuum which had existed since 382. There is no
sign that they were related to previous leaders of the Tervingi and
Greuthungi, and both again failed to establish themselves. At a
banquet, their rivalry erupted into violence; Eriulf was killed, and
Fravittas forced to flee Gothic society (Eunapius fr. 59; see further
Ch. 6).

After 395, the situation began to stabilize under Alaric. It has
been argued that since his name alliterates with those of Ariaric
and Athanaric, probably grandfather and grandson, who ruled the
Tervingi before the advent of the Huns, Alaric came from the
same ruling family.[45] This would suggest that the dynasty had in
some way survived the Hunnic invasions, and provide some
support for the *Getica*'s view of the Balthi. There is nothing in
favour of this hypothesis except the alliteration, however, and this
is flimsy evidence indeed. For as scholars who pioneered the study
of naming-patterns using the evidence of Carolingian (and later)
noble lines have shown, conclusions based on anything other than
a large sample of names are very unsound. In addition, naming-
patterns can provide only supporting evidence; identifications of
family lines must be based primarily on historical circumstances.[46]
In this case, the great political discontinuity which separates

[45] Wolfram, 32–3, 64–5, 143–4; Wenskus, 'Balthen'.
[46] Cf. Werner, 'Important Noble Families', 149 ff.; Schmid, 'The Structure of
the Nobility', 38 ff. The possibilities (cf. Wolfram, 144) that the Gothic Alaric
might have been named somehow after a king of the Heruli supposedly defeated
by Ermenaric, or that he was the son of the Alavivus who disappears so
mysteriously from the historical record in 376 (see Ch. 4), seem equally remote.

Tervingi from Visigoth makes it highly unlikely that Alaric and Athanaric were related. It is also far from certain that these names would have alliterated in their original Gothic forms,[47] nor even is it clear that the Goths used alliteration to signal family relationships. The only families for which we have secure evidence are later generations of the Amals and Balthi, and neither of these seem to have used systematic alliteration. The Visigothic king Theoderic I gave his children a wide variety of names (Theoderic, Thorismud, Fredericus, and Euric), and the descendants of Thiudimer were equally varied; some were given variants of his name, others named after mythical ancestors.[48]

Alaric definitively united the Visigoths, fighting off the challenge of one Sarus (p. 197), and handed on power to a designated and related successor: his brother-in-law Athaulf.[49] Alaric and Athaulf ruled for twenty years, but there was another break before a dynasty established itself. When bad relations with the Empire caused serious difficulties, opposition to Athaulf surfaced from within the Visigoths, culminating in an assassination attempt. Mortally wounded, Athaulf tried to transfer power to his brother, but it was usurped by an outsider, Sergeric, who slaughtered Athaulf's children and probably also the brother, since he is not mentioned again. Sergeric was the brother of the Sarus who had consistently opposed Alaric, so that the coup against Athaulf probably represents a rival line's attempt to reassert itself. As it was, Sergeric himself failed to hold on to power, being murdered after only seven days. He was succeeded by Vallia, for whom there is no record of family ties with previous leaders.[50] Sergeric and Vallia interrupted a nascent dynastic succession, and only in the thirty-three-year reign of Vallia's successor, Theoderic I, did a

[47] Cf. Schönfeld, *Wörterbuch*, 25; the original Gothic name behind Ariaric could be either **Arjareiks* or **Harjareiks*. The latter could not alliterate with **Alareiks* by old Germanic rules, under which *h* is a full consonant alliterating only with itself: so uniformly in Old Norse, Old English, Old Saxon, and Old High German. I am very grateful to Leofranc Holford-Strevens for pointing this out to me.

[48] Cf. Heather, 'Cassiodorus', 106 n. 10.

[49] *Getica* 30. 158 uses *consanguineus* of Athaulf and Alaric, implying that they were blood-relatives (Wolfram, 165), but this is probably a misunderstanding of their well-documented relationship by marriage (Zosimus 5. 37. 1).

[50] Cf. *PLRE* ii. 1147–8; see further p. 220.

dynasty establish itself. Theoderic's family ruled the Visigoths for
the rest of the century.[51] Theoderic seems to have married Alaric's
daughter, so that, to some extent, his dynasty was a continuation of
Alaric's. But Sergeric and Vallia had intervened, and nothing
suggests that Theoderic was elected because he had married
Alaric's daughter. We know of the marriage only because a later
panegyric portrays Theoderic's son Thorismud as Alaric's grandson.[52]

There is thus no sign of dynastic continuity between fourth-
century Gothic leaders and the rulers of the Visigoths, so that the
Getica's first view of the Balthi (that they had ruled since the third
century) seems mistaken. Likewise, while closer to the truth, there
is some exaggeration in the view that the Balthi quickly came to
lead all the Goths who had fled into the Empire in 376. If Alaric
was a Balth, as Jordanes maintains, it was nearly twenty years after
the Danube crossing before a representative of the family first
asserted himself. Alternative lines, particularly that of Sarus and
Sergeric, still had to be defeated over another twenty-year period
before the family's position was secure. Even then, Theoderic I
was probably related to Alaric only by marriage, and must again
have owed his position primarily to his own ability. Like the
Amals, the Balthi were originally one noble line among several
competing for the overall leadership of a new group.

Despite the undeniably Gothic nature of some of its material,
then, any reconstruction of Gothic history between 350 and 500
based on the *Getica* will be misleading. Contemporary sources, as
Wenskus and Wolfram have done much to show, demonstrate that
there was no real continuity between Gothic political units of the
fourth century, and the two groups who founded successor states
to the Roman Empire. Visigoth and Ostrogoth were the product of
the fundamental realignment that the Huns caused in Gothic
society. Against this background, it is hardly surprising to find
that, contrary to the *Getica*, the ruling families of these later
groups had no long histories of pre-eminence. Amals and Balthi

---

[51] Cf. *PLRE* ii. 1070–1 and Stemma 40, p. 1332.

[52] Sidonius Apollinaris, *Carm.* 7. 505. Wenskus, 'Balthen', 14 suggests that
Theoderic I was Alaric's son, but the sources would surely say so.

emerged from struggles with a number of rivals, at exactly the same time as the new groups were forming. The Hunnic invasions were a watershed in Gothic history, at the end of which the people had been redefined. This poses a further question. Why does the *Getica*, drawing uniquely on the Goths' own understanding of their past, contain such a misleading account of Gothic history?

2

THE HISTORICAL VALUE OF JORDANES' *GETICA*

Complete explanation of all the problems in the *Getica*'s account of Gothic history is impossible. Jordanes' dependence on the lost histories of Cassiodorus and Ablabius leaves us with too many unknowns. Nevertheless, the interaction of the authors' interests with the sources available to them can largely explain at least the two major difficulties we have observed in the *Getica*'s framework for Gothic history: its anachronistic account of the division of the Goths into Ostrogoth and Visigoth, and the exaggerated historical role accorded the Amal and Balth dynasties. It would be quite impossible, and in any case undesirable, to limit the discussion to just this line of enquiry, however, since Jordanes has been the focus of a great deal of scholarly activity. Certain technical arguments concerning the date and composition of the *Getica* will of necessity require considerable attention in the pages which follow. The argument will also attempt to follow less well-trodden paths, however, in its more general discussion of Jordanes' historical methods and the materials he had to hand. At times, this will take us some way from Gothic history, but without it we cannot begin to understand this most perplexing text.

A. *Source-Material and the Role of the Author*

In the early 550s, Jordanes interrupted labour on his other extant work, the *Romana*, to write a Gothic history for one Castalius (*Getica*, praef. 1). Both men seem to have been serious Christians (possibly even monks), since Jordanes addresses Castalius as *frater* (ibid.), and also refers to his own *conversio* (50. 266), almost certainly one to a more religious life.[1] This is in accord with the

---

[1] Wagner, *Getica*, 18 ff.; cf. Hachmann, *Goten und Skandinavien*, 35 ff.; Goffart, *Narrators*, 43–4.

strongly Christian tone of the *Romana*, which stresses the dismal course of world history.[2] Jordanes also seems to have worked in Constantinople,[3] probably belonging to a primarily Latin-speaking, Christian community there in the mid-sixth century.

Jordanes was thus isolated in time and space from that part of Gothic history which concerns us here. Gothic social organization before the Hunnic invasions was dictated by events of the third century, occurring nearly 300 years before Jordanes wrote; of the groups who established successor states, the Visigoths had by *c.*550 been settled in the west for almost 150 years, and the Ostrogoths for sixty. Both held territory hundreds of kilometres from Constantinople, so that Jordanes was dealing with personalities and events that were entirely beyond his compass. Not surprisingly, major mistakes can be found; he made them himself, or was unable to correct his predecessors. The two western usurpers defeated by Theodosius I are conflated (28. 145), for instance, as are Alaric's separate invasions of Italy (29. 147 ff.).[4]

Jordanes partly compensated for his ignorance by reusing earlier writers. Some of this material may appear in the *Getica* through Cassiodorus or Ablabius, but some he probably added himself. He claims as much (*Getica*, praef. 3), and the *Romana* is a compilation, stitching together extracts largely from Florus and Festus.[5] In the *Getica*, the influence of many earlier works is apparent: Greek and Latin writers from Josephus and Tacitus to Priscus of Panium and Ammianus Marcellinus. Some of these are reliable sources in their own right, increasing the *Getica*'s historical value, especially where the original is now lost. Thus the *Getica* preserves material from Priscus not in the collections of Byzantine epitomators.[6]

But the *Getica* is much more than a series of excerpts from earlier writers. Gothic oral history has also left its mark, and some passages combine these disparate sources. Where comparative evidence exists, the threads can be disentangled. For instance, in about nine lines of Mommsen's edition, the *Getica* summarizes

[2] O'Donnell, 'The Aims of Jordanes', 224–5; Goffart, *Narrators*, 45–6.

[3] *Getica* 5. 38 refers to Constantinople as 'our city'.

[4] See also Croke, 'Jordanes' Understanding'; Goffart, *Narrators*, 64.

[5] Cf. Mommsen, pp. xxiii ff.; O'Donnell, 'The Aims of Jordanes', 233; Goffart, *Narrators*, 47 ff.

[6] Mommsen, pp. xxx ff.; Blockley, i. 113–14.

Priscus' embassy to Attila (34. 178–9). Of this, Byzantine epitomators preserved a much longer version, and a simple comparison
demonstrates that not only is the *Getica*'s account greatly abbre-
viated, but also that a note has been added about where 'long ago'
the Gothic hero Vidigoia was killed in battle.[7] This probably did
not appear in Priscus' original, but was added in the course of the
Getica's composition.

A second example can be reconstructed from the *Getica*'s
description of Dicineus, who supposedly brought the blessings of
civilization to the Goths (11. 67 ff.). Dicineus was, in fact, the
mythical teacher of the Getae, who occupied the lands above the
Black Sea before the birth of Christ. The *Getica*'s account of him
has been borrowed from Graeco-Roman traditions, probably
originating in Dio Chrysostom's *Getica*. Dicineus thus entered
Gothic (as opposed to Getic) history through the artificial equation
of Goth and Geta (see below). For present purposes, the point is
that Jordanes' account closely follows other extant versions of
Dicineus' activities until it gets to the point where he designates
priests *pilleati* ('cap-wearers'). Here, the parallel accounts stop,[8]
but the *Getica* goes on to say that Dicineus named the rest of the
people *capillati* (11. 72), a recognized class of men within the
Ostrogothic kingdom (Cassiodorus, *Variae* 4. 49). This suggests
that the author of this part of the *Getica* has not simply used the
equation of Goth and Geta to add Dicineus to Gothic history, but
also a word-play between *pilleati* and *capillati* to make Dicineus
the founder of a genuine Gothic institution.

The author's role was thus much more than one of selecting and
ordering extracts. Such intervention perhaps made no substantial
difference to the material's historical value in the two cases just
discussed, but in a third it did. For the reign of Ostrogotha, two
wars are described in contrasting styles. One fought against the
Gepids seems to betray the marks of oral history. The action is
highly personalized around two kings, Ostrogotha and the Gepid
king Fastida. No other individuals are mentioned, and there is
little incidental detail. Only the site of the battle is recorded, Galtis
on the river Aluhas, and even this cannot be located. According to
Jordanes, Fastida was motivated purely by jealousy of the Goths,
and it is explicitly the point of the story to explain that, by going to

---

[7] Compare *Getica* 34. 178 with Priscus fr. 11. 2 (esp. 260, 264).

[8] e.g. Dio Chrysostum *Disc.* 72. 3; Cassius Dio 68. 9.

war, the Gepids had broken the bonds of kinship first (17. 96–100; cf. p. 6).

In Ostrogotha's second war against the Roman Empire, the action is much less personalized. He appoints two other men, Argaith and Guntheric, to lead the Goths in battle, and two Roman leaders, Philip and Decius, are also named. The account is far from exhaustive, but there is more detail than for the war with the Gepids. Decius expels troops from the Roman army after the first attack, and the second, led by Argaith and Guntheric, centres on a siege of Marcianople which lasts for some time before the Goths are paid to depart (16. 90–2). The contrast with the Fastida narrative suggests that this information came originally from a written source, and there is just enough correspondence with Graeco-Roman sources to confirm the point. Decius' measures to discipline troops of the Danubian army are reported by Zosimus (1. 21. 2–3) as well as Jordanes.[9] The *Historia Augusta* also mentions one 'Argunt' king of the Scythians (20. 31. 1), normally taken as the Argaith of the *Getica*.[10] Given this text's sense of humour and predilection for playing with names, 'Argunt' perhaps hides both Argaith and Guntheric, having taken the first syllable from each name.[11] The ultimate source here may have been Dexippus' *Scythica*,[12] but the main point is that Ostrogotha's war with the Romans seems to have been inspired by a written source.

But Ostrogotha, as an eponymous hero, never existed (p. 22), and hence presumably did not appear in the original source. The name appears nowhere in Graeco-Roman accounts of these years, some of which are dependent upon Dexippus,[13] providing additional confirmation that an Ostrogotha did not really play a part in

---

[9] The *Getica* has manipulated these events slightly; the troops did not flee to Ostrogotha, but supported Decius against Philip.

[10] Cf. Barnes, *Historia Augusta*, 64.

[11] Syme, *Ammianus and the Historia Augusta*, 165 ff. (esp. 8 ff.), add weight to the suggestion of Köpke, *Anfänge*, 98; cf. Hachmann, *Goten und Skandinavien*, 112.

[12] See generally, Millar, 'Dexippus'. *Getica* 18. 101–20. 109 may also be from Dexippus. Again, Graeco-Roman sources confirm the passages' literary origin. Dexippus fr. 19 and *Getica* 18. 103 both mention Priscus, commander of Philippopolis, and refer to differences between himself and Decius. See also Hachmann, *Goten und Skandinavien*, 112–13.

[13] Particularly not in Zosimus, for whose debt to Dexippus see Blockley, 'The First Book of Zosimus' New History', esp. source C, pp. 399–400.

the wars of Phillip and Decius. Again, the editorial role seems clear. The flight of Roman troops to Ostrogotha and the appointment by Ostrogotha of Argaith and Guntheric to lead the second attack are our author's devices for enabling Ostrogotha to appear in information taken from a written narrative. The point of this, of course, was to give the Amal Ostrogotha a role in the run up to what was, apart from Hadrianople, the Goths' most famous victory over the Roman Empire. The importance of the author's role emerges clearly here. Disparate sources have been carefully combined, and, in Ostrogotha's case, the author's intervention has completely undermined the historical value of a passage taken presumably from an originally reliable written source.

Understanding precisely how this editing process has affected the *Getica*'s view of Gothic history is complicated by the question of authorship. Jordanes, as we have noted, refers to two previous works of Gothic history by Cassiodorus and Ablabius. Cassiodorus is well known. Servant of successive Ostrogothic kings, he came to Constantinople in *c.*540, before founding a religious community on the southern coast of Italy. Many of his other works are still extant, including a collection of correspondence, the *Variae*, from his days at the Ostrogothic court. Ablabius, however, is quite mysterious. We do not know when and where he worked, although Mommsen saw him as the Goths' Herodotus, who first collected material from their oral history.[14] Neither Cassiodorus' nor Ablabius' history is extant, so that it is impossible to be precise about their exact contributions to the *Getica* as it now stands. Nevertheless, an examination of the role of Cassiodorus does shed some light on why the *Getica* should contain such a distorted view of Gothic history, Ablabius will be considered later.

B. *Jordanes and Cassiodorus*

Jordanes wrote the *Getica* in response to Castalius' request for an abridgement of Cassiodorus' history, but the task was not entirely easy:

The overriding burden . . . is that I have no opportunity of using the history (of Cassiodorus) in order to attend to his meaning. Still, to speak

---

[14] Ablabius is mentioned at *Getica* 4. 28, 14. 82, 23. 117; cf. Mommsen, pp. xxxvii ff.

truthfully, through the favour of his steward I previously read through the history over a three-day reading period.[15] Although I do not recall the words, nevertheless I believe I preserve intact its meaning and narrative. To this I have also added relevant material from several Greek and Latin histories, while mixing in a beginning, a conclusion, and a good deal in between in my own words. (*Getica*, praef. 2–3.)[16]

Jordanes thus relied on a previous reading of Cassiodorus' history, which he had borrowed for three days. Nevertheless, he felt that he had preserved Cassiodorus' general drift (*sensus*) and the sequence of events (*res actas*), even while adding some material of his own. Jordanes carefully modelled this preface on Rufinus' preface to his translation of Origen's *Commentary on the Epistle to the Romans*. Rufinus was concerned to explain why his translation was not as close to Origen's original as he might have wished. Similarly, Castalius had requested a simple summary of Cassiodorus' work, but Jordanes had produced something a little different. He is telling his friend that the *Getica* is not a line-by-line paraphrase, but neither does it depart too far from its model. At face value, Jordanes' general meaning seems clear enough, even if he does not specifically identify his own additions.[17]

His words, however, have aroused great suspicion. Three days has been seen as too short a reading-period, and many have suspected that Jordanes is hiding the fact that he had just copied Cassiodorus. This line of argument culminated in a famous lecture by Momigliano which denied Jordanes any substantial role in the writing of the *Getica*.[18] Following a previous suggestion, he identified Jordanes with the Bishop Jordanes of Crotone in Italy, who was in Constantinople in *c*.550 in the entourage of Pope Vigilius. The preface of the *Romana* dedicates that work to one Vigilius, whom it was then natural to identify with the pope. Having attached Jordanes to a circle of important Italians in Constantinople, Momigliano went on to argue that Jordanes was merely acting as a 'front man' for Cassiodorus, another Italian in the city at this date. For Momigliano, the *Getica*'s target was the

[15] The Latin is *relegere*, but this does not imply two readings: Croke, 'Cassiodorus', 120–1; Goffart, *Narrators*, 60–1.

[16] Trans. Croke, 'Cassiodorus', 120.

[17] Cf. Goffart, *Narrators*, 58 ff.; Croke, 'Cassiodorus', 118 ff.

[18] 'Cassiodorus and the Italian Culture of His Time', 215 ff.; ibid. 223, '[Jordanes] probably added the initial quotation from Orosius, the final paragraph, and a few details in the middle'; cf. id., 'Gli Anicii', 231 ff.

imperial court; Cassiodorus was trying to persuade Justinian to adopt a conciliatory policy towards the Italian Goths. Momigliano also argued that Cassiodorus had himself brought his own work down to 550, because *Getica* 60. 313 describes the marriage of Theoderic's granddaughter Matasuentha and the Patrician Germanus as a union of the Amals and Anicii. For Momigliano, the description could only reflect Cassiodorus' obsession with this noble family, to whom he was perhaps related. This thesis was all the more easily accepted because Ensslin had already argued that the *Romana* was really the lost *Roman History* of Symmachus, which Jordanes had similarly plagiarized.[19]

That the *Getica*'s preface is deliberately misleading has also been argued by Goffart. In his view, the *Getica* is totally different from Cassiodorus' *Gothic History*, and is only masquerading as a faithful summary of it for propaganda purposes. The *Romana* and *Getica*, he argues, were designed to circulate together among Italian senators and Latin-speaking Goths, to convince them that Justinian's reconquest was inevitable. The *Romana* reveals an author with a thoroughly Roman outlook. Chauvinistic sources (Florus and Festus) have been chosen to show that imperial victory over barbarians is inevitable, and a strong strand of Christianity emphasizes that God's will upholds the Empire (*Narrators*, 47 ff.). The *Getica* is much less pro-Gothic than has been supposed. Its last paragraph celebrates Justinian's final victory over the Goths, and this, Goffart maintains, informs the tone of the whole work. Gothic triumphs are played down, and Amal Gothic kingship is portrayed as an impediment to good relations between Romans and Goths. The marriage between the Amals and the Anicii underlines the fact that Gothic leaders should raise themselves no higher than noble Romans (ibid. 62 ff.).

The marriage is also seen as playing a more arcane role. For Goffart, underlying the *Getica* is a tale of two lovers, the Gothic and Roman peoples, who can exist happily only if the Goths take a female role in response to the Roman male lead (exemplified again in Matasuentha and Germanus). The fulfilment of their destiny (this happy marriage) is hampered by bad emperors and by the Gothic kingship, an illegitimate assertion of masculinity, and the whole of the narrative has been conceived around this plot (ibid.

---

[19] *Des Symmachus Historia Romana*; followed notably by Wes, *Das Ende des Kaisertums*, 89 ff.

68 ff.). Omissions and blunders are not accidental; characters and events appear only to advance or hinder the plot. The tone is consistently ironic; the *Getica*'s picture of Goths revolting when their subsidies are withheld is meant to make the reader laugh (ibid. 79–80). A further element in the fun is Jordanes' deliberately adopted pose as an unlearned Goth, designed to make the underlying message more palatable for its Italian audience (ibid., esp. p. 68). Jordanes was in fact in the employ of Justinian's court.

Two other specific frauds can be identified. First, by explicit dates in his two works (see p. 47), Goffart argues, Jordanes is trying to convince us that he wrote before 31 March 551, before Narses' expedition departed in order finally to crush Gothic resistance in Italy. But both works mention later events, leading Goffart to suggest that a better context for them is provided by the real end of the Italian war, winter 553–4. For him, Jordanes' writings reinforce the message of the Pragmatic Sanction of summer 554, that imperial victory really was inevitable (ibid. 97 ff.). Second, the names associated with these texts (Jordanes, Castalius, and Vigilius) have connotations which are too well suited to the roles they play, and may well be fraudulent, hiding Jordanes' closeness to the imperial court. 'Vigilance', for instance, is an attribute of Justinian, according to Procopius, and Goffart wonders if Justinian is the Vigilius who had sponsored the whole project (ibid. 103–4).

Goffart and Momigliano come to different conclusions, but the arguments turn on the same points. For both, Jordanes' autobiographical passages hide his closeness to an important political circle. For both, Jordanes' work is a piece of propaganda, arguing a case before a specific audience. And in both cases, the marriage of Matasuentha and Germanus is crucial. It is either diagnostic of Cassiodorus' continued involvement in Italian politics, or provides the key to Jordanes' elaborately contrived love-story.

The two hypotheses also have in common major problems. Above all, they require works of history to have functioned as propaganda. At Justinian's court, public readings seem to have been common, and more seditious material could always be passed round privately.[20] It is hard, however, to see the *Getica* circulating as propaganda in this context. Jordanes is not illiterate, but the Latin of the *Getica* is low-level and does not conform to classical

[20] On this literary context, Cameron, *Procopius*, ch. 2.

norms, reflecting the everyday language of military administration, where the author learnt his craft.[21] Corippus' poetry is more indicative of the elevated and recherché style required of Latin court literature in Constantinople.[22] Eastern court circles are unlikely to have been much impressed by the *Getica*, a work so obviously composed by a social inferior. The same argument applies in part to Goffart's reconstruction. Again, it seems highly unlikely that his proposed audience, including men of similar status to Cassiodorus, would really have been ready to listen to Jordanes' Latin, especially since echoes of Cassiodorus intrude to create almost a pastiche of his style.

For Goffart's hypothesis, another problem is still more damaging. To extract his message, it is necessary to be exposed to the *Romana* and *Getica* in their entirety, but it is difficult to imagine how precisely this might have been achieved in an Italy just emerging from twenty years of war. There seem to be two possibilities. Either all the remaining senators and important Goths were to be gathered in one place to listen to a full reading of the texts, or multiple copies were to be passed among them. The second method has the drawback that the audience might not read the crucial passages, and the message Goffart identifies is anything but obvious. Neither mechanism for disseminating the supposed message seems at all likely.

This reflects the fundamental problem inherent to approaches such as those of Momigliano and Goffart. Histories are not good vehicles for propaganda; that is, trying to convince a given audience of the validity of certain policies, or of a particular way of looking at a sequence of events. In the Late Empire, the major vehicle of court propaganda was the panegyric, delivered on all major state occasions. At such moments, a substantial portion of the politically important classes of the Empires were present: court officials, praesental military officers, and such senators and other distinguished men as happened to be around the Emperor at the given moment. There was then delivered an oration of encompassable length (to judge by surviving examples, taking about an hour to read) which presented important issues of the day as the

---

[21] Croke, 'Cassiodorus', 120–1 with refs.; cf. more generally, Wagner, *Getica*, 46; Reydellet, *La Royauté*, 259 ff.
[22] *In laudem Iustini Augusti minoris*, trans. A. M. Cameron; *Iohannis*, ed. Diggle and Goodyear; cf. Cameron's introd., esp. 1–20.

emperor wished them to be seen. Such occasions had the pre-requisties for successful propaganda: the right audience and a suitable literary and rhetorical form for addressing them.[23] Histor-ies certainly contain reflections on events, and must echo their authors' distinctive points of view, but this is a very different matter from political propaganda, with a specific agenda aimed at the susceptibilities of a well-defined audience.[24]

Momigliano and Goffart are equally unsuccessful in discredit-ing what Jordanes has to say of himself. The identifications with the bishop of Crotone and the pope do not convince. The *Romana* addresses Vigilius as 'most noble and magnificent brother', appro-priate for a layman rather than the Pope; Momigliano's counter-argument that Jordanes was a boorish provincial bishop who would not have understood such matters is unattractive. The *Romana* is also in part a homily on the vanities of worldly glory, which a pope is unlikely to have commissioned.[25] Momigliano's context for the *Getica* thus evaporates, and, with it, any reason to think that Jordanes was addressing Justinian's court. Goffart's attempt to turn Jordanes into an employee of that court seems equally flawed. The *Romana*, in particular, is really quite critical of important aspects of Justinian's reign. Justinian, triumphing in the spoils he had won from internal enemies (364), is unfavourably contrasted with Belisarius, victor over the Vandals (366). *Romana* 381 is equally insistent that Justinian had made a mistake in recalling Belisarius from Italy, and *Getica* 5. 37 comments that the Bulgars have been able to damage the state because of 'our' (=imperial) neglect. This is not enough to turn Jordanes into a dissident,[26] but it does make him an improbable court employee. Goffart's deductions from the personal names mentioned thus become even less likely. Many names have connotations, and they are insufficient to attach Jordanes to court circles against the run of the other evidence.

[23] *Menander Rhetor*, esp. 368 (pp. 76 ff. Russell–Wilson) on the imperial oration, shows that Greek and Latin traditions heavily influenced each other; cf. Nixon, *Pacatus*, 1–13. On panegyrics and ceremonial, see MacCormack, *Art and Ceremony*, esp. 1–14; cf. McCormick, *Eternal Victory*, 4–5, 37, 41, 45–6.

[24] Goffart, *Narrators*, 33 nn. 58, 59 makes similar points about Cassiodorus' *Gothic History*, but does not apply them to his own view of Jordanes.

[25] Cf. e.g. Wagner, *Getica*, 31 ff.; Reydellet, *La Royauté*, 257 ff.; Barnish, 'Genesis and Completion', 354–5; Goffart, *Narrators*, 44–6 with refs.

[26] Cf. Goffart, *Narrators*, 57–8.

In addition, neither account of the marriage of Germanus and Matasuentha is persuasive. The marriage produced a posthumous son, Germanus, in whom, Jordanes declares, the lines of Anicii (*Aniciorum genus*) and the Amals (*Amala stirpe*) are joined to bring hope for the future *utriusque generi*. Momigliano translated this as 'both peoples' (Goths and Romans), so that Germanus junior became the culmination of the *Getica*'s doctrine of reconciliation.[27] But, in context, the natural translation of the phrase is 'both families' (Amals and Anicii), which removes the phrase's political force. A doctrine of reconciliation was in any case out of place in *c*.550. By 549, the pope and other important Italians, including one of Cassiodorus' friends, the senator Cethegus, wanted the Ostrogoths annihilated (Procopius, *Wars* 7. 35. 9–11). The point of the marriage was in fact to confuse Gothic loyalties on the eve of Germanus' expedition to Italy (ibid. 7. 39. 14 ff.).[28]

Goffart views the marriage as the key to the *Getica*'s love-story. There is no way to 'disprove' something as personal as a reading of a text, but I am unconvinced by his analysis of the *Getica*, primarily because the story-line he detects is not all marked. Sexuality is explicitly an issue only twice in the whole work (the Amazons as Gothic wives, and the final marriage), and it is unclear why these two short sections should be given such emphasis. As we have seen, the marriage is simply a historical event, to which Jordanes' language attaches no great symbolic significance. The stress Jordanes gives to the Amazons may reveal this section to be not the other great clue to the lovers' tale, but one of Jordanes' own additions. The Amazons are made relevant to Gothic history because they are the 'wives of the Scythians'. The *Getica* uses a series of such bogus equations to make material about Scythians, Amazons, Getae, and Dacians relevant to its story. Goths had been

[27] Momigliano, 'Cassiodorus and the Italian Culture of His Time', 218 ff. (cf. 'Gli Anicii', 239 ff.); Barnish, 'Genesis and Completion', 352 ff.

[28] Cf. Croke, 'Cassiodorus', 131 ff.; Reydellet, *La Royauté*, 266, 286–7. For other criticisms of Momigliano, see Bradley, 'Composition of the Getica', 67 ff.; Baldwin, 'Purpose of the Getica'. O'Donnell, *Cassiodorus*, 103 ff. and 'The Aims of Jordanes', 235–6 argues that after an intense religious conversion, Cassiodorus lost interest in political affairs, but this has been rightly criticized by A. M. Cameron, 'Cassiodorus Deflated'. Momigliano, 'Cassiodorus and the Italian Culture of His Time', 220 virtually acknowledges that his translation begs a question, adding: 'It seems to me clear that this passage is a shortened version of something more circumstantial about the same subject.'

equated with Scythians and Getae in the fourth century, and Cassiodorus seems to have used the Dacian material (p. 57), but there is no known precedent for making the Amazons relevant in this way. The length at which Jordanes dwells on the Scythians as the Amazons' husbands might well reflect the fact that he used this device to add something of his own to the Goths' story.[29] We know, for instance, that he searched through Josephus for usable material on the early history of the Goths, and was disappointed by what he found (*Getica* 4. 29), so that it is not at all unlikely to picture him importing the Amazons in this way. Such activity would also have been quite in line with Jordanes' claims to have mixed in material of his own (ibid., praef. 3).

Goffart bolsters the evidence for his reading by detecting an ironic tone to two incidents where Gothic masculine self-assertion is mentioned: Alaric's elevation to kingship over the Visigoths, and Theoderic the Amal's departure from the eastern Empire. But the episodes are not obviously ironic, and the second can, with some certainty, be ascribed a different purpose. Having Theoderic's Goths voluntarily give up a life of ease in the east to defeat Odovacar is part of the *Getica*'s careful fabrication of Theoderic's time in the Balkans. This hides the fact that he had spent long periods in open rebellion, and also seeks to justify his assertion of independence in Italy (see p. 56). The *Getica* is thus simply following Cassiodorus' narrative here in all probability,[30] rather than constructing an ironic love-story.

The other elements of Goffart's love-story are similarly unconvincing. The consistent theme that Goths revolt every time the Romans cut off their pay is a good device for blaming the Empire for part, at least, of the violence that had plagued Roman-Gothic relations. Rather than delaying the lovers' consummation, this seems to have a more serious point, and we might again detect the hand of Cassiodorus.[31] It is also far from clear that the *Getica*'s part-Gothic emperor, Maximinus Thrax, is really meant to be a comic boor. His career is quite distinguished until he starts to persecute Christians (*Getica* 15. 83–8), which, coming from an

---

[29] *Getica* 5. 44, 7. 49–52, 8. 56–9, 58; 5. 44 and 9. 58 are self-justificatory in tone. The stories originated with Herodotus 4. 110–17.

[30] Cf. Barnish, 'Genesis and Completion', 343–4.

[31] *Getica* 13. 76, 16. 89, 29. 146, 52. 270–1, 53. 272; cf. Barnish, 'Genesis and Completion', 342. *Contra* Goffart, *Narrators*, 79–80.

overt Christian such as Jordanes (or Cassiodorus), is not obviously ironic.

The elements from which Goffart creates his love-story are thus all open to alternative, and more convincing interpretations. His reading also encompasses only certain episodes within the text, making much of the *Getica* incidental to such a purpose. Details about Alaric, the Ostrogothic succession after Ermenaric, and the wars of Valamer and Thiudimer are all irrelevant to the supposed love-story. Above all, as Goffart acknowledges, his love-story makes the *Getica*'s first seventy-odd paragraphs (about one-quarter of the whole) irrelevant to the author's central purpose (*Narrators*, 75–6). Yet it is Goffart's sensible contention in his book as a whole, that Jordanes and the other writers produced self-conscious, coherent works (ibid, ch. 1). He is thus forced to identify a different, second reason for Jordanes to have written about the Goths' origins and early history. This too is unconvincing (see below), an additional confirmation that the main purpose which Goffart ascribes to the *Getica* is probably artificial.

In sum, neither Momigliano's nor Goffart's attempt to attach Jordanes to a milieu where we might expect to find someone writing propaganda is at all successful, and neither makes a convincing case for Jordanes' having been something more than he claims to be. The marriage was no doubt an important event, but the fact that it comes last does not necessarily mean that it is a vital cipher for decoding the work. It and its offspring are simply the last major events that Jordanes wished to record.[32]

The reason for this choice, indeed, is not very difficult to detect. The *Getica* concentrates much attention on the Amal family, or rather one particular line of it: Thiudimer, Theoderic, and his offspring. Its vision of them as uniquely prestigious demigods is very misleading, as we have seen, but the point is that the *Getica* recounts highly 'Amalocentric' Gothic history. Scholars have sometimes been puzzled by the fact that Jordanes ends his account of Justinian's Italian war in the *Getica*, though not the *Romana*, with the surrender of Wittigis and Matasuentha in 540, but this merely reinforces the point. As Jordanes explicitly states when laying out the Amal genealogy, the *Getica* is concerned not with Gothic (or even Ostrogothic) history, but with the 'kingdom of the

---

[32] Cf. Croke, 'Cassiodorus', 135.

Amals' down to its destruction (*quomodo autem aut qualiter regnum Amalorum distructum est*, 14. 81). Wittigis, married to Theoderic's granddaughter, is the last Ostrogothic king who can be regarded as in any way an Amal. The wars of Totila and other non-Amals after 540 are irrelevant to Jordanes' purpose in the *Getica*, whereas the *Romana*, a more broadly conceived work, refers to them briefly.[33] Tracing the fortunes, subsequent to the surrender, of the last direct descendant of this line, Matasuentha, is thus a very suitable postscript to the *Getica*. This concentration on the Amal family also confirms that Germanus junior is being seen as the hope of the Amal family and not the Gothic race.[34]

The passage remains somewhat enigmatic in that it avoids noting that Germanus belonged to the house of Justinian. This seems to be a deliberate depoliticization of a marriage which could have been described as a union of the ruling families of both Romans and Goths. Jordanes may even be echoing imperial propaganda. Since the Goths had already offered their crown to Belisarius (Procopius, *Wars* 6. 29. 17 ff.), it may have been necessary to emphasize that the marriage of Matasuentha and Germanus was not to prepare the way for a semi-independent kingdom in Italy. This is not a fully satisfactory explanation, but the *Getica*'s emphasis on a particular branch of the Amals means that no great mystery need surround Jordanes' decision to conclude with the birth of its newest generation.

We must turn finally to the date of the *Getica*. Datable events in both the *Romana* and *Getica* suggest that 551 was a crucial year in the process of composition. The *Getica* closes with the birth of Germanus junior, which can have occurred no later than spring 551,[35] and records that the plague (of 542) occurred 'nine years ago' (19. 104). The Preface of the *Romana* (4) records that Jordanes brought this work down to the twenty-fourth regnal year of Justinian; this ended on 31 March 551. Many have therefore taken 551, and particularly 31 March, as the *terminus ante quem* for

---

[33] Attempts—e.g. Goffart, *Narrators*, 102; Barnish, 'Genesis and Completion', 359–60—to attach a deeper significance to the *Getica*'s ending in 540 are thus misconceived. Ideas that Jordanes was embarrassed by post-540 events are also undermined by the fact that the *Romana* mentions some of them.

[34] The fact that other branches of the family were still fruitful (Barnish, 'Genesis and Completion', 353) is not really relevant.

[35] Germanus senior died in late summer 550 (Procopius, *Wars* 7. 40. 9).

both works, since Vigilius was receiving a copy of each. As Stein
pointed out, however, two later events are mentioned, one in each
work. The despatch of Liberius to Spain (*Getica* 58. 303) most
likely occurred in autumn 551, but certainly not before this, and
perhaps as late as spring 552,[36] while a battle between the
Lombards and Gepids (*Romana* 386) is probably to be dated to
spring or summer 552.[37]

These are, however, insufficient grounds to justify Goffart's
accusation of fraud. For Jordanes does not actually say that he was
writing the *Romana*'s Preface during the twenty-fourth year of
Justinian. He does not specify when he was writing at all, merely
that this was the termination date of his work.[38] The fact that he
felt the need to state this so explicitly might well indicate that this
was indeed different from the moment that he sent the completed
work to Vigilius. We must also look again at what Jordanes tells us
of the process of composition. In the *Getica*, he reports that he had
already started the *Romana* when he interrupted his work to write
the *Getica* (praef. 1). He thus composed in three stages; he began
the *Romana*, wrote the *Getica*, and then completed the *Romana*.
This is neatly confirmed for us by the fact that the *Getica* is at
certain points a source for the *Romana*.[39] We can suggest, therefore, the following solution to the dating question. Jordanes
commenced his work meaning to write only the *Romana*, and his
final choice of termination-date might indicate that this project
was begun in Justinian's twenty-fourth year. He interrupted it to
write the *Getica*—in 551, to judge from the reference to the plague
and the fact that it ends with Germanus junior. Two points need
to be stressed here. First, 31 March of this year need not be
regarded as a *terminus ante quem* for the *Getica*. Justinian's twenty-
fourth year is the termination date of the *Romana*, and does not
apply to the *Getica*. Secondly, Stein's best guess dated Liberius'
departure for Spain to autumn 551. A reference to this event is
entirely consistent with the *Getica* having been written in 551,

---

[36] Stein, ii. 820–1.

[37] Stein, ii. 553–4; cf. Goffart, *Narrators*, 99 n. 363 with refs.

[38] *Romana*, praef. 3–4, esp. 4: the phrase *ab ipso Romulo aedificatore eius
originem sumens, in vicensimo quarto anno Iustiniani imperatoris* is clearly defining
the scope of the work, so that Jordanes' *in anno* would seem to be a solecism for *in
annum* rather than *anno*. Cf. Barnish, 'Genesis and Completion', 352.

[39] Cf. Mommsen, pp. xxix f. Goffart, *Narrators*, 107, claims that both works
were always designed to circulate together, but this is pure assertion.

even if not before the end of March. There is thus nothing obviously deceptive in the *Getica*'s chronological indications.

Having completed the *Getica*, Jordanes returned to the *Romana*, perhaps in winter 551/2, but still retained his original termination-date. The point of this, as Goffart argues, was surely to avoid having to mention Narses' expedition, which left for Italy in April 551, but there is no need to ascribe this a sinister motive. Narses achieved decisive results only in 552: in late June when Totila was killed, and in October with the death of Teias. Even then, the war continued in earnest until winter 553/4, when Cumae finally surrendered.[40] I would suggest, therefore, that, when finishing off the *Romana*, Jordanes had not yet heard any definite news of Narses' campaign, and kept to the date he had originally chosen, rather than refer to incomplete events. This reconstruction fits the available evidence, and the fact that one later event, of spring or early summer 552, crept into the *Romana* (in virtually its last paragraph) should not be accorded undue significance.

There is thus little reason not to take Jordanes at face value, both as a former military secretary with Gothic family connections, and with regard to when and why he wrote the *Getica*. We can now return to his own account of the work. The purpose of the *Romana* was perhaps to bring his friend Vigilius to convert to a more religious life by stressing the folly of worldly vanities, and there may be eschatological overtones to the *Getica*'s account of the Goths' downfall.[41] But we must not ignore the author's and his audience's strong interest in Gothic history. In the preface, for instance, Jordanes urges Castalius to add to the text where he had extra information (3), suggesting that Castalius was concerned with Gothic history *per se*. This is confirmed by Jordanes' note a few paragraphs later that he was writing about Scandinavia in response to Castalius' demands to learn of the Goths' origins.[42] The preface also refers to Castalius as *vicinus genti* (3). This could mean several things, but is most naturally interpreted metaphorically, implying that Castalius, like Jordanes, had some connection to the Gothic race. We are faced, then, with the coherent picture of

[40] Stein, ii. 597; cf. Goffart, *Narrators*, 99–100, but I do not agree with the significance he attaches to Jordanes' choice.

[41] O'Donnell, 'The Aims of Jordanes', 230 ff.

[42] *Getica* 1. 9 *cuius originem flagitas*: this can only mean Castalius, who is addressed in the second person in the preface.

two men with Gothic connections enquiring into Gothic history, at a moment when one of the two Gothic kingdoms in western Europe was being extinguished. The general reluctance to take Jordanes at face value reflects the realization that the *Getica*'s account of Gothic history is not straightforward. As Goffart puts it, it is so tendentious that it must be trying to convince somebody of something (*Narrators*, 23, 47, 97 ff.). But such responses to Jordanes' text fail to take full account of its relationship to Cassiodorus' *Gothic History*.

The debate generated by Momigliano has identified a number of ways in which Jordanes was his own man. Croke has successfully shown, for instance, that the *Romana* is not Symmachus' lost *Roman History*. As several scholars have recently argued, it in fact reveals Jordanes as a competent abbreviator who made careful choices from the sources available to him.[43] A number of features of the *Getica* indicate that this work is, likewise, no mere plagiarism of Cassiodorus. The first person is used extensively, notably when signalling cross-references, of which there are a large number. All match up, and must be Jordanes' own work; it is very unlikely that he could have imported them wholesale from Cassiodorus without leaving some loose ends. Their number emphasizes that Jordanes took a keen interest in his subject.[44] In addition, there is no good reason to doubt Jordanes' claim to have added material from other sources (praef. 3). Many Greek and Latin authors are named in the text, and, although some may have been cited indirectly from Cassiodorus, even the most sceptical have always allowed that he took his geographical introduction first-hand from Orosius (*Getica* 1. 4–9). As we have seen, adding the Amazons to Gothic history may also have been Jordanes' own idea, and many citations refer to material which digresses from his main theme. It is natural to interpret these additions as his own.[45]

If Jordanes had simply copied Cassiodorus, this would also imply that their views of Gothic history were the same. Cassiodorus, however, was working at the court of Ostrogothic kings,

[43] Croke, 'AD 476', 90 ff.; cf. Várady, 'Jordanes-Studien'; Goffart, *Narrators*, 47 ff.; Reydellet, *La Royauté*, 290 ff.

[44] e.g. Croke, 'Cassiodorus', 122 ff.; O'Donnell, 'The Aims of Jordanes', 230 and n. 15. It used to be argued that the first-person references were from Cassiodorus, e.g. Hachmann, *Goten und Skandinavien*, 60–1.

[45] Croke, 'Cassiodorus', 123 ff.; cf. O'Donnell, 'The Aims of Jordanes', 235, and *Cassiodorus*, 215 ff.

whereas Jordanes wrote the *Getica* at a time when the Italian kingdom was doomed. Some difference in approach is likely, and in part demonstrable. Jordanes reserves his ultimate accolade for Justinian, conqueror of the Goths (60. 315),

This glorious race (the Goths) yielded to a more glorious prince and surrendered to a more valiant leader, whose fame shall be silenced by no ages or cycles of years.

The *Getica*, especially when combined with the *Romana*, champions outright Imperial victory over the Goths.[46] Cassiodorus' *Gothic History* cannot have taken such a line. Similarly, the *Getica* lacks a full account of Theoderic's achievements (after he conquers Italy, at least), where Cassiodorus would surely have praised at length this most successful of Ostrogothic kings.[47] The *Getica* also diverges at certain points from Cassiodorus' *Chronicle*. Cassiodorus could have changed his mind in between, but the simplest explanation is that Jordanes has pursued an independent line.[48]

Yet we must not minimize Cassiodorus' influence. Castalius, it should be remembered, wanted an abbreviation of Cassiodorus' history, and, as we have seen, Jordanes was confident of having followed his model in broad outline. In addition, Schirren showed long ago that the *Getica* contains strong echoes of Cassiodorus' Latin style. The influence is too general for specific passages to be identified as Cassiodorian, but this suggests strongly that Jordanes really had read Cassiodorus very closely.[49] The *Getica*'s conclusion, strikingly, reuses a flower metaphor which Cassiodorus had applied to his own Gothic history. Here at least, then, Jordanes seems to have copied out a piece of prose he found particularly appealing.[50] On questions of content, too, there is strong evidence of Cassiodorus' influence. A reference in the *Variae* makes it all but certain that Jordanes took the Amal genealogy from his model

[46] Croke, 'Cassiodorus', 127; Reydellet, *La Royauté*, 256 ff., 289 ff.; Goffart, *Narrators*, 67–8; Barnish, 'Genesis and Completion', 354 ff.

[47] Reydellet, *La Royauté*, 268–9, 289; Goffart, *Narrators*, 67–8.

[48] Croke, 'Cassiodorus', 129 ff.; Goffart, *Narrators*, 40–1.

[49] *De ratione, passim*; cf. Momigliano, 'Cassiodorus and the Italian Culture of His Time', 222–3 with refs.; O'Donnell, *Cassiodorus*, 52–3; Barnish, 'Genesis and Completion', 348–9.

[50] *Getica* 60. 316; *Variae* 9. 25. 5; cf. O'Donnell, *Cassiodorus*, 52–3.

(p. 19). It was probably also Cassiodorus who added Ermenaric to Amal history from Ammianus, which implies, of course, that the passages of the *Getica* which display a strong verbal dependence on Ammianus do so because Jordanes has here more or less copied Cassiodorus.[51] Three days is not a long time, but if Jordanes was able to devote himself entirely to the task of reading Cassiodorus, seventy-two hours is more than long enough to make good notes on its contents and arguments, and even to copy out some favourite passages.[52]

I would argue, therefore, that much that is tendentious in the *Getica*'s account of Gothic history has actually been inherited incidentally from Cassiodorus. Jordanes, a competent but unlearned ex-military secretary, has simply culled information from his acknowledged model, without realizing that this text, written at the court of Gothic kings, distorts history to praise them. This much can be demonstrated, at least, in the case of the two major distortions which concern us here: the anachronistic account of the division into Ostrogoths and Visigoths, and the exaggerated historical prestige accorded Amals and Balthi. This argument also allows us to circumvent the problem of Jordanes' dependence on Cassiodorus. Since in these two instances, he can be shown to have followed his model's approach closely, anything he added himself must have been harmonized with what he had already learnt from Cassiodorus.

C. *Pro-Amal and Pro-Gothic Distortion in the* Getica

In a letter of 533 written for Athalaric, king of Italy and grandson of Theoderic, Cassiodorus announced his own elevation to the praetorian prefecture. The letter recalled some of the factors which had led to this promotion, and these included his Gothic history, described in the following terms (*Variae* 9. 25. 4–5),

He set out our [Amal] lineage from antiquity, gaining by reading that which even the grey-haired wisdom of our [Gothic] elders scarcely

---

[51] Heather, 'Cassiodorus', 126 ff. For other examples of dependence, see Barnish, 'Genesis and Completion', 348 ff., although I am unconvinced that Cassiodorus continued his work past *c*.535.

[52] Cassiodorus' work came in 12 books (*Variae* pr. 2), but these were probably more on the scale of a Eutropius than an Ammianus: cf. Goffart, *Narrators*, 39.

recalled. He drew forth from the hiding place of antiquity long-forgotten kings of the Goths. He brought the Amal family back into view, showing clearly that our ancestors have been royal for seventeen generations. He made Gothic origins[53] to be Roman history, collecting as into a single wreath the varied flowers that were formerly strewn here and there in the fields of books.

These few lines can only hint at the whole, but we may suppose them to transmit what Cassiodorus saw as his work's most important features.

The meaning of the first part is clear enough, and its effects on the historical value of Jordanes' *Getica* will be examined shortly. The significance of the second comment (*originem Gothicam historiam fecit esse Romanam*) is less obvious, but Jordanes' text suggests its main point. Much of the early part of the *Getica* is taken up with material from Graeco-Roman traditions, recalling episodes in the histories of Scythians, Amazons, Getae, and Dacians.[54] These people are all equated with the Goths, the point being that they, like the Goths, had all occupied lands north of the Black Sea. Material from classical traditions could thus illustrate the Goths' ancient history, and it is surely to this that Cassiodorus refers.[55]

Cassiodorus was not the first to make such equations. Orosius had viewed the Goths as Getae (1. 16. 2), and such equations perhaps made tribal peoples of the migration period less frightening. There could be no new barbarians; the Mediterranean world

---

[53] *originem*: this could simply mean 'history'; cf. Goffart, *Narrators*, 35–6.

[54] *Getica* 5. 44–13. 78; mostly from Justinus and Pomponius Mela; cf. Mommsen p. xxx and nn.

[55] This is the accepted general interpretation, although views of its more particular significance vary: e.g. Reydellet, *La Royauté*, 262 ff.; Schirren, *De ratione*, 71; Barnish, 'Genesis and Completion', 339–40. Goffart, *Narrators*, 37 ff. interprets the phrase to mean that Cassiodorus rearranged Gothic history into a Roman-style serial biography, but this seems too precise, and Cassiodorus' history included at least some of this material. The *Ordo generis* specifies that the history provided an account of Gothic origins, the reference to *capillati* is surely Cassiodorian since such men were known in Ostrogothic Italy (11. 72; p. 36), the material on the Dacians is important for the rise of the Amals (p. 57), suggesting that this is again the senator's work, and it was probably Cassiodorus who placed the origins of the Gothic kingdom in *c.*1500 BC: Heather, 'The Two Thousandth Year', 171 ff. He thus needed to fill 2000 years between his starting-date and AD *c.*500; the material made available by these equations performed this role admirably.

had conquered them before, and would do so again.[56] Cassiodorus, however, was writing for a Gothic king, and must have had a different aim. He was perhaps attempting to give the Goths cultural respectability, showing that they belonged to the mainstream of Graeco-Roman history. His approach may also have been designed to create a past where Roman and Goth had belonged together, finding historical justification for their coexistence in Italy.[57] More simply, the Graeco-Roman material also gave the Goths a more glorious past: defeating Egyptian kings, and, under the rule of Telephus, a son of Hercules, waging war upon the Greeks.

By the time Jordanes had made his contribution, perhaps importing the Amazons, these equations had made Gothic history longer than its Roman counterpart. According to Jordanes, when the Amal realm came to an end with Wittigis in AD 540, this was nearly its 2,030th year (*Getica* 60. 313). It thus began in *c*.1490 BC, which, according to late-antique conceptions, made it significantly older than Rome. For both Cassiodorus and Jordanes, Rome was founded only in *c*.760 BC, and according to these sixth-century chroniclers, 1490 BC was about the time that Moses was leading the Children of Israel through the wilderness.[58] Bogus identifications and their chronology gave the Goths historical precedence over Rome.[59]

Cassiodorus' glorified Gothic history should probably not be accorded too serious a purpose. It is hardly propaganda, since it is not subtle or powerful enough to have influenced its audience's attitudes and actions. Italian aristocrats are unlikely to have been much impressed by the Goths' new-found historical prestige, nor can it have had much serious effect on the Goths' own view of

---

[56] Maenchen-Helfen, 5 ff. Goths appear as Scythians in 4th-c. writers such as Eunapius. Another tradition identified them with Gog and Magog: Ambrose, *De fide* 2, 16, 495. 138 (Migne, *PL* 16. 611–12). Denied by Jerome, *Quaest. Hebr. in Genes.* 10. 2, and Augustine, *De civ. Dei* 20. 11, the identification remained influential: Anderson, *Alexander's Gate*, 9 ff.

[57] Momigliano, 'Cassiodorus and the Italian Culture of His Time', 223.

[58] Cassiodorus, *Chronicle* 29 (Moses), 73 (Rome) (*CM* ii. 121–2); Jordanes, *Romana* 27–8, 52.

[59] The figure of 2,030 is probably calculated from a notice of the kingdom's 2,000th year: Heather, 'The Two Thousandth Year', 171 ff.

themselves. But that was probably not its purpose. The level of argumentation suggests that Cassiodorus was attempting more to flatter and amuse a Gothic court, than to shape opinion in any important way.[60] Roman and Gothic aristocrats mixed freely at Theoderic's court, where a not insignificant literary culture flourished.[61] Cassiodorus' work would have appealed to this audience, among whom many Goths entered the Senate (Cassiodorus, *Variae, passim*) and the Roman family of Cyprian was fluent in Latin, Greek, and Gothic (*Variae* 8. 21–2). Romanized Gothic aristocrats would have been interested in the Graeco-Roman past, and enjoyed the gibe at Roman pretension implicit in Cassiodorus' extended chronology. Any political point may have been more personal: like his panegyrics, the history was a means of advancing Cassiodorus at court: reflecting official views, rather than propagating them.[62] As we have just seen, the history was considered an important factor in his promotion to the praetorian prefecture.

On the historical value of the *Getica*, the effects of all this are negative. The equations are false, giving the Goths an extended history in lands above the Black Sea, and the probably oral record of their migration there (under Filimer: 4. 26–8) had naturally to be placed before this material. A move of the second and third centuries AD was placed, therefore, in the second millennium BC. The same desire to glorify the Goths' part in Graeco-Roman history also distorts the *Getica*'s view of the more recent past, if on a smaller scale. That some of this originated with Cassiodorus is suggested by his *Chronicle*, where items from Jerome and Prosper have been adjusted to suit the sensibilities of the Ostrogothic rulers of Italy. Claudius defeats 'barbarians' rather than Goths, Ambrose's strictly anti-Arian Catholicism is downplayed, and the battle of Pollentia becomes a Gothic victory rather than a draw.[63] Similar manipulations are apparent in the *Getica*. The Goths fight for Constantine in his civil wars, and are primarily responsible for

---

[60] Cf. Barnish, 'Genesis and Completion', 338 ff.; Cassiodorus probably worked largely 523–6, and this political context would have been reflected in his work, if more as flattery than real propaganda.

[61] See generally, Momigliano, 'Cassiodorus and the Italian Culture of His Time', 208–17; Deichmann, 'La corte dei re Goti'; Moorhead, 'The Decii'; cf. Staab, 'Ostrogothic Geographers'; Barnish, 'Maximian'.

[62] Cf. O'Donnell, *Cassiodorus*, 33 ff.

[63] Cassiodorus, *Chronicle*, 982, 1133, and 1172, altering Jerome and Prosper twice respectively; O'Donnell, *Cassiodorus*, 38–9.

his victory over Licinius (21. 111). In fact, they supported Licinius (Anon. Val. 5. 27). There is also a tendency to overstate the Goths' contribution to Roman military success (e.g. 21. 110–12; 28. 145–6; 32. 166), and the idea, strongly marked in the *Getica*, that Romano-Gothic military alliances brought success to both parties, probably originated with Cassiodorus.[64]

A more pointed example is the *Getica*'s account of the Ostrogoths' time in the Balkans. Byzantine sources show that the Goths were unwelcome, and that, apart from fighting Theoderic Strabo, Theoderic the Amal also clashed with the Empire itself, tension escalating into open conflict from 478 to 483, and again between 486 and 488 (see Part III). None of this appears in the *Getica*, which portrays the relationship between the Amal and the emperor Zeno as one of uninterrupted harmony (57. 289 ff.). The ultimate point of this was to legitimize Theoderic's seizure of Italy. The picture of harmony allows the *Getica* to stress that the Amal went there at Zeno's invitation, and it also has the emperor tell Theoderic to rule as king over both Goths and Romans (57. 292). It seems clear, however, that, while Zeno had agreed to the move, he did not agree to Theoderic's ruling independently. The proclamation of Theoderic as King of Italy thus led to a further diplomatic breach, which the *Getica* again conceals (cf. p. 306). This is surely an example of Cassiodorus' rewriting recent history to suit his employers.

Devoting attention to seventeen generations of Amal kings, the other feature of his History which Cassiodorus chose to mention, also led to historical distortion, which remains equally apparent in the *Getica*. As we have seen, the Amal genealogy (14. 79–81) has surely been copied from Cassiodorus, and the *Getica* places much emphasis on Amal kingship from the time of Ostrogotha onwards.[65] But the family probably rose to real prominence only under Valamer, and could boast of no more than two or three generations of royalty. Here again, Jordanes has been misled by a major interpretative outline of Cassiodorus' history. Its perspective, of course, was shaped by the fact that Cassiodorus was a

---

[64] Momigliano, 'Cassiodorus and the Italian Culture of His Time', 223–4.

[65] The *Getica* mentions some non-Amal kings before the Hunnic invasions (Cniva, Respa, Vedar, Thuruar, Gerberich, Ariaric, Aoric). Jordanes may have added this material to what was originally a narrative of Amal domination in Cassiodorus.

leading civil servant of Amal kings. Their Italian kingdom had been established only in the 490s, and their last major Gothic rival, Recitach son of Theoderic Strabo, overcome only in the 480s (p. 301), so that the point of this distortion seems clear. The Amals wanted to present themselves and to be presented as natural rulers, legitimized by centuries of royal status. In this case, the word 'propaganda' seems more appropriate, but we might again doubt whether such historical distortions had any practical effect. Did they really strengthen the loyalties of the Amals' Gothic and Roman subjects?[66] It is perhaps more likely that they were just pleasing to Amal ears. Either way, we can distinguish four specific ways in which the *Getica*'s account of Gothic history has been distorted by the idea that the Amals had long enjoyed unchallenged supremacy.

The Amal genealogy, first of all, greatly exaggerates the length of Amal pre-eminence. As we have seen, the majority of names between Gapt and Athal are unhistorical, and Ermenaric was not an Amal. In addition, Hunimund, Thorismud, and Vinitharius were probably independent non-Amal rulers of the different Gothic groups which Valamer united in *c.*450 (p. 240). Other names must remain mysterious: Achiulf, Oduulf, Ansila, Ediulf, Vultuulf, and Valavrans appear only in the genealogy, and are accorded no famous deeds. This suggests that, like Valamer's father Vandalarius, they were not prominent Gothic kings, even if perhaps genuine Amals; some Germanic families could remember many non-royal ancestors.[67] There is no reason to suppose that Jordanes thought the genealogy and related sections of narrative (all presumably taken from Cassiodorus) anything other than historically accurate.

To digress slightly, it is perhaps worth noting that the genealogy and related narrative sections display the same dependence on a mixture of oral and written sources which we have observed before, suggesting that this kind of material perhaps all originated with Cassiodorus. Ermenaric, for instance, was taken from a literary work, the history of Ammianus Marcellinus, and then attached to a genealogy which drew in part on oral tradition. This pattern also characterizes the victory in battle, which, according to

---

[66] Cf. Wallace-Hadrill, *Early Germanic Kingship*, 10–11.

[67] The Lombard King Rothari could recall 12 non-royal generations of his family: Dumville, 'Kingship, Genealogies', 94.

Jordanes, led their Gothic followers to regard the Amals as demigods (13. 78). Victorious Germanic leaders do seem to have been regarded as specially favoured by the gods, and, in that sense, semi-divine.[68] This much, then, may reflect the Goths' own traditions. But the battle to which the *Getica* refers is drawn from Graeco-Roman history: a first-century battle in which Dacians killed the Roman commander Fuscus (13. 76 ff.). The Goths may well have viewed their victorious kings as semi-divine, but the *Getica*, again probably following Cassiodorus (since we are dealing with a crucial moment in Amal history), anchors Gothic tradition firmly within Graeco-Roman historiography.[69]

Returning to our main theme, Jordanes' inherited view of the Amals also concentrates attention upon one branch of the family at the expense of others. Other Amals were prominent in the eastern Empire, for instance, at the same time as Valamer and his successors were creating the Ostrogoths. These men do not appear in the *Getica*.[70] Jordanes similarly mentions only briefly that Beremud son of Thorismud left the Goths (33. 174–5; 48. 251), and states that it was decided by lot that Vidimer should go west in 473 (56. 283–4). In both these cases, brevity probably conceals political dispute; these other branches of the family seem to have been ousted by Thiudimer and Theoderic (p. 250).

Thirdly, bias in favour of the Amals undermines the *Getica*'s account of Gothic leaders from other families. We have no means of knowing how many families competed for the leadership of different Gothic groups between the third century and the emergence of the Amals and Balthi. But the *Getica* has suppressed the importance of at least one of these potentially alternative ruling lines, virtually omitting the power struggle fought out between Theoderic the Amal and Theoderic Strabo. Bitter rivalry between them lasted for an entire decade after 473, and nothing in the

---

[68] Schlesinger, 'Lord and Follower', 76; Moisl, 'Anglo-Saxon Royal Genealogies', 218 ff.

[69] Having extended Amal pre-eminence to 17 generations to echo Romulus and Aeneas (p. 21), Cassiodorus perhaps counted back a suitable number of years, and picked out the nearest victory of a trans-Danubian tribe over the Romans to mark the advent of Amal kingship. The defeat of Fuscus took place in AD 76, so that if Cassiodorus counted from the birth of Athalaric (the 17th Amal king) in *c*.520, he allowed *c*.26 years per generation. He perhaps first tried 25 years per generation, and then looked for the nearest suitable battle.

[70] Wolfram, 32: Andag, Andela, and Sidimund.

contemporary sources suggests that the Amal was bound to prevail
(Part III, *passim*). In the *Getica*, Strabo receives one brief mention
in the reign of Marcian (451–7) and then disappears (52. 270).
This was probably designed to preserve the fiction of the Amals'
ancient pre-eminence, concealing the extent of their struggle with
the equally legitimate line of Triarius. Again, it is hard not to see
this as the work of Cassiodorus, imported by Jordanes in all good
faith.

Finally, we must examine the *Getica*'s assertion that the Goths
as a whole regarded the Balthi as a less prestigious dynasty than
the Amals (28. 146; cf. 33. 174–5). Wolfram has taken this at face
value, suggesting that while, to Gothic eyes, the Amals were *Ansis*
or demigods, the Balthi were not. He also suggests that the son of
the Balthic king Alaric II and his Amal wife Theodegotha was
called Amalric because of the Amal family's historically superior
prestige. Subsequent events suggest, however, that this was more a
question of immediate political ingratiation than a reflection of
long-established inferiority. Under pressure from the Franks, the
Visigoths required Theoderic's support to maintain their realm.[71]

More generally, it is most unlikely that the Visigoths looked on
the Amals as superior to their own rulers. In a letter of 476, written
when he was detained at the Visigothic court, Sidonius Apollinaris
cites some of his own poetry which claims that the Ostrogoths,
presumably meaning the Amal-led Goths, had defeated the Huns
only because of the Visigoths' intervention,

With the men of this place [the Visigoths] as his champions, the
Ostrogoth flourishes and, crushing again and again his neighbours the
Huns, he is enabled to lord it over those enemies by being subject to
those friends [the Visigoths again].[72]

In the great days of Euric, the Balthi were thus not only unwilling
to admit Amal superiority, but asserted the opposite. The wars
referred to must be those which established Gothic independence
after Attila's death (see Ch. 7). Quite how Sidonius envisaged the
Visigoths as the Ostrogoths' champions in these wars is uncertain.
He was perhaps thinking of the Visigothic intervention which led
to the Huns' defeat on the Catalaunian Plains and started the

---

[71] Wolfram, 33; cf. Goffart, review of Wolfram.

[72] *Ep.* 8. 9. 36 ff.; Anderson's alternative translation in the Loeb edition
(slightly adjusted).

break-up of Attila's empire.[73] Alternatively, there may have been some subsequent contact between the two Gothic groups of which we are ignorant. Either way, quite contrary to the *Getica*, Sidonius is claiming superiority over the Ostrogoths on behalf of the Visigoths.

Given his precarious situation at court, Sidonius was no doubt flattering his Visigothic masters. We need not take the claim too seriously, but this only reinforces the general point. Neither of these contradictory views of the relative importance of Amal and Balth had its origin in historically determined Gothic attitudes. Both are examples of court propaganda, reflecting the changing balance of power which allowed first one and then the other to claim pre-eminence. This is not to deny that successful Amal kings were looked on as semi-divine; this, as we have seen, seems to have been a general Germanic phenomenon. The point is rather this: while successful Amals such as Valamer and Theoderic may well have been regarded by their followers as *Ansis*, this is equally likely to have been true of the Visigoths' attitude towards leading Balthi such as Alaric I and Euric.

Looking at the question more broadly, Amal claims to unique pre-eminence fit closely the general political context of the second half of Theoderic the Amal's reign in Italy. After their defeat by Clovis in 507, the Visigoths put on the throne Gesalic, Amalric's non-Amal half-brother. Theoderic at first accepted him, but in 511, replaced Gesalic notionally with Amalric, although he in fact ruled both kingdoms himself, establishing Amal tutelage over the Visigoths.[74] The *Getica*'s view that Amals were historically superior to the Balthi might well echo Theoderic's propaganda after 511, when this extension of Amal power, including the deposition of a Balthi, required justification.

When composing the *Getica*, then, Jordanes simply adopted Cassiodorus' means of incorporating the Goths into the Graeco-Roman past, and took at face value his exaltation of the Amals. Both undermine the historical value of his work, reflecting history as the Amals liked to hear it told, rather than reality. One major problem in the *Getica*'s account of Gothic history—the position

[73] Wolfram, 266 (cf. 196–7) interprets the passage to mean that a few Ostrogoths had found refuge at the Visigothic court, but the poem asserts Visigothic world-dominance, dealing with peoples, not individuals.

[74] Procopius, *Wars* 5. 12. 43 ff.; Gregory of Tours, *HF* 2. 37.

given to the Amals—is thus readily explicable. Looking for advancement at Theoderic's court, Cassiodorus produced a version of history which flattered and amused the Amals, and perhaps also attempted to legitimize their recent seizures of power. Jordanes faithfully incorporated it in his work, probably without realizing that it was propaganda rather than history. In part, Amal propaganda also explains the *Getica*'s anachronistic view of Gothic social divisions, our second major problem. The existence of such a ruling family over seventeen generations presupposes that the group they ruled had also existed. As the next section will suggest, however, this anachronism, the inflation of the ruling families' prestige, and even the *Getica*'s internal contradictions can only be fully understood when account is taken of the likely workings of Gothic oral history.

D. *Oral Tradition and History*

As we have seen, Gothic oral history does seem to be present in the *Getica*, if at some remove. Of contributors to the *Getica* as it now stands, Ablabius seems to have gathered at least some of this material, particularly the story of Gothic migration into lands above the Black Sea (*Getica* 4. 28; cf. p. 18). At the same time, Cassiodorus knew many Goths, and Jordanes was himself of Gothic origins. Knowledge of their oral traditions would have been as widespread as the Goths themselves in the sixth century, and Jordanes told his friend Castalius to add to the *Getica* any extra information that he had gained from his own Gothic contacts (praef. 3).

The *Getica* includes only part of its author's knowledge of oral history. *Getica* 4. 26 notes that Filimer was the son of Gadaric and 'about' the fifth after Berig, suggesting that Jordanes knew stories about intervening kings, but included merely the name of one of them, Gadaric. One reason for this was a desire for brevity: Castalius had urged Jordanes to produce something smaller than Cassiodorus' twelve volumes (praef. 1). But Jordanes was also suspicious of the historical value of this material. He refused to believe, for instance, tales of the Goths' supposed captivity in Britain or some other island, and of their redemption at the cost of a horse (5. 38). On these he comments, 'for myself, I prefer to believe what I have read, rather than put trust in old wives' tales (*fabulis anilibus*)'. The approach is applied consistently. At another point, Jordanes makes it clear that he was disposed to believe oral accounts of the migration under Filimer because Ablabius' history provided written confirmation,

for so the story is told in their early songs, in the manner almost of a history. Ablabius also, a famous chronicler of the Gothic race, confirms this in his most trustworthy account. (4. 26–9.)

Jordanes was not to know that Ablabius' source had probably also been oral history, but his working principles seem clear: written sources carried more weight with him than oral tradition.

Modern anthropological studies suggest that Jordanes' instinct was sound. Oral traditions do preserve memories of the past, but often in stylized form. For instance, Gothic oral history seems to have remembered the move into lands above the Black Sea, but the independent movement of any number of small groups became a tribal migration (p. 6). More fundamentally, pre-literate societies tend to preserve stories of the past to explain the present. Oral history is not unalterable, but reflects current social configurations; as these change, so must collective memory. The most extreme effects of oral transmission can be found in segmentary lineage societies, where all claim descent from a single ancestor, and subgroups use genealogy to define their relationship to the whole. As relations change, with groups disappearing or new ones being defined, so do later generations of the genealogies. New branches are added to take account of new groups, and irrelevant lines dropped, so that the genealogies do not reflect any historic sequence of events. The oral context makes these adjustments simpler, since there is no independent, written record of the past. A similar process applies to politically more centralized societies (more relevant to the Ostrogoths and Amals), where oral narratives and attendant genealogy legitimize both current kings and the different subgroups they rule. Elements fade in and out of tales as monarchical institution(s) change. Any material from a non-literate record of the past must thus be treated with particular care.[75]

[75] A commonplace, but see for instance, Goody (ed.), *Literacy in Traditional Societies*, esp. 31 ff., 44 ff.; Bohannan, 'A Genealogical Charter', esp. p 312; cf. Dumville, 'Kingship Genealogies', 85 ff. A good recent approach to history in oral tradition is Willis, *A State in the Making*, pt. 1; cf. Miller, 'Listening for the African Past', 1–5 for current debate.

A considerable margin for error must be allowed when importing insights derived essentially from Polynesian and African studies to something as remote as the migration period. Nevertheless, the *Getica* is partly dependent on orally transmitted information, and these insights help to make sense of the fallacious claims advanced by the Amal family. These were not only promulgated by Cassiodorus, but had probably also followed naturally from the family's rise to prominence. Modern parallels suggest that this would have generated adjustments in oral history, legitimizing Amal claims to rule by extending it back into the distant past. A centralized rule that had been built up only in stages since *c*.450 was antedated to lands above the Black Sea, particularly, we might guess, through stories about the eponymous Ostrogoths and Amal. By the 490s, Theoderic was referring to these eponymous heroes in the names he gave to his children (Amalasuentha and Ostrogotho Areagni); he also had a sister called Amalafrida.[76] Cassiodorus made his own additions to the Amal propaganda campaign, but it was already under way.

This helps to explain the *Getica*'s anachronistic account of Gothic social organization. Essentially, the *Getica* has applied the pattern of its own day (when the Ostrogoths ruled Italy, and the Visigoths Spain) to a much earlier period. This is exactly the way in which sixth-century Gothic oral history is likely to have rationalized the past. Once the two major groups had established themselves, oral history is likely to have adjusted itself and remade its account of the past, and particularly the Goths' occupation of lands above the Black Sea, accordingly.

This cannot, of course, be proved beyond doubt, but there is a little evidence that the *Getica*'s account of the division of the Goths came from oral history. Jordanes tells us that Ablabius thought it originated in the third century (14. 82), and he did gather some material from Gothic oral history (p. 61). The simplistic and symmetrical explanation of the names given in the same passage might also point in this direction. Presumably again according to Ablabius, the 'Ostrogoths' were the 'Eastern Goths' and the Visigoths the 'Western Goths', named from their geographical positions. 'Ostrogoth' may well have meant Eastern Goth, but 'Visigoth' is a later form of 'Vesi' or 'Visi' (last attested

[76] Cf. Wolfram, 32.

in *c*.450: App. A), which meant something different. Ablabius' explanation must thus belong to the late fifth century, after 'Visigoth' had come into use. It may also represent another rationalization of oral history, since it again reflects the actual situation of *c*.500, when the Visigoths held lands to the west, in Gaul and Spain, and the Ostrogoths were east of them in Italy.[77]

The workings of oral history suggest in addition an explanation for the self-contradiction we have observed in the *Getica*. Whereas its strongest current indicates that the Goths had been united under the Amals before the Hunnic invasions, it also once makes the contradictory statement that even then Visigoths and Ostrogoths lived apart under Balth and Amal rule, placing the dynasties on an equal footing (5. 42). Since the anachronism of Amal rule over both Gothic groups originated in a combination of oral-historical and literary propaganda from the Ostrogothic kingdom, it seems reasonable to suggest that the equal anachronism of ancient Balth rule over the Visigoths had its origins in the Visigothic kingdom. Again, this cannot be proved, but it is a logical and economic explanation of the contradiction.

This would indicate, of course, that the *Getica* must have drawn in some way on a Visigothic source. No such work is extant, but it is worth stressing that one is likely to have been written in the late fifth century. After his triumphant assertion of Visigothic power, Euric's court became a centre of literary patronage. A number of Sidonius Apollinaris' highly educated friends were drawn there to further their careers,[78] and Sidonius' own poem discussed above confirms that there was a market for Latin expositions of the glories of Visigothic kings. Its assertion that the Ostrogoths flourished through Visigothic patronage is part of a sustained attempt to portray Euric's people as politically dominant over all the major groupings within their orbit (Saxons, Burgundians, Herules, etc.). More specifically, Leo of Narbonne, chief adviser to Euric, tried to persuade Sidonius to write a history at about this time. We have only Sidonius' response to Leo (*Ep.* 4. 22), which does not make it explicit that the work was to concentrate on Visigothic kings, but it was certainly to include contemporary events (allowing Sidonius to suggest that Leo was better placed to

---

[77] Wolfram, 25–6 similarly dates the system, but attributes it to Cassiodorus. The reference to Ablabius (*Getica* 14. 82) seems to deny this suggestion.

[78] e.g. Leo of Narbonne, *PLRE* ii. 662–3; Lampridius, ibid. 656–7.

write it himself). Given Leo's position at the Visigothic court, it is only natural to suppose that the recent triumphs of Visigothic kings were to loom large. A circle at Euric's court was thus looking for someone to play the role that Cassiodorus later fulfilled in Italy, and there is no reason to suppose that someone was not eventually found.

That such a work may have been used, presumably in the first instance by Cassiodorus, is also not unlikely. After 511, Theoderic ruled both Ostrogoths and Visigoths, and there had been considerable contact between the two kingdoms since the 490s.[79] Such a work could easily have found its way to Italy, and a history extolling Visigothic kings may even have prompted a desire in Theoderic for something similar for his own dynasty. One of the *Getica*'s three parts, of course, is precisely devoted to Visigothic history (*Getica* 25. 131–47. 245), and may well reflect our lost Visigothic source.[80] We can perhaps also put a name to its author. Of the two passages asserting that the division into Ostrogoths and Visigoths existed before the Hunnic invasions, one is specifically ascribed to the mysterious Ablabius (14. 82). This implicitly contradicts the rest of the *Getica*, but is in harmony with the second passage we have considered before, where it is stated that Balthi even then ruled the Visigoths (5. 42). This second passage, seemingly from our Visigothic source, does not mention Ablabius, but agrees with the first passage where he is named, and disagrees with the rest of the *Getica*, so that Ablabius may well have been the author of them both. If so, Ablabius is likely to have been our now lost Visigothic historian.[81]

The argument cannot be pressed, but it is worth stressing a more general point. The content of Gothic oral tradition will have varied according to which Goths were preserving it: Visigoths having some versions, Ostrogoths others. The *Getica* confirms the point. Of early Gothic history, for instance, there would seem to

[79] Cf. Wolfram, 281 ff., 309–11.

[80] Goffart, *Narrators*, 65–6 notes that much of this section deals with other tribes, taking this omission of Visigothic history as another element in his love-story. Cassiodorus may have had to make the omissions, however, because a Visigothic history which was anything like Sidonius' poem (p. 59) would have asserted Visigothic pre-eminence over the Ostrogoths.

[81] Cf. Hachmann, *Goten und Skandinavien*, 59 ff. for the same conclusion to a different argument. It has been thought that Ablabius wrote in Italy, but on the basis only of an unconvincing emendation; cf. Goffart, *Narrators*, 62 n. 208.

have existed not one set of stories, but several. *Getica* 4. 26 tells us that Filimer was 'about (*pene*) the fifth king after Berig'. The use of *pene* suggests that Jordanes knew of alternative accounts. This would be quite in line with what anthropologists have found in modern oral histories; different views of and claims concerning the present demand different reconstructions of the past.

Similarly, apart from recounting the story of Gothic origins on the 'island' of Scandinavia, Jordanes also mentions other legends 'which tell of [the Goths'] subjection to slavery in Britain or in some other island, or of their redemption by a certain man at the cost of a horse' (5. 38). There was thus more than one version of Gothic origins current in the sixth century. Jordanes, as we have seen, made his choice because he found written confirmation of it, but this is hardly authoritative: the Scandinavian origin of the Goths would seem to have been one sixth-century guess among several. It is also striking that Jordanes' variants all contained islands: Scandinavia, Britain, 'or some other island'. In one strand of Graeco-Roman ethnographic and geographic tradition, Britain, Thule, and Scandinavia are all mysterious northern islands rather than geographical localities.[82] 'Britain' and 'Scandinavia' may well represent interpretative deductions on the part of whoever it was that recorded the myths. The myths themselves perhaps referred only to an unnamed, mysterious island, which the recorder had then to identify.[83] The Scandinavian origin-tale would thus be

---

[82] Goffart, *Narrators*, 88 ff. I agree with Goffart 88–96 that these paragraphs are not straightforward Gothic oral history, and in finding the mention of Scandinavia suspicious. He is also surely right in seeing Jordanes as concerned to refute rumours that the Goths originated in Britain. Much less convincing is the suggestion that Jordanes was really arguing—against Procopius' account of Herules who had returned to 'Thule' (*Wars* 6. 14–15)—that Goths could not be got rid of back to the far north. Nothing suggests that Procopius was advocating the act of the Herules as a general solution to the barbarian problem. The wealth of detail and involvement of Justinian's court show that this is a piece of history, not (Goffart, 99) 'a beguiling evocation of barbarians who set off for the distant north'. Belisarius did offer Britain to the Goths in 538 during the siege of Rome (*Wars* 6. 6. 28–9), but this was clearly not meant seriously and the Goths ignored it. It was simply another way of saying that the emperor was not interested in a compromise peace, the substance of the rest of Belisarius' remarks.

[83] Hachmann, *Goten und Skandinavien*, shows that there is no archaeological or philological evidence that the Goths really came from Scandinavia. But for those who view Gothic oral history in Jordanes as a window into the authentic past, Scandinavian names at *Getica* 3. 21–4 and the Berig story nevertheless guarantee the Goths' Scandinavian origins: e.g. Wolfram, 21 ff.

similar to much else in the *Getica*, depending upon a complex mixture of material from Gothic oral and Graeco-Roman literary sources.

The *Getica* provides some evidence, therefore, that the workings of Gothic oral history were congruous with modern examples, remaking the past to explain the present and to add historical legitimacy to contemporary rulers. The anachronistic division of the Goths into Visigoth and Ostrogoth, and overstating the length of Amal and Balth rule, can both be partly understood in this light. What seems to be a strain of Visigothic oral history, and the variety of tales known to Jordanes, also confirm that different Gothic groups remade the past to explain their own circumstances. There was no uniform Gothic oral history for writers simply to record, and choices had to be made between differing accounts. Not only that, but the *Getica* also draws on a wide variety of literary material, and the two kinds of sources have been carefully intertwined by authors—Cassiodorus certainly, and Ablabius probably—who had very considerable axes to grind. Both would seem to have been in the employ of Gothic dynasts and had to produce Gothic histories of a kind that their employers wished to hear. Jordanes stands apart, for no convincing political context has been found for him, and in all probability he incorporated Cassiodorus' historical distortions into his own work in good faith. Parts of the *Getica* are singularly Gothic, but this must not lead us to think that Jordanes' text contains a uniquely authoritative account of Gothic history.

PART II

THE FORMATION OF THE VISIGOTHS

GOTHS AND ROMANS, 376–418

INTRODUCTION TO PART II

By the mid-fourth century, the Goths had established kingdoms in and around the Carpathian chain, and out on to the Pontic Steppe, a world about to be shattered by the nomadic Huns who were to overturn the prevailing social and political order. This second part of the study will look in more detail at the impact of these events upon a series of largely Gothic groups which, between 376 and 418, eventually united themselves to create the political unit commonly known as the Visigoths. Broadly speaking, these were all Goths who successfully fled Hunnic domination, so that most of the events with which we are concerned take place inside the defended frontier of the Roman Empire, many of them in the Balkans. The following chapters will investigate not only the new relationships with the imperial authorities of east and west which this geographical situation necessitated, but also the processes which brought the Visigoths into being. It is important first, however, to take stock of the available source material. Archaeological evidence underlies much of what we can reconstruct of the fourth-century Gothic kingdoms, but cannot assist our political study of the Goths in migration. For this, we must rely almost entirely on literary evidence from the Graeco-Roman world.

Ammianus Marcellinus

The *Res Gestae* of Ammianus Marcellinus deals with only a few of the events which concern us. One chapter of book 27 describes Valens' first Gothic war between 367 and 369, and book 31 concentrates on the first impact of the Huns upon the Goths, and events leading to the battle of Hadrianople in 378. It would be impossible to overstate the importance of Ammianus as a source. His information on Gotho-Roman relations is unmatched for the period he covers. In particular, Ammianus alone distinguishes between the Tervingi and the Greuthungi, the two Gothic groups who appeared on the Danube in 376. More generally, his history as a whole provides an enormous amount of information on the dealings of emperors with foreign tribal groups. The institutions and general approaches which can be reconstructed from his account of innumerable encounters on Rhine and Danube allow us to draw out the full significance of particular events in Gotho-Roman relations.[1] As Sabbah has convincingly shown, much of this wealth of detail stems from Ammianus' use of official documentary sources. As a former military man himself, he also knew many of the soldiers involved,[2] and, as we shall see, there is even a suspicion that for his account of the Hadrianople campaign he had access to the report of some kind of official enquiry into what had caused such an unprecedented defeat.

That said, Ammianus' work is a coherent and consciously articulated piece of literature. It cannot simply be used as a quarry for facts, without taking account of the demands of its genre and Ammianus' personal approach to the subject matter. A general study of Ammianus is not to our purpose (and redundant in the light of Matthews's recent book), but some of its historiographical features can cause problems for the modern historian seeking to reconstruct events. As the title *Res Gestae* indicates, historical writing in the Late Empire was a rhetorical genre, which sought to draw lessons from the failings and strengths of past individuals.[3] This tends to personalize the action even to the extent of distorting it, and also explains a certain vagueness in accounts of mass action. It will be argued, for instance, that Ammianus' account of the outbreak of the Goths' revolt in 376 concentrates too much on individuals, ignoring the involvement of the central imperial authorities. Subsequent battles are described in splendidly dramatic style, but the lack of precision makes it impossible fully to understand their course. Ammianus also avoids giving a detailed chronology for the Hadrianople campaign,[4] and precise figures (with important exceptions) on the numbers of the Goths and their Roman opponents. The wealth of other detail suggests that Ammianus cannot have been ignorant of these facts, but chose to omit them in accordance with the norms of his chosen genre. His choice was of course a valid one, but causes problems when it

---

[1] See generally: Thompson, *The Historical Work of Ammianus Marcellinus*; and above all Matthews, *The Roman Empire of Ammianus* (esp. ch. 14).

[2] Sabbah, *La Méthode d'Ammien Marcellin*, pt. III.

[3] See generally Blockley, i, pt. 1 and *Ammianus Marcellinus, passim*. Though writing in Latin, Ammianus belongs with the Greek tradition; cf. also Matthews, *The Roman Empire of Ammianus*, ch. 18.

[4] Cf. Austin, 'The Adrianople Campaign'.

comes to reconstructing events. Similarly, ethnographical digressions were an obligatory feature of the genre, and had to fall into traditional patterns. Thus while Ammianus' account of the lifestyle of the Huns is the starting-point for any discussion of them, it reuses much material from traditional Graeco-Roman ethnography, producing a complex mixture of the relevant and anachronistic.[5]

Distortions caused by the author's position and outlook are often impossible to detect, but two merit discussion. Ammianus never seems to have served in the Balkans, and his grasp of its geography seems much less secure than for the Rhine and Mesopotamian frontiers. This poses a particular problem in reconstructing the battle of Ad Salices. It also seems clear that Ammianus preferred not to mention Christianity wherever possible. In part, this again reflects the genre since the vocabulary of Christianity was foreign to his classical models and could not be allowed to lower the tone of his work. It would also seem to mirror Ammianus' personal preference for more traditional religious observance.[6] Thus Ammianus gives only the barest hint that Christianity played a role in relations between the Goths and the Empire, whereas other sources make it clear that it was quite significant. Ammianus shaped his sources to fit a genre and his own outlook, but he took tremendous pains to gather an extraordinary amount of detailed information.

Eunapius of Sardis

Eunapius' history seems originally to have covered the period *c*.270–404. A full text has not survived, but the encyclopaedists of medieval Byzantium took many excerpts from it under a variety of headings. It was also used by a number of later authors, of whom the most important for reconstructing the original text is Zosimus. Up to *c*.404, Zosimus did little more than paraphrase his model.[7]

Eunapius thus covered a broader sweep of our period than Ammianus, but his work is in other ways an inferior source. He

---

[5] Cf. the opposing views of Thompson, *Attila and the Huns*, 6 ff. and Maenchen-Helfen, 9 ff.

[6] Cf. most recently Hunt, 'Christians and Christianity in Ammianus'; more generally, A. D. E. and A. M. Cameron, 'Christianity and Tradition'.

[7] On reconstructing the text, see Blockley, i. 1 ff., 97 ff.; Paschoud, *passim*, esp. i, pp. xxxii ff.

was a philosopher living at Sardis in Asia Minor, and generally had less information to hand. There are exceptions; particularly for Julian's Persian campaign, Eunapius provides an independent and highly valuable account.[8] With Gothic affairs, however, he always seems to be making the most of limited information. A battle in Lydia between troops transferred from Egypt and recently recruited barbarians receives much coverage, seemingly because it took place within fifty kilometres of Sardis. The revolt of Gainas and Tribigild, similarly, is recorded at very great length, again, it would seem, because it unfolded largely in Eunapius' neighbourhood. Eunapius also wrote in highly rhetorical Greek, which even Photius found overblown (*Bibliotheca* 77), and the significance of events can become lost in the verbiage surrounding them.[9] As we shall see, most of these faults come together in his account of the Gothic war between 376 and 382. Eunapius seems to have included no chronological indications, and the surviving fragments confirm what can be deduced from Zosimus, namely that Eunapius failed to distinguish between the Tervingi and Greuthungi, and the different circumstances of their entries into the Empire.

The historian's interpretation of the genre and personal prejudices create further difficulties. Hatred of both barbarians and Christians is marked, and deeply affects Eunapius' account of Gotho-Roman relations. Not only were the Goths barbarians, but they also converted to Christianity, and a conciliatory policy towards them was pioneered by the Christian Emperor Theodosius. Gothic affairs thus aroused Eunapius' ire in the two areas where he was most sensitive, and this in part distorts his account.[10] Goths are 'faithless barbarians' out to destroy the Empire, and Eunapius' favourite Goth is Fravittas, who fled Gothic society and adhered to traditional Graeco-Roman paganism (frr. 69. 1–4). Eunapius also adopted a rigid interpretation of the classicizing genre. For instance, he refused to use vocabulary he considered inappropriate, so that Goths are always 'Scythians'. Likewise, contemporary technical terminology rarely appears, and there is a disinclination towards precise factual detail.[11] Partly generic, this also reflects the author's lack of information.

[8] Most recently, Matthews, *The Roman Empire of Ammianus*, 161 ff.
[9] Blockley, i. 13–14.
[10] Cf. Blockley, i. 18 ff. (with refs.).
[11] Ibid. 14–15.

The problems are only too evident, but should not be over-stated. It is easy, in fact, to damn Eunapius for what, on reflection, must be Zosimus' mistakes (cf. p. 148). The very fact that Zosimus could make such errors suggests that Eunapias' original was somewhat obscure, but, in general, Eunapius' account of events after 376 was wide-ranging and contemporary, preserving much important information. His anti-barbarian prejudice also gave him a strong interest in Gothic affairs, to which he devoted some space. To Eunapius we owe our only connected narrative of the Gothic war between 378 and 382, a detailed account of the quarrel between Fravittas and Eriulf which tells us much about Gotho-Roman relations under the 382 treaty, and important details about Alaric's revolt in 395.

Olympiodorus of Thebes

Olympiodorus dealt largely with the years 407 to 425, but did include a summary of events from at least 395. A complete text of the work has not survived, and, in this case, no sizeable fragments have been preserved by Byzantine excerptors. Instead, we have to rely on Photius' summary account, and what can be learned from writers who used Olympiodorus as a source. From *c.*405 to the sack of Rome in August 410, Zosimus and the Church historian Sozomen transmit much of Olympiodorus' original narrative. After the sack, Olympiodorus continued to be copied by at least Philostorgius, but this author's work itself survives only in short fragments.[12]

Olympiodorus served as a diplomat for the eastern Empire, his work recounting missions to the Huns, and to the Blemmyes on the fringes of Roman Egypt. He wrote in Greek, but had visited Rome, and clearly had access to good information about western events.[13] In particular, he reports in great detail the negotiations between Alaric and the western Empire surrounding the sack of Rome. Enough has survived through Zosimus and Sozomen to allow us to reconstruct the Goths' major concerns. Olympiodorus'

---

[12] On reconstructing the text, see e.g. Matthews, 'Olympiodorus of Thebes'; Blockley, i. 27 ff., 107 ff.

[13] See generally, A. D. E. Cameron, 'Wandering Poets'; Matthews, 'Olympiodorus of Thebes'; Blockley, i. 27–8, 34–5; Thompson, 'Olympiodorus of Thebes'.

narrative also charts the growth of Alaric's forces, and some of the dynastic rivalries this entailed. After the sack of Rome, some valuable information on the Goths' activities in Gaul survives through Photius and Philostorgius.

As with the other historians, Olympiodorus shaped the information according to his own views and preconceptions.[14] He was a convinced pagan, for instance, which sometimes intrudes.[15] Rather like Ammianus, however, he was a man of affairs with a detailed knowledge of the Empire and its workings, so that even if his own explanations are insufficient, the narrative usually contains enough detail for alternatives to be reconstructed. He also flouted some of the literary conventions which Eunapius adopted so enthusiastically. As Photius reports, Olympiodorus was aware of this, characterizing his work as 'materials for history' (ὕλην συγγραφῆς), rather than formal history. This is in part a pose of modesty, for the work included learned digressions and each book had a preface written in high style, but Olympiodorus did generally write less rhetorically, and technical terms appear. He also included statistics, detailing the monetary payments involved in alliances, and the steady growth in Alaric's following.[16] These have been seen as wildly inaccurate, but it will be argued that much of the difficulty is due to those reusing the work, rather than Olympiodorus himself.

Zosimus

Zosimus' *Historia Nova* is important because, as we have seen, it reuses the histories of Eunapius and Olympiodorus. Starting in the mid-third century, it continues down to 410, at which point Zosimus was probably interrupted, since his work is not brought to a conclusion, and later parts have not reached the same state of completion as the earlier books. Little is known of him, but he was a pagan, probably writing in Constantinople in *c*.500, who was determined to show that Christianity had led the Empire to disaster. To some extent, his choice of subject explains his choice of sources. Eunapius was similarly hostile towards Christianity,

---

[14] See esp. Matthews, 'Olympiodorus of Thebes', 96–7.
[15] Cf. Blockley, i. 38 ff.
[16] Cf. Matthews, 'Olympiodorus of Thebes', 86–7; Blockley, i. 32 ff.; Thompson, 'Olympiodorus of Thebes', 48–9.

and while Olympiodorus concluded his work on a high-point of imperial unity and recovery, his work was at points markedly pagan. This probably combined with its detailed account of the event symbolizing imperial decline, the sack of Rome, to make Olympiodorus' work an attractive choice.[17]

The extent of Zosimus' personal contribution has occasioned some discussion. For the period which concerns us here (*c*.376–410), Zosimus was largely the slave of his two major sources. Particularly revealing is his attitude to the western general Stilicho, which changes markedly with that of his sources. Whereas Eunapius was hostile, Olympiodorus approved of the policy Stilicho pursued. Zosimus' narrative first criticizes him and then changes to measured praise at precisely the point it moves between sources.[18] But Zosimus did make his own additions. Book 4, essentially taken from Eunapius and dealing with the reigns of Valens and Theodosius, contains two doublets: of the Gothic war between 376 and 382, and of Odotheus' attempted crossing of the Danube in 386. In the first of these cases, Zosimus seems to have imported material from another source; its overall effect is to make nonsense of an otherwise coherent narrative, something for which the contemporary Eunapius is unlikely to have been responsible. The doublet of Odotheus may have a similar origin. It has similarly been argued that the first book was compiled from a number of sources, but the point is incapable of absolute proof.[19]

This would not deny that Zosimus rewrote his source material. Olympiodorus seems to have caused him little trouble, but a whole series of mistakes occur where he is following Eunapius.[20] Some may have originated with Eunapius, but many probably reflect Zosimus' difficulties in interpreting his source. Zosimus failed to grasp, for instance, that all the Roman campaigns in the Balkans between 378 and 382 were directed against essentially the same group of barbarians, the Goths who had crossed the Danube in 376. Thus Modares is reported to have wiped out the enemy in Thrace, and when further wars follow, Zosimus is forced to explain them by having more invaders cross the Danube (cf. p. 152).

---

[17] Cf. Paschoud, i, pp. xvii ff. with refs.
[18] Ibid. xxxiii ff.
[19] Blockley, 'The First Book of Zosimus' New History'.
[20] See the examples cited by Matthews, *The Roman Empire of Ammianus*, 493 n. 32.

He would seem to have been confused, perhaps by the overblown praise Eunapius had given to Modares' limited success, into thinking that the general had won a war.

One other example of Zosimus' intervention is worth noting. He combined his two major sources by connecting two mentions of Alaric's Goths in Epirus: one in Eunapius (cf. Zosimus 5. 7. 2: events of 395–7) and one in Olympiodorus (Zosimus 5. 26. 1 — with an explicit cross-reference: events after 405). This was Zosimus' first use of the latter, and he states here that the Goths had remained inactive in Epirus since 395–7 when he had last mentioned them. This provided Zosimus with a means of joining his sources, but creates historical chaos. Between 395 and 405, the Goths had occupied different areas of the Balkans, allied themselves briefly to Eutropius, and unsuccessfully invaded Italy. Zosimus has omitted any Eunapian account of these events.

Jordanes

Much space has already been devoted to the *Getica*, but it is important to deal briefly with the passages describing so-called 'Visigothic' history between 376 and 418. This comprises the section 25. 131–3. 172, which is typically vague and prone to error. The one passage it devotes to the Gothic war between 376 and 382 mentions few specific events, and what is probably a misleading juxtaposition between an illness of Theodosius I and a peace agreement has led to the supposition that Gratian made peace with some Goths in 380. Jordanes also mistakes the position occupied by Athanaric in Gothic society by 381, and separate but similar events are conflated: the usurpations of Maximus and Eugenius, and Alaric's two invasions of Italy.[21]

To these problems, we can add a series of anachronisms. Most important, Jordanes' account of the peace treaty of 332 between the emperor Constantine and the Goths is very misleading. It describes an agreement which turned the Goths into favoured imperial *foederati*, in receipt of annual pay in return for military service. This was the pattern of some later federate treaties, but contemporary sources show that the peace of 332 was quite different in character. In similar vein, a third-century Gothic leader, Gerberic, seems to have been imported into the fourth

[21] Cf. Ch. 2 n. 4.

century. We also find examples of the *Getica*'s characteristically biased rewriting of history. Ermenaric, for instance, appears in these pages as the ruler of all the Scythian and German tribes. Less blatant, perhaps, Jordanes maintains that Alaric became leader of the Goths because he was a member of an ancient, eminent clan, the Balthi. He was really the first of a dynasty which established itself only in subsequent generations.

Despite these problems, the *Getica* remains an interesting source, if only for the different materials it combines. Written sources underlie parts of the narrative; the Gothic revolt in 376, for instance, is taken largely from Ammianus. At the same time, the influence of Gothic oral material seems clear. Jordanes gives, for example, a depoliticized version of the slaying of Alaric's successor, Athaulf. Olympiodorus states that he was mortally wounded by a groom avenging his former master, whom Athaulf had killed (fr. 26. 1), and who, as we shall see, had probably been a rival for the kingship of the Goths. According to the *Getica*, Athaulf was killed by one Euervulf, who resented the mockery he had directed at his short stature (31. 163). Gothic oral tradition would seem to have cleansed itself of any trace of the struggle which surrounded the establishment of a ruling clan, the real context for Athaulf's assassination. This suggests that our estimation of how Gothic oral history is likely to have reworked the past is not too far from the mark (see Ch. 2).

Secular Oratory

Logical, eloquent speech was considered the mark of civilized life in the Graeco-Roman world, and by *c*.350 the different types of prose and verse oratory had been carefully differentiated. The chief opportunity for eloquent public address was provided by verse or prose panegyric, and it is this particular manifestation of secular oratory which requires discussion.[22] In panegyric, stylized praise was arranged under a number of set headings dealing with everything from an individual's lineage to his personal achievement. Where the individual concerned was an emperor or another major political figure, a speech's contents had to be in accord with the wishes of the ruling regime. Such speeches portray events as the imperial authorities wished them to be seen, and illuminate

---

[22] See generally Kennedy, *Greek Rhetoric*, 3 ff.

official policies. This is even more valuable than any factual information panegyrics might contain.[23]

For our purposes, a series of speeches by Themistius form the most important corpus of such material. He was an academic philosopher, famous for contributions to Aristotelian studies, but at the same time, used his skill in public speaking in the service of successive eastern emperors from Constantius II to Theodosius I. In these speeches, he consistently presents himself as an independent philosopher commenting objectively on events, and this has sometimes been taken at face value. Scrutiny of their contents renders such a view untenable, however, and it was essentially for the falseness of this pose that Themistius was criticized in his own lifetime. He faithfully served a series of regimes, service which brought him imperial favour and eventually office (he was urban prefect of Constantinople in 384). And when Constantius II decided to expand the Constantinopolitan senate in 357, Themistius headed the commission charged with finding suitable candidates. His surviving orations are important to this study because he regularly justified imperial policy towards the Goths. Orations 8 and 10 illuminate the changing course of Valens' first Gothic war (367–9), and four later orations cover the period from Theodosius I's elevation in 379 to the peace of 382. The speeches contain potential pitfalls as well as opportunities; many references would presumably have been obvious to contemporaries, but are somewhat enigmatic to the historian. The speeches are also polemical, but this is their chief virtue, giving us vivid insight into the presentation of imperial policy.[24]

Three other panegyrists demand attention: Pacatus, Synesius of Cyrene, and Claudian. From Pacatus has survived only one prose panegyric, delivered in Rome to Theodosius I in summer 389. This describes Maximus' usurpation and its suppression, in which Goths played a major role. As such, it presents us with an official view of the peace-treaty of 382 in action, when Goths served *en masse* in an imperial army.[25] Much more of Synesius' work has

---

[23] Cf. A. D. E. Cameron, *Claudian*, esp. 46 ff. See also Augustine, *Confessions* 6. 6. 9.

[24] See generally, Dagron, 'Thémistios'. The relevant parts of oration 8 and the whole of oration 10 have been translated by D. Moncur in Heather–Matthews, *The Goths in the Fourth Century*, ch. 2.

[25] *Pan. Lat.* 12(2); cf. Galletier's introduction; Nixon, *Pacatus*, 1–11.

survived, but we are again concerned with essentially one speech (or, at least, pseudo-speech), the *De Regno*. This presents itself as the oration which accompanied the presentation to the emperor Arcadius of the crown-gold from Synesius' home city in *c.*400. Instead of a speech in praise of the emperor, however, its contents are highly critical of the emperor's lack of martial vigour and choice of ministers (it includes a very disparaging reference to the eunuch chamberlain Eutropius, who headed a regime under Arcadius between 395 and 399). As Barnes has recently argued, it cannot be the speech it claims to be, but is a seditious political pamphlet, perhaps circulated in early 399 when Eutropius' regime was beginning to crumble.[26] Its importance for us lies in the fact that the conciliatory policy Eutropius had followed towards Alaric's Goths since 397 was an issue of major political debate. The *De Regno* illuminates both the policy and the degree of opposition it aroused.[27]

From Claudian, a large corpus of poetry is still extant, and the author is an excellent Latin poet, despite Greek origins. As Cameron's fine study demonstrated, between 396 and 404, Claudian also wrote ten poems as propaganda for his patron, the *magister militum* Stilicho. This was not confined to panegyric, but also included savage invective directed against Stilicho's enemies. In these poems, Claudian employed a full range of propaganda techniques, readily altering his account of events as circumstances changed. The poetry is particularly important for what it reveals of relations between Alaric's Goths and Stilicho in two stages: between 395 and 397, when Stilicho intervened twice in the Balkans to curb Gothic ravages, and again when the Goths invaded Italy in 401/2.[28]

Ecclesiastical Sources

For the Goths before the Hunnic invasions, ecclesiastical sources provide information of unique interest. In particular, the *Passion of St Saba*, one Gothic Christian's experience of persecution in the 370s, provides insight into the life of rank-and-file Gothic villagers. No other surviving text complements the picture of

[26] Barnes, 'Synesius in Constantinople'.
[27] Cf. Heather, 'The Anti-Scythian Tirade'.
[28] Cameron, *Claudian*, esp. 46 ff.

everyday life presented by the archaeological evidence gathered by Soviet and Romanian archaeologists. The *Passion*'s detailed account of the mechanisms of persecution also illuminates aspects of government and lordship among the Goths, and of the leadership's ties with local communities. To Gothic Christianity we also owe most of what we know of the Gothic language, and extant fragments of Ulfila's Gothic Bible can help to identify fourth-century Gothic institutions. This is not straightforward, however, since our surviving texts are all sixth- rather than fourth-century.[29]

From the period after 376, when the Goths were established on imperial soil, no comparable sources survive. Church writers generated a vast quantity of material, but the Goths were rarely their primary concern. They do nevertheless illustrate facets of the interaction between Empire and Goths. Of these, the Church histories are the most consistently important, belonging to the narrative genre established by Eusebius of Caesarea. The most original of the relevant authors is Socrates, who gathered many disparate sources. His work naturally concentrates on the Church, but briefly refers to significant secular events, some of which involved Goths. Although less original than Socrates', Sozomen's history is nevertheless more valuable because, as we have seen, he reused Olympiodorus.[30] And, despite surviving only in fragments, the work of the 'Neo-Arian' Church historian Philostorgius shows great interest in the Goths and their bishop Ulfila, presumably because Philostorgius was sympathetic to Ulfila's doctrinal position. Like Sozomen, Philostorgius also reused material from Olympiodorus, and some important passages survive, such as a description of Athaulf's marriage to Galla Placidia.[31]

Orosius' *History against the Pagans* provides complementary insight into western events. Orosius is not a Church historian in the tradition of the Greek writers, but attempts, rather than a history of the Church, to provide a Christian interpretation of major secular events. He wrote specifically to counter the charge that conversion to Christianity had destroyed the prosperity of the Empire. Divine providence naturally plays an important role in its

---

[29] For an English translation (the first) of these sources, and an introduction to the Gothic Bible, see Heather–Matthews, *The Goths in the Fourth Century*, chs. 4–6.

[30] See generally, Chesnut, *The First Christian Histories*.

[31] Bidez, 'L'historien Philostorge'; Blockley, i. 99, 108.

account of cause and effect, but the work devotes much space to political events, and provides important information about the Goths in the west, supplementing what survives from Olympiodorus.[32]

Beyond such narrative sources, the variety of ecclesiastical writing defies convenient summary. Letters in Greek and Latin illuminate individual episodes, and provide insight into contemporary views: Ambrose, for instance, describes aspects of the Gothic war between 376 and 382, and the quarrel between bishop and empress in which Arian Gothic soldiers were involved in the 380s. Other letters exemplify contemporary Graeco-Roman cultural chauvinism. Pastoral and theological materials also make some reference to the Goths. Taken together these writings fill in the background to political events, and place historical reconstruction on a surer footing.

[32] Cf. Goetz, *Orosius*.

3

GOTHS AND ROMANS
BEFORE THE HUNS

A broad picture of the territory under Gothic domination in the fourth century has emerged from the efforts of Soviet and Romanian archaeologists, who have successfully identified it with the Sîntana de Mureş—Černjachov culture (Fig. 3). Over 3,000 settlements are known, and, of these, about 150 have been investigated.[1] These finds coincide with what can be learnt of the Goths from Ammianus, where their power spreads over an area between the Danube and the Don; the Alans bordering the Greuthungi are the 'Tanaites', the 'Don People' (31. 3. 1). Amphorae and other objects date the emergence of the culture firmly to the second half of the third century when the Goths were establishing themselves in the area, and, like them, it flourished throughout the fourth.[2]

A. *Gothic Subdivisions of the Fourth Century*

On the basis of Jordanes' *Getica*, it has been normal for scholars to distinguish two Gothic groups within this area: the Visigoths and Ostrogoths. This is anachronistic (Ch. 1): the political geography of the Goths before the Hunnic invasions must be reconstructed from contemporary evidence. As we have seen, Ammianus mentions the Tervingi led by Athanaric, and the Greuthungi of Ermenaric and his successors. In 376, Alatheus and Saphrax, new leaders of the Greuthungi, retreated to the Dniester, and Athanaric advanced to meet them there (31. 3. 3–5), so that the river perhaps acted as some kind of frontier between them. We should

[1] Kropotkin, 'Chernyakhovo Tribes', 47. For a general introduction to the physical remains of the culture, see Heather–Matthews, *The Goths in the Fourth Century*, ch. 3.

[2] See generally Todd, *Northern Barbarians*, 90 ff.; Ščukin, 'Das Problem der Černjachow–Kultur'; id. 'Current Aspects of the Gothic Problem'; Gej, 'Date of the Chernyakhovo Culture', 87.

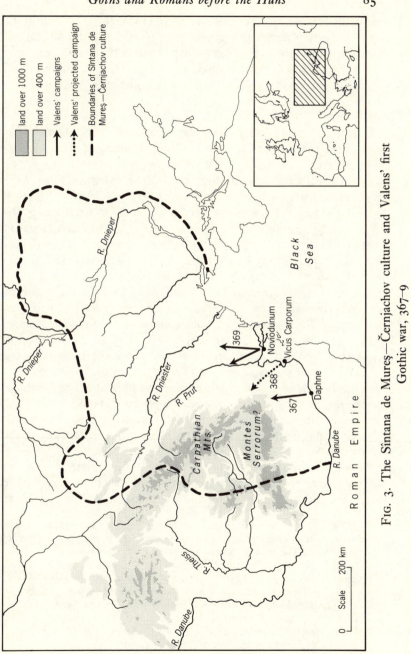

FIG. 3. The Sîntana de Mureş—Černjachov culture and Valens' first Gothic war, 367–9

probably beware, however, of envisaging too rigid a distinction. In later periods, Gothic subgroups readily exchanged political allegiances, and this may well have happened in the fourth century.[3]

Of the domain of the Tervingi, west of the Dniester, literary and archaeological evidence paint comparable pictures. Archaeological finds suggest that settlements were concentrated in Moldavia and Wallachia.[4] The Moldavian sites seem to be the oldest, and the culture continued to develop as it extended south and west. And it was in precisely this area, to judge from Ammianus' account, that the emperor Valens fought the Tervingi in the 360s. In 367 he crossed the Danube at the fort of Daphne, but the Goths were forewarned, and escaped to the *Montes Serrorum* (AM 27. 5. 2–4), which must be the south-eastern Carpathians.[5] Valens was probably aiming, therefore, to trap a population concentrated in western Wallachia. In 368, flooding prevented serious campaigning, but in 369 the emperor crossed further north-east at Noviodunum (modern Tulcea) opposite Moldavia (27. 5. 6), so that his campaigns would seem to have encompassed all the main centres of the Tervingi. The extent to which the Tervingi had also penetrated Transylvania, the upland heart of old Roman Dacia, is less clear. Some Romanized life still continued in the region, protected by the Carpathian mountains,[6] but the mountains are pierced by many passes, and a power settled in the adjacent plains can easily extend its domination into the uplands. The Tervingi knew the mountains well enough to escape Valens in 367, and archaeologists have uncovered a Gothic presence in south-eastern Transylvania, so that it may well have fallen under the sway of the Tervingi.[7]

The Greuthungi are less of a presence in the literary sources, so that we have to rely almost entirely on physical remains for the area east of the Dniester. The many settlements of this region are

[3] At face value, for instance, Ammianus 27. 5. 6 might suggest that in the 360s Athanaric, ruler of the Tervingi, also exercised hegemony over at least some of the Greuthungi. The passage, however, is problematic: see below.

[4] Ioniţă, 'Sîntana de Mureş–Tchernéakhov', 189 ff.; Diaconu, 'Socio-Economic Relations', 67–8; cf. the detailed accounts of finds in Mitres–Preda, *Necropole*; and Diaconu, *Tîrgşor*. A map showing individual find-spots can be found in Heather–Matthews, *The Goths in the Fourth Century*, fig. 2.

[5] Cf. Cazacu, 'Montes Serrorum'.

[6] Conea, 'Interprétations géographiques'.

[7] See further Horedt, 'Quelques problèmes', 590–1.

concentrated in river valleys, on the better agricultural land.[8] Political boundaries cannot, however, be reconstructed from archaeological remains, nor can different ethnic groups sharing a similar material culture be distinguished from one another with any certainty. Thus some of the territory covered by the Sîntana de Mureş—Černjachov culture may have been controlled not by Goths but by related Germanic peoples, such as the Heruli. The latter were active in the Black Sea region in the third century, and, although not mentioned in fourth-century sources, reappear in the fifth and sixth centuries after the collapse of the Hunnic empire of Attila. It seems likely, therefore, that they were somewhere in the vicinity of Rome's Danube frontier in the fourth century, but we have no firm archaeological criteria for distinguishing them from the Goths.[9] As we shall see, it also seems certain that indigenous, non-Germanic groups remained a very substantial presence in these lands, and hegemony can of course be exercised beyond any actual settlement area; occasional finds of Černjachov objects among groups living further north, on the edge of the steppe-forest zone, it has been suggested, may reflect Gothic political domination.[10]

The Sîntana de Mureş–Černjachov culture is thus only an approximate guide to the settlement of the Goths, and even to the extent of their power. The fact that this area as a whole shared a common material culture tells us little about the political units into which it was divided, and without further literary (or epigraphic) evidence, not much can be deduced of the political organization of the Goths (and, perhaps, other Germanic groups) east of the Dniester. One crucial question, however, must at least be addressed. Were the Tervingi and Greuthungi the only Gothic political units to exist before the Hunnic invasions? Or, putting the same question a different way, did Ermenaric, king of the Greuthungi, rule all Goths who were not Tervingi?

[8] Cf. Symonovič, 'La verrerie', 184 and the detailed publication of material in Rybakov, *Černjachovskaja kul'tura*. For a fuller account of the literature, Heather–Matthews, *The Goths in the Fourth Century*, ch. 3.

[9] In 3rd c.: Zosimus 1. 42, cf. Wolfram, 52 ff.; 5th c. (e.g.) Jordanes, *Getica* 50. 261; Procopius, *Wars* 6. 14–15. The panegyrist of 291 also mentions Vandals, Gepids and Taifali involved in fighting with the Tervingi (*Pan. Lat.* 11(3). 17. 1), and the Černjachov culture possibly encompasses areas dominated by these groups as well as Goths.

[10] Symonovič, 'Chernyakhovo Culture', 102.

The *Getica* answers in the affirmative, and on the basis of Jordanes, Ermenaric is normally considered to have ruled 'all the Scythian and German nations' (23. 116–20). But this picture was built up from Ammianus' brief account of the king, and is quite untrustworthy.[11] When read without preconceptions derived from the *Getica*, Ammianus' description of Ermenaric is decidedly vague. He is a 'most warlike monarch' who ruled 'extensive and rich lands' (31. 3. 1). He was clearly an important ruler, but it is difficult to say exactly how important. The question can perhaps be resolved using less direct evidence.

After the Hunnic invasions, as we have seen, at least two, and perhaps three major groups of Greuthungi threatened the Roman frontier at different moments. If Ermenaric ruled all these Greuthungi, the Huns must have fragmented his realm. This is not impossible, but Ammianus' narrative suggests that all Ermenaric's Goths crossed the Danube in 376 (31. 3. 1–3; 31. 4. 12; 31. 5. 12). Ammianus was concerned not with the Greuthungi *per se*, but with the build-up to Hadrianople, and may simply have ignored any split. He did, however, mention one among the Tervingi (31. 3. 8). In addition, other large Gothic groups also came into contact with the Roman empire in the seventy-five years after Ermenaric's death (cf. p. 13).

If Ermenaric ruled all Goths except the Tervingi, these groups—or, at least, their ancestors—must have been his subjects (assuming that there was no Gothic population explosion). Put alongside the known groups of Greuthungi, the list which follows emphasizes exactly how large a realm encompassing all Goths, except the Tervingi, would have been. Within it would have been found the force of Alatheus and Saphrax (perhaps *c.* 10,000 men), Odotheus' Greuthungi (of unknown but significant size), the ancestors of Radagaisus' group (over 10,000 men), those of Theoderic Strabo's followers (at least 10,000 men), those of the Amal-led Goths (*c.* 10,000 men), and various other units such as the Crimean Goths totalling perhaps another 10,000 men. These figures are rough approximations, but give an indication of the order of magnitude involved. To have combined them all, Ermenaric's empire would have had to be enormous, with a potential

---

[11] Cf. Ch. 1, and, in more detail, Heather, 'Cassiodorus', 110 ff. on Ermenaric's victories and the peoples he is supposed to have ruled.

army of at least 60,000 men. Such an empire seems very unlikely; it would be much larger than any other known Gothic political unit,[12] and would surely have made a much greater impact in our sources. At no great distance from the Roman frontier (Valens fought some Greuthungi in 369, AM 27. 5. 6), it would have been many times more powerful than the Tervingi, who caused Valens so much trouble (see below), and would surely have been the main object of Roman policy in the region. The Empire was much more concerned, however, with the Tervingi, so that we should proba-bly envisage several smaller Gothic political units east of the Dniester.

There is a little more evidence in favour of this view. In 399, according to Claudian, 'Ostrogoths mixed with Greuthungi' in-habited Phrygia at the outbreak of Tribigild's revolt (*Eutr.* 2. 153). It is impossible to know what precisely Claudian meant, but, at face value, he distinguishes Ostrogoth as a third category of Goth apart from Tervingi and Greuthungi. This would be fully in line with what we have already seen of the realignment that the Huns caused in Gothic society; we might envisage, for instance, that some of the ancestors of the Gothic groups of the fifth century were such Ostrogoths, but this is pure hypothesis. Russian archaeologists have also identified five Černjachov sites as political centres on the basis of size, fortification, and topography.[13] It would be rash to declare these the capitals of politically autono-mous areas, but this is quite possible. In any case, a realm uniting all Goths except the Tervingi would surely have left much more trace in the contemporary historical record.

B.   *The Cultural Substructure of the Gothic World*

The single most striking feature of the Sîntana de Mureş–Černja-chov culture as a whole is its uniformity. Apart from a few short-lived local variants, more or less the same physical culture has been found in sites and cemeteries all the way from the Danube to the Ukraine, and even out on to the steppe. The constituent elements of this uniformity, however, have differing origins. Certain el-ements either clearly attest the presence of a Germanic population,

---

[12] Cf. pp. 302 and 214 for the later Ostrogoths and Visigoths.
[13] Kropotkin, 'Chernyakhovo Tribes', 47 and fig. 3.

or are strongly reminiscent of Germanic cultures to the north and west. A spindle-whorl inscribed with runes was discovered in grave 36 of the cemetery at Letçani, and other runes have been found on pottery.[14] Similarly, certain types of hand-made pot are paralleled only in Germanic cultures, and combs, not found in earlier indigenous cultures of the region, but common in Germanic ones, are a striking feature of the archaeological record. A type of house found in some of the areas dominated by the culture—so-called *Wohnstallhaüser*, combining living space for animals and humans—seems, likewise, to have come from the north. So too, the habit of wearing two brooches (*fibulae*), rather than one, would seem to have originally been Germanic, and some types of pendant and amulet are paralleled only in the north.[15]

But other characteristic features of the culture have different antecedents. Many of the styles and, above all, the basic techniques used in the wheel-made pottery, the single most common artefact in sites and cemeteries, are indigenous to the Carpathian and perhaps also to the North Pontic region. Descending from La Tène Iron Age cultures, and strongly affected by Roman influence, the ceramic wares have little to do with the Germanic north.[16] Sunken huts (the so-called *Grübenhäuser*), which are the commonest type of dwelling found on Černjachov sites, similarly are strongly attested in earlier cultures of the Carpathian region.[17] Some elements of the culture were also inherited somehow from (Iranian) Sarmatian steppe nomads. Certain burials in Černjachov cemeteries are marked by such characteristic Sarmatian features as cranial deformation, or the use of a platform on which grave-goods were placed, and some items of jewellery and ornamentation have as their models items from earlier Iranian steppe cultures.[18]

Despite the homogeneity of the end result, then, the diverse origins of different elements of the culture suggest very strongly

[14] Bloşiu, 'Nécropole de Letçani', 219; cf. Diaconu, 'Zwei Gefäße', 269 ff.; Diaconu–Anghelescu, 'Radu Negru', 167 ff. Runes are also inscribed on a torque of the Pietroasa treasure: Harhoiu, *Treasure from Pietroasa*, 13–14.
[15] Combs: Heather–Matthews, *The Goths in the Fourth Century*, ch. 3, esp. fig. 13; Housing: Diaconu, 'Socio-Economic Relations', 69–70; *Fibulae*: Bichir, *Carpi*, 91; amulets: Werner, 'Dančeny und Brangstrup', 262–3.
[16] Palade, 'Eléments géto-daces', esp. 230 ff.
[17] e.g. Bichir, *Carpi*, 11 ff.
[18] Burials, Diaconu, *Tîrgşor*, 137–9; jewellery, Werner, 'Dančeny und Brangstrup', 262.

that a number of ethnic groups made a substantial contribution to the physical culture unearthed by archaeologists. This raises, of course, the question of how to measure the contribution to the end result of the different ethnic groups from whom these elements originally came. It is always difficult to decide ethnic identities on the basis of material objects, but this is more than usually the case here, where we are dealing with a culture where a number of strands with different origins fused to create homogeneity. Whatever the original groups from whom particular cultural elements were taken, the homogeneity indicates that all groups within these lands quickly adopted much the same material culture. Nevertheless, a combination of archaeological and literary evidence can at least hint at the identity of some of the non-Gothic groups to be found north of the Black Sea in the fourth century.

Within the realm of the Tervingi, Romanian archaeologists have discovered certain burials which, while seemingly Germanic in character, differ markedly from the norm of the culture. In some cases (e.g. grave 147 at Tîrgşor), it is a case of isolated burials with weapons; in the overwhelming majority of cases, such items were not buried with the dead. At Cozia-Iaşi, Todireni, and Branişte, however, groups of burials have been uncovered with grave-goods or funerary practices which, though Germanic, do not belong to the mainstream of Černjachov finds. In no case are these burials very numerous, and they can probably be explained as small groups of non-Gothic Germanic outsiders, who maintained separate customs for just a short period.[19] Sarmatian influence also seems marked. This is not surprising: these nomads were the natural users of the steppe over which the Černjachov culture spread, and groups of Sarmatians may have been included in the confederation of the Tervingi.[20]

Local Dacian groups seem to have continued to occupy parts of Wallachia, Moldavia, and Transylvania; as we have seen, their influence is marked on the wheel-made pottery of the culture. Important evidence of a different kind has also emerged from three sites in the eastern Carpathian area of Romania. On these sites— Costişa-Mănoaia, Botoşana-Suceava, and Dodeşti-Vaslui—settlement was continuous from the period of our culture (or even

[19] Ioniţă, 'Die Römer-Daker', 126–7; id., 'The Social-Economic Structure', 79–80.

[20] Id., 'Sîntana de Mureş–Tchernéakhov', 257.

before in the case of Dodeşti-Vaslui) right through the period of
upheavals associated with the Huns, and into the Middle Ages
proper. There are also clear links between these and a group of
related sites in western Romania (the so-called Bratei culture). If
further work confirms these findings, this would suggest that an
indigenous Daco-Getan population lived in and around the Carpathians before, during, and after the period of our culture.[21]

The Tervingi also ruled former Roman citizens: Romanized
Dacians from Transylvania, perhaps, and above all Roman prisoners captured in raids. Most famously, Ulfila's ancestors were
taken from a village in Cappadocia, and Roman prisoners may
have formed a distinct group within Gothic society, at least until
347/8, when persecution forced Ulfila to move south into the
Empire with many followers.[22] Their influence would have been
out of proportion to their numbers, and is perhaps reflected in one
aspect of daily life. Farmers in these lands used a type of plough
previously found only within the Empire.[23] In the person of Ulfila,
the former Roman population was also responsible for transform-
ing Gothic into a written language, and his 'semi-Arian' Christianity was to be long a feature of Gothic tribal life. Formally
adopted, it seems, in 376 (see Ch. 4), it remained official practice in
the Visigothic kingdom until the Third Council of Toledo in 589.

East of the Dniester, Soviet archaeologists have long maintained
that the Černjachov culture cannot be explained simply as a mass
migration. Nomadic Iranian Sarmatians were again a strong
presence,[24] and descendants of Roman prisoners were probably
also to be found there. More distinctively, Goths in these lands
came under the influence of the ancient Greek cities of the Black
Sea, for whom the first two and a half centuries AD had been

---

[21] Teodor, *East Carpathian Area of Romania*, 3 ff. On the Bratei culture, see
Zaharia, 'La culture Bratei et la culture Dridu'. Other local groups, such as so-
called Free Dacians, Bastarnae, and Carpi may also have remained in the lands of
the Tervingi, for when the literary sources say that 'all' the Bastarnae and Carpi
were transferred to the Empire in the third century, they probably mean 'large
numbers'. Thus *Cons. Const.*, s.a. 295 (*CM* i. 230) reports that all the Carpi were
transferred in that year, yet Galerius fought four campaigns against them
between 301 and 306: Barnes, 'Imperial Campaigns', 191.

[22] Philostorgius, *HE* 2. 5; Auxentius 244 ff.

[23] Ioniţă, 'The Social-Economic Structure', 77.

[24] Gej, 'Date of the Chernyakhovo Culture', 87; cf. Sulimirski, *Sarmatians*,
passim.

largely prosperous.[25] From the mid-third century, however, they came under increasing pressure; their coinages deteriorated, and many coin-hoards testify to the insecurity of the times.[26] Nevertheless, their roots were too strong for the cities to disappear overnight, and they left their mark upon the Goths. It was from these cities that the Goths extorted the ships (and presumably the sailors) to raid across the Black Sea in the third century (Zosimus I. 31. 1 ff., 32. 3, 42. 1 ff.). They were probably also another source of Christianity. Sessions of the Council of Nicaea in 325 were attended by a bishop, 'Theophilus Gothiae'. The signatories generally followed a geographical order, and Theophilus signed before Domnus of Bosporos, suggesting that he was from somewhere in the Crimean region.[27]

Quite how all these different groups were incorporated into the Gothic kingdoms is a question of critical importance for our understanding of the social and political structure of the Gothic world. More or less contemporary situations present us with a range of possibilities. We know, for instance, that ethnic groups of the migration period could on occasion absorb outsiders. Priscus met a Greek merchant who had become to all intents and purposes a Hun, graduating from slavery to freedom as a warrior, and marrying a Hunnic wife (fr. 11. 2); he retained his Greek culture, but legally and politically he was a Hun, and his children would certainly have been primarily Hunnic. The Slavs likewise gave released prisoners a chance to stay with them as full members of their tribal groups.[28] On the other hand, the Huns are also known to have exploited the agricultural surplus of Goths under their control, and, as might be expected, such a relationship, involving superior and inferior partners, kept the identity of both quite distinct.[29] The question to ask of the available evidence, therefore, is to what extent the Goths of the fourth century established equal relations with the complex mix of peoples among whom they lived, or whether they rather dominated and exploited them as subjects.

[25] Minns, *Scythians and Greeks* and Rostovtzeff, *Iranians and Greeks* are good accounts of the literary evidence. For more recent archaeology, Mongait, *Archaeology in the USSR*, 179 ff.; Sulimirski, *Sarmatians*, 142 ff.

[26] Frolova, *Coinage of the Kingdom of the Bosporos*, esp. 97 ff.; Anokhin, *The Coinage of Chersonesus*, *passim.*

[27] Cf. Schmidt, 233–4; Wolfram, 78; *contra* Vasiliev, *Goths in the Crimea*, 11 ff.

[28] Maurice, *Strategicon* 11. 4. 12–16 Dennis–Gamillscheg.

[29] Priscus fr. 49, discussed in more detail in the Conclusion.

No conclusive answer to this question seems possible at this point, and it is also not unlikely that the Goths established a variety of relationships with different groups. Nevertheless, a few observations are worth making.

As we have seen, there is a little evidence for small numbers of Germanic outsiders on certain sites, who quickly disappeared from the archaeological record. These may represent heterogeneous Germanic groups who were absorbed into Gothic tribal units. The same process is perhaps also suggested by the occasional finds of Sarmatian burials. Whether large numbers of indigenous Dacians and others were absorbed by the Goths on more or less equal terms seems much more questionable. This much has been argued by Romanian scholars, who suggest from their analysis of particularly two elements of the archaeological record—funerary rites and the pottery—that the different ethnic elements of the population lived cheek by jowl in mixed villages. The cases of outsiders being absorbed into tribal groups mentioned in our sources, however, refer only to individuals and not populations *en masse*, and, on closer examination, the archaeological evidence cited is far from conclusive.

The argument from funerary rites stems from the fact that Sîntana de Mureş–Černjachov cemeteries are largely bi-ritual in nature; that is, they consist of both cremations and inhumations. The two basic practices, it has been argued, reflect different ethnic identities, as do other, less obvious variations in funerary ritual.[30] It now seems probable, however, that behind the bi-ritual pattern of the cemeteries, there is a chronological trend towards inhumation which has little to do with race, and much more to do with changing beliefs; none of the other rituals supposedly diagnostic of ethnic identity has won much support either.[31] With regard to the pottery, great stress has been laid upon the fact that it is heavily dependent on indigenous forms and techniques. From this, it has been argued that local so-called 'Daco-Getans' played a leading role in the creation of the culture, and that they were present on most sites (the pottery is found everywhere).[32] There is no

[30] e.g. Diaconu, 'Archäologische Angaben über die Taifalen'; id., *Tîrgşor*, 136 ff.; Ioniţă, 'The Social-Economic Structure', 79 ff.

[31] Bierbrauer, 'Zur Gliederung des Ostgermanischen Fundstoffs', 132 ff.; cf. Heather–Matthews, *The Goths in the Fourth Century*, ch. 3 with further refs.

[32] Palade, 'Eléments géto-daces', esp. 250–3.

doubting the origins of the pottery, but it was clearly used by Germanic Goths. The usual pottery was discovered, for instance, alongside the rune-inscribed spindle-whorl in Letçani grave 36, and this must surely be the grave of a Goth. It is also hard to see why potters among the Gothic immigrants (and the Goths had their own word for 'potter'[33]) should not have been able to learn the superior techniques practised by the people with whom they had now come into contact. Neither argument from the archaeological record thus makes a strong case for mixed villages. Indeed, on closer inspection, they merely reinforce the point that ethnic identities are almost impossible to deduce from archaeological remains.

In the face of that fact, our enquiry is greatly handicapped, but there are a number of indications that the Goths in fact established themselves as a dominant and hence separate group within the mix of peoples north of the Black Sea. To start with, it is worth reflecting on the fact that fourth-century literary sources for the most part refer only to Goths and Gothic political units. As we have seen, this cannot mean that no other peoples lived in the region, but it does suggest that, viewed from the Roman perspective, the Goths were its dominant military and hence political power.[34] If this inference is correct, we are unlikely to be dealing with a polyethnic confederation of more or less equal partners.

A similar conclusion would also follow, should further work confirm the inference drawn from the three excavations in the eastern Carpathians that indigenous groups lived in the region before, during, and after the period of the Sîntana de Mureş– Černjachov culture. The existence and survival of such a local population would be a powerful indication that these groups, at least, had never become inextricably mixed up with the Goths, most of whom, as we shall see, left for areas further west in the course of the upheavals associated with the Huns. We also have just a little evidence that Gothic hegemony in the region had to be established by force. In the mid-third century, at least one local Dacian group, the Carpi, regarded the Goths as their rivals,[35] and it is hard to imagine, more generally, that a new and militarily

---

[33] *Kasja*; cf. Matt. 27: 7 (in Heather–Matthews, *The Goths in the Fourth Century*, ch. 6).

[34] cf. Daicoviciu, *Dacica*, 490–1.

[35] Petrus Patricius fr. 8 (*FHG* iv. 186–7).

powerful people was welcomed to the area by those already occupying it. Archaeologists, moreover, have also uncovered levels of burning, perhaps an indication that both Sarmatian cultures in the south-western USSR and indigenous Daco-Getan in western Romania were driven out forcibly by Gothic and other Germanic immigrants.[36]

Other ethnic groups were certainly a presence within the Sîntana de Mureş–Černjachov culture, and some may well have been absorbed more or less fully by the Goths, as the Huns did Priscus' merchant, or the Slavs their prisoners. To judge by Ulfila, for instance, descendants of Roman prisoners among the Goths retained some consciousness of their origins (it was known from which Cappadocian village Ulfila's parents had been taken) as well as their Christianity, but were substantially affected by their time in Gothic hands. South of the Danube after 348, if those who fled were indeed largely this group, they did not reintegrate into mainstream Roman society. Rather, they formed a distinct social unit around Nicopolis ad Istrum which seems to have survived until the mid-sixth century.[37] They also spoke Gothic—Ulfila's name means 'Little Wolf'—and had clearly become Gothic to a considerable extent.

The archaeological evidence does not, however, as has sometimes been argued, require us to envisage all the peoples of the Sîntana de Mureş–Černjachov culture as having established this kind of more or less equal relationship with the Goths.[38] It is not unlikely that the Goths had had to establish themselves at least partly by force, and some local groups do not seem to have become integrated, remaining in the area after the Goths moved on. The emphasis in Roman literary sources upon the Goths makes it probable that they were a dominant power in the racially mixed landscape, rather than mere name-givers to a confederation of

[36] Gej, 'Date of the Chernyakhovo Culture', 87; Bichir, *Geto-Dacii*, 107 ff.

[37] Apart from Theodoret, *HE* 4. 37, nothing is heard of them until Jordanes, *Getica* 51. 267, but he specifically refers to his own time (*hodieque*); their survival has often been doubted, e.g. Liebeschuetz, *Barbarians and Bishops*, 79–80.

[38] See below, p. 145 for a further example. The Taifali are often said to have been part of the confederation of the Tervingi on highly flimsy archaeological grounds. The literary sources make it clear that they were quite independent in the normal course of events.

equals. No doubt the Goths established a wide range of relationships with the other peoples of the region, but it seems likely that many groups were subdued and exploited by the Goths, just as, at a later date, they themselves were to be by the Huns.[39]

C. The Bonds of Gothic Society

By the mid-fourth century, the Goths were the dominant force in the Pontic region, operating in substantial political groupings such as the Tervingi and Greuthungi. Within these groupings existed smaller social units with their own leaders. *The Passion of St Saba* (pp. 219–20) describes one such local leader among the Tervingi, Atharid, and refers to his father Rothesteos as βασιλίσκος. A second document from this persecution describes atrocities committed by another such leader, Winguric.[40] Less helpfully, Eunapius and Themistius refer generally to Gothic tribes and their leaders, while Ammianus indicates by the plural *regibus* that more than one person was involved in decision-making among the Tervingi.[41] To judge from Ulfila's Bible, these component parts of the Tervingi may have been called *kunja*, a term which originally designated kin-groups.[42] The *Passion* suggests, however, that the social unit controlled by Atharid was larger than a single extended family, and in the Gothic Bible the term would be used of the Twelve Tribes of Israel. As we shall see, the enforcers of the persecution against Saba did not know conditions in the village well, so that each unit was probably composed of several villages.[43]

At the same time, a single figure also occasionally appears as pre-eminent among the Tervingi: not a king, but a 'judge' (*iudex*). His title is attested by three independent sources: Ammianus,

[39] The Goths had their own words for 'customs-' or 'tax-point' and 'tax-collector' (*mota* and *motareis* respectively), which might suggest that they evolved these institutions independently of Roman influence. Such arguments are not conclusive.

[40] Achelis, 'Der älteste deutsche Kalender', 318–19.

[41] Eunapius frr. 48. 2, 59; Themistius *Or.* 16, p. 301. 2; AM 26. 10. 3. Cf. Köpke, *Anfänge*, 10; Schmidt, 244; Thompson, *Visigoths*, 43 ff.

[42] Claude, *Adel, Kirche, und Königtum*, 17–18; Wolfram, 96–7. On the social organization of the Tervingi and Ulfila's Bible, Wolfram's history summarizes his 'Gotische Studien II'.

[43] The villages were probably called *haimos*: Wolfram, 103 ff.

Ambrose, and Auxentius.[44] Of these, Ambrose characterizes him as a 'judge of kings' (*iudex regum*), which partly clarifies the situation. The Goths would seem to have been using *rex* (Gothic *reiks*) with the original Celtic, sense of 'leader of men' (their number not specified) rather than as 'monarch' or 'overall leader'. Hence the judge occupied a position superior to that of the ordinary nobility, presumably to be equated with men such as Atharid, and Winguric.[45] The Gothic for 'judge' is uncertain.[46] Again with the Gothic Bible in view, it has been suggested that it may stand for *kindins*. Related obviously to *kunja*, it originally designated the ruler of a kin-group, but the Gothic Bible uses it, for instance, of Pontius Pilate. The ruler of the fourth-century Burgundians was also called *hendinos*, a derivative of the same root (AM 28. 5. 14).[47]

There were thus two distinct levels of leadership among the Tervingi, and it is of crucial importance to our understanding of their basic political organization to discover, as best we can, how these levels related to one another. It is now generally held, not least because of the work of E. A. Thompson, that real power was

[44] AM 27. 5. 6, 9; Ambrose, *De Spiritu Sancto*, prol. 17; Auxentius 246; cf. Schmidt, 243–4; Thompson, *Visigoths*, 45; Claude, *Adel, Kirche, und Königtum*, 11–12; Wolfram, 67, 91–2. Themistius has been taken as a fourth witness, but see n. 57.

[45] In the Gothic Bible, similarly, *reiks* translates ἄρχων not βασιλεύς. A hierarchy of kings of different sorts is a well-attested phenomenon among Germanic tribes of the migration period; see, for instance, James 'The Continental Evidence', 42 ff.

[46] The fact that *iudex* is a common term in the Late Empire for a high official must at least raise the question of whether it really is a technical Gothic term. The agreement of diverse sources, and particulary Ammianus' consistent usage (27. 5. 6, 9; 31. 3. 4: all referring to Athanaric) suggest that it is, but Ammianus does also refer generally to tribal leaders of the Sarmatians and Alans as *iudices* (17. 12. 21 and 31. 2. 25 respectively).

[47] Wolfram, 'Athanaric', 266 ff. This essentially translates his 'Gotische Studien I'. The need is to find a suitable term for an authority higher than that of a *reiks*: *kindins* is one possibility, *piudans* is another, translating βασιλεύς in all its usages in the Gothic Bible. Wolfram discounts *piudans* because, following the established interpretation, he considers a passage in Themistius to mean that Athanaric rejected the title βασιλεύς; see, however, n. 57. Wolfram would also see the judge's position as too weak to merit such a title, but it will be argued below that his authority was permanent, so that the question should perhaps be left open; cf. Claude, *Adel, Kirche, und Königtum*, 13.

concentrated in the hands of the lower-level leaders. The judge of the Tervingi, it is argued, was the relatively powerless head of a temporary confederation that came into being only to meet the pressing demands of immediate warfare and was then dissolved. Thompson argued this at some length specifically for the Tervingi ('Visigoths' in his terminology), but this was only one case-study forming part of a much broader argument tying together evidence from Caesar, Tacitus, Ammianus, and others.[48] It will be argued here, however, that the evidence better lends itself to an alternative interpretation.

It seems clear, first of all, that the office of judge descended through a single family. Thompson denied this, but the evidence, while scattered, seems clear enough. Ammianus records that Athanaric swore a great oath, which was in accord with his father's orders, not to tread on Roman soil (27. 5. 9). This makes most sense as the admonition of one ruler to his successor. More important, we know that Constantine had erected a statue to Athanaric's father behind the Senate at Constantinople (Themistius, *Or.* 15, p. 276, 7 ff.). Themistius does not state that he had been ruler of the Tervingi, but the erection of the statue indicates that he was a figure of considerable importance. Anonymous in Themistius, Athanaric's father can be plausibly equated with 'the son of King Ariaricus' who came as a hostage to Constantinople in 332 (Anon. Val. 6. 31). If not conclusive, the identification is seductive; the father resented the time spent as hostage, issuing orders to his son accordingly. The period as a hostage in Constantinople also provides a suitable context for erecting the statue.[49] We seem, then, to have three generations of a ruling family: Ariaricus (king in 332), his anonymous son, and Athanaric (Ariaricus' grandson).[50]

[48] Thompson, *Visigoths*, 43–55; cf. id., *Early Germans*, 29–41.

[49] *ILS* i. 840 ff. for statues raised to barbarian kings.

[50] Wolfram, 62 ff. and 'Athanaric', 261 ff. (suggesting a name for the anonymous son); *contra* Thompson, *Visigoths*, 45. *Getica* 21. 112 mentions two Gothic kings as co-rulers, Ariaric and Aoric. Co-rulership is unattested among the 4th-c. Goths, Wolfram argues, so that Jordanes has perhaps confused two consecutive rulers. Germanic families also sometimes used alliterative names, which would be the case were Aoric Ariaric's son. This is possible, but naming-patterns alone are very inconclusive. Schönfeld, *Wörterbuch*, 23 suggests that Gothic *Háuhreiks* may lie behind Aoric; Ariaric might be *Arjareiks* or *Harjareiks*—in the latter case they would alliterate, cf Ch. 1 n. 47.

Jordanes mentions a further fourth-century Gothic leader, Gerberic, dated only by the fact that he precedes Ermenaric. Taken to belong to a family other than Athanaric's, he has been seen as proof that the judgeship did not approximate to a hereditary monarchy.[51] But the fact that he is succeeded by Ermenaric (23. 116), would, at face value, make him a leader of the Greuthungi. The *Getica* also records only one event in Gerberic's reign: an attack on the Vandals, then led, we are told, by King Visimar of the Asding family, who were a most warlike race. This last piece of information (together with a further comment on the extent of Asding domination) is explicitly stated to have come from Dexippus (22. 113). Dexippus, of course, did not take his work past *c.*270, so that if, as seems likely, the whole account of Gerberic comes from Dexippus,[52] he is in fact a third-century king, misplaced into the fourth by the *Getica*. Gerberic is mentioned by no fourth-century source.

It seems best, therefore, to put him to one side and follow what must be the natural conclusion when we see father, son, and grandson all occupying the same position; namely, that it was hereditary in some way through their family. This is supported by explicit references in Zosimus (following Eunapius) to a royal clan of the 'Scythians' (as usual, 'Scythians' are Goths), one of which specifies that Athanaric was its head (Zosimus 4. 25. 2; 4. 34. 3).[53] The contemporary Greuthungi also had a royal clan. Alatheus and Saphrax thought it worthwhile to rule through the previous king's young son, Vitheric, even though they faced difficult circumstances, where a minor was a liability.[54] The observation is only relevant if we suppose the Tervingi and Greuthungi to have been affected by parallel social developments, but this is surely not unlikely.

---

[51] *Getica* 21. 112–23. 116, considered an outsider because his name does not alliterate: Wolfram, 'Athanaric', 266. Wolfram can thus retain Thompson's view of the Tervingi in its essentials despite having shown that the judgeship probably descended through three generations of the one family.

[52] See generally, Miller, 'Dexippus', 12–39. The war is recounted with some circumstantial detail, suggesting that the *Getica* is probably relying on a written source (cf. p. 37).

[53] Thompson, *Visigoths*, 54 n. 1 and *Attila and the Huns*, 10 is too dismissive.

[54] AM 31. 3. 3. Vithimer may well have been closely related to his predecessor Ermenaric: Heather, 'Cassiodorus', 117.

That the office was hereditary does not tell us much about a judge's powers, or precisely how a particular son came to inherit it. Nor even does it prove that the office was held continuously, though a single house (even if only *de facto*) is far more compatible with a permanent headship than with an *ad hoc* command in war, when at any given time the available members might be less suitable than other candidates in age or character. Nevertheless, many who accept the evidence for a royal clan would still argue, essentially on two counts, that the institution was activated only when the Tervingi needed to fight wars. First, we hear of no tribal confederation among the Tervingi in peacetime, and secondly, the sources are held to provide examples of underleaders acting quite independently of any judge.[55]

The first, however, is merely an argument from silence. There are in fact no references at all to the Tervingi in normal times of peace. They appear in narrative histories in times of war, and in ecclesiastical sources only during persecutions or conversions; as we shall see, such religious crises had distinctly political overtones. The point cannot be stressed too highly. No one was interested in the Goths so long as they kept quiet, and no source ever makes the positive statement that, because an event was occurring in peace-time, no judge was then in office.

The nature of the judge's position must stand or fall, therefore, on the two examples generally cited to show independent activity on the part of smaller scale rulers. The first is from Ammianus, who records that the 'kings of the Goths' sent troops to aid the usurper Procopius in 365 (26. 10. 3). This has been taken to mean that the aid was sent independently of any judge. But Ammianus also blames Athanaric for the same act (31. 3. 4), leaving us with a choice between ostensibly contradictory statements. A priori, the second seems preferable because it is more specific; the first is a brief allusion to a complicated sequence of events. The second is also more in tune with the wider context. As we shall see, aid to Procopius was only one aspect of consistent Gothic hostility towards the Roman Empire in the 360s. For all of this, Valens held

---

[55] Older work (e.g. Schmidt, 243 ff. and Klein, 'Frithigern, Athanarich', 43 ff.) noted the instances where more than one leader of the Tervingi is mentioned. The case is argued fully in Thompson, *Visigoths*, 43 ff. followed by Claude, *Adel, Kirche, und Königtum*, 11–12; Wolfram, 'Athanaric', 261 ff.; Demougeot, ii. 332 ff.; Burns, *The Ostrogoths*, 36 ff.

Athanaric responsible, and the treaty which halted the conflict was made with him (see below). It thus makes good sense for Athanaric to have attempted to exploit divisions in the Empire's ruling élite by sending aid to Procopius. Eunapius confirms the point; for him, it was the 'king of the Scythians [= Goths]' who assisted Procopius (fr. 37; cf. Zosimus 4. 10. 1–2). And in any case, Ammianus' two versions are not incompatible. The judge of the Tervingi did not rule without assistance; men such as Atharid, probably kings in the lesser sense of *reiks*, continued to play an important role in society, and were consulted on occasion by overall leaders.[56] To use the plural would thus accurately describe decision-making among the Tervingi, even where the judge was involved.

The second example of independent action by lesser leaders is similar. In a panegyric to Constantius II, Libanius reports that the emperor had calmed the anger of the kings of the Scythians without recourse to battle, persuading them to fight against the Persians (*Or.* 59. 89–90). Libanius was highlighting the emperor's skill, not commenting directly on the Goths, and is unlikely to have been over-worried about what his words implied of Gothic social organization. This oration was given in 348/9, and a judge of the Tervingi was certainly in office just before this in 347/8 (Auxentius 246). It was probably this judge, then, who dealt with the hitch in Gotho-Roman relations. Libanius, like Ammianus, is simply being imprecise; it sounds more impressive (and is not inaccurate) for the emperor to have dealt with barbarian kings.

That this leader was called a judge, rather than a king, in itself says nothing of his powers or permanence.[57] More significant is the fact that Graeco-Roman sources found him eminently confusable with the kind of king more familiar to us (Latin *rex* rather than Gothic *reiks*). Themistius describes Athanaric as 'lord' or 'ruler' (δυνάστης), suggesting a permanent leader (*Or.* 11. p. 221. 9; *Or.* 15. p. 276. 5). The Anonymous Valesianus distinguished two levels of leader among the Goths, a certain *regalis* Alica (5. 27), and the

---

[56] AM 31. 6. 4, 12. 9 (referring to Fritigern); cf. Thompson, *Visigoths*, 47–8.

[57] Themistius, *Or.* 10. p. 204. 16 ff. commenting that a βασιλεύς is distinguished by power, but a judge (δικαστής) for his wisdom, has been taken as Athanaric's gloss on his own position; cf. the varying interpretations of Köpke, *Anfänge*, 111; Claude, *Adel, Kirche, und Königtum*, 12; Wolfram, 'Athanaric', 266 ff. Themistius is conceivably punning here, knowing that Athanaric was a judge, but it is Valens who is being referred to; cf. the translation of D. Moncur in Heather–Matthews, *The Goths in the Fourth Century*, ch. 2.

rex Ariaricus (6. 31). Eunapius and Zosimus, similarly, consistently refer to the 'King of the Scythians' ($\beta\alpha\sigma\iota\lambda\epsilon\grave{\upsilon}\varsigma$ $\tau\hat{\omega}\nu$ $E\kappa\upsilon\theta\hat{\omega}\nu$). These sources fail to use an equivalent of the correct Gothic term, but provide impressive testimony that the ruler of the Tervingi looked to the Romans very much like a monarch.

We hear, then, of the Tervingi on essentially three occasions before the Hunnic invasions: in the 330s (when they made peace with Constantine); the late 340s (the expulsion of Ulfila and the incident referred to by Libanius); and the 360s (Valens' first Gothic war). On each of these occasions, they had an overall leader (whether styled judge or king), and we have no evidence that such a leader had not continued in office in between. On the basis of this contemporary evidence, therefore, it seems perverse to conclude that the judge and confederation of the Tervingi were anything other than permanent. Any comparison of this situation with the temporary confederations found particularly in the time of Caesar can only be misleading.[58]

Having established this point, we may attempt to explore the judge's role in more detail, questioning the extent to which central direction impinged upon everyday life, and whether the judge was the major impetus behind such activity. *The Passion of St Saba* provides our only evidence for the first line of enquiry; it suggests that the central authorities of the Tervingi could enforce a decision to uphold traditional religious observance at village level. Public acts of conformity were demanded; the villagers had to eat meat offered to idols, and subsequently to swear oaths that there were no Christians among them. In the final stage of enforcement, Atharid, representing the central authorities in the village, used his retinue against two recalcitrant villagers, Saba and the priest

---

[58] Temporary Germanic confederations existed in Caesar's day (*BG* 6. 23. 4–5), but that is 400 years before our period. Wolfram, 'Athanaric', 272 ff. also makes comparisons between Athanaric and the ancient Celtic *vergobretos*, but they are not compelling. This was a regular, annual magistracy, with chiefly judicial duties, whose occupant did not leave tribal lands while in office (Wolfram, 'Athanaric', 272 ff. after Caesar, *BG* 1. 16. 5–6; 7. 32 ff. etc.). But Athanaric held office for much more than one year (at least ten: 365–75), with a wide range of duties (see below). Wolfram, op. cit. 273–4 sees Athanaric's refusal to meet Valens on Roman soil as perhaps reflecting such an institutional tying of the Gothic judge to tribal territory. While possible, this does not make Athanaric into an annually appointed legal officer, and Ammianus' words (27. 5. 9) seem specifically anti-Roman, rather than a general ban on foreign travel.

Sansala (*St Saba* 3 ff., pp. 217 ff.). Atharid was acting 'on the orders of the unholy ones' (4, p. 219. 2), who are elsewhere referred to as 'the great among the Goths' (3, p. 217. 26–7). We have only this example, but central policy decisions clearly were enforced among dispersed Gothic villages. Attempting to create ideological unity among a diverse population is, by any standard, an ambitious act of government.

The *Passion* also provides much evidence for the effective limits of the central authorities' power. Their main difficulty seems to have been that there was little direct contact between the great men and the villages. None of them actually lived in Saba's village, and they were consequently ignorant of conditions within it. Thus the villagers could attempt to defeat the persecution by merely pretending to have offered meat to idols, and by swearing false oaths. It was only because Saba would not co-operate that these deceptions failed,[59] which implies that those enforcing the persecution had no real knowledge of the village's affairs. The village was also, to some extent, self-regulating, having a council to facilitate collective action (3, p. 218. 7).[60] The local community would seem to have been the villagers' first concern. As we have seen, they were willing to deceive the central authorities to preserve Christian members of their own community. When Saba refused to co-operate, they themselves threw him out (3, p. 217. 26 ff.), presumably because he was putting the rest of the village at risk. On a second occasion, we find the villagers hiding other Christians from persecution, although they had by then lost patience with the still stubborn Saba, whom they refused any longer to protect (3, p. 218). The *Passion* thus provides us with a remarkably vivid picture of local solidarity, which there is no reason to think exceptional.

Yet, as we have seen, mechanisms did exist by which the great men could direct their people, and they certainly pursued a consistent policy in religious matters. According to the Church historians, the Goths were converted by Constantine, but this is mistaken. It was probably not until 376 that the leaders of the Tervingi officially adopted Christianity, after half a century or more of missionary work;[61] before the Hunnic invasions, the great

---

[59] *St Saba* 3, p. 217. 28 ff.; cf. Thompson, *Visigoths*, 70 ff.
[60] Cf. Thompson, *Visigoths*, 66 ff.
[61] Heather, 'Gothic Conversion', esp. 315 ff.

men of the Tervingi even resisted the spread of Christianity in at least two periods of persecution, in 347/8 and from 369 onwards. The first receives only brief mention in the sources, so that its causes can only be guessed at, but two related motives are recorded for the second. Socrates and Sozomen report that Athanaric ordered it because the ancestral religion was becoming debased, and, according to Epiphanius, the persecution was to spite the Romans, since their emperors were Christian.[62] The Goths would seem to have been afraid that Christianity would undermine that part of Gothic identity which was founded in their common inherited beliefs, so that religion was not just an individual spiritual concern, but also a political issue standing in some relation to Gotho-Roman affairs. This finds some confirmation in the way that persecutions followed important events in Gotho-Roman relations. That of 347/8, for instance, seems to be associated with the diplomatic dispute referred to by Libanius.[63] More strikingly, the better-known persecution from 369 to at least 372 (when Saba was martyred) was launched in the very year that Valens recognized renewed Gothic independence (Jerome, *Chronicle*, s.a. 369). The persecution would seem to have been an attempt to rid Gothia of the religious as well as the political influence of the Empire.[64]

The actual role in all this of the judge, as opposed to his great men, is harder to evaluate. The latter did contribute to important decisions. The *Passion* records, for instance, that 'impious *magistanes*' (in the plural) ordered the persecution (pp. 217. 26–7; 218. 3, 16–17), so that from the *Passion*'s 'village-eye' view, the judge did not stand out as uniquely responsible. Ammianus, it has often been noted, also portrays a later leader, Fritigern, urging and persuading his followers, rather than simply issuing orders (p. 179). It is a false conclusion, however, to suppose that the judge of the Tervingi was powerless because he was unable simply to

[62] Socrates, *HE* 4. 33. 7 (= Sozomen, *HE* 6. 37. 12); Epiphanius, *Panar. Haer.* 70; cf. Thompson, *Visigoths*, 98 ff. The persecution of 347/8 was possibly caused by evangelism; Philostorgius, *HE* 2. 5 might imply that Ulfila was appointed for those already Christian, and Auxentius 244 ff. suggests that he spread Christianity among the Goths as a whole.

[63] Thompson, 'Lower Danube Frontier', 379 ff.

[64] Roman emperors sponsored Ulfila's missions, and Gothic Christians had contacts with Roman Christians, so that there were grounds for suspicion: Heather, 'Gothic Conversion', 316–17.

command people to do his will.[65] He ruled a Germanic tribal society, lacking aids to strong government such as widespread literacy and developed communications. Any ruler's power in such a society was necessarily bound within strong limits, and direct contact between himself and his subjects always interrupted by men powerful in their own right. It should occasion no surprise that the *Passion* and Ammianus reveal that the ruler of the Tervingi could not just issue commands. This reflects the quality of the sources, rather than any singularity in the situation. The judge's need to consult what might be called his nobility does not contradict his existence, nor define him as powerless. Detailed case-studies would be required to assess the exact balance of power between them, and the necessary evidence does not exist. Failing this, all we can do is survey the judge's range of activity.

He certainly played a central role in foreign policy. As we shall see in a moment, it was Athanaric who initiated the war with Valens in the 360s, and ended it in 369 when he met the emperor on board a ship in the middle of the Danube. The peace was binding on all his followers. In the 370s, similarly, we find Athanaric directing measures to deal with the Huns, including pre-emptive military action and the attempt to build a huge defensive fortification (AM 31. 3. 4–8). He was ultimately unsuccessful, but the episode emphasizes the judge's responsibilities in this area. Hand in hand with this went an important military role. In 369 Athanaric attempted to harass Valens' army, and in 376 he led a force east against the Huns (AM 27. 5. 6; 31. 3. 4–5). Graeco-Roman sources, the *Passion* notwithstanding, also report that Athanaric played a major role in the persecution of Christians after 369, and there seems no reason to doubt their word.[66] We are told by Auxentius (246) that the judge had also ordered the persecution of 347/8. It seems unlikely that the judge was any kind of priest-ruler, but he clearly had a religious role. He probably also played an important part in the settlement of disputes. We have no specific evidence for this, but judicial power is a common function of lordship, and is of course suggested by his title. The judge thus played an important role in most major facets of tribal life.

Although much of the internal workings of their confederation cannot be recovered, the Tervingi were much more than a

---

[65] Cf. Thompson, *Visigoths*, 47 with refs.
[66] Jerome, *Chronicle*, s.a. 371; Socrates, *HE* 4. 33. 7–8.

temporary alliance of groups with an overall leader only in wartime. The judge's position was permanent, and seems to have passed through at least three generations of the same family. This is not to deny that other men exercised real authority, and power will surely have ebbed and flowed between the judge and his great men. We have no explicit evidence of direct competition between them,[67] but an heir, for instance, cannot immediately match the prestige built up by his predecessor, and Athanaric, for his part, is likely to have strengthened his position by the war against Valens (see below), and his prestige probably remained high until the Huns broke his power. The Huns, however, were too severe a test for many rulers, and Athanaric's failure in 376 must not lead us to think that the institution of the judge was in itself powerless. It seems much more likely that his power and the loyalties this enabled him to generate were the forces which really bound together the Tervingi.

D. *Gotho-Roman relations to c.375*

For over thirty years in the mid-fourth century (*c*.332–65), a peace treaty between Constantine and the Goths dictated the nature of Gotho-Roman relations. The emperor made clear his commitment to safeguarding the Danube frontier when, after defeating Licinius, he constructed a bridge over the river between Sucidava and Oescus. Inaugurated in July 328, it was 2,437 m. long, and a triumph of engineering; henceforth, Roman troops and heavy equipment could move quickly across the Danube.[68] North of the river, Sucidava and other forts such as Daphne (also inaugurated in 328) provided secure bases for military operations.[69] Coin-issues commemorating both the bridge and fort depict a barbarian kneeling in supplication, so that the projects were clearly designed

---

[67] It has been suggested from Socrates, *HE* 4. 33 (= Sozomen, *HE* 6. 37) that Fritigern resisted Athanaric's attempts to turn the judgeship into a monarchy after 370; e.g. Wolfram, 70. But Socrates has misplaced a quarrel which only broke out in 376: Heather, 'Gothic Conversion', 293 ff.

[68] Aur. Vict. 41: 13; *Chronicon Paschale*, s.a. 328 (*CM* i. 233), cf. Seeck, *Regesten*, 178; Tudor, *Ponts romains*, 5 ff.

[69] Tudor, *Sucidava*, 71 ff. This followed Tetrarchic building: Mócsy, *Pannonia and Upper Moesia*, 266 ff.; Scorpan, *Limes Scythiae*, 117 ff., 134–5.

to strengthen Rome's strategic position.[70] Such a purpose and effect are also ascribed to an earlier Constantinian bridge over the Rhine by the panegyrist of 310. He declared that peoples across the river would henceforth live in a state of constant fear, since Roman troops could quickly avenge any outrage, and that many of them had already submitted (*Pan. Lat.* 7(6). 13. 1–5).

The Danubian bridge had similar results. The 330s saw not only the treaty with the Goths, but also an agreement with neighbouring Taifali. By 358 they were imperial allies (AM 17. 13. 19), whereas they had previously been hostile (Zosimus 2. 31); the 330s provides the most likely moment for this change of status.[71] Constantine likewise intervened in the middle Danube region to pacify the Sarmatians.[72] How far the emperor extended Roman power into Transylvania is uncertain, but he crowned his general pacification of the Danube region by taking the title Dacicus Maximus in 335/6.[73]

Of Constantine's particular agreement with the Goths, Jordanes reports that it was a *foedus* confirming a special relationship of long standing. Under its provisions the Goths were to send 40,000 men to help the Empire whenever required, this group (the *foederati*) becoming so famous that their deeds were still remembered in his own day (*Getica* 21. 112). But Jordanes envisages all satisfactory phases of Gotho-Roman relations, before and after Constantine, to have been organized on the basis of Gothic military assistance in return for annual gifts. Good emperors from the first century onwards grant the Goths their dues, bad emperors are too greedy or foolish to pay up.[74] Jordanes even claims that by *c.*300 the Empire had 'for a long time' found it difficult to fight without Gothic assistance (21. 111).

Much of this is nonsense. Jordanes imagines Constantine's treaty to have affected all Goths, when it applied primarily to the

---

[70] *RIC* vii. 574–5 (Daphne); 283–4, 331 (the Bridge).

[71] Schmidt, 546.

[72] Anon. Val. 6. 31–2 (also AM 17. 12. 17 ff.); cf. Harmatta, *Sarmatians*, 54 ff.; Bichir, 'Les Sarmates', 194 ff.

[73] Barnes, 'Victories of Constantine', 151.

[74] Good emperors: Gallus and Volusianus (19. 106), Maximian (21. 110), Constantine (21. 112), Theodosius (28. 145), Leo (52. 271). Bad emperors: Domitian (13. 76), Philip (16. 89), Arcadius and Honorius (29. 146), Marcian (52. 270). Cf. Mommsen, 'Das römische Militärwesen', 227 n. 4.

Tervingi. The agreement of 369, which replaced it, was signed by Athanaric, leader of the Tervingi. Since he was probably a descendant of the leader who treated with Constantine in 332, it is only natural to suppose that both treaties were made with the same group.[75] Similarly, while Goths did fight alongside the Roman army after 332, they never sent anything like 40,000 men. Three thousand Goths were sent to Procopius in 365 (AM 26. 10. 3), and this is usually taken as a more correct order of magnitude. Jordanes also tells us that Constantine greatly valued the Goths' help, and that it enabled him to defeat Licinius, whom they actually killed (21. 111–12). In reality, Constantine had first defeated Gothic raiding parties in the 320s, and then overcome still more Goths who were in fact fighting for Licinius (Anon. Val. 5. 21, 27). The peace of 332 followed further conflict, in the course of which the Goths made a complete surrender, Constantine celebrating his success with a column and annual games.[76]

Nevertheless, Jordanes' picture of Constantine making the Goths into favoured *foederati* has won general acceptance,[77] and is usually supported with more contemporary evidence. Ammianus applies a case-form of *foedus* to the Goths' position (27. 5. 1), Gothic troops campaigned for the Empire on three known occasions while the treaty was in force,[78] and the Goths also received annual payments. Eusebius claims that Constantine warred against the Goths to end tribute (*VC* 4. 5), but Julian (*Caesares* 329 A) clearly states that the emperor continued to pay 'tribute of some kind'. This is confirmed by Themistius, who reports that money, provisions, and clothing were handed over to the Goths (*Or.* 10, p. 205. 13 ff.). From this it has been argued that the Goths really did fight for the Empire as *foederati* in return for annual payment, if not quite on the scale that Jordanes envisages.[79]

---

[75] Some Greuthungi fought Valens in the 360s (AM 27. 5. 6), and may also have treated with Constantine.

[76] Anon. Val. 6. 31; Eusebius, *VC* 4. 5; Eutropius 10. 7. 1; Aur. Vict. 41. 13; *Cons. Const.*, s.a. 332 (*CM* i. 234); cf. Wolfram, 62.

[77] e.g. Schmidt, 226 ff.; Wolfram, 61–2; Demougeot, ii. 327–8.

[78] In 348 (Libanius, *Or.* 59. 89), 360 (AM 20. 8. 1), and 363 (AM 23. 2. 7). Libanius, *Or.* 12. 62 also claims that Constantius attempted to mobilize the Goths against Julian; they sent 3,000 men to Procopius (AM 26. 10. 3).

[79] The frontier was left open for trade, where imperial policy normally controlled cross-border trade through designated centres: Themistius, *Or.* 10, p. 205. 24 ff.; cf. Thompson, *Visigoths*, 15 n. 2.

A legal framework for this relationship has also been constructed. Coins marked *Gothia* were issued by Constantine. This style of coin-legend seems to have been reserved for actual conquests, so that the agreement of 332 involved—however notionally—the annexation of Gothic land. The point is confirmed by Julian, who reports that his uncle claimed to have reconquered Trajanic Dacia (*Caesares* 329 C), on part of which the Goths were established.[80] Given (from Jordanes) that the Goths were also *foederati*, Constantine's claim has been glossed from the sixth-century Procopius, who describes *foederati* in much the same way as Jordanes: foreigners incorporated into the Roman state as equals, not slaves, performing military service for annual salaries (*Wars* 3. 11. 3–4; 8. 5. 13–14). The 332 treaty has thus been seen as an important innovation which turned Goths into Roman soldiers: the first example of a type of agreement which was to have a wide currency in the period of imperial collapse.[81] More contemporary evidence does not suggest, however, that Constantine granted the Goths such a special relationship.[82]

Ammianus indicates that Gothic military service was not an obligation clearly defined by the treaty. In 360, Constantius 'asked the Scythians [= Goths] for *auxilia*, either for pay or as a favour' (*mercede vel gratia*, 20. 8. 1). Jordanes' picture of constantly available Gothic support is thus misleading; precise terms were negotiated on each occasion. Nor does Ammianus' use of the words *foederibus* . . . *pacis* imply a special relationship: Ammianus uses *foedus* in its different forms quite indiscriminately of every kind of agreement that the Roman state made with its neighbours, although two broad types are distinguishable. Much the rarer usage is of agreements involving no submission to the Roman state; the best example of this is Jovian's treaty with the Persians in 363.[83] But Ammianus uses *foedus* and its derivatives much more

---

[80] Cf. Eusebius, *VC* 1. 8. On the coins, see *RIC* vii. 215–16 (Trier); cf. Chrysos, 51 ff. and 'Gothia Romana', 60–1; Bernhardt, *Handbuch zur Münzkunde*, 103 ff.

[81] Mommsen, 'Das römische Militärwesen', 228–9 first identified it as an innovation; cf. Chrysos, 58 ff. (with refs.) and 'Gothia Romana', 53 ff. For Schenk von Stauffenberg, *Das Imperium*, 107 ff. the 332 treaty asserted a Christian conception of world empire, but see Stallknecht, *Untersuchungen*, 16 ff.

[82] Cf. (with different arguments) Stallknecht, *Untersuchungen*, 16 ff., and the excellent study of Brockmeier, 'Der große Friede', 79–100.

[83] AM 25. 7. 14; 8. 4; 9. 11; 26. 4. 6; 27. 12. 10; 12. 18; 29. 1. 3; 30. 2. 3.

frequently of agreements following capitulations; this is because the majority of treaties he mentions stem from the Rhine and Danube frontiers, where Roman strength was sufficient to maintain its hegemony. For instance, the submission of Gundomadus and Vadomarius in 354 was followed by a *foedus* (14. 10. 1–16; cf. 21. 3. 1); or after his complete surrender to Julian (17. 10. 6–9), the subsequent peace made Hortarius a *rex foederatus* of the Empire (18. 2. 13). There are many similar examples.[84] The usage is entirely in accord with precedent. In earlier periods, an act of submission by a foreign power (often signalled by the use of *deditio* and related terms) was routinely followed by a negotiated agreement: *foedus*, *pax*, or something similar.[85] It is thus insufficient to say that Constantine's treaty with the Goths was a *foedus*; the question is what kind of *foedus*.[86]

Some, as we have seen, adduce the evidence of Procopius, but he glosses *foederati* as 'those . . . who had come into the Roman political system not in the condition of slaves, since they had not been conquered by the Romans, but on the basis of complete equality' (*Wars* 3. 11. 3; cf. 8. 5. 13). His definition is thus irrelevant. The treaty of 332, it will be remembered, was preceded by a total surrender, and Eusebius and Libanius both use the language of slavery (δουλεύειν) of the Goths' status afterwards.[87] It is necessary to find a form of unequal alliance, current in the fourth century, which Ammianus would have been willing to describe as a *foedus*, and which would have allowed Constantine to claim that he had added the Goths to the Roman Empire.

[84] e.g. Rhine frontier: 15. 4 (referred to as a *foedus* at 31. 10. 2); 17. 1. 12–13; 17. 6. 1; 17. 10. 3–4 (referred to as *foedera* at 18. 2. 7). Middle Danube: 17. 12. 9 ff. (called *foedus* at 29. 6. 16); 17. 13. 20–3 (*foedus* at 19. 11. 5). The pattern of submission followed by a peace seems consistent even where different vocabulary is used: e.g. 16. 12. 15; 18. 2. 16–19.

[85] Cf. Brockmeier, 'Der große Friede', 80. Older work considered *deditio* to entail total legal dissolution, so that a formal treaty (*foedus*) after *deditio* was inconceivable: Mommsen, *Römisches Staatsrecht*, iii. 716 ff.; Taubler, *Imperium Romanum*, 2 ff. But *deditio* never ruled out a *foedus*: e.g. Horn, *Foederati*, 5 ff., 16–17; Dahlheim, *Struktur und Entwicklung*, 107 ff. (with refs.).

[86] There have been many attempts to produce a single definition of *foederati* (starting with Mommsen, *Römisches Staatsrecht*, iii. 645 ff. esp. 653–4) but, as we might anyway expect, Roman foreign policy was highly flexible. This was just as true in earlier times: Klose, *Klientel-Randstaaten*, 135 ff.

[87] Eusebius, *VC* 4. 5; Libanius, *Or.* 59. 89; cf. Brockmeier, 'Der große Friede', 93–4 (with refs.).

This in fact poses little problem, the Latin panegyrics helping to establish three related points. First, any people brought to submission by the imperial army was afterwards considered part of the Empire.[88] Second, this was equally true if that submission was caused by fear of Roman arms, rather than actual defeat.[89] Third, once they had submitted, a people remained part of the Empire (at least according to the Romans) even if no provincial organization was established and the existing social order continued as before. For instance, the panegyrics describe the surrender of the Frankish king Gennobaudes, and how Maximian restored him to rule his people. It is emphasized throughout that the king nevertheless remained in servitude to the Empire, and he is seen encouraging his followers to take a good look at their true lord, Maximian. Such acts of restitution after surrender had long been a part of Roman diplomacy.[90] Similar ideas were aired when Symmachus celebrated the Rhine campaigns of Valentinian I (*Or.* 2. 12 ff.), and Libanius those of Julian (*Orr.* 13. 27, 30–1; 15. 32–3; 18. 75 ff.). Eunapius also records that Julian told his men (fr. 18. 1), '[that] while they must regard as enemy territory that which belonged to those at war with them, they must treat as their own that which belonged to those who had submitted to them'. Equally important, Ammianus' account of Julian's campaigns reveals that submissions of Alamannic kings were usually followed by other agreements which settled precise peace-terms. These are exactly the kinds of agreements which Ammianus labels *foedera*, and all left established kings in place.[91] Yet these kings were also subject to imperial dominion, and we are told that Julian had treated them as 'common slaves' (25. 4. 25).

A Roman victory and Gothic surrender, followed by a treaty (*foedus* in Ammianus' usage) which maintained the existing social order, is a sequence of events matched on numerous occasions in the fourth century along Rhine and Danube. Such a surrender left people permanently dependent on the Roman state. A distinction is sometimes drawn between this method of adding subjects to the

[88] e.g. 2(10). 7. 2 ff., 9. 1; 3(11). 5. 4; 4(8). 1. 4, 10. 4; 5(9). 21. 1–3.

[89] e.g. 2(10). 10. 3 ff.; 3(11). 5. 4; 7(6). 12. 1 ff.; 9(12). 22. 3, 25. 2.

[90] *Pan. Lat.* 2(10). 10. 3 ff.; (3(11). 5. 4); cf. Dahlheim, *Struktur und Entwicklung*, 77 ff.

[91] Suomarius: 17. 10. 3–4 (cf. 18. 2. 7); Hortarius: 17. 10. 6–9 (*rex foederatus* at 18. 2. 16); Macrianus and Hariobaudes: 18. 2. 16–18; Urius, Ursicinus, and Vestralpus: 18. 2. 18–19; Vadomarius: 18. 2. 16 (cf. 14. 10. 9 ff.; 21. 3. 1).

Empire and a full-scale conquest followed by the creation of a Roman province.[92] Nevertheless, groups beyond the fortified frontier who submitted to imperial power were in a sense part of the Empire, not as full citizens but as dependent subjects.[93] These contemporary ideas fully explain Constantine's claim to have added *Gothia* to the Empire.

That this is the correct way to understand Constantine's relations with the Goths is confirmed by the other instance where his coinage claimed that territory had been annexed. From the mid-310s appear similar coin-legends referring to the Rhine: *Gaudia Romanorum Alamannia* and/or *Francia*. A first example is dated *c*.310–13, and the series continued into the 320s.[94] The chronological coincidence leaves little doubt that the legends commemorated in the first instance Constantine's activities on the Rhine after the battle of the Milvian Bridge. He then defeated a hostile coalition which had taken advantage of his preoccupation with Maxentius to break its existing agreements. Constantine's subsequent victory was won partly on the field of battle and partly through the submission of unfought, but suitably cowed tribal groups.[95] A previous Constantinian use of the *Gothia*-type coin-legend marked not an equal agreement, but the assertion of Roman power over uncooperative tribal neighbours.

There was thus nothing out of the ordinary in Constantine's relations with the Goths. The agreement of 332, affecting primarily the Tervingi, can be called a *foedus*, but only in the broad sense predominant in Ammianus. A *foedus* after submission, it left the Goths at least notionally under Roman dominion. Its special trading-arrangements[96] were probably a palliative. Constantine had forced this agreement upon the Goths after a major victory, and by incorporating an item to their benefit may have hoped to give them a positive reason for keeping it. Having expended much

[92] Panegyrics to Constantine stress that force is required to make such groups keep faith: e.g. 6(7). 8. 4–5; 7(6). 10. 1–7, 11. 4–5; 9(12). 3. 2, 22. 3 ff. Roman freedom of action could also remain limited. In two cases (AM 28. 2. 1 ff.; 29. 6. 2 ff.) the building of forts was contrary to the terms agreed.

[93] For earlier periods, see Braund, *Rome and the Friendly King*, esp. 181 ff.; cf. Millar, 'Government and Diplomacy', 351 ff.

[94] From 310–13: *RIC* vi. 323 (cf. Christ, *Antike Münzfunde*, i. 154 ff. and *RIC* vii. 224 ff.); *RIC* vii, Trier (143–221), Ticinum (349–87), Siscia (411–16).

[95] *Pan. Lat.* 9(12). 22 ff., 10(4). 18; cf. Demougeot, ii. 59 ff.

[96] See above, n. 79.

time and money, Constantine wanted his Danubian settlement to last. This also explains the respect shown Gothic hostages, such as Athanaric's father, who, it will be remembered, was immortalized in stone at the back of the Senate. The careful treatment of hostages had long been a feature of Roman diplomacy, strengthening the agreements which had brought them to Roman territory.[97]

Likewise, the gifts (cf. p. 109) may have been at least partly designed to win Gothic acceptance for the treaty. Annual payments or gifts were not special concessions, but a constant feature of Roman diplomacy, used in different ways for centuries.[98] Historians have tended to minimize their use, interpreting such payments as 'tribute'—a mark of subjection which cannot be reconciled with demonstrable Roman supremacy. But a display of generosity—giving more than the recipient can afford to return— in itself asserts superiority, and gift-giving or exchange has long been a means by which relationships are maintained.[99] In Germanic society in particular, of course, lordship was often equated with the giving of gold. Moreover, such gifts also increased the powers of patronage available to the leaders to whom they were granted, and so reinforced the position of those with whom the treaty had been made. This was obviously to Rome's benefit, since the loss of face inherent in any surrender might otherwise have led to the ousting of these leaders. Gifts such as those made to the Goths after 332 are evidence of Rome's willingness to adapt diplomatic forms to the needs of the frontier. Ammianus similarly refers to treaties whose form was dictated by native custom: the gain once more being greater security, since tribal groups were more likely to uphold relationships they understood.[100] Even Julian's subjugation of the Alamanni in the 350s, for instance, left them with rights to annual gifts, and Julian had been in a position to enforce his will as he chose.[101] This may seem surprising given Julian's disparaging reference to Constantine's paying of 'tribute' to the Goths, but gift-giving, while standard, was also—if labelled 'tribute'—a

[97] Braund, *Rome and the Friendly King*, 9 ff.

[98] e.g. Klose, *Klientel-Randstaaten*, 138 (cf. Syme, review of Klose, 97–8); Braund, *Rome and the Friendly King*, 62–3.

[99] Mauss, *The Gift*, esp. 37 ff.

[100] AM 14. 10. 16; 17. 1. 13; 17. 12. 21 (cf. 17. 10. 7; 30. 3. 5).

[101] The Alamanni revolted in 365 because Valentinian I reduced their gifts (AM 26. 5. 7; cf. 27. 1. 1 ff.); Julian's arrangements had not been revised before this date.

useful stick with which to beat any emperor whose achievements needed to be disparaged. Annual gifts—and, indeed, occasional service alongside Roman armies—are a standard part of fourth-century treaties which maintained Roman hegemony on Rhine and Danube and do not require particular explanation.[102]

The treaty of 332 thus established the Tervingi as a Roman client power. Jordanes' rather contradictory characterization of Gothic *foederati* greatly resembles, in fact, the relationship that certain Gothic groups established with Constantinople in the fifth century (see Ch. 7). The *Getica* has probably backdated this later meaning of *foederati*, therefore, to the fourth century.

We are now in a better position to understand the attitude of the Tervingi, or at least their leaders, to the Roman Empire. The *Getica* implies that the Goths were willing participants in a close relationship, but contemporary sources suggest the opposite; Roman victory forced them into submission. The victory was also won on Sarmatian soil, where an imperial army finally trapped the Goths, who seem to have been migrating.[103] This may be further evidence of the Goths' distaste for the Empire. They were moving perhaps from lands where Roman power—manifest in Constantine's building programme of the late 320s—was encroaching too closely. If so, their attitude remained consistent up to 376. Dependence on Rome was to be resisted.

The treaty seems to have remained in force down to the 360s, when Ammianus described the Goths (again presumably meaning primarily the Tervingi) as 'a people long friendly to the Romans, and long bound by treaties of peace' (27. 5. 1). Apart from small-scale raiding,[104] there had been one incident of greater significance in the late 340s, which was resolved by negotiation (Libanius, *Or.* 59. 89–93).[105] In the 360s, however, Valens' first Gothic war and the peace of 369 overturned Constantine's settlement. This second treaty was in some ways the antithesis of 332. Payments and special trading arrangements ceased; two towns only were designated as trading-posts. Imperial propaganda also stressed the

---

[102] Cf. Stallknecht, *Untersuchungen*, 18–19; Brockmeier, 'Der große Friede', 82.

[103] Anon. Val. 6. 31; Jerome, *Chronicle*, s.a. 332; cf. Schmidt, 226–7; Wolfram, 61.

[104] Cf. AM 22. 7. 7; 26. 4. 5; Themistius, *Or.* 10, p. 207. 20 ff.

[105] On this incident, see Chrysos, 77 ff.; Wolfram, 63; Brockmeier, 'Der große Friede', 83 ff., 96–7; *contra* Thompson, *Visigoths*, 13 ff.

importance of an impenetrable frontier. It is surely correct to view this separation of Roman and Goth as reversing Constantine's policy, which had attempted to safeguard Roman interests through close relations with the Tervingi.[106] Some have argued that Valens imposed this separation upon the Goths, but the evidence suggests that the peace of 369, if not actually a Gothic victory, did incorporate more of the will of the Tervingi than had that of 332.

According to Eunapius, Valens attacked the Goths because they had supported Procopius in 365 (fr. 37; cf. Zosimus 4. 10), but this was only a pretext. Even before Procopius' usurpation, Valens had sent troops to the Danube because the Goths were threatening the frontier. Procopius suborned these troops at the outbreak of his revolt (AM 26. 6. 11–12), so that the sequence of events cannot be doubted. Trouble had in fact been brewing since the reign of Julian. Brief allusions to Gothic hostility in Ammianus (22. 7. 7–8) and Eunapius (fr. 27. 1) might on their own be dismissed, but Libanius records that in 362 a Gothic embassy came to Julian asking for alterations to the terms of their treaty. The emperor dismissed the embassy, telling them that the treaty could only be changed by warfare (*Or.* 12. 78). No clash occurred in Julian's reign, and Goths did serve on the Persian campaign, but the accession of Valens, after Julian's defeat and Jovian's death, perhaps offered the Goths more hope of changing the relationship by force. There is no inconsistency between this hostility and the Goths' later decision to assist Procopius, when they were notionally responding to a request which stressed the usurper's relationship to the Constantinian dynasty (AM 27. 5. 1). Supporting Procopius offered more chance of real gain than confronting the Empire directly; the Goths preferred to intervene in the civil war (much as they had done for Licinius against Constantine), hoping for concessions from a victorious Procopius.[107] Gothic hostility to

---

[106] The main sources are AM 27. 5 and Themistius *Or.* 10, esp. pp. 205. 11 ff. (payments); 206. 7–8 (trading); 206. 8 ff. (fortifications). All agree on the main effects of the treaty: e.g. Schmidt, 232–3; Wolfram, 68–9; Thompson, *Visigoths*, 13 ff.

[107] Chrysos, 97 ff. and Wolfram 66–7 view Constantine's treaty as welcome to the Goths, and hence make Valens the aggressor, stressing that there was no Gothic attack. They fail to take proper account of AM 26. 6. 11 ff., and neither refers to Libanius, *Or.* 12. 78. Supporting Procopius was anyway an attack on Valens.

the treaty of 332 was thus the real cause of Valens' first Gothic war.

The war itself was conducted over three campaigning seasons, in none of which was Valens able to engage the Goths decisively. In 367, as we have seen, they escaped to the Carpathians, in 368 unusual flooding of the Danube prevented a major attack, and in 369, although Athanaric resisted for a while, seemingly aided by some Greuthungi, he fled after only light skirmishing (*leviora certamina*). Ammianus says that Athanaric used only part of his army in 369, which might suggest that he was seeking merely to harass Valens (AM 27. 5. 3–6).[108] Despite a three-year campaign, Valens had not won so complete a victory as had been achieved in 331/2.

His response to these frustrations is illustrated by Themistius' eighth oration. This was delivered at Marcianople in late March 368, so that Themistius was standing in Valens' field-headquarters after one fruitless campaign (367), at a time when the coming of spring was making it obvious that the Danube flood was going to interfere with the next (368). Themistius here 'advises' Valens that the Empire lacks the resources for constant campaigning. Reconquering lost territories and fighting on menaced frontiers, he argues, distract the emperor from the true interests of state, furthering common welfare. The point is couched in the language of economic necessity: military action benefits only the areas concerned, not the Empire as a whole, and real achievement lies in minimizing the overall tax-burden.[109] It has been thought that Themistius was censuring Valens, but the speech makes better sense when he is viewed (properly) as the emperor's mouthpiece. Through Themistius, Valens was preparing opinion for the change of policy which the frustrations of 367 suggested might be necessary. Mobilizing the army proclaimed aggressive intent and aroused expectations of victory; if it was not to be forthcoming, public opinion had to be prepared.[110]

[108] Ammianus' account of 369 (27. 5. 6) is problematic, seeming to describe Athanaric as leader of the Greuthungi, and not making explicit the relationship of the skirmishing to the activities of Athanaric's band; I interpret them as the same, not separate incidents.

[109] *Or.* 8, p. 172. 11 ff. Celebrating Valens' Quinquennalia, the speech was delivered on 28 Mar. 368: Dagron, 'Thémistios', 21.

[110] See McCormick, *Eternal Victory*, esp. 35 ff. for the emphasis on military success as an emperor's greatest attribute.

The propaganda campaign continued in the next two years. In oration 10 of 370, Themistius reports that, on behalf of the Senate, he continued to advocate negotiating with the Goths in 369, and again makes the point that Valens had been persuaded by Themistius' embassies to accept a diplomatic solution to the conflict (p. 202. 4. ff.). All this has been taken to reflect the independent will of the Senate, but to be believed sixteen hundred years later is probably a greater coup than Themistius managed in his own lifetime. Set against Valens' inability to win a decisive military victory, Themistius' speech has an obvious significance. It was clear to all that Valens' policy had changed from one of confrontation to negotiation; Themistius was attempting to hide the fact that Valens compromised because he had been unable to win on the battlefield. Instead, Valens is portrayed as having changed his mind of his own free will, and the placing of responsibility for this firmly on Themistius and the Senate may have been designed to divert attention away from the emperor's military performance.[111]

Valens' failure must not be overstated. The Goths did not defeat him, and his campaigns hit them hard. Harvests were disrupted, and commercial contacts halted, so that the Goths were deprived of their major sources of food (AM 27. 5. 7). Themistius claims that Valens could have destroyed the Goths if he had so chosen, and that he anyway dictated the terms of the peace, defeating the Gothic leader in debate on board the ship.[112] This should not be taken seriously. When he made this claim, Themistius was standing in the Senate of Constantinople, before the ruling class of the eastern Empire, with the task of justifying Valens' actions. He would not have wished to admit that imperial armies had been frustrated by mere barbarians. And despite his attempt to build up Valens' performance in the debate, Themistius twice admits that the peace-settlement conceded something of the Goths' demands (pp. 202. 21–2, 205. 7 ff.). Imperial policy was not changed without a struggle, Valens turned away several

---

[111] On the context of the oration: Dagron, 'Thémistios', 22. Dagron, esp. 95 ff. and Daly, 'The Mandarin and the Barbarian', 351 ff. do not realize that he was a mouthpiece for successive eastern emperors.

[112] *Or.* 10. *passim*, esp. pp. 198. 15 ff. (conquest); 201. 10 ff. (military exploits); 203. 11 ff. (the debate).

embassies (cf. AM 27. 5. 8), before finally accepting that matters should be resolved by negotiation.

His original aims are uncertain; he perhaps wanted to make the Goths abide by the terms of the 332 agreement, and punish them for assisting Procopius. When outright military victory proved elusive, the emperor made virtue of necessity, and claimed in his propaganda that separation from the Goths was actually beneficial for the Empire. The argument found some contemporary accept-ance. Both Ammianus (27. 5. 8) and Zosimus (4. 11. 4, from Eunapius) are probably echoing Valens' propaganda in stating that the peace-agreement was a reasonable outcome to the war. The emperor was also under pressure to end it because of events on the eastern front. After a brief period of quiet, Sapor had, since 368, ousted the rulers of Armenia and Iberia (Arsaces and Sauro-maces), who had been Roman allies, attempting to replace them with his own creatures (AM 27. 12). These events were more urgent than subjugating the Tervingi.

The causes of the war, its course, and Valens' propaganda thus present a coherent picture. The agreement of 369 (called a *foedus* by Ammianus) was a compromise in the face of military stalemate and the pressure Valens faced from other quarters. Themistius does claim that the Goths 'consented to submit to [Roman] rule' (*Or.* 10, p. 212, 20) and Ammianus reports that the Goths 'sent submissive deputations to beg for pardon and peace' (27. 5. 7). But fourth-century emperors demanded subservience from barbarians, and some kind of submission probably had to be made before friendship could be formally re-established.[113] No source describes a formal surrender, however, and, as we have seen, Valens conceded some of Athanaric's demands. Any submission was more notional than in 332.

A final point of interest is the peace-ceremony itself. Claiming that he was constrained by an oath and his father's orders from entering Roman territory, Athanaric dictated that the treaty should be signed on a ship in the middle of the Danube (AM 27. 5. 9). This again seems to emphasize the comparative strength of Athanaric's position. It was usual for an emperor who had achieved a significant victory either to make the enemy come to him on Roman soil, or to parade imperial standards in the defeated

---

[113] AM 31. 4. 13 refers to the time *cum foederaretur concordia*; *concordia* is here probably a synonym for *amicitia*, the usual diplomatic term.

people's territory, compelling their leaders' attendance upon him there.[114] This second means of displaying Roman might remained open despite Athanaric's oath, but the leaders instead met in the middle of the river in a ceremony which accorded Athanaric some kind of symbolic diplomatic equality.[115] Themistius attempts to divert our attention by picturing Goths beside the river cowering in fear (p. 201. 21 ff.), and praising Valens' fortitude for standing in the sun (p. 203. 11 ff.), but Ammianus did not miss the point. When discussing events of 376, he noted that Athanaric feared that the ceremony of 369 would have left Valens with a grudge (31. 4. 13). It is even possible that Athanaric's excuses for not leaving Gothia were invented to save Valens' face, and to hide the fact that dominion had not been asserted in the usual fashion. The whole episode strongly recalls the treaty of friendship made between Valentinian I and the Alamannic king Macrianus in 374. Ammianus calls this a *foedus* (30. 3. 4, 7), but describes no formal submission (30. 3). Valentinian had twice previously failed to destroy Macrianus' power: in 371 (28. 5. 8 ff.), and 372 (29. 4). In 374 he needed to deal with troubles in Illyricum, and courteously summoned Macrianus to a meeting where symbolic equality was maintained. Valentinian conducted negotiations by boat in acknowledgement of Macrianus' rights over territory beyond the Rhine. The similarities are obvious, further evidence that Athanaric had thrown off some elements of Roman dominion.

This had its drawbacks. Annual gifts ceased, and it has been argued that, because of this, Athanaric's policy aroused hostility among other leaders of the Tervingi, who enjoyed the annual income which was part of Constantine's settlement. For this there is no evidence. In 376, Fritigern led a large group of Tervingi into the Empire, when Athanaric wanted to keep them north of the Danube, but by that time the Huns had invaded Gothic lands. Nothing suggests that these people would have been hostile to Athanaric's desire to throw off imperial subjection before the Huns were a factor. Indeed Athanaric could not have pursued his aggressive policy towards the Empire in the 360s without widespread support among those leaders, such as Winguric and Atharid, who also enforced the persecution. Unity could not otherwise have been maintained during these three difficult

---

[114] Cf. e.g. AM 17. 12. 9 ff., 21 ff.; 18. 2. 15 ff.; 30. 6. 1–2.
[115] Cf. Schmidt, 233; Wolfram, 68.

years.[116] And, as we shall see, even the Goths who entered the Empire in 376 showed little desire to become Roman, maintaining independence over several generations.

The attitude of the Tervingi, or, at least, their leaders thus seems consistent. Despite economic blandishments, they resisted imperial domination. Much of their motivation must remain uncertain, but the sources suggest some lines of thought. After 376 these Goths, or rather their descendants, were not keen to fight for the Empire, Theodosius provoking major revolts when he recruited them for campaigns (see Ch. 5). If it is legitimate to backdate this attitude, then each time that the Goths fought against Persia would have aroused great resentment. It would also seem that the Tervingi simply did not relish incorporation into the Roman state. As we have seen, they had a powerful and ambitious central authority, which resisted the spread of imperial culture in the form of the Christian religion, and probably also controlled a subservient non-Gothic population. Athanaric's oath and his father's orders, both of which forbade him to set foot on Roman soil, seem to confirm that, among the political leadership of the Tervingi, there was a current of hostility towards Roman power. Defeat had forced them to accept Constantine's treaty for a time, but in the 360s they were ready to reassert independence. We are already dealing with a nascent Gothic state, rather than a temporary and amorphous confederation, whose one aim in life was to extract large subsidies from the Roman Empire.

---

[116] *Contra* Thompson, *Visigoths*, esp. 49 ff., 98 ff. followed (with variations) by Wolfram, 70; id., 'Athanaric', 261 ff.; Demougeot, ii. 332 ff. They have misplaced the quarrel between Athanaric and Fritigern (p. 137).

4

THE DANUBE CROSSING
AND GOTHIC WAR

In c.375 the Gothic kingdoms we have just surveyed collapsed in upon themselves. After the deaths of Kings Ermenaric and Vithimer, the Greuthungi moved west under Alatheus and Saphrax, regents for Vithimer's son Vitheric. The Tervingi then came under so much pressure that political unity collapsed. Athanaric attempted to resist the Huns, but was abandoned by the majority of his people, who preferred, under Alavivus and Fritigern, to seek asylum in the Roman Empire (AM 31. 3). Early in 376, the larger part of the Tervingi, followed closely by the Greuthungi, approached the Danube and requested permission to cross. Local commanders referred the matter to the Emperor Valens in Antioch, and Gothic embassies went to Syria. Eventually an answer came back; the Tervingi were to be admitted, but the Greuthungi excluded (31. 4): the Tervingi being ferried across the Danube, probably early in summer 376. On 9 August 378, however, these Goths fought and killed Valens on a plain outside the city of Hadrianople. Why had peaceful co-operation degenerated into violence?

A.   *Terms of Agreement*

Orosius tells us that no formal treaty was signed in 376 (7. 33. 10), but the Tervingi did enter the Empire on mutually agreed terms, Roman forces helping them to do so (AM 31. 4. 5 ff.); the lack of diplomatic formalities may simply reflect Valens' absence in Antioch. Some of what had been agreed is known: the Romans were to supply the Goths' immediate needs from imperial stores, and land was subsequently to be allotted them in Thrace (31. 4. 8). In return, they gave guarantees of peace and promised to do military service if required (31. 4. 1). Such a summary hides the administrative nightmare of finding suitable farmland for the many Tervingi. The sources also fail to make clear on what basis this land was granted.

The Empire resettled immigrants in ways more or less favourable to the group concerned. Peoples defeated *en masse* were not treated the same as allies, and with regard to land, there seems to have been a basic economic distinction. More favoured groups received land in freehold, while the less fortunate were, at best, settled as tenant farmers (*coloni*) on private or public estates.[1] All had to pay taxes, but a tenant farmer also owed rent, and by 376 was already acquiring a semi-servile status, as the Empire sought to tie producers to their lands.[2] As the examples of the Franks and Sciri show (late third and early fifth centuries respectively), less favoured immigrants were also usually disarmed, and settled in small groups over a wide area, to neutralize any military threat, and eventually destroy all sense of group identity. As *coloni*, they remained (at least to *c*.400) subject to the draft, but did not serve in units of their own kinsmen.[3] Of the more favoured, some individuals rose to positions of distinction, but these were often displaced chieftains.[4] More relevant to the present enquiry are larger groups, especially those known as *laeti*. The first *laeti* of *c*.300 seem to have been prisoners taken by Germanic tribes who then returned to the Empire, but by *c*.350 true barbarians were also being settled with this title.[5] As such, they had to do military service, but the 'laetic lands' (*terrae laeticae*) were freehold.[6] And while kept under supervision (the *laeti* of the *Notitia Dignitatum* are all commanded by presumably Roman Prefects), they served to some extent according to tribal origins. Occasionally treated as individual recruits for different regiments (AM 20. 8. 13), they did also form their own unit in the army of Constantius (21. 13. 16),

---

[1] They were also sometimes sold as slaves; Orosius 7. 37. 6; Sozomen, *HE* 9. 5.

[2] The generally accepted account is Jones, 795 ff.; cf. de Ste. Croix, *Class Struggle*, 226 ff. (esp. 247 ff.). Goffart, *Caput and Colonate*, proposes an alternative, but still sees a tied colonate emerging by *c*.370 (77 ff.).

[3] See *Pan. Lat.* 4(8). 9. 1–4 dealing with Franks; Sozomen, *HE* 9. 5 with *CTh* 5. 6. 3 on the Sciri. On the recruitment of *coloni*, Jones, 614.

[4] Thus Alamannic refugees include Fraomarius, Bitheridus, and Hortarius (AM 29. 4. 7), and Vadomarius (*PLRE* i. 928). Gothic refugees include Munderich (AM 31. 3. 5), Modares (*PLRE* i. 605), and Fravittas (*PLRE* i. 372).

[5] Jones, esp. 620; Demougeot, 'A propos des lètes', 101–13. The earliest reference to *laeti barbari* is AM 16. 11. 4 (357).

[6] De Ste. Croix, *Class Struggle*, 247–8; cf. *CTh* 13. 11. 10 (399).

and by *c*.400, the *Notitia* catalogues them by race (Sarmatians, Taifali, Franks, and others: Occ. 42. 33–70). To be settled on freehold land and serve alongside one's tribesmen was much preferable to the fate of the barbarian *colonus*, separated from friends and relatives under a harsh economic regime. On what terms, then, did Valens grant lands to the Tervingi in 376?

The sources are unanimous in describing the Goths as fugitives seeking the protection of Rome. Ammianus reports that the Goths 'humbly begged to be admitted to [Valens'] dominions' (31. 4. 1), and Eunapius' account is similar (fr. 42). This language directs us to think in terms of *deditio*, as Ammianus confirms by having the Goths describe themselves as a people 'submissive (*obnoxiam*) and well-disposed towards [Roman] power' (31. 5. 5). It is now commonly held that this implies that the Tervingi agreed to become Roman *coloni*, with all that this entailed, and, in particular, that their independent existence was to end. The most important piece of evidence for this interpretation comes from Eunapius (fr. 42; cf. Zosimus 4. 20. 6), who reports that Valens ordered the Goths to be admitted only if they laid down their arms, a report echoed in other sources.[7] Disarmament was a feature of the treatment of Frankish and Sciri *coloni*, so that, if Eunapius can be believed, he would confirm that the Tervingi were so frightened of the Huns in 376 that they agreed to subject themselves entirely to the Emperor's will, accepting the status of *coloni* with all its drawbacks.[8] Unfortunately, Eunapius' report is not trustworthy.

It is hard *a priori* to believe that the Goths agreed to disarm. They were moving into the lands of the powerful Roman Empire with whom they had a long history of conflict. However much they feared the Huns, it is unlikely that they would have agreed to leave themselves defenceless. This is confirmed in three ways by Ammianus, a more reliable source than Eunapius. First, he

[7] Jerome, *Chronicle*, s.a. 377 and Orosius 7. 33. 10 report that the Goths did not disarm, but suppose that they should have done; cf. Thompson, *Early Germans*, 119 n. 1. Failure to disarm the Goths has been seen as the cause of their victory at Hadrianople by e.g. Thompson, op. cit. 119; Burns, 'Battle of Adrianople', 336; Demougeot, ii. 138–9; Chrysos, 129–30.

[8] This is the current consensus: Stallknecht, *Untersuchungen*, 24 ff., 65–6; Cesa, 'Romani e barbari', 66 ff.; Demougeot, ii. 138 ff.; Wolfram, 117 ff. Chrysos, 124 ff. sees the agreement as a renewal of Constantine's *foedus*.

mentions no Gothic agreement to disarm. Second, while referring with outrage to the frontier being opened to 'columns of armed barbarians' (31. 4. 9), he makes no suggestion that their arms were concealed and should have been confiscated. His anger is rather directed against Valens for admitting them in this state, implying that this was imperial policy. Finally, Ammianus places the economic exploitation of the Goths in a quite different context, which incidentally undermines Eunapius' account of a supposed disarmament. Eunapius (and Zosimus) report that the Imperial officials were too busy exploiting the Goths' distress to disarm them properly. In Ammianus, Roman corruption is important only after the crossing. Food-shortages occur once the Tervingi are on Roman soil, and, when exploited by certain officers, provoke the ill-feeling which causes the revolt (31. 4. 11). As usual, Ammianus must be preferred to Eunapius; Roman corruption did not enable the Goths to retain their weapons, but prompted the later revolt.[9] Eunapius' account of a botched disarming thus seems mistaken; he was perhaps confused by the fact that a symbolic surrender of arms was an important element in the ceremonial act of *deditio*.[10]

More fundamentally, the whole view that *deditio* necessarily implies acceptance of life as *coloni* is much too simplistic. As we have seen, formal submissions were often the precursor of specific agreements which either left the established social order of a tribe in place, or notionally restored it. Understood in this way, *deditio* underlay much of the Late Empire's dealings with tribal groups on Rhine and Danube, and did not mean that indigenous tribal structures were destroyed (p. 112). The treatment of the Franks and Sciri is in fact an inappropriate model for understanding the institution of *deditio*. Neither of these groups surrendered voluntarily, as the Tervingi did in 376, but were taken prisoner in the course of military campaigns. The ancient world made a strong distinction between this situation and one where a negotiated capitulation preceded conflict. In the latter case, applicable to the

---

[9] Cf. Paschoud, ii. 2. 376 n. 143. Eunapius may have used failure to disarm the Goths to explain the Roman defeat at Hadrianople.

[10] Thus in 358, the prince of the Sarmatians threw down his arms and fell on his face before Constantius; when he was pardoned, his people in turn threw down their shields and spears: AM 17. 12. 8 ff.

Tervingi, terms were arranged which were binding on both parties, while in the former the victors could do exactly what they wished with any prisoners.[11] The act of *deditio* is by itself insufficient to indicate the nature of the 376 agreement, and we must look again more carefully at the sources to reconstruct its terms.[12]

The Tervingi seem to have exercised considerable influence over the location of their new homes. While still north of the Danube, they decided that Thrace would make a good refuge because it was fertile, and separated from the Huns by the Danube (AM 31. 3. 8). And it was in Thrace that Valens eventually agreed to cede them land (31. 4. 5, 8). We do hear elsewhere of barbarian volunteers who served in the imperial army only on condition that they did not campaign too far from their homes (20. 4. 4; cf. 20. 8. 8), but barbarians—whether as unwilling captives or volunteer *dediticii* (e.g. the Limigantes, AM 19. 11. 6)—were customarily settled wherever the emperor chose. The degree of choice exercised by the Tervingi is striking.[13]

The Tervingi also, it seems, handed over hostages to guarantee good behaviour. This characterizes bilateral agreements where the

---

[11] In siege-warfare, for instance, defenders were often offered the chance to negotiate a surrender, giving them a higher status than captives: AM 16. 7. 10; 19. 1. 6; 20. 7. 3; 20. 11. 11; 21. 12. 4; 24. 1. 8; 24. 2. 1; 24. 4. 11. The distinction had a long history: Eckstein, *Senate and General*, 180 ff.

[12] Those accepting the reigning consensus (n. 8) refer to the Limigantes, who in 359 offered to become 'tributaries' (AM 19. 11. 6 ff.), but a *tributarius* is not the same as a *colonus*. The *colonus* paid both rent and tax, but even freeholders paid tax, and 'tribute' (*tributum*) is the standard term for tax in the 4th c. The Limigantes may simply have committed themselves to paying taxes. The Theodosian Code seems to use *colonus* and *tributarius* as synonyms twice (10. 12. 2; 11. 7. 2), but most of the time (nine occasions) *tributarius* simply means 'taxpayer': 3. 5. 8; 5. 11. 9; 7. 4. 32; 11. 22. 5; 11. 36. 19; 12. 6. 21; 13. 5. 32; 13. 10. 8; 13. 11. 4). Ammianus similarly uses *tributum* for tax (references as in Chiabo), and *tributarius* for taxpaying subjects of the Empire: 14. 8. 15; 17. 10. 10; 20.4. 1; 27. 8. 7. Likewise, agreeing to be resettled wherever Constantius chose is not the same as agreeing to the dissolution of tribal life; when the Franks and Sciri (p. 123) are left to one side, there is no necessary presumption here that Constantius would choose small plots of land in widely separated places.

[13] Cf. Wolfram, 118. Cesa, 'Romani e barbari', 70–1 takes Ammianus' report that Valens gave the Goths 'parts of Thrace' to mean the Tervingi were to split up into small groups of *coloni*. But there were probably too many Tervingi for land to be found for them all in one locality.

Empire was to have subsequent need of means of enforcement, rather than situations where its dominance was complete.[14] There is, however, a problem. Eunapius reports that the Empire originally took Gothic children, distributing them among the cities of the east. Having grown up extremely quickly, these children were slaughtered after Hadrianople because they were planning to rebel. It is impossible that they should have grown up in two years (376–8), and Ammianus indicates that the Goths killed in the east were in fact troops serving in the eastern army (31. 16. 8), so that Eunapius is confused.[15] But the Empire did sometimes take drafts of recruits for the army as hostages.[16] If this happened in 376, it would both explain Eunapius' confusion and add another dimension to their killing; hostages were killed when agreements broke down.[17]

Little is known of the conditions under which the Tervingi agreed to do military service, but our one indication suggests that they were treated quite favourably. Apart from perhaps an initial draft of recruits, any further military service had to be negotiated. Before the Tervingi rebelled, Valens, continuing to contemplate war with the Persians, wished to obtain Gothic auxiliaries. He was unable, however, simply to command their attendance, as he could have done had they been *coloni*, and looked instead to hire them.[18]

Finally, the new leaders who replaced Athanaric seem to have converted to Christianity as a further guarantee that they would abide by the agreement. At first sight, the sources provide a variety of dates for a Gothic conversion in the reign of Valens, but a close comparison of them with Ammianus suggests strongly that Fritigern and other leaders of the Tervingi changed their religion to that of the Emperor as they crossed the Danube in 376. Religion had been an issue in Gotho-Roman relations since the time of Constantine, and the decision to convert at this moment was probably a gesture of good will.[19] Doctrinal niceties may have mattered little to Gothic nobles who had recently persecuted

[14] Eunapius fr. 42; cf. Zosimus 4. 26. 2. Cesa, 'Romani e barbari', 68 makes too clear a distinction between *foedus* and *deditio*; hostages were often a feature of *foedus* after *deditio*, e.g. Anon. Val. 6. 31; AM 17. 12. 11, 13, 16.

[15] Cf. Paschoud, ii. 2, 389 n. 154.

[16] AM 17. 13. 3; 28. 5. 4; 30. 6. 1; 31. 10. 17. See also Jones, 620.

[17] The implication, for instance, of AM 28. 2. 6–9.

[18] AM 30. 2. 6; cf. Wolfram, 118–19.

[19] Heather, 'Gothic Conversion'.

Christians, and it can surely be no accident that they chose the branch of Christianity favoured by Valens.

The agreement of 376 was never put fully into operation because of the rebellion, so that it is hardly surprising that much of it remains elusive. We can, however, draw some conclusions. The Tervingi approached Valens respectfully; having thrown off his hegemony in 369, they needed to conciliate him in 376. Athanaric, instigator of war in the 360s, decided in 376 that there was no point in even asking Valens for sanctuary (AM 31. 4. 13). The Tervingi thus adopted the formal submissiveness that fourth-century emperors regarded as their right. It was probably not part of the agreement, however, for the Tervingi to become *coloni*. They were not captives taken on campaign, and an act of submission merely paid lip-service to imperial might before the real business of negotiation got under way.[20] The choice exercised by the Tervingi over their place of settlement, conditions of military service, hostages, and conversion are all suggestive of a much more equal agreement. This leaves us with essentially two possibilities; either it was agreed that the Tervingi should be resettled on favourable, but still traditional, terms such as those granted to *laeti*, or alternatively, and perhaps less likely, Valens sanctioned a new departure in imperial diplomacy by allowing the creation of a Gothic kingdom on Roman soil.[21] It is a mistake, however, to concentrate too much attention on the diplomatic form of the agreement and its terms. These details are less important than the fact that neither Valens nor the Tervingi were committed to making their new relationship work.

B. *Imperial Policy*

The agreement of 376 not only reversed a policy towards the Tervingi established only seven years before (p. 116), but is also exceptional when compared with other occasions where foreign tribal groups were admitted to the Empire. This is obviously true if Valens agreed to the creation of a semi-independent Gothic

[20] Ammianus disapproves, for instance, of over-confident Quadi and expresses compassion for the Sarmatian prince who could hardly speak for fear (17. 12. 9); cf. Millar, 'Emperors, Frontiers', 6 on Eunapius fr. 18. 6.

[21] Schmidt, 403–4; Chrysos, 124 ff.

kingdom, the less likely of our two possibilities. More fundamentally, the admission of the Tervingi, whatever its form, stands out from established Roman practice, because the Goths had not been subdued, and Valens could not closely control events.

Taking a broad historical perspective, and concentrating on the Balkans, it is clear that barbarians were incorporated into the Empire only with great care, in ways that reduced any threat they might pose to the Roman state. In the first two centuries AD, imperial administrators broke up dangerous tribal confederations among the indigenous peoples of the Balkans, and tribal leaderships, though largely retained, were carefully Romanized to neutralize independent tribal identities.[22] Settlements of outsiders were also made under close supervision. In the first century, Dacians and other *Transdanuviani* were compelled to pay tribute, and never seem to have revolted, suggesting that their tribal loyalties had also been carefully dismantled. The similar fate of the Carpi is representative of later groups. Their military power was smashed in a series of campaigns, and, in small units, they were then settled the length of the Danube. Settlements of Goths made by Claudius and Aurelian were likewise preceded by successful campaigns.[23] In the 330s, Constantine brought many Sarmatian Agaragantes into the Empire, but again they were thoroughly subdued first. Many campaigns had been mounted against them since *c.*300, and the 330s saw a Gothic assault upon them, a civil war, and the intervention of imperial troops north of the Danube. The Sarmatians were then spread across Thrace, Scythia, Macedonia, and Italy.[24] Imperial control was equally pronounced when Constantius contemplated admitting Limigantes in 359. Preceding years had seen a major campaign, asserting imperial hegemony over these tribes (17. 12–13), and as soon as the emperor heard of their request for asylum, he hurried to the scene with enough troops to dominate the situation. When trouble broke out, the unfortunate would-be immigrants were massacred (AM 19. 11).

[22] On this, see Mócsy, *Pannonia and Upper Moesia*, 53 ff.; Alföldy, *Noricum*, 62 ff.; Wilkes, *Dalmatia*, 153 ff.

[23] De Ste. Croix, *Class Struggle*, app. III, 509 ff. with refs. is an invaluable list of barbarian settlements, recording ten affecting the Danube region: nos. 3, 5A, 5B, 8, 10–15. Carpi were resettled as far apart as Scythia Minor and Pannonia (AM 27. 5. 5; 28. 1. 5).

[24] Anon. Val. 6. 31–2; AM 17. 13. 1; 12. 18 ff., cf. Barnes, 'Imperial Campaigns', 174 ff., id.; 'Victories of Constantine', 149 ff.

Compared with these examples, the Tervingi were quite unsubdued in 376. Fear of the Huns obviously affected their attitude,
but they had not been brought under close control by imperial
forces.[25] No imperial campaign had prompted their decision to
seek asylum, and Valens was not present with his field-army as
they began to cross the Danube; he was detained in the east, where
the pick of his troops continued to be deployed against Persia.
Events on this front had halted Valens' first Gothic war, and by
the mid-370s head-on conflict seemed inevitable when Valens
issued an ultimatum that Sapor should either remove his troops
from Iberia or be forced to.[26]

The sources suggest that the resulting lack of close control over
the Goths did not matter, because Valens positively welcomed
them for two reasons. First, they would provide him with many
recruits, who, with his existing forces, would create an irresistible
army. Second, the Goths would be such a ready source of
manpower that recruitment levies, taken annually from the countryside, could be commuted into gold to fill the Treasury.[27] These
reasons have often been taken at face value, but should be doubted
a priori. While the Empire had always been willing to receive
immigrants on its own terms, an uncontrolled Gothic immigration
is unlikely to have been welcome. A fourth-century example
demonstrates any emperor's likely attitude. In the course of
Magnentius' revolt, Salian Franks occupied Roman land and then
suggested to Julian that 'since they were peaceful, as if in their own
territories, no one should attack or molest them'. Julian immediately attacked them, refusing to sanction a situation that had not
come about under close Roman supervision (AM 17. 8. 3–4).

We can deduce, in fact, that Valens' reacted less positively to the
Goths than the sources would have us believe. First, he attempted
to limit the number of Goths admitted to the Empire. While the
Tervingi were allowed to cross, the Greuthungi were not, and
many imperial troops were positioned on the Danube to enforce
their exclusion (AM 31. 4. 12–13; 31. 5. 2–3). Ammianus does not
tell us why the Tervingi were preferred to the Greuthungi, but it
was probably because, as we have seen, the former had a history of

---

[25] *Contra* Stallknecht, *Untersuchungen*, 65–6; Cesa, 'Romani e barbari', 68 ff.
[26] AM 26. 4. 6; 27. 12; 29. 1; 30. 2. See also p. 119.
[27] AM 31. 4. 4; Eunapius fr. 42; Socrates, *HE* 4. 34; Sozomen, *HE* 6. 37; cf.
Cesa, 'Romani e barbari', 64–6 on the sources' unanimity.

closer relations with the Roman state and were the better-known quantity. Whatever the case, Valens clearly gave only a guarded welcome to Gothic refugees, accepting only one out of the two groups. Secondly, when dissent began to appear among the Tervingi, and the local commander wanted to move them to Marcianople, he had to transfer to this area the forces who had been watching the Greuthungi. He was then able to impose his will on the Tervingi, but had left the way clear for the Greuthungi, who duly crossed the river (31. 5. 1–3). The sequence of events is instructive. The Roman commander had sufficient troops to dictate only to one of the two Gothic groups. When he deployed his forces to exclude the Greuthungi, he was powerless to constrain the Tervingi; when he shifted his forces to move on the Tervingi, the Greuthungi were able to cross the river. Imperial policy in 376—admitting the Tervingi and excluding the Greuthungi—thus matches the general military situation in the Balkans. There seem to have been enough troops available to exclude only one of the Gothic groups.[28]

It is hard to believe that this correspondence is accidental, even though it raises the difficult question of how accurately imperial policy could have been formulated in such chaotic circumstances. The sources record that the local commanders referred the whole matter to Valens, and no doubt included what intelligence they had on Gothic numbers. This information must have been imprecise, but Valens would have been aware—as their subsequent embassies confirmed—that there were two discrete Gothic groups to be dealt with.[29] He would have had some idea of the forces immediately available to him from military listings and the pay-returns required of unit commanders,[30] and he was also aware that few reinforcements could be rushed to the area, because of the situation in the east. Valens and his advisers may well have had sufficient information, therefore, to conclude that, at best, they

[28] It might be argued that the situation after the Tervingi had crossed the river was different, but two large Gothic groups at separate points of the Danube would have stretched imperial forces quite as much as did the situation after the crossing.

[29] AM 31. 4. 1, 5; Eunapius fr. 42; Zosimus 4. 20. 6; cf. Austin, 'The Adrianople Campaign', 78–9. AM 31. 4. 6–7 comments on the impossibility of counting even the Goths who crossed legally.

[30] Antoninus deserted to the Persians in 359 with detailed information on military dispositions and numbers: AM 18. 5. 1; cf. Jones, 626–30.

could hope to exclude only one of the two Gothic groups. In accepting the Tervingi while barring the Greuthungi, Valens was probably attempting merely to minimize the number of barbarians penetrating the frontier. Any notion that Valens would have been moved by pity rather than power politics can be safely left aside. As we have seen, only closely controlled immigration was acceptable to the Roman state. The new relationship with the Tervingi was forced upon Valens, and there is no reason to suppose he wanted it.

This is confirmed by two indications that Valens was already planning to regain control in the Balkans. Plans, first of all, were put into operation to control food-supplies. By summer 377 these had been moved into secure fortifications beyond the reach of the Goths (AM 31. 8. 1). Moving bulky foodstuffs required a major administrative effort, which, to be successful by summer 377, is likely to have been under way since the previous year. Lacking land, the Goths had to rely on their own reserves and on what they could extract from the Romans, so that control of food-supplies would, in the long term, allow the Empire to starve the Tervingi into submission. This might even explain the food-shortages that generated the first unrest among the Tervingi and prompted their revolt. Ammianus blames these shortages on the greed of local Roman commanders, who withheld supplies to run a profitable black market (31. 4. 11; 31. 5. 1–2). There surely was corruption, but the original shortages, which the officers duly exploited, may have been caused by the fact that a higher priority was being given to transferring foodstuffs to secure places. The Romans' primary aim may have been long-term control of the Goths rather than feeding them.

The senior military commander in the area, Lupicinus— perhaps *comes rei militaris* in Thrace[31]—also seems to have had orders to strike at the leaders of the Tervingi. Lupicinus invited Alavivus and Fritigern to dinner in Marcianople, once their people had finally moved there from the Danube. Lupicinus seems always to have had in mind some mischief, for he posted troops to keep the Gothic rank and file at a distance, and Ammianus gives no indication that the Goths were mistaken in perceiving this as an attempted kidnap (31. 5. 5). Lupicinus partly lost his nerve after killing some of the leaders' attendants, and rather than provoke

[31] AM 31. 4. 9 with *PLRE* i. 520.

open conflict at that particular moment, released Fritigern. Alavivus, however, is never mentioned again, and was presumably held when Fritigern was released. It was contemporary imperial practice to remove leaders around whom dangerous confederations were coalescing, before any conflict could occur, and we know of several important tribal leaders hijacked while enjoying Roman banquets.[32] Lupicinus was just possibly acting on his own initiative—Ammianus reports one example of an unauthorized attack (29. 6. 5)—but several others were ordered by the central authorities, and it is very unlikely that Lupicinus would have kidnapped leaders he knew to be the joyfully received allies of his emperor.

The attack on the leaders of the Tervingi and control of food-supplies seem to confirm the deduction from the military situation; the Tervingi were accepted because Valens had no choice. The sources' unanimous reports that Valens saw the Tervingi as beneficial to the Empire would seem to record not Valens' real motives, but justifications given out to allay fears naturally aroused by this sudden influx of Goths. Such justifications were a constant feature of life at the imperial court, and were recognized as such by at least some contemporaries. Cassius Dio, senator and *assessor* of the emperor Severus, referring specifically to foreign affairs, provides a succinct account of the imperial propaganda machine,

After [the establishment of the Empire], most things that happened began to be kept secret . . . and even though some things are made public, they are distrusted because they cannot be verified; it is suspected that everything is said and done with reference to the wishes of the men in power at the time and their associates.[33]

In 376 the emperor would not have wished, and perhaps could not afford, to admit that mere barbarians had forced him to act against his will, especially when the act held obvious dangers for the Empire. Hence Valens' propaganda had to make virtue of necessity. Similar justifications had been put forward in 359, when it was decided to accept Limigantes into the Empire.[34] Referring to the

---

[32] AM 21. 4. 1–5; 27. 10. 3; 29. 4. 2 ff.; 29. 6. 5; 30. 1. 18–21; cf. Austin, 'The Adrianople Campaign', 78–9. In the first case, abduction was ordered in a letter to be opened only if the leader was found on Roman territory; similarly contingent instructions might explain Lupicinus' change of mind.

[33] Dio, *Roman History*, 53. 19. 3; cf. Augustine, *Confessions* 6. 6. 9; Millar, 'Emperors, Frontiers', 2.

[34] AM 19. 11. 7; cf. Cesa, 'Romani e barbari', 69; Wolfram, 118.

benefits of numerous recruits and the commutation of recruitment
levies into gold may well have been a topos of imperial propaganda, brought out whenever barbarian immigrants appeared.

The propaganda effort would have been carried on at many
levels, but one of its components was perhaps a now lost political
oration of Themistius. In a markedly veiled reference, Ammianus
records that justifications for the Goths' admission were put
forward by 'learned flatterers' (*eruditis adulatoribus*, 31. 4. 4), who
remain anonymous. Apart from the plural, which is no objection
since Ammianus is being deliberately less than explicit, this phrase
exactly describes Themistius. He was both an academic of distinction—his orations stress that his words are the contribution of
philosophy to the running of state affairs—and the propagandist of
successive emperors from Constantine to Theodosius.[35] Before
and after 376, Themistius justified other major changes in imperial
policy towards the Goths. In 370 he explained why it was better
for Valens to have turned from his original purpose of utterly
defeating the Goths, and in a sequence of orations between 379
and 383 later highlighted the wisdom of the emperor Theodosius'
conciliatory approach to the Gothic problem (see Ch. 5). There
was thus none better to justify a 'soft' line towards the Tervingi in
376 than the man who declared both in 370 and 383 that different
emperors were morally right not to crush them.[36] The reason why
such an oration has not survived may well have been embarrass-
ment. By 356 Themistius was already publishing his orations, and
giving copies to the library of Constantinople (*Or.* 4. 72); later
speeches would also have been collected by himself or admirers.[37]
To be remembered as the man who said it was a good thing to
admit Goths in 376—an event closely followed by the battle of
Hadrianople—would not have been attractive.

The more general point at least seems secure. In recording
Valens' joy, the sources are echoing imperial propaganda, which
was designed to put the best face on events, hiding as much as it
revealed. Valens had no choice but to admit the Tervingi, and our

[35] Dagron, 'Thémistios', 1 ff.

[36] In 370 *Or.* 10 p. 199. 9 ff.; in 382, *Orr.* 16. p. 296. 10 ff., 34. p. 226. 7 ff.
Sabbah, *La Méthode d'Ammien Marcellin*, 348 ff. found no specific examples of
contact between Ammianus and Themistius, but thought that the historian often
reacted to the official views for which Themistius was a mouthpiece.

[37] Dagron, 'Thémistios', 17.

sources are recording justifications designed to convince a perhaps sceptical public that the emperor was still in control. How many contemporaries were convinced is hard to say: not those, at least, with the insight of a Dio. But if Valens was less than thrilled at the arrival of the Tervingi, what was the reaction of the Goths to the prospect of coexisting with imperial power?

C. *The Goths*

As the Tervingi and Greuthungi described in their petitions to Valens, they came to the Danube because the Huns had destroyed their hold on lands north of the Danube. In the words of Eunapius (fr. 42, 58. 1 ff.), 'The Scythians [= Goths] had been defeated and destroyed by the Huns and were being utterly extirpated. Those who were captured were massacred with their wives and children. There was no limit to the savagery employed in the killings.' Their old lives were collapsing around them, and the Goths wanted new lands where they would be safe (AM 31. 3. 8).[38] This much is well understood, but more can be reconstructed of the Goths' state of mind in 376.

The magnitude of the revolution taking place north of the Danube can hardly be underestimated, but its nature must be understood. The sources' rhetorical descriptions have led to visions of panic-stricken Goths fleeing before a solid mass of Huns, who had suddenly swept all before them.[39] This seems mistaken. There is no space here to investigate the Huns in detail, but some important points must be picked out. The Tervingi were able to wait beside the Danube while an embassy travelled to Antioch, and Valens' decision was made and communicated to them (AM 31. 4. 1). Involving a round trip of over 1,000 km., this process must have taken more than a month. In the longer term, Gothic and not Hunnic groups remained the major threat to the lower Danube for at least the next decade. An independent Gothic

---

[38] Cf. Zosimus 4. 20. 3 ff., 26. 1; Ambrose, *Expositio Evangelii secundum Lucam* 10. 10 (CSEL 34. 4. 458); Synesius, *De Regno*, 21. 50.

[39] e.g. Maenchen–Helfen, 26–7; Schmidt, 400 ff.; Wolfram, 71–2; Demougeot, ii. 138–9, 383 ff.

kingdom under Arimer existed north of the Danube after 383,[40] and it was primarily a Gothic group which attempted to cross the river under Odotheus in 386 (Zosimus 4. 35. 1; 4. 37–9). The first large body of Huns found in the area are those of Uldin, who appear only in *c*.400, a quarter of a century after the Tervingi crossed the Danube.[41]

The decision of some Goths to seek sanctuary south of the river in 376 does not mean, therefore, that a solid mass of Huns had advanced to the Danube. Rather, incessant smaller-scale warfare over a lengthy period had provoked the first major convulsion in what was to be an extended crisis. There had been a considerable time-lag between the first attacks on Ermenaric and the retreat of the Greuthungi; Ermenaric resisted 'for a long time' (*diu*), and Vithimer, his successor, died only after 'many . . . defeats' (AM 31. 3. 2–3). In 376 some Goths decided to leave their homes in the Ukraine and Moldavia, but many remained: some attempting to enter the Empire at a later date, others eventually absorbed by the Huns. The imperial authorities faced not a panic-stricken rabble, as the sources' rhetoric might suggest, but two organized Gothic groups who had made a careful decision to move into imperial territory.

Ammianus describes the circumstances of the retreat of the Greuthungi only briefly. Vithimer was killed in battle leaving his son Vitheric, a minor, to succeed. Control passed to Alatheus and Saphrax, who moved the group westward (31. 3. 1–3). The full ramifications of the crisis are unclear, but the decision to move may have split the Greuthungi, as it did the Tervingi (p. 14). Ammianus also distinguishes a third leader of the Greuthungi on the Danube in 376, Farnobius (31. 4. 12), who, after allying with some Taifali, met a separate fate from the rest of the Greuthungi (31. 9. 3 ff.). Farnobius may have refused to recognize Alatheus and Saphrax, but, as we shall see, subgroups did operate separately for periods under their own leaders, so that Farnobius' independence may have been partial.[42] Either way, the Greuthungi who arrived at the Danube in 376 acted largely as a single unit.

---

[40] Arimer is mentioned in Achelis, 'Der älteste deutsche Kalender', 300 ff.; cf. Wolfram, 135.

[41] See Maenchen-Helfen, 59 ff.

[42] Cf. Austin, 'The Adrianople Campaign', 88.

More is known of how the Hunnic crisis affected the Tervingi. After some defeats, the majority (*populi pars maior*) rejected the policy of resistance championed by Athanaric (AM 31. 3. 4 ff.). It is a clear sign of the severity of the situation that, just a few years after his successful defiance of Valens, most of his followers rejected the measures he proposed to deal with the Huns. The hold of a family which seems to have controlled the Tervingi for at least three generations was thus destroyed by the Huns.[43] Rivalries among the ambitious nobles who wished to take Athanaric's place took some time to work out. To begin with, the Tervingi were led jointly by Alavivus and Fritigern: perhaps a compromise to appease rival factions. They brought the Tervingi across the Danube, and both were invited to Lupicinus' banquet (AM 31. 5. 5). As we have seen, Alavivus is never mentioned again, and Ammianus seems to imply that Fritigern was happy to leave him in Lupicinus' hands. Fearing to be held hostage 'with the rest' (*cum ceteris*), Fritigern told Lupicinus that he could prevent bloodshed if he were released (31. 5. 7). Ammianus stresses that Fritigern was quick-witted, and it seems that he did a deal with Lupicinus which left Alavivus in Roman hands. There is likely to have been little love lost between the rival Gothic leaders, and it was perhaps useful for Fritigern to be able to blame Lupicinus for Alavivus' disappearance, avoiding any prospect of a feud.

Small groups may well have drifted away from the main groups in this political reordering, but the leadership rivalries let loose by Athanaric's deposition did not destroy the cohesion of the Tervingi who had deserted him. Most gathered behind leaders who saw a new relationship with the Roman Empire as the solution to their problems. They then advanced to the Danube and conducted negotiations as a unit with the imperial authorities, Ammianus' words underlining the orderliness of their decision-making (31. 3. 8):

The majority of the people . . . were looking for a home beyond all reach of the barbarians [= Huns], and after long deliberation (*diuque deliberans*) about what place to choose, decided that Thrace offered them a

---

[43] Some Tervingi followed Athanaric to 'Caucalanda', described as a place of 'high mountains and deep forests' which suggests the Carpathians: AM 31. 4. 13.

convenient refuge for two reasons, both because it has very fertile soil, and because it is separated by the mighty waters of the Danube from [the Huns].

We are not dealing with a panic-stricken rabble.

None the less, their position was precarious. Compared with the Goths and other tribal peoples, the Roman Empire of *c*.375 was massively powerful. Significant portions of Ammianus' narrative, for instance, describe a series of imperial victories over such tribal neighbours. The Goths' chosen refuge thus posed nearly as much of a threat to their security as did the Huns. It is inconceivable that the leaders of the Tervingi were unaware of this. They had been unable openly to resist the imperial field-army between 367 and 369; they were first-hand witnesses of its powerful fortifications along the Lower Danube; and many Goths had served with Roman armies after the treaty with Constantine. It is thus hardly surprising that, while determined to escape the Huns, the Tervingi also took precautions against the Empire.

Above all, they acted in close co-operation with the Greuthungi. The two may have worked together previously, since Greuthungi seem to have become involved in Athanaric's war against Valens (AM 27. 5. 6), and Athanaric perhaps tried to support the Greuthungi against the Huns (31. 3. 4). In 376, this relationship was carefully maintained. Ammianus reports, for instance, that after the Tervingi had decided to seek refuge in Thrace, 'the remainder, too, had this same thought as if in a common mind' (*hoc quoque idem residui velut mente cogitavere communi*). This seems to imply that the Greuthungi in some way adopted the idea from the Tervingi, but it is unclear whether we should view this as joint planning. Once both groups had adopted the same plan, their leadership kept in close touch, even when one was admitted to the Empire and the other not. Fritigern knew, for instance, that the departure of the Tervingi for Marcianople had allowed the Greuthungi to cross the Danube. He therefore advanced the Tervingi only slowly to give the Greuthungi time to catch up (31. 5. 3–4). Despite an agreement which ostensibly favoured his followers over the Greuthungi, Fritigern was thus clearly envisaging a united Gothic front against the Romans. The motivation here seems clear enough; the Empire's superior resources made it advisable for the Goths to work together. At its simplest, this perhaps doubled the number of Gothic troops available.[44] The Goths gave hostages and made some concessions to reinforce good will, but the circumstances of their asylum were unusual, and they probably suspected that Valens had had little choice but to admit them. Co-operating with the Greuthungi was a sensible attempt to ensure that the balance of power in the Balkans did not swing back too markedly towards the Empire.

According to Eunapius, the Goths' leaders also swore a great oath before crossing the Danube,[45]

that, even if they were to receive the greatest kindnesses from the Romans, they would plot against them in every way and use every treacherous device to harm [them], in order that they might gain possession of all their territory.

This presents a number of problems. It is unclear to which Goths Eunapius is referring, since he makes no distinction between Tervingi and Greuthungi, and he is so hostile to barbarians that he may have invented or altered the oath to stress Gothic perfidy. A complete fabrication is perhaps unlikely, however, and oath-swearing does seem to have been an important means of rallying Gothic rank and file support behind particular policies. It was used during Athanaric's persecution of Christians (*St Saba* 3, p. 218. 4 ff.), Athanaric swore a great oath (or at least, said that he had) not to set foot on Roman soil (AM 27. 5. 9), and Priscus records that later hostility of Goths to the Huns was encapsulated in an oath (fr. 49).[46] It would not be surprising for the same

---

[44] Valens was deceived into advancing because he received intelligence putting the number of Gothic warriors in his vicinity at 10,000 (31. 12. 3). These were led by Fritigern (31. 12. 8), and probably represented most of his command, since he had previously ordered them to concentrate (31. 11. 5). Lacking any other indication, one is left with the impression that Alatheus and Saphrax led a force of similar size; cf. Schmidt, 403; Austin, 'The Adrianople Campaign', 83. Reconstructions based on Eunapius' 200,000 Goths (fr. 42), will be misleading; cf. Paschoud, ii. 2. 376 n. 143.

[45] Fr. 59. 86. 8 ff.; clumsy editing has confused events of 376 with the treaty of 382: Thompson, 'Fritigern to Euric', 107 n. 7.

[46] Later Visigothic and Ostrogothic kings extracted oaths of allegiance from their subjects, and swore to govern well in return: Claude, 'Oath of the Allegiance'. Theoderic the Amal used oaths in relations with the Emperor Zeno: Malchus fr. 18. 2. None of this, of course, makes the case conclusive; cf. (most recently) Liebeschuetz, *Barbarians and Bishops*, 48–9.

mechanism to have been used to rally the Goths as they entered the Empire in 376.

But even if the oath's wording is entirely historical, it cannot be taken at face value. The idea that the Goths might one day conquer the Empire appears occasionally in the sources,[47] but the only moment when total conquest even came close to becoming genuine policy was after the Goths' shock victory at Hadrianople. Before the battle, even the most optimistic Goths were willing to settle for Thrace (p. 175). This should cause no surprise; it is inconceivable that the Goths' leaders can seriously have been planning to conquer the Empire in 376. Yet, as we have seen, they were (correctly) suspicious of Valens, and the oath might fit such a context. Fritigern and his circle may have been worried not only about overt Roman power, but also that the attractions of Roman wealth might in the long term destroy group solidarity. The exhortation to conquest can perhaps be viewed as an attempt to bolster Gothic unity in the face of new dangers, by defining the group ideologically in opposition to the Empire. The oath would have publicly committed all the leading Goths to maintaining Gothic independence against every manifestation of Roman power. This perhaps makes too much of some dubious evidence, but, like Valens, the Tervingi clearly had considerable doubts about their new relationship. It enabled them to escape the Huns, but carried its own risks. Cooperation with the Greuthungi was essential if the Goths were not to be swallowed up by the Empire.

This mutual distrust allows us to reconsider the breakdown in relations between Valens and the Goths. As reported by Ammianus, it had a simple cause. Roman officers first withheld food supplies to make money out of the hungry Tervingi. When they were moved on to Marcianople, all available troops were mobilized to supervise the operation. This increased tension, because these troops had previously kept watch on the Greuthungi, who now also crossed the Danube; a second Gothic group had moved illegally into the Balkans. Tension flared into violence after Lupicinus' ill-fated banquet. Although Fritigern was released, hostilities had already begun, and, shortly afterwards, the Tervingi routed Lupicinus' forces (31. 4. 11; 31. 5. 1 ff.).

---

[47] Eunapius fr. 59. 86. 8 ff.; Claudian, *De bello Getico*, 78 ff., 518 ff., *VI cons. Hon.* 295 ff.; Orosius 7. 43. 3 ff.

Implicitly in the narrative, and explicitly in a section devoted to that purpose, Ammianus blames corrupt Roman officials—Lupicinus and Maximus—for the eruption of violence (31. 4. 9–10). This has rightly been considered a fairer account than that of Eunapius, for whom the war was caused by faithless barbarians, who refused to keep promises (fr. 42; cf. Zosimus 4. 20. 7). But both explanations probably over-personalize the action. Ammianus concentrates on the actions of Roman commanders, and fails to highlight the role of the central imperial authorities. The Empire received the Goths only under duress which can be deduced from, but is not explicit in, his narrative. This, rather than individual greed, perhaps explains the shortage of food, and Lupicinus' attack on the leadership of the Tervingi was probably not a personal whim. It may have involved something less than a direct order, but is highly unlikely to have contradicted the will of the central authorities. Similarly, the barbarians were not faithless by nature as Eunapius and Zosimus suggest, but they did look after their own interests in preference to following the agreement. By co-operating with the Greuthungi, the Tervingi acted against the conditions of their admission.

Part of the explanation for this is the genre of classicizing history itself, which concentrates on the great deeds or failings of significant individuals. It was written to provide moral lessons, and concentration on individuals made for high drama and a strong moralizing tone.[48] Eunapius, obviously enough, is pointing out the futility of trying to make agreements with barbarians. This is also applicable to Ammianus' account of the Roman officers, but here the concentration on two individuals may have an individual significance. Ammianus wrote of the Hadrianople campaign in tremendous detail, and clearly had access to official sources.[49] The Roman defeat is very likely to have spawned an enquiry into what went wrong,[50] and Ammianus may be echoing an official pronouncement on the individuals' guilt. Any enquiry would have been conducted after the war, or as peace was being negotiated, by

[48] Cf. Blockley, i. 90 ff.; Crump, *Ammianus Marcellinus*, 31 ff.; Austin, 'The Adrianople Campaign', 77–8.

[49] Sabbah, *La Méthode d'Ammien Marcellin*, 115 ff. and pt. III.

[50] These were a feature of Late Roman government: e.g. AM 27. 5. 1 (why did the Goths support Procopius); 28. 6. 28 (misgovernment in Africa); 30. 5. 2 (into incursions on the Middle Danube).

which time there was every reason to blame certain individuals rather than imperial policy as a whole. The government was by then seeking to maintain (or negotiate) a peace with the Goths which depended heavily on mutual trust (cf. p. 177). In such circumstances, it would have been very embarrassing to have it known that war was not a mistake, but the natural consequence of Valens' plans to subdue the Goths.[51]

The breakdown in relations was really caused by a lack of commitment on both sides; the agreement of 376 lacked stability because neither Goths nor Romans really accepted its conditions. The personalized judgements of Ammianus and Eunapius combine to make the point. Ill will on the part of the imperial authorities had its counterpart in 'barbarian faithlessness'. The judgements are the expression in language and concepts suitable to classicizing history of something more fundamental. Both sides were determined to revise the agreement in their own favour.

D. *From Marcianople to Hadrianople*

The rebellion of the Tervingi began, perhaps, in early 377, since Valens could still contemplate hiring Gothic auxiliaries in winter 376/7 (AM 30. 2. 6). The defeat of Lupicinus brought damage to areas immediately around Marcianople (AM 31. 5. 7–9), but the Tervingi quickly widened the scope of their operations. Fritigern next appears some 250 km. to the south at Hadrianople, adding to his command the Goths of Sueridas and Colias, a unit of the Roman army who were in winter quarters there (AM 31. 6. 1). They seem to have had no previous contact with Fritigern, but joined the revolt because of the hostility of the citizens on whom they had been quartered (AM 31. 6. 1–3). After a costly attempt to capture the city, Fritigern persuaded the Goths to attack softer targets instead, 'reminding them that he kept peace with walls'. The Goths then raided throughout Thrace (AM 31. 6. 4 ff.).[52]

In spring and summer 377, the Empire responded. Valens sent Traianus and Profuturus with troops from Armenia, who drove

---

[51] If (cf. Matthews, *Western Aristocracies*, 96) the Maximus mentioned here is the later usurper, he may have rebelled in part to avoid becoming a scapegoat.

[52] Zosimus 4. 22 reports an attack on Constantinople before Hadrianople, but it is probably the same incident placed afterwards by Ammianus (31. 16. 4 ff.); cf. Schmidt, 412 ff. But see also Paschoud, ii. 2. 378–9 n. 145.

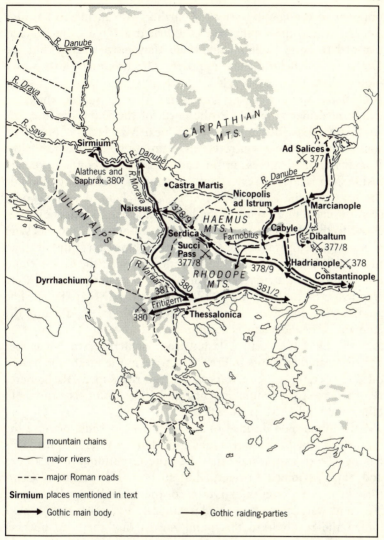

Fig. 4. The Gothic War from *Ad Salices* to the conclusion of peace, 377–82.

the Goths out of the province of Haemimont, confining them to the Haemus Mountains and the Danube Plain (31. 7. 1–3). When western reinforcements arrived under Frigeridus and Richomeres, imperial forces counter-attacked further. Advancing to *oppidum Salices*, where the Goths had established a laager, the Romans planned to harry their enemy when they moved camp, but the Goths stayed behind their rampart. The eventual battle was a bloody draw (AM 31. 7. 3 ff.).

Oppidum Salices is usually indentified with *Ad Salices*, which the Antonine Itinerary places in the north of the Dobrudja (227. 1). Ammianus describes it, however, as 'near Marcianople' (31. 8. 1), some 150 km. to the south. He may simply be mistaken, but the Romans' limited success in the battle forced the Goths to remain inside their laager for seven days, allowing the Romans to blockade the passes of the Haemus (31. 8. 1). This chain of events would seem to make more sense if the battlefield, like Marcianople, was closer to the mountains than *Ad Salices*. Either way, the blockade was designed to starve the Goths into submission. Supplies had previously been taken to fortified centres, which the Goths could not capture (cf. Fritigern's comment), so that the Goths were trapped in a confined area with little food (AM 31. 8. 1). The passes were fortified in late summer (AM 31. 8. 2), and the Romans retreated again as autumn turned to winter (31. 10. 1), so that the blockade perhaps lasted from September to November 377. Repeated attempts to break out were in the meantime beaten off (AM 31. 8. 4), and imperial forces regrouped. Richomeres returned west for reinforcements, and Valens sent Saturninus to take command (AM 31. 8. 2 ff.).

Saturninus soon decided to abandon the blockade, because the Goths had allied with some Huns and Alans (AM 31. 8. 4 ff.). This has been seen as the moment when the Greuthungi of Alatheus and Saphrax joined Fritigern, but such an interpretation seems mistaken. The Greuthungi crossed the Danube as Fritigern's Tervingi were moved on to Marcianople. For them not to have joined the revolt until this point means that they did nothing during the campaigning season of 377 when they were already south of the Danube. Since, as we have seen, Fritigern had advanced the Tervingi only slowly towards Marcianople to allow the Greuthungi to catch up, it is much more likely that they joined the revolt shortly after Lupicinus' defeat. To equate these Huns and Alans with Alatheus and Saphrax also runs into the problem that the Greuthungi were Goths. To circumvent this, it has been argued that Alatheus and Saphrax led a mixed Gothic, Hunnic, and Alan force, and that when Ammianus mentions one or more of these peoples, the others are present, even if unspecified. The argument is based partly on an Iranian etymology for the name Saphrax, from which it is concluded that he must have led an Alanic component within the group, and mostly on Ammianus' mentions of Huns and/or Alans allied to Goths. Both arguments are unconvincing. Such etymologies are never conclusive; there is also a gap between proving Saphrax an Alanic name and showing that he led Alans within the Greuthungi (cf. Jordanes, *Getica* 9. 58 on names being swapped between races). More important, Ammianus never implies that Goths, Huns, and Alans were normally part of the same political unit. Huns fought with the Greuthungi against Alans at 31. 3. 3 because they were paid to, and it was promises of booty which caused Huns and Alans to join the Goths here (31. 8. 4). Likewise, at 31. 12. 17 Ammianus specifies that the Gothic cavalry of Alatheus and Saphrax were at this point combined with some Alans, implying that the Alans were usually separate, and at 31. 16. 3–4 Huns and Alans are again distinguished from Goths.[53] It seems likely, then, that Fritigern ended the blockade by tempting more tribal groups to cross into the Empire.

Concluding that the alliance would undermine the Romans' grip on the Haemus, Saturninus ordered a withdrawal, so that his dispersed troops would not be overwhelmed piecemeal (31. 8. 4 ff.). The Huns and Alans had probably overturned a delicate balance. Whereas the Romans had previously coped, their enemies' increased numbers meant that they were likely to be swept aside.[54] In consequence, the Goths were able to return to the Thracian plain, and recommenced foraging raids, which spread as far as Rhodope; some withdrawing Roman units were also ambushed outside Dibaltum (AM 31. 8. 6–10). Imperial forces could only occupy the Succi Pass to prevent the Goths moving

---

[53] *Contra* Várady, *Das letzte Jahrhundert*, 20–6, 31 ff.; cf. Wolfram, 120–2; Cesa, 'Romani e barbari', 77 ff. (with other refs.). Other brief references to Huns, Goths, and Alans (*Cons. Const.*, s.a. 379 (*CM* i. 243); Pacatus 12(2). 32. 4; Themistius, *Or.* 16, p. 297. 11 ff.) must be taken generally; cf. Nagy, 'Last Century', 313.

[54] For an alternative suggestion, Seeck, *Geschichte*, v. 109; cf. Burns, 'Battle of Adrianople', 340.

into the western Balkans, although, in setting up this barrier, Frigeridus defeated Farnobius' force and killed its leader (AM 31. 9). In the meantime, Gothic camps were established between Nicopolis and Beroe (31. 11. 2).

For 378, Valens and Gratian organized a major effort; both emperors and their field-armies were to be involved. Advancing from the west, Gratian was held up first when the Lentienses raided Raetia (AM 31. 10), and again when he unexpectedly encountered Alans at Castra Martis (31. 11. 6).[55] By early summer, only Valens was ready to attack the Goths, having reached Constantinople by 30 May. As summer progressed, he concentrated his forces, the Goths doing the same under the impetus of losses inflicted on them by Sebastianus. The Gothic camp moved to Cabyle and then on to the Thracian plain (AM 31. 11. 4–5; 31. 12. 1 ff.). Uncertain what to do, Valens advanced to Hadrianople, while the Goths converged from the north. Roman spies reported their advance, estimating their numbers at 10,000, much less than expected; Valens perhaps thought himself opposed by only the Tervingi. On top of his jealousy of Gratian, the chance to attack half the Goths was too attractive to miss, and after much debate, imperial forces advanced from Hadrianople on the morning of 9 August (AM 31. 12. 1–10). Valens was still willing to contemplate peace, and responded positively to offers of a truce, but, as hostages were being arranged, Roman troops started hostilities, at which point at least part of the Greuthungi suddenly arrived (AM 31. 12. 11–17). Valens was forced to fight on bad terms, facing the entire Gothic force alone, with some of his forces still stretched out along the road (AM 31. 12. 12). Things went from bad to worse, and the emperor perished with two-thirds of his army (AM 31. 13. 18).

Roman losses cannot be calculated precisely. Thirty-five tribunes and *rectores* were killed and, on the guess that each commanded 1,000 men, total losses have been put as high as *c.* 30,000. A thousand men per unit, however, is a notional figure, and some

---

[55] Since Várady (refs. as n. 53), these have been seen as the Alans of the supposed mixed confederation. But Alans also fought at Hadrianople (AM 31. 12. 17), to do which they would have had to cover the 400 km. to the battle with amazing speed. The Alans were composed of many separate groups (AM 31. 2. 12 ff.), however, so that these Alans are probably different from those who fought at Hadrianople.

of the officers were *vacantes* (that is, did not command units).[56] Hoffmann has shown that there are sixteen western regiments of *seniores* in the *Notitia Dignitatum* whose corresponding eastern *iuniores* are missing, and convincingly argues that these represent units never reconstituted after Hadrianople (*Bewegungsheer*, 450–8). Fourteen of the sixteen were infantry of the *comitatenses*, who were left unprotected after the Roman cavalry had fled (AM 31. 13. 2 ff.), so that this makes good sense. His argument that Valens led 30,000–40,000 men, implying losses of 20,000–26,000 (*Bewegungsheer*, 444 n. 138) is less convincing. The combined strength of the Tervingi and Greuthungi was probably *c.* 20,000 (p. 139), and such a victory could surely not have been won with odds of 1 : 2. Hoffmann's estimate of the total number of regiments available to Valens cannot be challenged, but we do not know how many units had to be left to face Persia, nor to what extent Roman units mustered less than their paper strength. Losses of *c.* 10,000–12,000, implying an original force of *c.* 15,000–20,000 seem more likely.[57] Whatever the figure, Roman strategy for 378 had gone disastrously wrong.

E.   *The Gothic War of Gratian and Theodosius*

After Hadrianople, Zosimus' summary of Eunapius becomes our main source. It is supplemented by some fragments of Eunapius' original history, chronicle entries, and panegyrics, but the quality of information available is much reduced. A little more, however, can be recovered from Zosimus than is generally allowed.

His account begins with the aftermath of Hadrianople at 4. 24. 3, and seems to run to 4. 34. 5. Chs. 4. 24–33, as we shall see, provide a coherent sequence of events, leading from Theodosius' elevation to a peace agreement with some 'Scythians', which it is natural to associate with the general peace of October 382. But having already given, seemingly, a full account of the war in these chapters, Zosimus returns to the subject again in 4. 34. This apparently gives us another account of the peace (4. 34. 5), in what

---

[56] *Contra* Stein i. 518–19 n. 189*, followed by Schmidt, 408; Wolfram, 124. On the first day of the Somme, the British lost 21,000 men; Hadrianople is unlikely to have been more destructive.

[57] Cf. Delbrück, *Geschichte der Kriegskunst*, 292; Grosse, *Römische Militärgeschichte*, 254; Austin, 'The Adrianople Campaign', 82.

is generally a garbled chapter. Fritigern, Alatheus, and Saphrax
are leaders of 'German peoples from beyond the Rhine', Athanaric's position in *c*.380 is misunderstood, and his funeral in
January 381 is made the cause of peace in October 382. Sense can
be made of much of this (App. B), but there is a more general
point. It is this confused chapter, coming after what is otherwise a
more orderly account, which makes Zosimus' narrative of the
whole war seem so absurd.

This chapter is also the only point in his entire account of the
Hunnic and Gothic invasions where Zosimus names Gothic
leaders; everywhere else, he fails even to make it clear that two
separate Gothic groups had arrived at the Danube in 376.[58] That
the leaders of these groups should suddenly be specified (along
with Athanaric) right at the end of Zosimus' narrative of 376–82 is
striking, and suggests strongly that the chapter has a different
source from the rest of Zosimus' material. This is at least partly
confirmed by the fact that, when disentangled, it is a summary of
the entire Gothic war, referring to simultaneous attacks on Rhine
and Danube, the Danube crossing of 376, Athanaric's arrival in
380/1, and the final peace of 382 (App. B). The chapter's
confusions are so great, indeed, that a contemporary, such as
Eunapius, can hardly have been responsible. Zosimus has probably added to his main, Eunapian account, a summary of the war
from one or more places. Its different character (providing
significantly more detail on the Goths) made Zosimus unaware
that he was repeating himself. Hence 4. 34 should be treated as a
misplaced and confused doublet.[59]

Faults inherited from Eunapius—a lack of detail, particularly
dates, and a marked hostility to Theodosius—continue to cause
problems. Zosimus, as we shall see, seems to have made things
worse by not realizing that the events involved the same barbarians, who did not return 'home' after each incident. Without the
confused chapter 4. 34, however, Zosimus' narrative is internally
coherent, and corresponds with our other information, such as it
is. This should not cause too much surprise: Eunapius, Zosimus'
main source, was a contemporary who ought to have been able to

[58] Cf. Paschoud, ii. 2. 407 n. 166.
[59] The same may have happened with the doublet of Odotheus at Zosimus 4.
35, 38–9. For an attempt to discern Zosimus' contribution elsewhere, see
Blockley, 'The First Book of Zosimus' *New History*'.

produce a reasonable account of such important events, some of
which he knew at virtually first hand.

Zosimus catches something of the eastern Empire's disarray
immediately after the battle of Hadrianople, reporting the circular
route (through Macedonia, Thessaly, and Moesia to Pannonia)
taken by the *magister equitum* Victor, seeking to inform Gratian of
Valens' death (4. 24. 3). This was presumably to avoid the Goths.[60]
In the meantine, the Goths attempted to take Hadrianople itself,
but failed, and marched towards Constantinople (AM 31. 15–16.
1). Among the forces available to defend the city were the Arabs of
Queen Mavia,[61] and, with the strength of the city's walls, these
proved sufficient to deter a siege. The Goths then returned to
raiding, spreading across the Balkans as far as the Julian Alps (AM
31. 16. 7). Of other events, we hear only that the *magister militum*
Julius massacred, on his own initiative, Gothic troops in the east;
these were perhaps hostages taken in 376.[62]

Gratian seems to have made no further move against the Goths
in 378. Alamanni were attacking across the Rhine (Sozomen, *HE*
7. 4; Zosimus 4. 24. 3), and the emperor and his advisers were
perhaps preoccupied with choosing an imperial colleague. They
eventually decided on Theodosius, who was elevated to the purple
on 19 January 379, after winning a morale-boosting victory over
some Sarmatians (Theodoret, *HE* 5. 5; *Pan. Lat.* 12(2). 12. 9–10).
After a period of joint activity, Gratian left for the west, reaching
Trier in September 379 (Seeck, *Regesten*, 250 ff.).[63] Theodosius
was left in charge of the Gothic war, and received control of
probably the Illyrican dioceses of Dacia and Macedonia, which
normally belonged to Gratian's western empire.[64] The Goths had
spread into Illyricum, so that Gratian probably wanted Theodosius to exercise unified command over the entire area under attack.

---

[60] Paschoud, ii. 2. 384–5 n. 150 calls this a 'geographical fantasy', but it
accurately describes a journey along the Via Egnatia and then north via Scupi and
Naissus through Moesia I to Pannonia.

[61] AM 31. 16. 5–6, to be preferred to Zosimus 4. 22. 1–3; cf. n. 52.

[62] AM 31. 16. 8, to be preferred to Zosimus 4. 26. 2 ff.; cf. Schmidt, 414.

[63] On Theodosius' elevation, see Matthews, *Western Aristocracies*, 91–2.
Ausonius, *Grat. Act.* 2. 11. 18 mentions Gratian's activities in the Balkans, but
provides no details.

[64] Sozomen, *HE* 7. 4; cf. Stein, 'Untersuchungen', 347 ff.; Grumel, 'L'Illyricum', 8 ff.; Paschoud, ii. 2. 386 n. 151; Vera, 'La prefettura dell'Illirico
Orientale', 392–3.

He had established himself at Thessalonica, within this area, by June 379 (ibid. 251).

The main confrontation of the 379 campaigning season seems to have occurred in Thrace, for after Theodosius' move to Thessalonica, Zosimus recounts the attack there on his own people by Modares, a Goth in Roman service (4. 25. 2–4). The passage is dated merely by association, and probably exaggerates Modares' success, but there is no reason to doubt that the incident occurred.[65] The victory was perhaps similar to previous, limited Roman successes before Hadrianople, when individual Gothic raiding parties had been defeated. The imperial authorities announced victories 'against Goths, Alans, and Huns' on 17 November 379, but peace did not follow for three years, so that we need not think in terms of a really significant Roman triumph.[66] Zosimus' conclusion that, after Modares' success, no barbarians were left in Thrace (4. 25. 4) may also be correct, if understood to mean that those Goths not defeated by Modares (i.e. most of them) were moving west into Illyricum. In oration 14 of spring 379, Themistius reports that the barbarians had already broken into Illyricum (p. 261. 4 ff.), and by 380 both the Tervingi and Greuthungi were operating there (see below). Modares' success may have encouraged the rest of the Goths to leave Thrace for the safer uplands of Illyricum, or, perhaps more likely, the move may already have been under way. Thrace had been raided in 377 and 378, reducing its value as a food-source, so that Modares may have been harrying stragglers.[67] Zosimus' conclusion thus makes sense, even if he did not understand its significance.

There are two main routes which the Goths could have followed from Thrace into Illyricum: the Via Egnatia from Constantinople to Thessalonica and beyond, and the main military road which crossed the Succi pass to Serdica and Naissus. No source makes it clear which alternative was chosen, and in principle, of course, the Goths might have used both. There are two indications, however, that suggest the latter, and this route has been shown on Fig. 4 First, the *magister militum* Victor's circular route through Macedonia and Thessaly after Hadrianople suggests that he felt unable to

---

[65] Seeck, *Geschichte*, v. 125–6; Schmidt, 415–16; Paschoud, ii. 2. 386 ff. n. 153.

[66] *Cons. Const.*, s.a. 379 (*CM* i. 243); cf. Demougeot, ii. 145–6.

[67] Eunapius fr. 47. 1 seems to imply that many Thracian cities held out, perhaps supporting the view that the Goths moved on for lack of food.

use the much more direct military road, presumably because it was infested with Goths. Second, before their campaign against Theodosius in 380, Fritigern's Tervingi seem to have occupied Moesia Superior; it was from here, reportedly, that they advanced south to defeat Theodosius in that year (App. B). The military road, of course, ran through Moesia Superior.

To return to Zosimus' narrative: the historian next devotes attention to Theodosius in Thessalonica (4. 27–31. 1).[68] First, we are told, the emperor increased the number of *magistri militum* from two to more than five, stimulating greater corruption (4. 27. 1–3). This prompts a digression on Theodosius' greed and mismanagement (4. 28–9). These passages are certainly biased against Theodosius, but comment on military restructuring is not out of place in a war narrative.[69] The next chapter describes how Theodosius recruited barbarians from beyond the Danube, and then, to minimize the potential for disloyalty, exchanged them with troops from the east (4. 30. 2). Much space is devoted to a fight between some of these recruits and the Egyptians by whom they were being replaced, when the two groups met at Philadelphia (4. 30. 3–5). This is anecdotal, but certainly to the point. Many eastern troops had fallen with Valens, and even if Gratian had given Theodosius some troops along with Illyricum, more were needed. Recruiting north of the Danube was standard Roman practice,[70] and Eunapius at Sardis, only 50 km. away from Philadelphia, had presumably heard of the fight from eye-witnesses,[71] so that there is no reason to doubt the nature of the action. Other steps were also taken. From 379, legislation was issued against deserters and others avoiding military service, and we hear of peasants and miners mobilized for war.[72] Troop transfers were also general; Libanius complains of Syrian units being drafted into the

---

[68] Zosimus 4. 26 seems misplaced; cf. n. 62.

[69] This has been taken to refer to the 2 praesental and 3 regional commanders of the eastern *Notitia Dignitatum*, which would make it anachronistic: Hoffmann, *Bewegungsheer* 460 n. 243, 494 ff. However, Demandt, 'Magister militum', 720 ff. has shown that Theodosius did appoint more generals than his predecessors even before this new system was established, and Zosimus says not five but 'more than five'; cf. Paschoud, ii. 2. 391–2 n. 155.

[70] Jones, 619 ff.; Hoffmann, *Bewegungsheer*, 131 ff., 450 ff.; Schmidt, 421–2.

[71] Cf. Paschoud, ii. 2. 390–1 n. 158.

[72] e.g. *CTh* 7. 13. 8–11; 7. 22. 9–19; Themistius, *Or.* 14 p. 261. 4 ff.; Libanius, *Or.* 24. 16; Hoffmann, *Bewegungsheer*, 460 ff.

Balkans (*Or.* 24. 28).[73] Hatred of both Theodosius and barbarians is evident in this digression, but its information is either confirmed elsewhere or entirely plausible. It is also relevant; Zosimus is describing how Theodosius rebuilt the army after Hadrianople.

We are then returned to the action. Barbarians 'cross the river' to reach Macedonia, overcoming Theodosius, whose new army falls apart. The barbarian recruits desert to the attackers, who, after a hard fight with the Egyptian transferees, defeat Theodosius (4. 31. 2–4). Zosimus supplies no chronology, and it is unclear who the mysterious river-crossing barbarians might be. Some of the difficulties can be resolved. The action is not dated explicitly, but the sequence ends with Theodosius' entry into Constantinople, dated by other sources to 24 November 380.[74] We are probably dealing, therefore, with the campaigning season of 380, during which Theodosius was absent from Thessalonica between early April and mid-June.[75]

This clarifies the action, because it was probably in 380 that the forces of Fritigern and Alatheus and Saphrax attacked south and north Illyricum respectively (App. B). Theodosius' enemy can thus be identified as Fritigern's Tervingi. Zosimus seems not to have grasped that they were already within the Empire, so that he has them cross (presumably) the Danube, but otherwise the action is coherent.[76] No other source describes these events—although Themistius does hint that Theodosius suffered a set-back in Thessaly[77]—so that we cannot confirm Zosimus' account. But there is again no reason to doubt that Theodosius confronted barbarians, probably Fritigern's Tervingi, somewhere in the south-west Balkans, and lost.

According to Zosimus, the Goths subsequently took over the cities of Macedonia and Thessaly, from whom they were content

[73] Seeck, v. 482–3 argued that the *Notitia Dignitatum* shows evidence of these transfers, but see Hoffmann, *Bewegungsheer*, 460–1.

[74] *Cons. Const.*, s.a. 380 (*CM* i. 243).

[75] Seeck, *Regesten*, 255; id., *Geschichte*, v. 141; Schmidt, 416–17; Paschoud, ii. 2. 398 ff. n. 159.

[76] The contemporary Eunapius must have known that the barbarians who left Thrace in 4. 25 did not go 'home', so that if the Danube is meant, the mistake is probably Zosimus'. Alternatively, the river could be the Axius/Vardar dividing Thrace from Illyricum, and the crossing an authentic detail.

[77] *Or.* 16, p. 298. 16 ff., describing Theodosius' evolving policy towards the Goths, refers to Achilles' response to the Trojans' burning of Thessalian ships.

with moderate tribute. Learning that the barbarians had gone home, Theodosius garrisoned the cities and forts, hurrying to Constantinople and requesting help from Gratian. He then levied so much tax from the cities that they called back the barbarians (4. 31. 5–32. 1–3). Hatred of Theodosius is again evident, and Zosimus is also confused in making the barbarians go 'home' for a second time.[78] Otherwise, there is nothing implausible here. Because they were at war, the Goths could not grow food, supporting themselves instead from the cities' surplus—Zosimus' 'reasonable tribute'. This makes good sense; an area can be ravaged only once, but more ordered exactions taken on a number of occasions. The Goths had perhaps learnt from their experience in Thrace. The point of Theodosius' countermove is also apparent. Having failed to defeat the Goths he garrisoned the cities to make them invulnerable to Gothic pressure. Since the Goths were not good at sieges, this cut off their only source of food.

Because Zosimus does not mention it, we know little of the simultaneous attack of Alatheus and Saphrax on Pannonia. Gratian returned from the Rhine, presumably to confront them, in summer 380 (Seeck, *Regesten*, 252), but with what outcome is unclear. Zosimus and Jordanes' *Getica* have been thought to show that Gratian settled the Greuthungi in Pannonia, but they securely document no more than the attack. Ammianus' report of an oracle suggests—although there is much room for doubt—that those of the invaders of 376 who reached Pannonia suffered a defeat there, and this might refer to the Greuthungi (App. B). If there was a settlement, it was perhaps on Gratian's terms, but many Goths may simply have been repulsed. Imperial victories were again announced in autumn 380.[79]

Gratian and Theodosius may also have met in this year. According to the law-codes, Gratian was at Sirmium in August 380, and Theodosius had arrived there by 8 September (*CTh* 7. 22. 1; cf. *CJ* 11. 47. 2). This has prompted the suggestion that they met.[80] Yet we might expect some reflection of such a meeting in other sources. Zosimus is more reliable than usually thought, and

[78] Cf. n. 76. See also Paschoud, ii. 2. 401–2 n. 161, but stationing garrisons in cities would have been expensive for their inhabitants; cf. the different demands mentioned in *CTh* 7. 8.

[79] *Cons. Const.*, s.a. 380 (*CM* i. 243).

[80] Seeck, *Regesten*, 254–5; cf. Paschoud, ii. 2. 401 n. 160.

he mentions only letters passing between them (4. 33. 1). Likewise, Themistius does not refer to a meeting in a speech of January 381, even when describing the great co-operation that the emperors had shown in the conduct of the war (*Or.* 15, pp. 280. 27 ff., 283. 11 ff.). He surely would have done if they had really met less than six months before, so that there probably was no meeting. Theodosius may have needed to consult Gratian's generals, who were to retrieve the situation in Macedonia in 381, or the codes may simply be misleading.[81]

By late 380, the emperors had returned to their capitals, Gratian to Trier and Theodosius to Constantinople. Zosimus complains that, despite his defeats, Theodosius still staged a grand entrance (4. 33. 1). While awaiting the next campaign, however, he did manage a propaganda triumph. Athanaric, former leader of the Tervingi, lost control even of those Goths who had not abandoned him in 376 (AM 27. 5. 10; cf. p. 337). Theodosius gave him asylum, and he arrived in Constantinople on 11 January 381, to an enthusiastic welcome, promptly followed by a funeral with full pomp on 25 January when he died shortly afterwards.[82] Some sources have been confused by Athanaric's importance before 376, and perhaps also by Theodosius' propaganda, into making too much of this episode. Thus Zosimus 4. 34. 4–5 makes it the main cause of the peace of 382, but Athanaric did not command many Goths at this point. Orosius (7. 34. 6–7) similarly has the death of Athanaric cause the Goths' surrender, but he mistakenly considers Athanaric king of all Goths in the Roman Empire in *c*.380. Jordanes (*Getica* 27. 141 ff.) has Athanaric succeed Fritigern and make a goodwill visit to Theodosius in Constantinople after peace has been made, but this is again precluded by Ammianus.[83] Athanaric's arrival is very unlikely to have substantially affected the balance of power in the war, although it did make good propaganda (see further Ch. 5).

[81] See generally A. D. E. Cameron in Bagnall *et al.*, *Consuls*, 71 ff. There are, however, no obvious inconsistencies in *CTh* 7. 22. 11.

[82] *Cons. Const.*, s.a. 381 (*CM* i. 243).

[83] Athanaric's position in *c*.380 has been clear since Kaufmann, 'Kritische Untersuchungen', 420–1; cf. Schmidt, 418; Cesa, 'Romani e barbari', 83–4. Some have nevertheless echoed the mistakes of Jordanes, Orosius, and Zosimus. Stallknecht, *Untersuchungen*, 75–6 and Demougeot, ii. 149 ff. both consider Athanaric to have succeeded Fritigern. See also App. B.

According to Zosimus, the next major episode of the war saw Bauto and Arbogastes attack 'Scythians' in Macedonia and Thessaly. Under the orders of Gratian, they drove their opponents, presumably Fritigern's Tervingi along with any refugee Greuthungi, out of Illyricum and back into Thrace (4. 33. 1–2; Fig 4. is merely guessing at the route). These events have generally been dated to 380,[84] but Zosimus places them after Theodosius' entry into Constantinople, and it is impossible to mount large campaigns in the Balkans in winter (cf. Themistius, *Or.* 15, p. 269. 18 ff.). This suggests that the date was actually 381, which makes good sense on other counts. In 380, Gratian had to deal with Alatheus and Saphrax, and his troops would have needed time to organize a second expedition. Zosimus also records no other action between this episode and a peace treaty with the 'Scythians' (i.e. Goths) expelled from Illyricum (4. 33. 2–3). This peace must surely be that of 382, so that dating Bauto and Arbogastes to 380 leaves no action for 381. It was surely in 381, therefore, that the Goths were driven out of Illyricum. Gratian was at hand in Aquileia, Theodosius remained mostly in Constantinople (Seeck, *Regesten*, 256 ff.).

Zosimus' final act is a peace between the 'Scythians' in Thrace and Theodosius. Bias is again evident, since the emperor is said to have been tricked by them (4. 33. 2–3), and the narrative sequence closes with a diatribe against his love of luxury (4. 33. 4). The venom can be discounted, but Zosimus is correct that peace came about without a second great confrontation. Military pressure brought the Goths to heel, but Themistius confirms that there was no major battle (*Or.* 16, p. 297 ff.). With the cities garrisoned, and western forces harrying them in the field, the Goths were perhaps worn down. The formalities of the peace were completed on 3 October 382.

Problems remain, but if we understand the tribal groups who fought at Hadrianople to have been involved throughout, Zosimus 4. 24–33 provides us with an internally coherent account of events. In 378/9, the Goths moved into Illyricum. Imperial counter-attacks were limited to small-scale actions such as that of Modares, while Theodosius reconstructed the army. In 380, the Goths attacked in

---

[84] Paschoud, ii. 2. 403 n. 163; Demougeot, ii. 147–8; Cesa, 'Romani e barbari', 87–8; Wolfram, 132.

different directions; Gratian perhaps checked Alatheus and Saphrax, but Theodosius' force fell apart against Fritigern's Tervingi. In 381 western forces drove the Goths out of Illyricum, and in 382 peace was made in Thrace. When its confusions are disentangled, 4. 34 fits within this framework, providing more detail on the events of 380.

5

THE PEACE OF 382 AND AFTER

Six years of conflict were brought to an end on 3 October 382.[1] This peace is usually thought to have involved only the Tervingi, the Greuthungi supposedly having come to terms with Gratian separately in 380. The fate of their raid on Pannonia remains mysterious, so that a separate peace cannot be ruled out completely. It is, however, very unlikely. The passage in the *Getica* normally taken to describe it really refers to the treaty of 382 (App. B), which was probably made with the bulk of both the Tervingi and Greuthungi.[2] Its terms may well have encompassed, in addition, the Huns and Alans who joined the Goths after the battle of Ad Salices.

For the Romans, negotiations were conducted by a group of officers including Saturninus and Richomeres,[3] but it is unclear whether Fritigern, Alatheus, and Saphrax survived the war; all three are last mentioned in the context of the raids of 380 (Zosimus 4. 34. 2 ff.; Jordanes, *Getica* 27. 140). One chronicle has been taken to show that Fritigern, at least, was alive, reporting that 'in [382] the whole people of the Goths with their king (*universa gens Gothorum cum rege suo*) surrendered to the Roman state'.[4] Just a few lines earlier, however, it records the surrender of Athanaric in 380/1, describing him as *Gothorum rex*, so that *cum rege suo* probably refers back to Athanaric—especially since, as we shall see, no Gothic king was recognized by the treaty. What happened to the three is unknown; they are equally likely to have been deposed by the Romans or to have lost out to Gothic rivals (see

---

[1] *Cons. Const.*, s.a. 382 (*CM* i. 243).

[2] Some groups had been neutralized separately during the war: Farnobius' group (AM 31. 9. 3–4), and those defeated by Sebastianus (AM 31. 11. 2–5) and Modares (Zosimus 4. 25. 2 ff.).

[3] Themistius, *Or.* 16, p. 288. 14 ff. (Saturninus) with the implication at 290. 13 ff. that the consul for 384 (Richomeres) had made an equal contribution.

[4] *Cons. Const.*, s.a. 382 (*CM* i. 243); cf. Schmidt, 419.

below). Other important aspects of the peace agreement can, however, be reconstructed.

A. *The Treaty*

According to Jordanes, the treaty of 382 renewed Constantine's special relationship with the Goths. They were again *foederati*, forming one body with the Roman army, in which they served faithfully in return for due reward (*Getica* 27. 141–29. 146). Once again, Jordanes' characterization is at least partly anachronistic. The peace did mark a new departure in Gotho-Roman relations, but its diplomatic form was not an equal *foedus*. Orosius and Latin chroniclers report that the Goths 'surrendered' to the Roman state (some using the language of *deditio*),[5] Pacatus refers to the Goths as 'in servitude' in the late 380s (12(2). 22. 3), Libanius calls them Theodosius' 'loyal slaves' (δούλων εὔνων, *Or.* 9. 16), Synesius his 'suppliants' (ἱκέτας, *De Regno* 21. 50. 12), and Themistius consistently uses language of surrender and subjection.[6] Oration 16 even implies that the Goths formally surrendered:

> We have seen their leaders and chieftains, not making token concession of a tattered banner, but giving up their weapons and swords with which up to that day they had held sway, and clinging to the knees of the Emperor . . . (p. 301. 2 ff.)

In outward form, the peace of 382, as these more contemporary sources affirm, was a *deditio*.[7] What were its more practical arrangements?

First and foremost, the Goths were granted land to farm. Synesius (writing within a generation) refers to Theodosius giving them Roman land (*De Regno* 21, p. 50. 12), Pacatus to the Goths

---

[5] Orosius 7. 34. 7 *Romano sese imperio dediderunt; Cons. Const.*, s.a. 382 (*CM* i. 243) *se tradiderunt*; Hydatius s.a. 382 (*CM* ii. 15) *se tradunt*; Marcellinus Comes s.a. 382 (*CM* ii. 61) *Romano sese imperio dedit*.

[6] *Orr.* 16. e.g. pp. 299. 4 ff., 300. 15 ff., 301. 2 ff.; 34, pp. 226. 10 ff., 24 ff., 227. 13 ff.

[7] Those who consider that *deditio* meant settlement as *coloni* deny this evidence and follow Jordanes: e.g. Stallknecht, *Untersuchungen*, 26 ff., 75 ff.; cf. Wolfram, 133 (others as p. 124).

serving the Empire as farmers (12(2). 22. 3), echoed by Themistius, who also reports the re-smelting of weapons into agricultural implements (*Or.* 16, p. 301. 27 ff.; *Or.* 34, pp. 227 ff.). This evidence is rhetorical, but unambiguous. The location of the lands also seems clear. Themistius refers to 'Scythians' in Thrace (*Or.* 16, esp. pp. 299 ff.) and Zosimus to barbarians keeping watch on the Danube (4. 34. 5), so that the Goths were probably spread along the river frontier-zone of Lower Moesia in the Thracian Diocese. Some were perhaps also settled a little further west in Dacia Ripensis (*Getica* 25. 133), and others in Macedonia.[8]

This much is uncontroversial, but we also need to know on what terms lands were granted. The sources are not specific, but the Goths were clearly not settled as individual *coloni*. After 382, Gothic tribal life continued *de facto* and probably also *de jure* (see below), which would have been impossible had the Roman state treated them as subject *coloni*. This is not surprising; the Goths were not prisoners of war, but had negotiated a surrender. They were probably given land in freehold, which may have been plentiful in a frontier zone which had seen six years of warfare.

The Goths seem to have agreed to pay some tax to the Empire. In oration 16, Themistius proclaims that the Romans will soon see the Goths sharing their tables, military ventures, and public duties (ὁμοῦ λειτουργοῦντας). This usually means taxes in Themistius.[9] In oration 34, similarly, Themistius' *apologia* composed in 384, the orator, now in the past tense, refers to the fact that under the 382 agreement, the Goths were not destroyed, but, having been turned into farmers and taught to bear burdens (φορτηγεῖν ἐθίσειε), they serve the Empire as farmers or soldiers (p. 227. 5 ff). The same point is made by Pacatus in 389 (22. 3). Serving as soldiers is straightforward, but Gothic farmers can be said to have served the Roman state only if they paid tax.[10] Quite what this meant in practice is uncertain. Gothic farmers were possibly not taxed as their Roman counterparts, and any contributions would have had

[8] Themistius, *Or.* 34. 24, pp. 228–9; a lacuna makes it unclear whether the text refers to a settlement, or to the Macedonians' having seen much of the war.

[9] *Or.* 16, p. 302. 23 ff.; cf. Cesa, 'Romani e barbari', 94 n. 83.

[10] Cf. Schmidt, 421 commenting on Libanius *Or.* 19. 16; Wolfram, 133 states that the Goths held tax-free land, but cites no evidence.

a powerful symbolic value. In late-antique diplomacy, the reception of any kind of annual gift from a foreign power could be used to 'prove' that the power was a 'tributary'.[11] Receiving some kind of payment from the Goths was *de rigueur* if they were to be presented as in subjection to the Empire. The Goths' economic contribution is mentioned only in speeches of Themistius and Pacatus,[12] and their more widely attested military service was perhaps the real *quid pro quo* for their lands.[13]

Their military service is described only in general terms; Synesius, for instance, just says that Theodosius made them allies (σύμμαχοι, *De Regno* 21, p. 50. 13). Its nature has to be deduced, therefore, from the ways in which Goths acted as part of the Roman army after 382. This has a major drawback. Those regulated by the treaty were not the only Goths within the Empire's orbit after 382. A large force of Greuthungi attempted to cross the Danube in 386 (Zosimus 4. 36, 38–9), the Goths of Arimer lived near the Empire between 383 and 392,[14] and the Tervingi who ousted Athanaric in 380/1 presumably continued to live around the Carpathians (p. 13). Large numbers of Goths also followed Radagaisus to Italy in 405/6, and must have lived fairly close to the imperial frontier before their attack. Substantial recruitment from Goths beyond the frontier is quite conceivable, and fully in accord with standard practice, so that we cannot simply assume that every Goth found in the Roman army after 382 was serving under the terms of the peace.

One aspect, however, does seem clear. When required, the treaty Goths served *en masse* in expeditionary armies, such as those sent against the usurpers Maximus and Eugenius. For the former, Pacatus describes the mobilization of barbarians (12(2). 32. 3–4, trans. Nixon, 42; cf. App. B).

---

[11] The Latin panegyrists portray the Persians as tributaries when gifts were sent: *Pan. Lat.* 3(11). 5. 4; 4(8). 10. 4; 12(2). 22. 5; cf. Rubin, 'The Mediterranean', 41 ff.

[12] Cf. Stallknecht, *Untersuchungen*, 26–7.

[13] Some have attempted to make land and military service mutually dependent. Demougeot, 'Modalités', 154–5 suggests that many Goths were made into *laeti* after 382; Chrysos, 152 ff. argues that they were *limitanei*. Either is possible, but both would make the Goths part of the regular army, which does not seem to have been the case (see below).

[14] Wolfram, 135; *contra* Thompson, *Visigoths*, 159–60.

(3) Finally you granted the privileged status of fellow-soldiers (*commilitii*) to the barbarian peoples who promised to give you voluntary service, both to remove from the frontier a force of dubious loyalty (*manus suspecta*[15]), and to add reinforcements to your army and they followed standards which they once opposed. (4) There marched under Roman leaders and banners the onetime enemies of Rome, and they filled with soldiers the cities of Pannonia which they had not long ago emptied by hostile plundering. The Goth, the Hun and the Alan responded to their names . . .

The mentions of Pannonia, Goths, Huns, and Alans show that Pacatus refers, at least in part, to the invaders of 376, so that this would seem to be a secure reference to groups settled under the 382 treaty. Pacatus also seems to say that it was only when these peoples were drafted for the campaign that they became part of the army. Before that, they had not shared 'the privileged status of (Roman) soldiers'. This would also seem to hold true for the campaign against Eugenius, when Theodosius' attempts to make them fight stimulated a violent quarrel (see below). In both cases, large numbers of Goths were mobilized only for the specific campaign.[16]

This perhaps accounts for a contradiction between the picture of the eastern army in the *Notitia Dignitatum*, and descriptions of it on campaign in narrative sources. The latter describe an army composed of distinct Roman and barbarian elements, while the *Notitia*, whose eastern part seems to date from *c*.394,[17] lists only Roman regiments. Although these units must have included many individuals not of Roman origin, that would seem insufficient to account for the distinct forces described by the sources. If, however, the barbarian element was mobilized only for specific

---

[15] Nixon renders *manus* as 'troops', implying that the group referred to was already part of the army, but Theodosius grants them military status as they join the campaign, so I have adopted a less specific meaning.

[16] This much is generally accepted; e.g. Schmidt, 320; Cesa, 'Romani e barbari', 96. Demougeot, ii. 154 ff. and 'Modalités', 155 ff. argues that Goths served in large numbers in the field-army up to 388, before Theodosius replaced them with western troops of whom (cf. Hoffmann, *Bewegungsheer*, 469 ff.) about 15 regiments were transferred to the east in *c*.390. But Pacatus seems to show that most barbarians were drafted into the army only for the campaign, and there is no other evidence of Goths serving in the regular army in the 380s.

[17] Hoffmann, *Bewegungsheer*, 516 ff.

campaigns, they would not appear in the *Notitia*'s listing of the regular army.[18]

Precisely how the Goths were organized while on campaign is problematic. Pacatus refers to Goths and others marching 'under Roman leaders and banners'. Interpreted precisely, it might suggest that foreign auxiliaries were incorporated into Roman units, but the words probably just emphasize that foreigners were fighting for the Roman state, since military service did not destroy existing power-structures among the Goths. Officers of the regular Roman army were ultimately in command,[19] but Gothic nobles remained important. Theodosius, for instance, approached these men first when mobilizing the Goths against Eugenius (p. 186), and, of these leaders, Alaric, at least, held a command on the campaign.

We also hear of Goths performing more regular service. 'Tervingi' and 'Visi' are listed among the palatine auxiliaries of the two eastern *magistri militum praesentales* (*Notitia Dignitatum*, Or. 5. 61, 6. 61). 'Tervingi' is the name of one of the invading groups of 376, and 'Visi' came to designate the new group that emerged from them inside the Empire (App. A). The natural conclusion is that two regular regiments were recruited from groups covered by the 382 treaty.[20] Further west, under the regime of the empress Justina, mother of Valentinian II, there were Goths among the presumably regular troops of the imperial bodyguard.[21] Less

---

[18] Liebeschuetz, 'Generals, Federates', 463 ff.; id., *Barbarians and Bishops*, 32 ff. The other possibility is that the Goths are disguised in the *Notitia*. The obvious troop category would be the palatine auxiliaries, where Visi and Tervingi are listed. This category contains many units raised from scratch by Theodosius (e.g. *Not. Dig.*, Or. 5. 62, 64–6, 6. 62–7), which could represent Goths notionally organized into Roman units. I prefer Liebeschuetz's view, however, since it better fits Pacatus' description of the Goths' recruitment. As palatine auxiliaries, the Goths would have been paid more than many Roman troops in less élite formations, which could only have spawned dissent. Gratian was murdered because of resentment at his turning Alans into highly paid troops: Zosimus 4. 35. 2–3; Aur. Vict. 47. 6.

[19] Timasius, Arbogastes, Promotus, and Richomeres commanded against Maximus (Philostorgius, *HE* 10. 8); Timasius, Stilicho, Gainas, Saul, and Bacurius against Eugenius (Zosimus 4. 57. 2).

[20] Cf. Liebeschuetz, 'Generals, Federates', 464; id. *Barbarians and Bishops*, 29.

[21] Ambrose, *ep.* 76 distinguishes them racially, but nowhere suggests that they were in a different troop-category. They perhaps belonged to the western Schola Palatina: *Not. Dig.*, Occ. 9. 4–8.

helpfully, Zosimus reports that a unit of barbarians was stationed, probably in the 380s, near the city of Tomi in Scythia Minor (4. 40). If these were Goths, and the fact Theodosius rewarded them, in Germanic fashion, with gold torques suggests they may have been, they were a unit of the regular army, perhaps *comitatenses* since they received higher pay than the Tomi garrison, who were probably *limitanei*.[22]

This evidence leaves us with a number of possibilities. We do not know whether any of these Goths were performing duties laid down by the treaty of 382. Recruitment from the many other Goths living in or around the Roman Empire would account for their appearance in the Roman army. The Tervingi and Visi of the *Notitia*, at least, must have something to do with the treaty Goths, but precisely what is uncertain.[23] In addition to mass mobilizations for campaigns, the Goths may also have been obliged to provide troops for more regular service. Alternatively, even these units may have nothing to do with the treaty, sustained instead by individual recruitment; the high pay of élite, palatine troop formations may well have attracted sufficient Goths to maintain their ethnic character.[24]

In sum, the Goths' military obligations after 382 may not have been dissimilar to those placed on them at an earlier date by Constantine's treaty (Ch. 3). In both cases, the mass of Goths were under a general obligation to fight for the Empire. They were not

[22] Jones, 607 ff. The 'barbarians' are normally considered to be Goths: Schmidt, 433; Wolfram, 134.

[23] Cf. Cesa, 'Romani e barbari', 95–6.

[24] A draft of recruits was often taken by the Roman state in peace-agreements (p. 127), and that of 382 may have involved similar arrangements. If such a draft founded the regiments, the favourable conditions of service perhaps sustained them. In essentials, these units may have resembled the élite Gurkhas of the British army. Liebeschuetz, *Barbarians and Bishops*, 27–9 suggests that substantial numbers of Goths—those of Alatheus and Saphrax settled in Pannonia, together with some of those settled under the treaty of 382—received different terms, being turned into regular soldiers (in part following Demougeot, 'Modalités'). The existence of units of Tervingi and Visi may well confirm this in part, but the evidence is unconvincing that large numbers of Goths were treated in this way. The Pannonian settlement is a myth (App. B), and Liebeschuetz otherwise rests his case on rhetorical references to Goths and Romans sharing houses (Synesius, *De Regno* 15; Themistius, *Or.* 34, p. 228). These are taken to refer to the billeting of troops, but it seems more likely that the authors were just stressing that Goths and Romans were living peacefully in close proximity to one another.

by and large part of the regular army, however, and, in practice, their participation had to be negotiated for each separate campaign. Under Constantine's settlement, the Goths had perhaps provided 3,000 men per campaign, but the numbers required after 382 are unknown. There is some reason to suppose them higher, since they are said to have lost 10,000 dead in the battle of the Frigidus.[25]

Our understanding of this military service is also directly relevant to the question of what financial payments the Goths received under the treaty. Jordanes reports that the Goths received regular annual payments for the upkeep of a designated number of men. But since, *en masse*, they were probably part of the army only for particular campaigns, this seems unlikely. Here again, the situation perhaps resembled Constantine's arrangements. Eunapius refers specifically to gifts rather than pay (fr. 59), and, as we have seen, the Romans seem to have been well aware that gift-giving played an important role in Germanic societies (p. 114). Gifts were probably handed over regularly to important Gothic nobles, but larger payments, recompense for military service, are likely to have been negotiated on each occasion that large numbers of Goths fought for the Empire.[26]

The sources also shed some light, finally, on the Goths' legal position. The act of *deditio*, however much *pro forma*, placed the Goths in a position of subjection to the Empire, as the payment of tax confirms. Yet in practice, much of the tribal life continued as before. In his diatribe directed primarily against Alaric's Goths, Synesius complains about the 'mass of differently bred youth', 'not born and brought up under (Roman) laws', who are 'pursuing their own customs',[27] and Gothic nobles were able to continue their usual struggles for pre-eminence (see below). The main point seems clear: the Roman state did not dismantle Gothic tribal life. Was this merely tolerated *de facto*, or recognized *de jure*? The sources do not allow us to answer the question with complete certainty, but Synesius reports that Theodosius 'considered the Goths worthy of citizenship and gave them a share in the honours of state' (*De Regno*, 21, p. 50. 13–14). Even if citizenship was limited only to the most important Goths (in accordance with established

[25] Orosius 7. 35. 19: untrustworthy, but suggestive of large-scale service.
[26] Liebeschuetz, 'Generals, Federates', 464–5.
[27] *De Regno* 19. 43. 5 ff. with Heather, 'The Anti-Scythian Tirade', 153 ff.

practice[28]), this would indicate a more formal recognition of the Goths' semi-autonomy.[29] The Roman state had evolved legal compromises long before this, which granted citizenship to foreigners in so far as it did not impinge upon other claims upon them, so that Gothic leaders could easily have held dual citizenship.[30] Synesius' evidence suggests that established practice was adapted to express the ambiguities of the Goths' position. They had been subdued, but not totally defeated; dependants of the Empire, they retained their own identity.

As many have noted, the peace of 382 was in some ways similar to that of 332. In reality, however, it marked a new departure, for the Goths were now a semi-autonomous unit on what was otherwise directly governed Roman soil. The peace of 332 had dealt with Goths beyond the imperial frontier, so that to concentrate on the similarities is to miss the point. We must consider further, therefore, the balance of power which underlay the treaty, and ultimately dictated the nature of this new relationship.

B. *Imperial Policy, 376–382*

Up to Hadrianople, the underlying aims of the imperial authorities remained constant, although outward appearances changed. While imperial propaganda celebrated the advent of the Goths, Valens really accepted them only because he had no choice. Hostility to the Goths is evident in the measures taken to control the food-supply and the attack on the leaders of the Tervingi, so that the Goths' revolt probably did not occasion any major change in imperial attitude. Valens' measures precipitated the revolt, and must always have been likely to; in 376/7, he had more or less committed the Empire to military confrontation anyway. In 377 east and west could free sufficient troops only to parry the Goths' attacks, but in 378 a much larger force was gathered seemingly to inflict total military defeat upon the Goths. Roman numbers are uncertain, but Valens probably mobilized something like

---

[28] Braund, *Rome and the Friendly King*, 39 ff.; Demougeot, 'Restrictions', 381 ff.

[29] Cf. Schmidt, 420; Wolfram, 133; Cesa, 'Romani e barbari', 96–7; Chrysos, 164 ff.

[30] Sherwin-White, *Roman Citizenship*, esp. 380 ff.

15,000–20,000 men, and Gratian was perhaps to provide similar forces. Since the Goths are unlikely to have had more than 20,000 men (p. 139), the emperors planned to attack with a considerable military advantage: perhaps 2:1 (if a higher estimate of Valens' forces is preferred, the planned superiority increases). Imperial field-armies were also better equipped than the Goths,[31] so that Valens and Gratian clearly meant to overpower their opponents.

The policy behind this general aim is less clear, but there are two main alternatives. The emperors may have intended simply to drive the Goths out of the Empire, an idea referred to by Themistius in 381 (*Or.* 15, p. 285. 25 ff.). At the same time, and the two approaches could have been followed simultaneously, the emperors were surely determined to dictate terms to any Goths who remained south of the Danube after the campaign. They would probably have received treatment towards the harsher end of the spectrum of possible methods of resettlement: perhaps being dispersed as individual *coloni*. Such at least, was the fate of the followers of Farnobius, defeated before Hadrianople by Frigeridus and resettled as agricultural labourers around Italian towns (AM 31. 9. 4).[32]

As events turned out, Gratian was delayed, leaving Valens without the planned superiority, and his resolve wavered; he was attempting to negotiate a truce as battle commenced (AM 31. 12. 13–15). By 382, this had become a permanent change in policy. The Empire won no military victory, and did not attempt to. As Themistius reports, peace was brought about not by arms, but by the confidence the Goths had in Theodosius' goodwill (*Or.* 16, p. 298. 9 ff.). Yet, as we have seen, the peace of 382 sanctioned a major departure in imperial policy, the Goths retaining their identity as an at least semi-independent tribal group. Somewhere between 378 and 382, it must have been decided that the Goths could not be defeated, or that the cost of doing so was too high. The evolution of this decision is strikingly reflected in the changing tone of Themistius' orations from the war years.

In oration 14, of spring 379, Themistius' tone is martial and aggressive. He celebrates the fact that Theodosius had been chosen emperor for his military ability, demonstrated in the defeat he inflicted on some Sarmatians. His appointment means that the

[31] Thompson, *Early Germans*, 116 ff.
[32] Cf. Demougeot, 'Modalités', 145.

tide of fortune in the war has now turned. Themistius notes that Theodosius has mobilized farmers to spread fear among the 'Scythians', and miners to produce more iron, and is confident that the new emperor will inspire the army to defeat the enemy. Theodosius' gentleness and love of mankind (φιλανθρωπία) are mentioned, but only briefly; the speech presents Theodosius as a military commander capable of winning the war.[33]

By January 381, there had been considerable modification. In oration 15 Themistius still expresses confidence that the 'Scythians' will be driven north of the Danube by Theodosius and Gratian, but military affairs this time receive only brief treatment.[34] Most of the speech is devoted to the argument that an emperor's main duty was not to fight, but to govern, war being the province of generals (esp. pp. 270. 19–275. 13). This can be explained partly by the fact that winter had halted military operations (p. 269. 18 ff.), but involves a clear shift of emphasis from 379, when Theodosius' main qualification for the purple had been his military ability.

That this is significant for the evolution of policy towards the Goths, is confirmed by the oration's account of Theodosius' reception of Athanaric. Abandoned in *c.*380 by even those who had followed him in 376, Athanaric fled to Constantinople, which he entered on 14 January 381. According to Themistius (p. 275. 14 ff.), the episode showed that Theodosius' love of mankind could subdue a hostile barbarian who had remained implacable when attacked by Roman armies. Since the main body of the Goths were still unsubdued in January 381, it is hard to escape the conclusion that this part of the speech was designed to prepare public opinion for a change in imperial policy. Themistius is putting forward the idea that enemies are best subdued non-violently, and generally stresses that war takes an emperor away from more important business. While briefly looking forward to the enemy being driven across the Danube, the bulk of the speech told its audience—the political classes of the eastern Empire, celebrating Theodosius' second anniversary—to expect a more peaceful solution to the war than that anticipated in 379.

[33] *Or.* 14, *passim*; cf. Dagron, 'Thémistios', 103.

[34] At two points: *Or.* 15, pp. 269. 18 ff., 285. 25 ff. Oration 15 marks the second anniversary of Theodosius' elevation, 19 Jan. 381.

Such expectations were confirmed in the actual treaty, and to its justification Themistius devoted part of oration 16, a speech celebrating the consulship of Saturninus, on 1 January 383; Saturninus had been instrumental in negotiating the peace. Restating the argument used for Athanaric, Themistius widens its scope, stressing that barbarians as a whole are better subdued by the emperor's love of mankind than by violence. Theodosius' virtue, we are told, has caused the enemy to yield where coercion failed. The populace should not worry that the Goths had not been destroyed; they have surrendered completely, and the land is better filled with farmers than corpses.[35] From a martial tone early in 379, Theodosius' propaganda came to justify an alternative policy of peace by negotiation.[36]

Why did policy change, and whose was the impetus behind it? According to Themistius, policy changed because Theodosius was wise enough to realize that barbarians are better subdued by persuasion than force (*Or.* 16, p. 297. 1–299. 3, esp. p. 297. 8 ff.). It was Theodosius' 'forbearance, gentleness, and love of mankind' which made the 'Scythians' ready to surrender (299. 4 ff.). Themistius does not hide that conditions were difficult (296. 17 ff. refers to 'the indescribable Iliad of woes on the Danube'), nor that the new policy was a response to this fact, but he minimizes the extent to which Theodosius was constrained to make peace. Even if it had been easy to destroy the 'Scythians', Theodosius would still have chosen not to (p. 301. 27 ff.). Policy changed because Theodosius thought that peace by negotiation was better than military victory. But, as the peace of 369 and the crossing of the Danube have warned us, this kind of propaganda cannot be taken at face value. Themistius probably also presents a distorted picture of the peace of 382.

It is very hard to believe that Theodosius was not really constrained by circumstances, or chose not to defeat the Goths out of love of mankind. After 382, he reacted more traditionally to tribal groups. In 381/2, a mixed group, seemingly led by Huns (Zosimus 4. 34. 6), was driven away from the Danube, while in 386

---

[35] *Or.* 16, esp. p. 299. 4 ff. On the context, Dagron, 'Thémistios', 23.

[36] Themistius' *apologia* of the mid-380s describes the peace in similar terms: *Or.* 34, p. 226. 10 ff.

a large force of Gothic Greuthungi approached the frontier and found no asylum. Thoroughly defeated as they attempted to cross, they were dealt with as the emperor chose. Some were drafted into the army, many were resettled as *coloni* in Asia Minor. When he was able to, therefore, Theodosius thoroughly subdued any would-be immigrants, returning to traditional means of dealing with tribal groups.[37] He is likely to have departed from them in 382, only because he was forced to.

A significant factor in his decision not to fight the war to a conclusion was Hadrianople itself, which destroyed two-thirds of Valens' army, upwards of 10,000 men from élite units. Theodosius made strenuous efforts to reassemble an army, but it fell apart in battle (p. 152). With help from Gratian, the Goths' worst excesses were curbed, but the emperors did not again confront them in open battle. Because of Hadrianople, Gratian and Theodosius were perhaps unable to assemble enough reliable troops to be sure of victory. Imperial armies had disappeared 'like shadows' in 378 (Themistius, *Or.* 16, p. 296. 17 ff.). The decision was probably also dictated by the fact that the Huns had altered the balance of power on the Danube frontier. The authors of our sources all understood that the Goths entered the Empire in 376 because they had been driven out of their old homes by the Huns. This was only the first manifestation of a much broader problem. In 378 Gratian's march east was disrupted by Alans in Dacia Ripensis (AM 31. 11. 6). In 378/9 Theodosius' first task was to deal with Sarmatians on the Middle Danube, who may have been displaced by Athanaric's Goths (AM 31. 4. 13), and over the next two decades the frontier was far from quiet. In the early 380s, a mixed tribal group was repulsed (Zosimus 4. 34. 6), and, as we have seen, Gothic Greuthungi sought asylum in the Empire in 386. In the mid-390s the Huns themselves, rather than those driven before them, began to threaten the Danube directly, if as yet on a limited scale.[38] Not all of this could have been envisaged in *c.*380, but it was

---

[37] Cf. Stallknecht, *Untersuchungen*, 78. The sources are Zosimus 4. 35. 1, 38–9; *Cons. Const.*, s.a. 386 (*CM* i. 244); Claudian, *IV cons. Hon.* 625 ff. For their resettlement as *coloni*, see Schmidt, 263, and, with additional arguments, Heather, 'The Anti-Scythian Tirade', 156–7.

[38] Maenchen-Helfen, 36 ff.; the Huns themselves became important on the Danube in the time of Uldin (*c.*400).

understood that the Huns were overturning the political geography of the western steppe,[39] and the imperial authorities must surely have grasped that the Danube would henceforth require stronger defences.

To shift the balance of imperial forces was no solution, because they were already fully stretched. As soon as troops moved to the Danube to confront the Goths, other operations had to be curtailed, and gaps appeared. Gratian was forced to return to Raetia in 378 because Lentienses were raiding in his forces' absence (AM 31. 10); eastern armies faced Sassanian Persia.[40] The peace of 382 may have offered the Empire a way out of these difficulties. In strategic terms, it established the Goths as an extra defence for the Danube. Instead of expanding the army, an undesirably expensive option,[41] or weakening other frontiers, the imperial authorities used the Goths to solve their security problems on the Danube: rather than resist each invasion, they set one wave of immigrants to confront the others. The Empire could thus escape a vicious circle in which ever more troops were drawn into the Balkans. In the absence of direct evidence, such as minutes of the Consistory, it is impossible to know what level of strategic analysis lay behind the Empire's approach to the peace of 382, but the idea of using Goths against the Huns does appear in one source (Zosimus 4. 34. 5), so that this line of thought may not be too far from the mark.[42] Traditional policy towards tribal immigrants was reversed in 382 because it was impossible or undesirable to apply it in this case; the Empire was much more constrained by circumstance than Themistius would have us believe.[43]

---

[39] AM 31. 3. 1 ff.; Eunapius fr. 42; Zosimus 4. 20. 3 ff.; Orosius 7. 33. 9–10; most strikingly Ambrose, *Expositio Evangelii secundam Lucam* 10. 10, 'The Huns threw themselves on the Alans, the Alans on the Goths, and the Goths on the Taifali and Sarmatians; the Goths, exiled from their own country, made us exiles in Illyricum, and this is not yet the end.'

[40] Millar, 'Government and Diplomacy', 345 ff.; Rubin, 'The Mediterranean', 32 ff.

[41] Jones, 448 ff.; cf. anecdotal evidence such as the complaint of the *comes largitionum* Ursulus before Amida (AM 20. 11. 5).

[42] Cf. Stallknecht, *Untersuchungen*, 78 ff. Themistius argues that the 'Scythians' will provide extra troops: generally in *Orr.* 16, 34, and also *Or.* 18, p. 320. 5 ff.; cf. Cesa, 'Romani e barbari', 90–1.

[43] Cf. Ch. 3 on the peace of 369. The emphasis on victory (McCormick, *Eternal Victory*, 35 ff.) probably made it impossible to admit publicly that an emperor had been forced into a course of action.

That Theodosius was entirely responsible for the change of course may also be misleading;[44] the treaty of 382 is likely to have been the agreed policy of both Gratian and Theodosius. This is suggested above all by the part Gratian, or at least his troops and commanders, played in the war. Gratian originally elevated Theodosius to the purple, giving him parts of Illyricum which normally belonged to the western Empire, and which perhaps contained troops as a core around which Theodosius could rebuild the eastern army. When that army failed, more of Gratian's troops under Bauto and Arbogastes retrieved the situation (p. 153); whether they continued operations in Thrace in 382 is unclear. Either way, the Goths could not have been forced to make peace without Gratian's help. He also spent part of every campaigning season between 378 and 382 in the Balkans; he was at hand throughout the second half of the war, and also when peace was finally negotiated.[45] Eastern propaganda acknowledged Gratian's role in January 381. In celebrating the second anniversary of Theodosius' accession, Themistius expresses the hope that the two emperors will crush the Goths between them in the coming campaign, and presents them as joint commanders, twin steersmen of the ship of state (*Or.* 15, pp. 280. 27 ff., 283, 11 ff.).

All this, and especially the fact that he was at Viminacium in Moesia Superior in summer 382 when peace was being negotiated, prompts the thought that Gratian was probably just as intimately involved in the peace-process as Theodosius. If Goths were settled in either Macedonia or Dacia Ripensis (see above), this would confirm the point, since settlement in these areas would have required Gratian's consent. No western panegyrics happen to survive from late 382 or early 383, so that we have nothing with which to balance Themistius' account, which gives all the credit to Theodosius. Themistius, however, was disseminating Theodosian propaganda, which by January 383 had particular reasons for minimizing the part played by Gratian.

[44] Following Themistius, the policy enshrined in the 382 peace is generally viewed as Theodosius' own; cf. Pavan, *La politica gotica, passim.*

[45] Seeck, *Regesten*, 250 ff. Gratian was in the Balkans early in 379 before travelling to Milan by 31 July. In 380 he reached Aquileia by 14 May and remained in the Balkans throughout the summer, before travelling to Trier, which he reached by 14 Oct. In 381, he was at Aquileia from April to December. In July 382 he was at Viminacium in Moesia Superior.

Gratian had originally promoted him, but Theodosius was not content with a secondary role alongside his western partner. This manifested itself first in religious affairs, where in 380/1 Theodosius seems to have undermined Gratian's plans for an oecumenical council, to prevent any chance of Gratian's wielding influence in the eastern half of the Empire.[46] A more serious dispute arose in winter 382/3 when Theodosius elevated his son Arcadius to the purple without Gratian's permission; numismatic evidence shows that Gratian never recognized Arcadius.[47] He was crowned Augustus on 19 January 383,[48] but on 1 January Themistius was already anticipating his promotion (*Or.* 16, p. 293. 26 ff.). The oration says nothing explicit about the quarrel this provoked with Gratian, but unmistakably reflects the issues involved. Responsibility for Theodosius' promotion is given solely to 'the Divinity' who 'summons to leadership the only man capable of resisting such an inundation of misfortune' (namely the aftermath of Hadrianople). Gratian merely proclaims the decision (*Or.* 16, p. 297. 4–7). This is in marked contrast to oration 15 of January 381, where Gratian is given full credit for having recognized in Theodosius all the virtues that would make a good emperor (*Or.* 15, p. 273. 10 ff.). The point of this changing view is obvious in the context of Arcadius' promotion. In 383, Themistius produced an account of Theodosius' own elevation which was in accord with his emperor's desire for total independence.

There is more than a possibility that, in giving Theodosius credit for ending the Gothic war, Themistius is again deliberately minimizing Gratian's contribution. Orations 15 and 16 present similarly contrasting pictures of Gratian's role in the war. Whereas in January 381 he is an equal partner (p. 338), two years later he is completely ignored. And, as we have seen, Gratian's part in the war—or at least that of forces under his command—is well documented. One of Themistius' purposes in oration 16 was thus probably to appropriate for Theodosius alone the credit for solving the Gothic problem. A point of irony is that it was the end of the war which removed Theodosius' need for military help, and gave him the breathing-space he needed to force a break with Gratian

---

[46] McLynn, 'Ambrose', 207 ff.

[47] Pearce, *RIC* IX. pp. xix–xxi (cf. 72); McLynn, 'Ambrose', 220 ff.

[48] *Cons. Const.*, s.a. 383 (*CM* i. 243).

by promoting Arcadius. Gratian's troops had previously played too important a role in containing the Goths.

The lack of a western account makes it difficult to allow for Themistius' bias, but the polemical nature of oration 16 is obvious, and from their role in the war we should expect Gratian and his advisers to have been closely involved in the peace-process. The initial impulse to negotiate may have been Theodosius', but Gratian's regime, responsible for much of the effective military resistance to the Goths, must have approved of the policy, or it would simply have continued the war. Themistius' comment that Theodosius was the first to entertain the notion that a negotiated peace should replace outright victory as the Empire's war-aim might well be a reference to the fact that others—especially at Gratian's court—then publicly adopted it (*Or.* 16, p. 297. 11 ff.).[49] Tension existed between the two courts and came to a head with Arcadius' elevation, but the negotiated peace of 382 was in all likelihood an agreed policy.

That said, the emperors were probably also planning, in the longer term, to undermine the semi-autonomy they had just granted the Goths. At the end of oration 16, Themistius looks forward to the complete absorption of the Goths into the Roman world, citing the Celtic tribes who had become Romans, once settled in what became Galatia (*Or.* 16, p. 302. 8 ff.). Envisaging a future in which the Goths had lost their independent identity was perhaps a necessary sop to public opinion. It probably also reflects long-term imperial hopes. It could not have been imagined in 382 that these Goths would play a major role in bringing the western Roman Empire to an end, and independent tribal groups were not usually tolerated on imperial territory. In at least one practical way, the peace of 382 attempted to further these hopes.

Between *c.*380 (when Fritigern, Alatheus, and Saphrax are last mentioned) and the mid 390s we hear of no individual recognized by the Empire as king of the Goths. The sources are not comprehensive, but Zosimus (following Eunapius), Pacatus, and Themistius between them devote much space to the Goths. In Themistius' description of their surrender in 382, for instance, no individual of particular importance is picked out; Themistius refers explicitly to 'leaders' in the plural (ἐξάρχους καὶ κορυφαίους,

---

[49] If the reception of Athanaric was used to prepare public opinion (see above), the policy may have been agreed as early as winter 380/1.

Or. 16, p. 301. 2). This has sometimes been seen as mere rhetoric,[50] but the contrast with oration 10, describing the individual confrontation between Valens and Athanaric in 369, is striking (p. 203. 11 ff.). The absence of anything similar in oration 16 indicates that no opponent was singled out in the peace ceremonies of 382.[51]

This has been noted, but not accorded much significance. Since it is generally held that the Goths elected overall leaders only in wartime, the absence of a king (or *iudex*) after the peace of 382 has seemed natural.[52] But overall leadership was a permanent institution among the Goths in the fourth century (Ch. 3), and the absence of any Gothic king leaves something to be explained. The point emerges from an incident on the eve of Hadrianople, when Fritigern sent messengers to Valens, saying that he hoped to become Valens' 'friend and ally' (*amicus . . . et socius*, AM 31. 12. 9). This phrase has a particular meaning in Roman diplomacy: *rex socius et amicus* was the title accorded foreign kings who stood in an established (if subordinate) position to Rome; their royal rights were fully recognized in so far as they were not incompatible with their duties as Roman allies.[53] Fritigern was thus asking Valens to acknowledge his rights as overall Gothic leader, using an established diplomatic formula. It is precisely this recognition that the Empire did not grant in the peace of 382.[54]

The Empire's acceptance of Gothic independence thus had its limitations. Semi-autonomy was acknowledged, and, as a whole, the Goths were considered allies; they were not, however, granted the status of an independent people under their own king. This must surely have been deliberate, since Fritigern's letter shows that the question of recognizing an overall Gothic king was raised in negotiations. In the short term, recognition might have made such a leader malleable, but, once he was firmly in control of his

[50] e.g. Schmidt, 419.

[51] Cf. e.g. Wolfram, 133; Liebeschuetz, *Barbarians and Bishops*, 50. Cesa, 'Romani e barbari', 89 plausibly argues that Themistius would have mentioned Fritigern, the victor of Hadrianople, had he been present.

[52] e.g. Schmidt, 425 ff.; Demougeot, ii. 153–4; Wolfram, 133.

[53] Braund, *Rome and the Friendly King*, 23 ff.

[54] Thompson, 'Fritigern to Euric', 107 ff. argues that the gifts to Gothic leaders were designed to divide their interests from those of their followers, but see below. Widespread settlement (if the Goths were distributed between Thrace and Illyricum) may also have been designed to disrupt social cohesion.

followers, their strength would have made him essentially independent of Roman control. It was standard fourth-century practice, when dealing with groups beyond the frontier, to remove leaders who were building up too powerful a following.[55] Inside the frontier, the potential threat posed by such men was obviously greater; the cases of Alaric (p. 209) and the two Theoderics (Part III, *passim*) show the kind of problems that such leaders, even when not implacably hostile, necessarily caused. The restriction was thus in part probably an attempt to forestall the rise of an over-powerful individual. In addition, the Hunnic invasions had broken the loyalties tying both the Tervingi and the Greuthungi to their former leaders, letting loose conflicts among those trying to fill the leadership vacuum. The refusal to recognize any particular individual may have been calculated to exacerbate these divisive struggles, which continued unabated after 382 (see below). Prolonged political chaos could only weaken the Goths, fuelling imperial hopes of eventually dismantling their independent identity.

In the peace of 382, therefore, the Empire was trying to preserve a careful balance. For good reasons, Theodosius and Gratian renounced any immediate attempt to destroy the Goths' identity, granting them quite favourable peace-terms. The refusal to recognize any overall Gothic leader, however, makes it clear that they were not fully reconciled to the existence of independent, tribally organized Goths on Roman soil.

C. *Gothic Aims in War and Peace*

In coming to the Danube, the Goths were not looking to change their way of life fundamentally, but seeking a new area in which to live as before. This aim could have been satisfied in a number of ways, as the simultaneous offers Fritigern made to Valens on the eve of Hadrianople illustrate. In his open letter, Fritigern requested that 'Thrace . . . should be granted as a habitation [to the Goths], with all its flocks and crops'; in return, there would be lasting peace (AM 31. 12. 8). The request for all the 'flocks and crops' shows that the Goths were not envisaging paying tax; they

---

[55] e.g. AM 21. 4. 1–5; 27. 10. 3; 29. 4. 2 ff.; 29. 6. 5; 30. 1. 18–21.

would not be Roman 'tributaries', but form an independent state.[56] Not surprisingly, Fritigern also made more conciliatory noises in a private message. Given a demonstration of the Empire's military might, he suggested, he would be able to persuade the Goths to accept terms favourable to the Romans (AM 31. 12. 9).

Valens thought this a ruse,[57] but the offer is plausible. Fritigern was not suggesting that Gothic tribal life should end, merely that Gothic aims could be satisfied by something short of an independent realm in Thrace.[58] Imperial prestige could never have countenanced such a loss of territory, so that Fritigern was attempting to avoid the conflict which, by itself, the open letter was bound to provoke. On the day of battle, he made a second attempt to avoid bloodshed, suggesting a truce. This time Valens reacted more positively, but Roman troops precipitated conflict while negotiations were still in train (AM 31. 12. 12 ff.). Even in 378, some Goths could conceive of achieving their aims by means other than the outright annexation of Roman territory. This kind of view prevailed in 382, when the Goths accepted a treaty which subordinated them to the Roman state. As we have seen, it provided them with agricultural land and sanctioned the continuance of Gothic tribal life, but stopped well short of the demands made in the open letter. Not a sovereign state, the Goths were imperial subjects, who, at least notionally, paid tax and performed military service. Nor were they united under a recognized king.

Fritigern's exchanges with Valens also illustrate the dynamics involved in any attempt to make peace. Roman emperor and Gothic leader had to trust one another. In addition, the Gothic commander had to reckon with his unruly followers. Fritigern's private message implies strongly that the demand for Thrace had been forced on him by his men. Likewise, when arranging the truce on the day of battle, Fritigern picked some nobles to act as

---

[56] Cf. Cesa, 'Romani e barbari', 75–6; Wolfram, 126. It was thus quite different from what was agreed in 382: *contra* Stallknecht, *Untersuchungen*, 26.

[57] Modern commentators such as Thompson, 'Fritigern to Euric', 106–7 have agreed with him.

[58] Cf. Cesa, 'Romani e barbari', 76–7. Fritigern was perhaps contemplating something similar to the compromise reached in 382, with the addition of himself as king. Demougeot, ii. 142 misinterprets the messages as referring to the same demand for Thrace.

hostages and said that he himself would 'fearlessly meet the threats of his soldiers', who presumably wanted to fight rather than talk (AM 31. 12. 14). Diplomacy is full of deception, but Ammianus refers several times to the fighting spirit of the Gothic rank and file, which often proved difficult to control.[59] For instance, the Goths quickly realized that they lacked the technology to reduce fortified cities, but, on occasion, enthusiasm nevertheless led them to make costly attacks. Enough other sources also refer to this to suggest that it was a constant feature of Gothic tribal life.[60] Any compromise peace required not only trust between Roman and Gothic leaders, but also that the Goths' bloodlust should be curbed, to give their leader room to negotiate.

None of these prerequisites was present in 378. Valens ignored Fritigern's secret message because he thought it deception, and the Goths had reason to distrust Valens. They had been exploited as food shortages grew, and an attempt had been made to kidnap their leaders. Fritigern seems to have been willing to compromise, but the Empire failed to provide the military demonstration which might have enabled him to convince his followers to moderate their demands. Instead of underlining Roman might, victory made the Goths impossible to control. An opportunity for peace had been lost, and years of warfare were required to make compromise again a possibility.

To start with, the social cohesion and military strength the Goths demonstrated in the war convinced the Empire that it was necessary to accept their semi-independence, the major concession it granted in 382. As we have seen, this new departure in foreign relations occurred only because Theodosius and Gratian decided that the Empire would have to pay too high a price fully to subjugate the Goths. For a compromise peace to work, the Goths had also to be convinced that policy had changed. After their experience in 376, imperial promises were no doubt subject to heavy scrutiny. Hence Theodosius' demonstrated 'love of mankind' probably was crucial to peace, making the Goths believe that an agreement could be genuine (Themistius, *Or.* 16, p. 298. 9 ff.). His treatment of Athanaric in winter 380/1 may also have been a

---

[59] AM 31. 5. 8–9, 6. 3–5, 7. 2–3, 7. 8–9, 12. 9–14, 15. 2 ff.
[60] e.g. Cassiodorus, *Variae* 1. 24, 38; 3. 43; 4. 2; 5. 27, 29.

general signal to the Goths that he was genuinely interested in a compromise.[61]

Thanks to Hadrianople, warfare was also necessary to convince the Goths that they could not defeat the Empire. Hadrianople stands as a uniquely decisive military confrontation in the history of Gotho-Roman relations after 376. On no other occasion did one side destroy the other so thoroughly as on 9 August 378; twice in the Balkans in 395 and 397, and twice more in Italy in 402, confrontations produced no decisive victory. After the battle, the Goths became very ambitious. The city of Hadrianople was attacked because they knew that Valens had left there his senior officials, insignia, and treasury (AM 31. 15. 2–15). The attack was launched against the counsel of Fritigern, and heavy casualties were incurred in a useless assault. This did not curb Gothic pride, however, and they turned to Constantinople, preparing siege-engines as they went. The size of the city and its defences restored a sense of reality; the machinery was destroyed and they marched away without attempting an assault (AM 31. 16. 3–7). The sequence of events is instructive. After their shock victory, Gothic martial vigour reached a fever pitch and they might even have thought of replacing the Roman Empire with their own, but such ideas were quickly sobered by the cold reality of imperial power. We cannot fully document the grinding campaigns which eventually brought the Goths to heel, but victories such as that of Modares sapped their strength, and nothing could have better outlined the impossibility of outright victory than to have destroyed imperial armies only to see others take their place. The Goths defeated and killed Valens, but Theodosius quickly appeared; they then defeated Theodosius, but still had to face western troops under Bauto and Arbogastes.

Six years of warfare thus convinced the Empire that the Goths could not be defeated, and demonstrated to the mass of the Goths just how strong the Empire was. This enabled the Goths' leaders (whoever they were in 382) successfully to negotiate a compromise, as Fritigern had desired to in 378. There is no fundamental contradiction here between the aims of Fritigern (and like-minded Gothic leaders), and those of the rank and file. Fritigern sought to

---

[61] Cf. Schmidt, 418. This might also explain why the event is given disproportionate coverage in the sources (cf. p. 335).

curb his people's spirit only to secure their long-term interests, which lay in an agreed relationship with the Empire. He had played a similar role in attempting to prevent attacks on fortified centres; in both cases, he wished to curb the Goths' aggression for their own good.[62]

The peace, and the events leading up to it, also began a transformation among the Goths. Previously separate, the Tervingi and Greuthungi co-operated closely: probably in the battle of Ad Salices (p. 144), and certainly at Hadrianople. The division reappeared in 380 when they attacked in separate directions, but does not seem to have been recognized in the treaty of 382. We know so little that this is not necessarily significant. If Goths were settled as far apart as Macedonia and Thrace, one cluster of settlements could represent the Tervingi, and the second the Greuthungi. Whether the distinction had already disappeared by 382, or whether the treaty established the conditions that were to lead to its disappearance is unclear, but also in a sense immaterial; never again do our sources differentiate between Tervingi and Greuthungi when describing the Goths who had crossed the Danube in 376.[63] Roman interference played a major role in this. Imperial forces defeated particular leaders and destroyed the coherence of groups gathered around them. Frigeridus ended the career of Farnobius before Hadrianople, and defeat in Pannonia may have weakened Alatheus and Saphrax (App. B). The Romans also affected the Goths by refusing to recognize any Gothic leader after 382, and perhaps even caused Fritigern's downfall by refusing to negiotiate with him in the later stages of the war.

At the same time, struggles for pre-eminence continued among leading Goths, who sought to fill this power-vacuum, caused first of all by the Huns, who broke the hold of established dynasties, and exacerbated by the Romans. Ammianus gives us some insight into this through the light he sheds on the nature of Fritigern's authority. Fritigern was unable simply to order Goths to do his bidding; he could give persuasive counsel, but, as we have seen, looked for Roman help to force the Goths to accept a compromise peace on the eve of Hadrianople. It is also implicit in Ammianus' account, although they are never named, that other Gothic leaders

---

[62] *Contra* Thompson, 'Fritigern to Euric', 106–7.

[63] 'Greuthungi' is used of a group who crossed the Danube in 386, and the *Notitia* distinguishes between Tervingi and Visi (Or. 5. 61, 6. 61); cf. App. A.

continued to co-ordinate action on those occasions when Fritigern's counsel was rejected. During the siege of Hadrianople,
other leaders issued orders (AM 31. 15. 13), and devised the
stratagem of infiltrating Roman deserters into the city (31. 15.
7 ff.). Fritigern's position was thus far from unquestioned; other
leaders were vying to influence policy, and advance their prestige
in Gothic society.

This gives us some idea of the difficulties facing any Gothic
leader. It was a position founded on the consistent wielding of
influence, but many leaders were competing for this role. In such
circumstances, the influence of any individual was bound to ebb
and flow, as Fritigern again illustrates. On the day of the battle, he
tried to negotiate a truce against the wishes of his excited warriors.
After the battle, which proved a triumph for those who had
advocated fighting, Fritigern was unable to prevent a costly assault
on the city of Hadrianople. The siege's failure justified his
position, but it was only after 'a great deal of talk and disagreement' that the Goths decided to move on to Perinthus (AM 31. 16.
1). In this context, Fritigern's attempt to win Valens' recognition
as *rex socius et amicus* has a second significance. After 376, the
Roman Empire loomed larger than ever in Gothic minds, and
establishing good relations with it was a high priority for any
leader. If Fritigern had won recognition from Valens, he would
have greatly strengthened his position at the head of the Goths. He
would have then been best placed to secure the needs of his
followers, and could have eclipsed his rivals who were advocating a
more aggressive stance towards the Empire. Whether Fritigern
was claiming recognition as ruler of the Greuthungi as well, and
how Alatheus and Saphrax may have reacted to this, is unknowable.

Nor do we know how the leadership struggle developed between
378 and 382. On the face of it, Fritigern should have gained in
standing as it became apparent that even Hadrianople had not
made Gothic victory possible. It is perhaps a sign of his renewed
influence that the Goths did not assault Macedonian cities, but
were content to take from them modest tribute (Zosimus 4. 31. 5).
But Fritigern was not recognized by the Romans in 382. Similarly,
we do not know what happened to Alatheus and Saphrax, nor to
Vitheric, in whose name they ruled.[64] These uncertainties are

[64] For a guess, see App. B.

frustrating, but the war clearly saw a further stage of political realignment among the Goths. Two previously independent groups had co-operated closely, and the peace seems to have ignored any distinction between them. In addition, the leaders who brought them across the Danube failed to maintain their position. They were ousted either during the war, or in the course of peace-negotiations. Established political groupings and the leadership around which they coalesced had thus been destroyed by Roman interference and the ambitions of Gothic nobles. The Romans refused to acknowledge any individual as Gothic king after 382, but otherwise left tribal life intact; left to itself, this power-vacuum at the top of Gothic society was bound to be filled, and, with it, a new political identity created.

D. *Goths and Romans 382–395*

The treaty of 382 thus provided a framework for coexistence which may not have been dissimilar to the kinds of arrangements discussed by Valens and the Tervingi in 376. What had previously failed to bring peace did so after 382 because six years of warfare had convinced both parties that a compromise peace was the only reasonable course of action. Nevertheless, such an untried relationship could not be expected to function entirely smoothly, especially after so much violence.

Conflicts and Contacts

Several kinds of conflicts are found in the sources, but underlying them all was a general racial tension. On the Roman side, cultural chauvinism designated all foreigners barbarians. This general phenomenon need not be examined here,[65] but the usual disdain was shown to the Goths after 382. Synesius of Cyrene, for instance, identified the Goths with the 'Scythians' arguing that they had never retained their lands, but were always fleeing. This, he claimed, proved that their natural state was slavery.[66] Libanius, likewise, called the Goths Theodosius' slaves (*Orr.* 19. 16, 20. 14). Perceptions of barbarians as dishonest and faithless were also applied vigorously to them by Eunapius (hence Zosimus), and in a

---

[65] See e.g. Dauge, *Le Barbare, passim*; Teillet, *Des Goths*, pt. 1.

[66] *De Regno* 21, pp. 49 ff.; cf. Heather, 'The Anti-Scythian Tirade', 154 ff.

letter to the Gothic *magister militum* Modares, Gregory Nanzian-zus contrasted his honesty with more usual Gothic behaviour (*Ep.* 136). Even Themistius refers to Gothic 'arrogance' and 'drunken abuse'.[67] If the Goths had stirred up anti-Roman feeling with an oath in 376 (p. 139), it was no more than a defensive response.

Such mutual hostility could always lead to violence. Libanius, for instance, twice refers to a riot in Constantinople where a crowd lynched a Goth (*Orr.* 19. 22, 20. 14). Another example is provided by the conflict between some barbarian troops and the garrison of Tomi in Scythia Minor. It is not certain that these were Goths regulated by the treaty, but the episode illustrates how hidden tensions could erupt into violence. According to Zosimus, the garrison commander Gerontius learnt that the barbarians were planning to attack the city and made such a successful pre-emptive strike that only a few of them, who found sanctuary in a church, survived. Gerontius received not praise but blame from Theodo-sius, who accused him of coveting the gifts made to his adversaries (4. 40. 1–8). It is quite unclear whether or not there really was a plot, but this only underlines the point. Suspicion was always liable to undermine the peace, especially if favour was shown to barbarians in preference to Romans.

Religious differences were also a potential problem. In 376 the Tervingi embraced what was then Christian orthodoxy in the eastern Empire: a traditional, non-Nicene Christianity sometimes described as 'semi-Arianism'. This was in line with Valens' Church settlement and the teaching of Ulfila,[68] but it contradicted Theodosius' Nicene beliefs. Between 382 and 395, however, the Goths' Arianism never seems to have caused serious problems. Despite the fierceness of his legislation against such heretics,[69] Theodosius seems to have practised *de facto* toleration. Gothic churchmen even continued to play a public role. Soon after 386 a split developed among moderate Arian churchmen over an old question: could God be called 'Father' before the Son had come to be? Selenas, bishop of the Goths, sided with the so-called Psathyrians, who held that God was eternally Father. A sign of *de facto* imperial toleration is that, in Constantinople, the dispute was

---

[67] *Or.* 16, p. 299. 11, 14–15. Cf. *Or.* 10, p. 212. 7 ff. where, although he admits that they are men, Themistius calls them an inferior breed.

[68] Heather, 'Gothic Conversion'; cf. Kopecek, *Neo-Arianism*, 422 ff.

[69] *CTh* 16. 5. 6 ff.; cf. Ensslin, *Religionspolitik*, 28 ff.

eventually healed by Fl. Plintha, and Arian Gothic *magister militum praesentalis*.[70]

In responding to these problems, Theodosius trod carefully. Libanius tells us that he was concerned to prevent the lynching from causing a general revolt, and the same motivation may have underlain his treatment of Gerontius. Coexistence was threatened much more seriously, however, on the two occasions that Theodosius mobilized the Goths against western usurpers, in the 380s against Magnus Maximus, and in the mid 390s against Eugenius.

Of the campaign against Maximus, Zosimus reports that 'barbarians enrolled in the Roman legions were contemplating treason under promise of great rewards from Maximus' (4. 45. 3). This diverted Theodosius' attention to Macedonia, where those implicated had fled, but enough of them were quickly dealt with to allow the campaign to continue. Zosimus' words have been taken to mean that regular troops were the cause of the trouble,[71] but this is probably too precise an interpretation. A similar phrase, for instance, is used by Pacatus, when there seems no doubt that he is referring to barbarians mobilized only for the campaign (*Pan. Lat.* 12(2). 32. 4; cf. p. 161). The words again probably just emphasize that the barbarians had become part of a Roman army.

It makes better sense on two further counts for Maximus to have suborned foreign allies rather than Theodosius' regulars. First, the eastern army had suffered heavily in the Gothic war which western troops eventually brought to an end. Yet eastern forces defeated western troops in both Theodosius' campaigns against usurpers. The large number of foreign auxiliaries available to Theodosius under the 382 treaty are the most probable cause of this change in the military balance of power. Themistius stressed their military potential (p. 170), and they were heavily involved in both campaigns. At the same time, these troops were only paid for the duration, and had a first loyalty that was not to the emperor at all. They were thus a much more obvious target for Maximus' machinations than regular troops who had been in receipt of Theodosius' donatives for nearly a decade. Secondly, Alaric's

---

[70] Socrates, *HE* 5. 23 (Sozomen, *HE* 7. 17); cf. Thompson, *Visigoths*, 135–8. Goths were involved in the conflict between Ambrose of Milan and the empress Justina, but only marginally (see above). Eastern bishops such as Chrysostom took a conciliatory line: Thompson, *Visigoths*, 133 ff.

[71] Liebeschuetz, *Barbarians and Bishops*, 51.

Goths were certainly involved in the trouble by the early 390s (see below), so that Goths of some kind seem likely to have started it. This would also explain why Pacatus was concerned to emphasize how well the barbarian auxiliaries had behaved during the campaign (12(2). 32. 4–5).

Although the campaign against Maximus was fought to a successful conclusion, Theodosius found on his return to the east, that matters were still precarious in Macedonia, the surviving deserters having seemingly sparked off a much larger-scale revolt. In a long passage reading almost like an historical novel, Zosimus describes Theodosius' part in the subsequent campaign: how he unmasked a spy, and narrowly escaped death (4. 48–9). Theodosius then (according to Zosimus) left the war to Promotus, who was killed in a barbarian ambush (4. 50–1). The account lacks an ending (we are not told if, or how the revolt was contained), and also a chronology; Theodosius did not return to the east until summer 391 (Seeck, *Regesten*, 279), so that three years separate Zosimus' two mentions of the revolt.

Other sources fill in part of the gap. In 390 a crowd in Thessalonica lynched the *magister militum* Bothericus.[72] We know nothing specific about his activities, and little more about the cause of his death (said to involve the imprisonment of a charioteer), but it would explain Theodosius' harsh response to the incident (the famous circus massacre) if Bothericus was engaged in subduing those suborned by Maximus. Thessalonica was not at this date a normal post for a top-ranking general, so that his presence there surely had something to do with the disturbances.[73] Claudian also alludes to incidents which must have occurred at this time. Alaric, we are told, successfully defied Theodosius on the river Hebrus in Thrace (*Get.* 524–5; *VI cons. Hon.* 104 ff.), and Stilicho, avenging Promotus (*Ruf.* 1. 314 ff.; *III cons. Hon.* 147 ff.), is said to have blockaded the enemy horde and been about to deliver the final blow when Rufinus tricked the emperor into making peace (*Stil.* 1. 94 ff.; *Ruf.* 1. 314 ff.). The reference to Promotus indicates that we are dealing with the events mentioned by Zosimus.

---

[72] The sources—Sozomen, *HE* 7. 25; Theodoret, *HE* 5. 18; Rufinus, *HE* 11. 18; Ambrose, *Ep.* 51 (the source of Paulinus, *V. Ambr.* 24)—leave much obscure; cf. Larson, 'The Thessalonian Massacre', 297 ff.

[73] McLynn, 'Ambrose', 465 ff.

Schmidt (p. 424) argued more specifically, and plausibly, that Alaric's defiance of Theodosius should be equated with the emperor's adventures in Macedonia.[74] We can also deduce from Claudian that the troubles were ended by negotiation, although any suggestion that Stilicho was frustrated by Rufinus must surely be discounted.[75] More problematic is the exact nature of these disturbances. Zosimus would suggest that guerrilla actions were fought against small numbers of enemies. Claudian, however, implies that Stilicho and Theodosius faced a large and mixed horde of barbarians in open revolt. Apart from Getae, his usual designation for Goths, the poems also mention Sarmatians, Dacians, Massagetae, Alans, Geloni, Bastarnae, and Huns.[76] This has been interpreted to mean that groups from across the Danube had by now joined the deserters in a huge revolt, but some of the tribes mentioned are certainly poetic anachronisms in this context (Massagetae, Geloni, and Bastarnae), and others may be (Sarmatians and Dacians).[77] One poem also emphasizes that Stilicho's victory was mainly a defeat of Goths, and it seems clear that Goths were central to the final negotiations (*Ruf.* 1. 316–22).[78] Non-Gothic groups must have rebelled too, but Zosimus' picture of smaller-scale warfare is probably closer to the truth than Claudian's poetry. After all Claudian had every interest in building up the number of enemies involved in order to heighten the achievement of Stilicho, his patron, in having subdued them. Huns and Alans were settled under the 382 treaty (p. 157), and Claudian is more likely referring to their participation than to fresh incursions from beyond the Danube.[79] Much remains obscure, but the original deserters of 388 were perhaps joined by some of those returning from the campaign against Maximus in the early 390s. How it ended is unclear. From Claudian we know that peace came

[74] Paschoud, ii. 2. 447 n. 196 doubts the identification because Claudian refers to Thrace, but Claudian must not be interpreted too precisely; cf. McLynn, 'Ambrose', 467ff.

[75] On this repeated topos, see Cameron, *Claudian*, 157 ff.

[76] *Ruf.* 1. 310 ff.: Sarmatians, Dacians, Massagetae, Alans, Geloni; *Stil.* 1. 94 ff.: Bastarnae, Alans, Huns, Geloni, Sarmatians.

[77] Cf. Wolfram, 431 n. 128.

[78] *Ruf.* 1 is dealing simultaneously with Gothic attacks in the early 390s, and Hunnic invasions in the middle of the decade; it is not entirely clear which of the peoples are meant to have taken part in which episode.

[79] *Contra* e.g. Liebeschuetz, *Barbarians and Bishops*, 52; Wolfram, 137–8.

about by negotiation (*foedera, Stil.* 1. 115), but we have no idea of the terms agreed. Perhaps the rebellious allies eventually returned to the agreements of 382, since the Goths' position in 395, as we shall see, shows no substantial improvement.[80]

For Zosimus, greed and faithlessness explain why the barbarians succumbed to Maximus' bribes. There is no doubt something in this, but dissent among the Goths (and others) continued, and probably grew, after Maximus' fall, indicating that it had a more general cause. Its nature is suggested by Eunapius' description of a later quarrel among Goths allied to Theodosius (fr. 59). Some wanted to uphold the agreements made with the emperor, while others, following the oath of 376, argued that, no matter what the kindnesses shown to them, they should continue to damage the Empire until they had seized it for themselves. Conflict exploded at a banquet given by Theodosius, when the leader of the first group, Fravittas, killed Eriulf, the most prominent of his opponents. Imperial troops intervened to protect Fravittas from Eriulf's followers. Eunapius implies that these contradictory opinions had existed since at least 382, but Zosimus' summary of Eunapius places the banquet immediately after the arrival in Constantinople of a first embassy from the usurper Eugenius, who was proclaimed on 22 August 392 (4. 55. 3–56. 1). The fight thus took place in late 392 or early 393.[81]

The banquet almost certainly had a causal connection with the embassy. Just before the embassy's arrival, Theodosius had begun preparations to fight Eugenius, appointing Richomeres overall commander, but the general died just as Eugenius' ambassadors reached Constantinople (4. 55. 3). Immediately after the banquet, Zosimus reports the appointment of Richomeres' replacements (4. 57. 1–4). The context suggests strongly that Theodosius' banquet for the Goths was another element in his preparations for war. The Goths were a crucial part of Theodosius' military establishment, and their support was again required for a major campaign. The revolt associated with war against Maximus had also shown how important it was to secure their allegiance. The banquet was very

---

[80] Alaric perhaps gained personally, but it is not clear that he was pre-eminent among the Goths before 395 (p. 195).

[81] Cf. Demougeot, ii. 158; Wolfram, 147; *contra* Thompson, 'Fritigern to Euric', 107–8; Schmidt, 422 n. 3.

likely part of the emperor's drive to secure Gothic participation in the coming civil war.

This allows us to re-examine the argument which exploded among the Goths. The position of Fravittas' faction seems straightforward. They simply considered that the benefits from the treaty with Theodosius were such that promises to provide military aid should be kept. That of Eriulf and his supporters is not so immediately obvious. It is unlikely that a significant element of the Gothic leadership ever seriously held the motive given to Eriulf of seizing the Roman Empire. If anything, the oath of 376 was originally designed to promote Gothic solidarity (p. 140). In 392/3, it can be suggested, Eriulf and his supporters saw no reason to endanger the Goths' continued independence by participating in a purely Roman quarrel. Autonomy ultimately depended on Gothic military power, which was what had prevented the Empire from enforcing its usual policies of pacification after 376. Taking sides in a quarrel between different groups of the Empire's upper classes could thus be regarded as folly. The events of the Eugenius campaign reinforce the point. At its climax on the Frigidus, the Goths found themselves in the van of Theodosius' army and suffered heavy casualties.[82]

It made little difference to the Goths whether a legitimate emperor or a usurper ruled in the west, yet, by supporting Theodosius in 394, they weakened their ability to maintain independence. Orosius, perhaps not atypical, rejoiced that the Frigidus had seen two victories: that of Theodosius over Eugenius, and that of the Empire over barbarians, because the Goths had suffered such heavy losses.[83] Where such attitudes prevailed, it made good sense for Eriulf to argue that there was no point in Goths dying in an attempt to win Roman friendship. Nothing is heard of how matters developed after the banquet, but potential casualties were perhaps considered less important than the loss of Theodosius' goodwill. For although Eunapius records that Eriulf's party was in the majority, and Fravittas seems to have been hounded out of Gothic society, many Goths, including Alaric, fought against Eugenius. Apart from natural greed, it was

[82] Orosius 7. 35. 19; Zosimus 4. 58. 2–3.
[83] Orosius 7. 35. 19; cf. Claudian, *VI cons. Hon.* 218 ff.

probably similar hesitations about participating in Roman civil wars which had made the Goths receptive to Maximus' bribery and prompted their subsequent revolt.

These disputes demonstrate the limits of the relationship established in 382, but do not present a full picture of it. We hear only of Goths involved in conflicts, but they spent much of their time as farmers, even if no account exists of how lands were assigned, and of the crop-production which probably occupied most of their lives. Similarly, no source describes the details of Gothic military service: who was chosen, and by whom. It is also only incidentally that we hear of one of the channels of communication which maintained the relationship. The banquet at which Fravittas killed Eriulf was particularly costly, Eunapius tells us, but he implies that Theodosius regularly invited Gothic leaders to dine with him. This is used to underline Theodosius' stupidity in continuing to favour the Goths even though they were plotting against him (fr. 59, esp. 17 ff., 34 ff.). But such feasts would have been an important point of contact. Feasting had a particular role in Germanic, as in many other societies. Sharing a meal built trust, and strengthened relationships, so that Theodosius' banquets provide a further example of Roman diplomatic practice adapting itself to the custom of its neighbours.[84] Such meetings must also have provided a forum where the many disputes generated by the day-to-day coexistence of Roman and Goth could be settled, ensuring that unfortunate incidents such as the lynching did not lead to more general conflict.

Transformations in Gothic Society

After 382 the lives of those who had crossed the Danube in 376 were transformed by close contact with the Roman Empire. Agriculture had to be pursued in a quite new context (and perhaps respond to the demands of Roman taxation), warfare was dictated by a Roman emperor, and a foreign religion took hold. As far as we can tell, Gothic Christianity firmly reflected its origins in the

---

[84] Cf. p. 114. *Beowulf* brings out the role of feasting in later Germanic society, and this is so general a phenomenon (cf. Homeric society) that there is no reason to think the 4th c. much different. Thus the revolt of the Tervingi was sparked off by a fatal banquet (AM 31. 5. 5–9), and Alamannic kings were surprised at a banquet beyond the Rhine: AM 18. 2. 13 ff.

Roman world. It was highly literate, and there was nothing specifically Gothic about its semi-Arian doctrines.[85]

It has also been argued that contact with the Empire quickly altered the whole structure of Gothic society, making it fundamentally more hierarchic. In a justly famous article, Thompson suggested that Gothic leaders' powers of patronage must have been greatly increased by control of the land-division under the 382 treaty, and of the gifts which Theodosius subsequently made to the Goths. Such men, he argued, probably took much larger estates and used the subsidies to reinforce this unprecedented social stratification. Thus antagonism grew between leaders and led. The former had every interest in close relations with the Empire, many of whom deserted to it, while their followers wished to maintain the anti-Roman stance of the oath of 376.[86]

Thompson's argument was limited by a lack of source-material, and this hampers any response. He probably overestimates, however, the effects of Roman wealth on the Gothic society. The division of lands, and distribution of moneys, may well have increased the leaders' powers of patronage, but this emphasized existing hierarchies and did not create new ones. Thompson started from a view of Gothic society which saw the power of later Gothic kings as a new phenomenon. As we have seen, however, even before 376, Gothic leaders had decided policy and enforced it with some determination upon local communities, and a permanent overall leadership was already in existence (Ch. 3).

There is also no evidence that Theodosius stimulated a significant number of desertions to Rome. We know of only three leaders who left Gothic society to enter Roman service before 395: Munderich, Modares, and Fravittas.[87] This does not amount to social collapse. Equally important, all three seem to have left because they were political outcasts. Modares and Munderich were both close supporters of Athanaric. Modares belonged to Athanaric's family, 'the royal clan of the Scythians' (Zosimus 4. 25. 2; cf. p. 100), and Munderich led Athanaric's scouting-party against the Huns (AM 31. 3. 5). The Tervingi who entered the Empire in 376 had deliberately abandoned Athanaric, so that it is

---

[85] Thompson, *Visigoths*, 115 ff.

[86] Thompson, 'Fritigern to Euric', 107 ff.

[87] Thompson, 'Fritigern to Euric', 108–9 finds a fourth case in Gainas, but he was probably not a Gothic noble: p. 197.

hardly surprising that Modares and Munderich did not rejoin them. Fravittas was strongly influenced by Roman culture (he took a Roman wife, and adhered to Graeco-Roman paganism), but even he was content to remain among the Goths until he slew Eriulf. Eriulf's retainers were looking for revenge at the end of the banquet, and it was probably the operation of feud which forced Fravittas to pursue an alternative, Roman career.[88] Fravittas and others like him were certainly more receptive to Roman culture, but, as we have seen, the quarrel seems to have been a dispute about what policy would best secure the future prosperity of the Goths as a whole.

A different element in the episode, in fact, seems more important. While the fight provides no real evidence of antagonism between leader and led, it is a very clear example of one leader quarrelling with another. Both Fravittas and Eriulf led factions, and were attempting to win the mass of Goths over to their point of view. The quarrel was not just a personal matter: Fravittas and Eriulf were rivals for influence over the Goths as a whole. That Eunapius recorded the incident suggests the same conclusion. We are not just dealing with a dispute between two individuals of little importance.[89]

Their quarrel almost certainly represents, in fact, a further round in the political upheavals which had affected the Goths since the 370s. As we have seen, the Huns undermined the existing leaders of the Tervingi and Greuthungi by 376, the Romans had toppled their successors by 382, and then refused to recognize any claims to pre-eminence in the peace-treaty. Fravittas and Eriulf were surely competing to fill this power-vacuum at the top of Gothic society. Leadership-struggles are as often fought out around issues as around personalities, so that Eunapius' concentration on the matter dividing them does not deny that the two were also personal rivals. Theodosius' response to the quarrel is also interesting. Zosimus records that 'the emperor was quite unmoved . . . and allowed [the Goths] to destroy themselves in their spite' (4. 57. 1). This is at first sight surprising, since we

---

[88] See most recently, Liebeschuetz, *Barbarians and Bishops*, 13.

[89] The likely connection between their quarrel (of 392/3) and Alaric's rise to power has generally been missed: e.g. Wolfram, 146–7, who discusses it after Alaric's rise to power (in 395), whereas I should see it as an integral part of Alaric's success (p. 196).

might expect Theodosius to have supported those who were willing to fight, and Zosimus may be misrepresenting his attitude. If not, this gives us precious insight into Theodosius' real attitude to the Goths. They were a useful weapon in civil wars, and too numerous for him to be overtly hostile. He may have been happy, however, to see them weaken themselves, reflecting long-term Roman hopes of thoroughly subduing the Goths.

Set in its full context, the quarrel between Fravittas and Eriulf tells us much. Rivals were seeking to fill the leadership vacuum, and the main issue at stake was how best to deal with the Roman state. This is not surprising: after 382 the relationship with the Empire was the most important element in Gothic political life. That they could still form factions confirms Synesius' report that they were allowed autonomy, since it presupposes considerable contact between Gothic leaders. The quarrel provides no evidence, however, that significant numbers of Gothic nobles had adopted a Roman allegiance.

Correspondingly, what evidence there is would suggest that Gothic subgroups, the power-bases of second-rank leaders such as Atharid and Winguric (cf. Ch. 3), had survived largely intact. Subgroups ($\phi v\lambda a\iota$) were recognizable as the Goths crossed the Danube,[90] and it is hard to see who the 'leaders and chiefs' ratifying the peace of 382 might have been if not the leaders of such units. The distribution of lands after 382 is also likely to have taken account of these pre-existing subdivisions, settling members of the same subgroup together. In accepting the Goths' autonomy, the Empire had renounced any major interference in Gothic society (such as resettling individuals as *coloni*). Thus, while the Roman state did not recognize a Gothic king, the basic social structure of the Gothic tribes had probably survived intact. Alaric's formidable army confirms that there had been no mass rejection of tribal society before 395.

Political allegiances, however, were redefined. In 376 two Gothic groups crossed the Danube, but the distinction between Tervingi and Greuthungi is never applied to Alaric's force.[91] It is also very striking that authors writing in *c*.400 and looking back

[90] Eunapius fr. 48. 2; cf. Heather, 'Gothic Conversion', 305 ff.

[91] Athaulf, who joined Alaric from Pannonia in 408 with a force of Huns and Goths, was already an integral part of his force, although others see in this the unification of Tervingi and Greuthungi (App. B).

over the events of the previous quarter-century did not make the distinction between Tervingi and Greuthungi, even when referring to the Danube crossing. The circumstances under which the two entered the Empire were quite different, but none of this appears in Eunapius (and hence Zosimus) or Synesius, who refer only to one crossing. By the time these authors wrote, therefore, the distinction was probably meaningless; Tervingi and Greuthungi were already inseparable.

Unification came about partly because established leaders had failed to survive; Athanaric, Fritigern, the dynasty of Vithimer, Alatheus, and Saphrax all fell by the wayside. As we have seen, Tervingi and Greuthungi represent not ancient subdivisions of the Gothic people, but confederations built up around particular dynasties. The end of these dynasties paved the way for political restructuring. The ground was further prepared by the fact that Tervingi and Greuthungi had fought together. Once the ties to different leaders, which had made them separate in the first place, were broken, it would have been natural for comrades in arms to move closer together. Rivals in leadership disputes henceforth played for higher stakes: command of both groups. At what precise moment the distinction between Tervingi and Greuthungi disappeared is unknowable, but it had already lost most of its meaning by 382, when their separate leaderships had been eclipsed, and they were settled under the same treaty, facing the same basic threat: the Roman Empire.[92]

The agreements of 382 thus provided a framework for coexistence, but could not make it trouble-free. Six years of war had made both parties ready for peace, but not solved fundamental problems. The imperial authorities still, in the long term, contemplated the total subjugation of the Goths, and the Goths were also far from content. Losses incurred on campaigns against usurpers threatened their independence. As memories faded of the pointless warfare between 376 and 382, the less either side was likely to keep an agreement which had resolved no conflicts, but merely created a *modus vivendi*.

---

[92] Political reorganization is paralleled by a change of name (App. A).

6

ALARIC AND THE MOVE
TO GAUL

Theodosius' death on 17 January 395 precipitated a generation of instability in Gotho-Roman relations. Alaric's revolt, which soon followed, exploited imperial disunity. Control of Theodosius' two sons, Honorius and Arcadius, and the western and eastern halves of the Empire, fell respectively to the *MVM praesentalis* Stilicho and the praetorian prefect Rufinus; the combined field armies of east and west, still together in Italy after the defeat of Eugenius, were controlled by Stilicho. Alaric's Goths thus had no army to face when advancing on Constantinople, and such was their rivalry that Stilicho did not rush to Rufinus' assistance.[1]

A. *The Rise of Alaric*

Alaric's revolt is usually seen as a general rising of Goths settled under the 382 treaty. It has recently been argued, however, that this is 'arbitrary' and that 'there is not a shadow of evidence that there had been a mass [Gothic] uprising . . .' in 395. Instead, Alaric is portrayed as the commander of a mutinous regiment of allied troops, who wanted his force to become regulars, essentially on the basis of a passage in Zosimus (5. 5. 4),

[Alaric was] angry because he did not command an army (μὴ στρατιωτικῶν ἡγεῖτο δυνάμεων), but had only the barbarians Theodosius had given him when he helped to put down . . . Eugenius.

This is taken to mean that Alaric commanded only one among several allied units, and that he simply desired a regular military appointment.[2] In the absence of an explicit statement, many

---

[1] See generally, Demougeot, *De l'unité*, 146 ff., ii. 161 ff.; A. D. E. Cameron, *Claudian*, 65–6; Matthews, *Western Aristocracies*, 253 ff.

[2] Liebeschuetz, *Barbarians and Bishops*, 48–85, quotations from pp. 51 and 57.

including myself[3]) have been too quick to assume that Alaric mobilized most of the Goths settled under the 382 treaty. When the relevant texts are considered with due care, however, they do yield clear indications that this was in fact the case.

Claudian, for instance, consistently describes Alaric's force as large,[4] and sometimes as a 'people' (*gens*).[5] The poet had reason to exaggerate; the larger Alaric's following, the greater Stilicho's achievement in containing it. Nevertheless, his evidence is clearly indicative of a large force rather than a mutinous regiment, and there is a limit to the amount of exaggeration that his audience might have accepted. In 395, similarly, Alaric is already found with a wagon-train, used to transport families and goods. This seems to confirm that we are dealing with a sizeable social phenomenon.[6] Claudian is also very specific that Alaric's force is directly descended from the Goths who crossed the Danube in 376 (*Get.* 166 ff., 610 ff.). This comes only in a poem of 402, but we know of no large reinforcement to Alaric's Goths in the mean time, so that there is no reason to suppose that the nature of his following had been radically transformed since 395. The passages have been taken as the Goths' view of themselves, the ideology which united Alaric's miscellaneous band,[7] but that is incorrect: they occur in a poem of Stilicho's propagandist Claudian, and thus represent a Roman view of Alaric's force. By 402 at the latest, then, Romans considered that force to be composed of the descendants of the Goths who had crossed the Danube in 376. The date can be pushed back a little further. Writing before summer 399, Synesius of Cyrene wrote a diatribe against some 'Scythians' who, for a number of reasons, can only be Alaric's Goths, citing

---

[3] Certainly in the doctoral thesis on which this study is based, and perhaps partly in my article 'The Anti-Scythian Tirade'. My argument there is saved from circularity, however, by the fact that the passages cannot refer to Gainas and Tribigild, and by the closeness of the fits between Synesius' ὅ σισυροφόρος ἄνθρωπος and Claudian's description of Alaric's position after 397, and between Synesius' account of the living conditions of the mass of Goths with which he was concerned and the terms of the 382 treaty.

[4] *Ruf.* 2. 36–8; *IV cons. Hon.* 459 ff.; *Stil.* 1. 94 ff, 183 ff.; *Get., passim*; *VI cons. Hon.* 104 ff.

[5] *IV cons. Hon.* 474; *Get.* 99, 134, 169, 533, 645–7.

[6] *Ruf.* 2. 124 ff.; *IV cons. Hon.* 466; *Stil.* 1. 94–5; cf. *Get.* 604 ff., 83 ff. for a rhetorical description of the effects of its partial loss in Italy.

[7] Liebeschuetz, *Barbarians and Bishops*, esp. 51, 76.

the history of those who crossed the Danube in 376 as the story of their past.[8] For Synesius, then, like Claudian, Alaric's force consisted of the Goths covered by the 382 agreements.

These indications are partly confirmed by the events which unfolded in summer 395, when Alaric was attacked by Stilicho, who had brought with him the combined field armies of east and west. The expedition failed partly perhaps because the two armies could not be controlled (see below), but Alaric's force was already sufficiently numerous to survive a confrontation with a large imperial army. The same held true in 397, when Stilicho confronted Alaric a second time, but again failed to subdue him. Alaric's following must already have been very substantial, then, or Stilicho would simply have nipped his revolt in the bud.[9] Thus even if Alaric did not necessarily mobilize every Goth settled under the 382 treaty, he galvanized enough of them to fend off Stilicho and for his followers to look from the outside as though they were the direct descendants of the Goths who had proved so hard to defeat between 376 and 382. As we shall see, his demands in 395 also make good sense as an attempt to improve the terms the Goths had been granted in 382. If the nature of the revolt seems clear enough, the position and earlier career of its leader require further investigation.

His ability to gather such a following so quickly after Theodosius' death suggests very strongly that Alaric was more than one among several Gothic commanders appointed by Theodosius. Alaric's own history, indeed, confirms that this is too simple a view of his position. He had, for instance, played a major role in the revolt which followed the campaign against Maximus. Some Goths had already accepted his leadership even then, when he 'barred the Hebrus to Theodosius' (p. 184). This makes it clear that although Theodosius appointed Alaric to some kind of

---

[8] *De Regno*, 19–21, pp. 43–51 (esp. 21, pp. 49–51. 3); cf. Heather, 'The Anti-Scythian Tirade', 154 ff.

[9] Liebeschuetz, *Barbarians and Bishops*, 52–3 suggests that some sense of solidarity between Alaric's followers and barbarians in the regular army may explain Alaric's escape (cf. Wolfram, 137). But barbarians were usually happy to fight one another in Roman service: e.g. Taifali and Free Sarmatians against Sarmatian Limigantes (AM 17. 13. 20–1); Burgundians against Alamanni (AM 28. 5. 8–14); Goths against Vandals (Hyd. 60 ff., s.a. 416 (*CM* ii. 19)). Liebeschuetz himself, *op. cit.* 22–5 refers to this striking lack of solidarity among Germanic groups of the period.

command against Eugenius, Alaric's pre-eminence did not solely depend on the emperor's favour; Theodosius was also in part recognizing a prestige among the Goths which Alaric had established independently. There thus seems no reason to doubt that by 395 Alaric had risen to some prominence among the Goths settled under the 382 treaty. According to Jordanes, it was because he came from the ruling 'Balth' family (*Getica* 29. 146), but this is anachronistic. There is no sign that he was related to any previous rulers of either Tervingi or Greuthungi; the Balthi, if Alaric was one, became important because of Alaric, and not vice versa (Ch. 1). We must therefore look a little more closely at Alaric's rise to power, in so far as that is possible.

Given the hierarchical nature of Gothic society, he presumably came from a family that was already important, but we have no explicit details. His rise can be set, however, in the context of broad political developments affecting the Goths since 376. Thus the quarrel between Fravittas and Eriulf in winter 392/3 (p. 190) probably marked an important stage in Alaric's advancement, removing two potential rivals: one killed, the other forced to flee. Alaric's policy throughout his reign, as we shall see, was in many ways a combination of the positions adopted by these two less fortunate leaders. He never hesitated to confront the Roman state, but at the same time always sought ordered relations with it, cultivating members of the imperial aristocracy.[10] This coincidence may not be accidental; a leader steering a path midway between the factions stood to gain considerable support.

As we have seen, Alaric was involved in the revolt which followed the defeat of Maximus. In its aftermath, he also commanded some Goths on the Eugenius campaign (Zosimus 5. 5. 4). How many is uncertain. The Goth Gainas, the Alan Saul, and the Iberian Bacurius had overall command of the foreign auxiliaries in this war (Zosimus 4. 57. 2–3), and each was perhaps responsible for contingents of his own countrymen. All three, however, were primarily Roman officers. Bacurius had been in the army since the 370s, Saul served until his death at Pollentia in 402.[11] The same seems true of Gainas. He was of Gothic origin, but joined the

---

[10] Cf. Thompson, 'Fritigern to Euric', 111 ff.

[11] Saul: John of Antioch fr. 187, *PLRE* ii. 981; Bacurius seems to have entered Roman service in winter 367/8: Heather–Matthews, *The Goths in the Fourth Century*, ch. 2 n. 56 (otherwise *PLRE* i. 144).

Roman army as an ordinary soldier, winning swift promotion (Socrates, *HE* 6. 6. 1; Sozomen, *HE* 8. 4. 1), suggesting, perhaps, that he was not a Gothic noble. After 393, he played an important role in the eastern Empire, seeking the Roman distinction of *magister militum*. Everything suggests, indeed, that he wished to emulate Stilicho, and only fled north of the Danube in *c*.400 with the few Goths who remained from his originally mixed army when all Roman avenues were closed to him. It seems unlikely, therefore, that Gainas should be seen as a potential rival for Alaric as leader of the Goths settled under the 382 treaty. The former was a Goth in Roman service with no strong ties to the tribal group, the latter primarily a tribal leader for whom Roman office was complementary and not an alternative to this role.[12] If this is correct, then Alaric may well already have been the most prominent of the Goths' tribal leaders by the time of the war against Eugenius. This is little more than a guess, however, and it is equally possible that Alaric established his pre-eminence only as the Goths revolted shortly after Theodosius' death.

Although it cannot be dated, one further episode is worth discussing in this context. At some point in his career Alaric seems to have forced a certain Sarus to abandon the Gothic tribal world, very much as Fravittas had done. From *c*.406 onwards, Sarus was a distinguished imperial general and an ally of Stilicho. After Stilicho's death, he demonstrated implacable hostility towards Alaric, undermining his negotiations with Honorius. Sarus' enmity also extended to Alaric's brother-in-law and successor Athaulf. He and Sarus, we are told, had quarrelled some time in the past (Zosimus 6. 13. 2), and Sarus eventually met his end at Athaulf's hands (Olympiodorus fr. 18). The feud continued after Athaulf's death, however, when Sarus' brother Sergeric slaughtered Athaulf's children in making himself (if briefly) leader of the

---

[12] On Gainas' career cf. *PLRE* i. 379–80; it will be studied in A. D. G. Cameron *et al.*, *Barbarians and Politics*, who note, amongst other things, that a quarter of Constantinople was named after him; cf. Ps.-Codinus 3. 109 (*Scriptores originum Constantinopolitarum*, 252 Preger). *Contra* e.g. Liebeschuetz, *Barbarians. and Bishops*, esp. 59 with refs. I accept with Liebeschuetz, 'Generals, Federates', esp. 446 (cf. id., *Barbarians and Bishops*, ch. 4) that the categories are not absolutely distinct. Roman generals of barbarian (and even Roman) origin increasingly kept bands of personal retainers, and (cf. p. 189) ousted Gothic nobles served as imperial officers. There is no evidence, however, that Gainas had ever had, or wanted, strong connections with Alaric's Goths.

Goths.[13] Sarus' obvious personal distinction, and the fact that his brother could contemplate seizing the leadership of Alaric's Goths, make it an obvious suggestion that the original source of hostility had been a leadership struggle of some kind from which Alaric emerged victorious, and after which Sarus fled to Roman service.[14] We do not know the date of this struggle, and it may well have occurred closer to 406 than 395, although Sarus could equally have been in Roman service for some time before he appears in our sources. Whatever the correct date, however, Sarus is both representative of the kind of challenges Alaric must have overcome in first establishing himself, and a further reminder that, as we have seen, Gothic leaders always faced rivals.

Much of Alaric's rise to power can only remain obscure. His involvement in the revolt which followed Maximus' defeat and command of Gothic troops on the Eugenius campaign suggest very much, however, a Gothic noble steadily advancing his prestige among the Goths settled in the Balkans by Theodosius. The disappearance of both Fravittas and Eriulf, leaders of rival factions, in 392/3 must also have cleared the way for a new star to rise. Whether Alaric had to beat off challenges from other potential leaders or not between 393 and 395, when we find him leading the treaty Goths in revolt is unknowable, but not unlikely. The line of Sarus and Sergeric, at least, seems to have made two bids for power (one at some point in Alaric's reign, the other after Athaulf's death), and there may well have been others. Whatever the case, Alaric's revolt is best seen as the first act of a leader who had consolidated the support of the bulk of the Goths who had crossed the Danube in 376.[15] Alaric stands in the long line of

[13] Sarus is *dux Gothorum* (Orosius 7. 37. 12) and *rex Gothorum* (Marcellinus Comes s.a. 406 (*CM* ii. 69)), cf. Zosimus 5. 34. 1. His hostility to Alaric is explicit in Sozomen, *HE* 9. 9. 3; Olympiodorus fr. 6; cf. Philostorgius, *HE* 12. 3. On Sergeric, see Olympiodorus fr. 26. 1; cf. Claude, *Adel, Kirche und Königtum*, 35–6.

[14] For alternative views, see e.g. Jones, 62; Liebeschuetz, 'Generals, Federates', 467; Wolfram, 152 who may well be correct on the date at which Sarus joined Roman service.

[15] Cf. Wolfram, 143–6, arguments persist about whether Alaric was a 'king' or not. As Wolfram argues, in the sense of being an overall ruler with recognized pre-eminent prestige, he surely was. The fact that 4th c. leaders of both the Tervingi and Greuthungi wielded permanent authority of a wide-ranging kind (Ch. 3) means that we need not here address questions of when the Goths first invented kingship (see Wolfram for references).

leaders from Alavivus, Fritigern, Alatheus, and Saphrax onwards who competed for pre-eminence amidst the political chaos engendered by the Huns.

B. *Alaric and Constantinople, 395–401*

When they revolted in 395, the Goths had just suffered heavy casualties in the battle of the Frigidus. Finding themselves in the van of Theodosius' forces, they became involved in heavy fighting.[16] As we have seen, there is some evidence, despite his propaganda, that Theodosius wanted in the long term to stamp out Gothic independence (p. 173). If so, he may have deliberately placed the Goths in a position where losses were likely. But it is the Goths' reaction which really matters, and however incurred, the losses must have stimulated great resentment among the tribes. The campaign against Maximus, for instance, had prompted a major revolt, although there is no record of heavy Gothic casualties on that occasion. Fighting Eugenius no doubt generated a similar hostility, this time intensified by the Goths' heavy losses; as we have seen, some Goths had resisted the idea of fighting even before the campaign began. By the time they returned to the Balkans, therefore, the Goths must have been feeling, at the very least, mistrustful of the Roman state. The Frigidus could only have fuelled suspicions that the treaty of 382 did not represent an irreversible Roman commitment to the Goths' continued independence.

Alaric's desire for a military command (Zosimus 5. 5. 4) makes good sense against this background. Zosimus' words are so vague that it is not obvious what precisely Alaric wanted, but the demand can probably be interpreted in the light of later events. After 397, Alaric extracted a high Roman command (probably the post of *magister militum*) from Eutropius, Stilicho paid a similar price for an alliance in *c*.405, and the same desire figured prominently in Alaric's negotiations with Honorius after 408. The same post is thus likely to have been at stake in 395. It was not, however, a substitute for Alaric's position in the Gothic tribal world. At no point, even when *magister militum*, did Alaric pursue a normal

---

[16] Orosius 7. 35. 19, referring specifically to Goths.

Roman military career (unlike Fravittas or Gainas), so that there is no reason to think that he was seeking the post for its own sake.[17] Rather, it carried specific benefits for himself as tribal leader, and for the people he led.

Since 376, the Goths had been conscious of the Roman threat, and this can only have increased after the Frigidus. The demand that their leader be recognized as a senior imperial commander amounted to a demand for greater official acknowledgement. The 382 treaty had refused to recognize any Gothic leader; in 395 the Goths demanded that this policy be reversed. If the demand in 395 (as later) was for the post of *magister militum*, this would have made Alaric a member of the decision-making establishment of the Empire. Valentinian I had ordained that a *magister militum* should be an *illustris*, figuring in the first rank of the Senate and Consistory.[18] A Gothic *magister militum* was potentially a significant figure in imperial politics, able to lobby for Gothic interests at the highest levels.[19] No doubt Alaric had personal ambitions, but it had become essential for any Gothic leader to be able to operate effectively as an imperial politician.

The demand for a generalship may also have been the mechanism for securing larger, regular payments from the Roman state. As we have seen, the Goths seem to have been paid for individual campaigns after 382, otherwise receiving only 'gifts' (which may have been substantial). We have no specific evidence for the era of Alaric, but it was certainly the case after 450, that, when a Gothic leader attained the status of *magister militum*, a designated number of his followers were placed on the army payroll (see Ch. 7). This may not have been the case in the 390s, but we can be sure that Alaric, in whatever form, was already seeking greater rewards, as well as greater security, for his followers.[20] We have much better information after 405, and, in all but his most modest set of

---

[17] Liebeschuetz, *Barbarians and Bishops*, 56 argues that Alaric wanted to command regular troops as a further attempt to distance him from the tribal world of the Goths. But this ignores the later occasions on which he demanded a generalship.

[18] Cf. Jones, 143, 333, 372, 378.

[19] Cf. Demougeot, ii. 168–9.

[20] Cf. Zosimus 5. 48. 3: payments in gold and the post of *magister militum* seem to have been separate issues in 409.

proposals, Alaric then demanded substantial payments for his followers.[21] Thus the fact that his most dramatic request was for a generalship does not make Alaric anything other than a newly established Gothic leader. Bringing in regular payments would have impressed the Gothic rank and file, and winning greater influence in imperial politics would have made him better able to serve his followers' interests.

It was probably with such aims in mind, then, that Alaric rebelled in spring 395 and advanced on Constantinople.[22] Claudian implies that he then made an agreement with Rufinus, which allowed him to ravage Macedonia and Thessaly (*Ruf*. 2. 54 ff.; cf. Zosimus 5. 5. 4). But Claudian consistently presents Rufinus as in league with various barbarians to destroy the civilized Roman world, and the reported agreement is surely a malicious fiction.[23] Alaric probably ravaged the area (Claudian, *Ruf*. 2. 100 ff.; cf. Socrates, *HE* 7. 10), not with Rufinus' agreement, but to force him to grant his demands.

In summer 395, Stilicho advanced from Italy to attack the Goths with the combined imperial army. He claimed that he was intervening to curb the Goths, but his main concern was to undermine Rufinus. Stilicho's designs are encapsulated in Claudian's poetry, which claims that, on his deathbed, Theodosius had made Stilicho regent for both his sons, Arcadius in the east as well as Honorius in the west. To enforce such a claim and make himself pre-eminent throughout the Empire, Stilicho had to destroy Rufinus, against whom Claudian also wrote two fierce invectives.[24] It is perhaps unlikely that Stilicho was planning to destroy the

---

[21] Both of Stilicho and his successors: Zosimus 5. 29. 5 ff.

[22] Philostorgius, *HE* 11. 8 seems to describe Hunnic incursions over the Danube in 395, and some have argued that the Goths rebelled, in fear of the Huns: e.g. Várady, *Das letzte Jahrhundert*, 88, 436; Demougeot, ii. 161–2, 389–90; Wolfram, 139–40. But no other source records this attack, and Philostorgius may have been confused by the fact that Huns attacked through the Caucasus in this year. Claudian, *Ruf*. 2. 26 ff. (recording two threats to the eastern Empire; one over the Danube, the other—obviously the Huns—to eastern provinces) is cited as supporting evidence, but ibid. 36 ff. shows that Alaric's Goths are the threat to the Danube, not a second group of Huns.

[23] Cameron, *Claudian*, 71 ff.

[24] Cameron, 'The Regency of Stilicho', 247 ff., *Claudian*, 63 ff.; cf. Matthews, *Western Aristocracies*, 270–1.

Goths, since this had proved too costly for Gratian and Theodosius, but he may have hoped to subdue them, and drive on to Constantinople in the wake of his triumph. He withdrew from the Balkans, however, before battle could take place. According to Claudian, the Goths were about to be destroyed when Arcadius ordered Stilicho to return the eastern half of the army, but this is not to be believed. Dissensions in his army (the two halves had fought each other at the Frigidus) were probably the real reason why eastern troops were returned.[25]

After Stilicho's departure, the Goths moved into Greece, presumably in a further attempt to pressurize the eastern government, headed by the eunuch Eutropius after Rufinus' assassination in November 395, into granting favourable terms.[26] The invasion itself saw much looting, and seemingly indiscriminate slaughter,[27] although major urban centres perhaps survived largely intact (Zosimus 5. 5. 6–8; 5. 6). These attacks seem to have occupied 396 and the early part of 397, while Stilicho was active on the Rhine and Eutropius dealt with Hunnic raids through the Caucasus.[28] Rufinus' death had led to a short period of co-operation between the two (Zosimus 5. 8. 1), which allowed some co-ordinated response to the Goths. Eutropius seems to have handed over western Illyricum (Pannonia and Dalmatia) to Stilicho,[29] perhaps freeing eastern troops from garrison duties there to fight Alaric.

By summer 397, however, hostility between east and west had resurfaced. Stilicho launched a seaborne invasion of Greece, forcing Alaric to retreat north towards Epirus. Apart from probably a genuine desire to curb the Goths, Stilicho was again, as in 395, seeking to undermine a hostile eastern regime. Eutropius, at

---

[25] Cameron, *Claudian*, 159 ff.; cf. pp. 474 ff. for a convincing unravelling of John of Antioch's and Zosimus' confused accounts of the campaigns of 395 and 397.

[26] Zosimus 5. 5. 5–6 suggests that Alaric entered Greece through the collusion of imperial generals, but again stresses the secrecy of these arrangements. It seems very likely, therefore, that, like Alaric's supposed alliance with Rufinus, this collusion is the product of Eunapius' imagination and desire to criticize those in charge of the Empire.

[27] Claudian, *Ruf.* 2. 186 ff., *IV cons. Hon.* 461 ff.; Eunapius, *Lives of the Sophists*, 482; Jerome, *Ep.* 60. 16.

[28] Cameron, *Claudian*, 168–9; Maenchen-Helfen, 51 ff.

[29] Grumel, 'L'Illyricum', 22; cf. *CTh* 15. 1. 34.

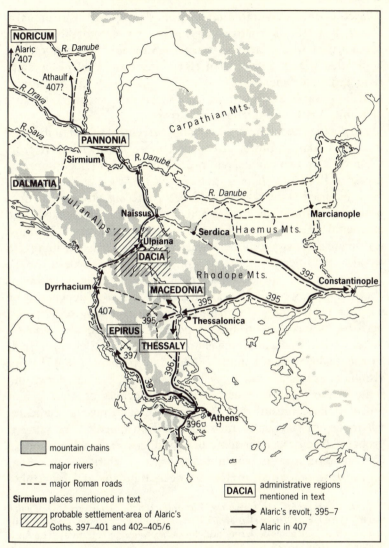

FIG. 5. Alaric's Balkan campaigns, 395–407

least, perceived his expedition as a threat, persuading Arcadius to declare Stilicho *hostis publicus*, and perhaps simultaneously negotiating with Alaric. Stilicho withdrew to Italy once more, and

Alaric obtained favourable terms from Eutropius.[30] Eutropius, it seems, had two alternatives for restoring peace to the Balkans: make a pact with Alaric, or sanction Stilicho's intervention. He chose the former, rather than risk being ousted by his western rival. A revolt, whose outbreak was facilitated by the hostility of Stilicho towards Rufinus, reached a successful conclusion because of enmity between Stilicho and Eutropius.

No detailed account survives of the agreement of 397, only some images of Alaric's power afterwards, most of which derive from Claudian. At two points, we hear that Alaric wielded supreme power in Illyricum (*Eutr.* 2. 216 *praesidet Illyrico*; cf. *Get.* 535–6). He is pictured as the ravager of Greece, entering cities he had once besieged to administer justice where he had previously raped and murdered (*Eutr.* 2. 211 ff.). We also see him using his now legitimate authority to force Thracians to forge arms for him (*Get.* 535 ff.). A different image is conjured up by Synesius, who pictures him as 'the skin-clad man' (ὁ σισυροφόρος ἄνθρωπος) alternating between barbarian dress and the toga depending on whether he is among his tribe or in the company of Romans: perhaps commanding troops or perhaps sitting in the Senate.[31] What we should make of this is not entirely clear. Synesius signals by the qualifications 'I think' (οἶμαι) and 'perhaps' (που) that his visions of Alaric are not to be taken literally. He has drawn out some of the potential, not actual, consequences of Alaric's new position; those, presumably, that would most outrage his audience, whom he was trying to turn against Eutropius.[32] The same is probably true of at least some of Claudian's images. The normal civilian administration continued to exist in Illyricum, one Anatolius being praetorian prefect between June 397 and November

---

[30] On these events, see Cameron, *Claudian*, 168 ff.; Demougeot, *De l'unité*, 170 ff.; Matthews, *Western Aristocracies*, 271–2. I follow Cameron, except for the reason behind Eutropius declaring Stilicho *hostis publicus*; cf. Heather, 'The Anti-Scythian Tirade', 167–8.

[31] *De Regno* 19–21, pp. 43–51; cf. Heather, 'The Anti-Scythian Tirade', 157 ff.

[32] *De Regno* 20, 46. 4 ff.: ἐπεὶ νῦν γε καὶ τὴν βουλαίαν Θέμιν αὐτήν, καὶ θεὸν δῖμαι τὸν στράτιον ἐγκαλύπτεσθαι, ὅταν ὁ σισυροφόρος ἄνθρωπος ἐξηγῆται χλαμύδας ἐχόντων, καὶ ὅταν ἀποδύς τις ὅπερ ἐνῆπτο κώδιον, περιβάληται τήβεννον, καὶ τοῖς Ῥωμαίων τέλεσι συμφροντίζῃ περὶ τῶν καθεστώτων, προεδρίαν ἔχων παρ' αὐτόν που τὸν ὕπατον, νομίμων ἀνδρῶν ὀπίσω θακούντων. See further Heather, 'The Anti-Scythian Tirade', 162 ff.

399.[33] Anatolius and his staff, rather than Alaric, will have dealt with legal cases. Claudian, again, is aiming to shock his audience, and literal truth is not of the essence.[34]

This material aside, the agreement surely gave Alaric a high-ranking military command, to judge by Claudian's words, in Illyricum. Claudian does also mention Thracian arms-factories (*Get.* 533 ff.), but this is perhaps poetic licence (cf. p. 185). Eutropius had ceded west Illyricum to Stilicho, and the Goths are unlikely to have been settled in Greece or Epirus, so that they were probably established in Macedonia and Dacia. Synesius describes Alaric's potential position in the Senate as alongside the consul, which suggests that he was made an *illustris*, most probably *magister militum per Illyricum*.[35] This would have allowed him to use the arms-factories, as Claudian reports, but this again is surely an image designed primarily to shock. Nevertheless, it seems clear that the treaty with Eutropius fulfilled most of Alaric's aims. The Empire had made him a general, acknowledging his pre-eminence, and perhaps entitling his followers to the pay and benefits of regular Roman troops. Above all, Eutropius' concessions implied greater acceptance of the Goths' independent position on Roman soil.

Of other aspects of the agreement, we have no information. No source tells us whether Alaric and his followers were resettled on the land to return to farming. Indeed, Zosimus' clumsy editing of Eunapius and Olympiodorus means that we lack any narrative account of Alaric's Goths between 395 and 405 (p. 78). Claudian partly fills the gap, but he wrote as Stilicho's propagandist, and is not trustworthy, especially when dealing with the aims of his master's opponents, a role often played by the Goths in these years. Not until Zosimus and others preserve material from Olympiodorus (largely dealing with events after 407), are we provided with reliable information about Alaric and the Empire. It is thus impossible to know whether the 397 agreements resettled the Goths on agricultural land, or guaranteed their economic livelihood by other means, such as the pay and rations allowed

---

[33] *PLRE* ii. 83; cf. *CTh* 4. 12. 7; 6. 28. 6; 11. 14. 3; 16. 8. 12.

[34] Top military officers presided over military courts, before which civilians tended to bring cases, so that the image is coherent; cf. Jones, 487–8.

[35] The accepted interpretation. Cf. Wolfram, 142: Claudian's use of *dux* (*Get.* 535–6) is probably not technical.

regular Roman soldiers.[36] We can be sure, however, that Alaric obtained sufficient financial support to satisfy his followers.

The new agreement had a short life. In autumn 401, Alaric marched into Italy.[37] The treaty of 397 had favourably answered the Goths' demands, but, late in 401, they abandoned the region in which they had occupied land for some twenty-five years, and all political contact with the authorities in Constantinople. They returned to their wagons, and entered new lands and an unfamiliar political context. To do this they must have been convinced that satisfactory relations with Constantinople were no longer possible. The full story of Alaric's expulsion from the east is irrecoverable, but, given no indication to the contrary, the treaty of 397 probably lasted until Eutropius' fall in August 399.[38] An extended political crisis followed, and some insight into how this would have affected Alaric's Goths is provided by Synesius' *De Regno*. Despite appearances, this is not a panegyric, but a political pamphlet denigrating Eutropius' regime, composed some time before its fall. Elsewhere, Synesius shows himself a convinced supporter of Aurelianus, who replaced Eutropius, and Synesius probably wrote the *De Regno* on his behalf.[39] The text devotes much attention to the dangers posed to the Roman state by a large group of autonomous foreigners providing a substantial part of the imperial army under their own leader, who had been given high Roman honours. There can be little doubt that the principal target here is Alaric, and that Synesius was making political capital out of the favourable treaty that Eutropius had been forced to grant the Goths in 397.[70] Synesius concluded that the foreigners should be expelled, or forced to disarm and cultivate the soil: a return to traditional policies for neutralizing dangerous groups of foreigners.

This suggests strongly that the Gothic problem was one of the major issues exploited by Aurelianus in his bid for power.

[36] Liebeschuetz, *Barbarians and Bishops*, 60 cites Claudian *Eutr.* 2. 196–201 to show that the Goths were billeted in cities rather than settled on the land. The passage is rather rhetorical, however, referring to wives showing off in the towns their husbands had conquered. See also p. 217.

[37] See e.g. Schmidt, 436–7; Demougeot, ii. 169 ff.; Wolfram, 150 ff.

[38] *CTh* 9. 40. 17 of 17 Aug. 399 confiscated Eutropius' property.

[39] Barnes, 'Synesius in Constantinople', 106 ff.

[40] *De Regno* 19–21, pp. 43–51; cf. Heather, 'The Anti-Scythian Tirade', esp. 166 ff.

Through Synesius, he indicated that, under a regime headed by himself, the Goths would no longer be part of the eastern Empire's military and political establishments. This was an astute move. While there had probably been little choice (p. 202), Eutropius had concluded a generous treaty with Goths who had just ravaged Greece, giving their leader a high imperial rank. Gothic policy had thus offered Eutropius' opponents a fruitful line of attack. It was also exploited by Claudian, who could find few other specific subjects on which to criticize Eutropius.[41] There can, of course, be a gap between manifesto and practice, but Synesius' evidence indicates that Aurelianus' regime would have broken with Alaric when it came to power in August 399.[42] Hostility between Alaric and Aurelianus was natural; Aurelianus could win power only by deposing Eutropius, to whom Alaric owed all his gains. After seizing power, Aurelianus was too busy holding on to it to attack the Goths directly (see below), so that the break in relations probably took the form of removing their privileges, especially withdrawing any regular payments that had been granted to them. How this was enforced in practice will have depended on the population of Illyricum, caught between imperial orders and the military power of the Goths.

There is a considerable time-lag between August 399 and Alaric's move to Italy, and we have no specific information on Alaric's activities. He may well have been hoping, however, that a regime would come to power with which he could re-establish favourable relations. In spring or summer 400, Gainas and Tribigild brought about the downfall of Aurelianus. An alliance between Aurelianus' brother Caesarius and Gainas produced a new regime, but this lasted only until July 400, when Caesarius seems to have organized a massacre of Gainas' supporters. After this, power was probably retained by Caesarius until 403.[43] Political turmoil continued, however, throughout 400; Gainas attacked Constantinople itself, only to be defeated by Fravittas.

[41] *Eutr.* 2. 194 ff. (esp. 214–18); cf. Cameron, *Claudian*, 126 ff.

[42] Aurelianus probably retained power until spring/summer 400 when ousted by Gainas (Cameron *et al.*, *Barbarians and Politics*). There are, however, many problems; cf. the contributions of Seeck, *Regesten*, 475; Jones, 'Collegiate Prefectures', 78 ff.; Albert, *Goten in Konstantinopel*, 183 ff.; Liebeschuetz, *Barbarians and Bishops*, app. 2.

[43] Cameron *et al.*, *Barbarians and Politics*.

Throughout this period, Alaric could reasonably have retained hopes of readmittance to the eastern Empire's political establishment. The Goths' decision to move to Italy in autumn 401 suggests that Caesarius had in turn refused an alliance on terms acceptable to the Goths.[44] Caesarius' motivation is likely to have resembled his brother's. The Goths were a powerful, independent force, and an agreement with them would have been unpopular after the damage they had caused. The brutal massacre of Gainas' Gothic supporters, some of whom were burnt alive in a church, must also have undermined Alaric's trust in the imperial authorities. Late in 401, the Goths attempted to break the impasse by moving to Italy.

C. *Alaric and Stilicho, 401–408*

In the *De Bello Getico*, Claudian insists that the Goths came to Italy to destroy. Rome, Alaric is made to say, is the only place left for the Goths to conquer (78 ff.; 518 ff.), and, in deliberate contrast, Claudian's employer Stilicho is portrayed as the defender of the civilized world (267 ff., 558 ff.). This cannot be taken as a true account of Gothic motivation.[45] The Goths plundered widely, but a desire for loot is an unlikely motive to induce a whole people to trek across the Julian Alps, and even Claudian hints that Alaric had something else in mind. As Claudian notes, he engaged in negotiations with both west and east (*Get.* 566–7), supposedly in bad faith, and his first move was to besiege Honorius in Ravenna to force him to come to terms (*VI cons. Hon.* 440 ff.). The Goths were probably looking for a new area in which to settle. After Stilicho had checked them in Italy, for instance, they attempted to cross into Raetia or Gaul (*VI cons. Hon.* 229 ff.). This seems to confirm that Alaric now considered it impossible to establish satisfactory relations with the eastern Empire, and needed a new centre for operations. The Goths' view of their own requirements is likely to have been constant, so that Alaric probably wanted the

---

[44] Liebeschuetz, *Barbarians and Bishops*, 61–2 suggests that war between Gainas and Fravittas meant that the Goths could not be supplied with rations, but the eastern Empire could surely have found and transported food if it had wanted to.

[45] Cf. Cameron, *Claudian*, 183–4.

kind of relationship from the western Empire that had come to an end in the east.

As events turned out, the Goths were unable to achieve their aims. An invasion of Raetia by some Vandals allowed them easy passage over the Julian Alps, but by spring 402 Stilicho was ready for battle. There followed two major confrontations: Pollentia on Easter Day 402, and Verona some time in midsummer of the same year.[46] Pollentia was an even contest, and Stilicho subsequently allowed Alaric to retreat with his army largely intact. Even Verona failed to destroy Gothic military power. Claudian presents Alaric bemoaning his losses, and his followers leaving him in droves, but Alaric still had enough strength to contemplate moving on to Gaul or Raetia, and when he next appears in the sources his forces are as formidable as ever.[47] After Verona, nevertheless, the Goths did retreat to the Balkans. Stilicho had not won an outright victory, but had avoided making concessions. In this he was probably aided by logistics. The Goths depended for food on what they had brought with them and what could be taken from the countryside; Stilicho had only to parry their attacks until food-shortages drove them out of Italy. By blocking the other Alpine passes, he could also guarantee that they would retreat to the Balkans.

Stilicho probably refused to come to terms with Alaric for reasons similar to those that had made the eastern Empire break its ties with him. Stilicho's own fall, and Claudian's poetry, suggest that there was an influential party within the governing circles of the western Empire which was hostile to compromising with such independent barbarians.[48] This view was shared by Honorius, who declared in 409 that he would never confer a generalship on one of Alaric's race (Zosimus 5. 48. 4). Practical considerations also made a Gothic alliance unattractive. The Goths were not necessarily violent, but they were a force for instability: a separate people whose loyalties were not given primarily to the emperor. They had their own aims, and between 376 and 382, and again after 395, had shown themselves destructive in pursing them. Always needing to satisfy his followers, Alaric was a dangerous political colleague. In

[46] Barnes, 'Prudentius' *Contra Symmachum*', redates Verona to 403, but the argument turns on whether Stilicho could travel, between Easter and midsummer 402, from north Italy to Rome and back again; this is surely possible.

[47] *VI cons. Hon.* 229 ff.; cf. Cameron, *Claudian*, 186–7.

[48] Christiansen, 'Claudian', 45–54; Bayless, 'Anti-Germanism', 74 ff.

402 tolerated Gothic autonomy must still have seemed an unwelcome departure from normal imperial policy.

Denying Alaric an alliance was also in line with Stilicho's policy towards the east, where relations had improved. In 401 Stilicho recognized the consulship of Fravittas, having spurned Eutropius and Aurelianus in 399 and 400. The year 402 saw the first joint consulship of the imperial brothers since 396, and coins celebrated renewed fraternal concord. Stilicho also seems to have dropped his claim to regency in the east, acknowledging the legitimacy of Caesarius' regime.[49] It was in tune with these developments for Stilicho to uphold in Italy the eastern Empire's decision to refuse Alaric's Goths a privileged position within the state.[50]

On their return to the Balkans, the Goths were thus outlaws. We know little of their activities between 402 and 450. In 405, they were in Epirus; from Zosimus, it has been supposed that they had occupied this area since 402. It is at precisely this point, however, that Zosimus makes the transition between Eunapius and Olympiodorus. Finding references to Alaric's forces occupying Epirus both in Eunapius (referring to events of 397) and in Olympiodorus (the later occupation of 405; cf. Zosimus 5. 26. 1), he supposed, quite incorrectly, that the Goths had been in Epirus for the eight years in between. The point is clarified by Sozomen, who used Olympiodorus but not Eunapius, and who tells us that Alaric went to Epirus in 405, from 'barbarous regions bordering Pannonia and Dalmatia' (*HE* 8. 25. 3–4; 9. 4. 2–4). A precise reading of this would place the Goths in west Illyricum in either Savia or Pannonia II between 402 and 404/5, interpreting the names as those of late-antique provinces.[51] Both Savia and Pannonia II were part, however, of the old, larger province of Pannonia, and it is just as likely that Sozomen is using 'Pannonia' and 'Dalmatia' as broad regional designations. In this case, the Goths returned from Italy to east Illyricum: the provinces of Dacia and Macedonia, where they had probably occupied territory before moving to Italy (see above).

---

[49] Claudian, *VI cons. Hon.* 581 ff. omits claims to regency over Arcadius; cf. Cameron, *Claudian*, 38–51; Bayless, 'Unity of the Roman Empire', 23 ff.

[50] The idea that the East had encouraged Alaric's invasion of Italy is based on a mistaken reading of Claudian: Bayless, 'The Visigothic Invasion', 65–6.

[51] Cf. Schmidt, 441; Liebeschuetz, *Barbarians and Bishops*, 64.

We have only one other reference to the Goths in these years. Relations between east and west quickly turned sour again, Stilicho refusing to recognize the eastern consuls for 404 and 405.[52] One of the issues at stake was the exile of John Chrysostom, about whom Honorius wrote to Arcadius in summer 404. The letter also complains that the eastern authorities had failed to notify the west of devastations in Illyricum.[53] This is surely a reference to Alaric's Goths, and it has been taken to mean that the Goths were supporting themselves by plundering the region.[54] But this was probably more or less the same area the Goths had occupied after 397, and an area repeatedly ravaged could not long remain productive. The Goths had previously shown themselves aware of this in taking only moderate sums from Macedonian cities in *c*.380 (p. 153). Alaric perhaps established a similar regime after 402, and may even have used the Roman administration to obtain what his followers needed. It would have been familiar to them from the years after 397.

Nevertheless, non-recognition implied some kind of long-term threat, and the Goths' position was precarious. It was transformed only when Stilicho decided to seize Illyricum from the eastern Empire; presumably east Illyricum is meant, since he already ruled the western half. Stilicho appointed Jovius praetorian prefect, and made an alliance with Alaric in 404 or 405,[55] granting him the military command he had coveted since 395. The Goths then marched to Epirus, to await Stilicho's arrival.[56] Stilicho's motives are far from transparent. The explanation proposed by Mommsen is that Illyricum was an important recruiting-ground

---

[52] Bayless, 'Unity of the Roman Empire', 30–1.

[53] Having placed the Goths in West Illyricum (n. 51), Liebeschuetz, *Barbarians and Bishops*, 64–5 argues that the devastations reflect their move to Epirus in east Illyricum, and that this was made originally on their own initiative. Sozomen, *HE* 8. 25. 3–4; 9. 4. 2–3 is explicit, however, that the Goths did not move to Epirus until they made an alliance with Stilicho in 404/5. The undated devastations probably correspond to their return to this area from Italy.

[54] *Collectio Avellana*, *ep*. 38 (CSEL 35. 1. 85); cf. Demougeot, ii. 176, 428–9; Wolfram, 152–3.

[55] Date as Liebeschuetz, *Barbarians and Bishops*, 65–6; Demougeot, *De l'unité*, 364 ff. (cf. id. ii. 176) mistakenly places the alliance in 406/7.

[56] Sozomen, *HE* 8. 25. 3 (cf. 9. 4. 2–4) suggests that he was appointed *magister militum*: Schmidt, 441; Matthews, *Western Aristocracies*, 274–5; Wolfram, 153.

and Stilicho wanted recruits.[57] It has also been argued that he was concerned to prevent further Gothic incursions into Italy, so that attacking the eastern Empire was designed to keep Alaric occupied.[58] Or again, Stilicho may still have had his sights set on wielding power in Constantinople.

It is equally possible that his main aim was in fact to add Alaric and his Goths to the military forces of the western Empire. This, in a sense, would be a modification of Mommsen's explanation, since Alaric's Goths were the most effective armed force in east Illyricum at this time. If Stilicho wanted to expand this army, the quickest method available to him was to enlist the Goths, which is exactly what he did in appointing Alaric *magister militum*. Moreover, in 408, Stilicho proposed to send Alaric against the usurper Constantine in Gaul (Zosimus 5. 31. 5), and a year later, after Stilicho's fall, Alaric offered to fight generally for Honorius against his enemies (ibid. 5. 42. 1). The prospect of using the Goths more widely may thus have been an important factor in promoting the alliance. If so, the attack on east Illyricum was perhaps incidental. The Goths had been established in primarily this area since 402, and we can assume that they would have wanted an agreement which gave them a legally recognized position on Roman territory. Later episodes in Italy demonstrate that Alaric was not satisfied with *de facto* control of an area (see below). Stilicho had thus either to move the Goths to lands under his legal control, or extend his control to lands they already held. The first alternative involved upheavals of the kind that Stilicho had resisted in 401/2 when the Goths had invaded Italy in search of a new homeland, so that taking east Illyricum from Constantinople may well have seemed preferable. Relations between east and west were already at a low ebb, and the whole of Illyricum had traditionally belonged to the west.

Plans were curtailed by events beyond Stilicho's control. In 405/6, Radagaisus invaded Italy, and on 31 December 406 several tribal groups crossed the Rhine in force. Perhaps in response, the Roman army in Britain supported a series of usurpers, disaffected

---

[57] 'Stilicho und Alarich', 517 ff.; Claudian frequently refers to his patron's need for manpower: Cameron, *Claudian*, 158, 374 ff. Cameron has shown (ibid. 59 ff. *contra* Mommsen) that these ambitions first surfaced in 405.

[58] Liebeschuetz, *Barbarians and Bishops*, 64–5.

elements eventually gathering behind one Constantine. The rebellion spread quickly across the Channel, taking in large areas of Gaul. Alaric was left in Epirus as Stilicho attempted to counter these invaders and usurpers.[59] A rumour also circulated that Alaric had died, leading Stilicho to delay further. Late in 407 Alaric finally lost patience and advanced on Italy for a second time. Stationing himself in Noricum, he demanded 4,000 lb. of gold as back-pay for the time spent in Epirus. Stilicho persuaded the Senate to pay, but the argument provoked much opposition and weakened his hold on the emperor (Zosimus 5. 29. 5–9). In May 408 Arcadius died, and the split between Stilicho and Honorius widened; both wanted to go to Constantinople. An opposition group won the emperor's confidence, and, in August 408, Stilicho was toppled. A new regime under Olympius committed itself not to compromise with the Goths.[60]

D. *Alaric and the Sack of Rome*

Stilicho's death led to an important reinforcement of Alaric's command. Foreign auxiliaries of the Roman army in Italy deserted to him after their wives and children were massacred (Zosimus 5. 35. 5–6). Zosimus reports that 30,000 men now joined Alaric, but this is too many. These auxiliaries were almost certainly some of Radagaisus' followers, whom Stilicho had incorporated into the army in 406/7.[61] According to Photius' summary of Olympiodorus, 12,000 'nobles' had at this point entered Stilicho's service (fr. 9). Like many other figures for Radagaisus' force,[62] this would suggest a total number that is obviously too high, but it is possible that Olympiodorus' 12,000 originally represented a total figure which Photius later confused. If so, Alaric was joined by about 10,000 recruits. Some confirmation that this is how we should interpret Photius is provided by Zosimus, who reports that, a year or so later, large numbers of slaves brought the total of Alaric's following to 40,000.

---

[59] e.g. Matthews, *Western Aristocracies*, 274–5, 307 ff.; Demougeot, ii. 421 ff.

[60] Zosimus 5. 30. 1–34. 5; cf. Demougeot, *De l'unité*, 397 ff.; Matthews, *Western Aristocracies*, 278 ff.

[61] Cf. Wolfram, 169–70.

[62] Zosimus says he led 400,000 (5. 26. 3 ff.), Orosius 200,000 (7. 37. 4 ff.); Orosius is copied by Marcellinus Comes s.a. 406 (*CM* ii. 68).

This is obviously not consistent with Zosimus' own report that 30,000 recruits had joined Alaric in 408/9, but the figures do add up if Zosimus' 30,000 is itself interpreted as another total figure for the size of Alaric's force. The combined strength of Tervingi and Greuthungi, Alaric's initial power base, was *c.* 20,000 (p. 139), so that if *c.* 10,000 men joined after the massacre, we would expect the total then to have been *c.* 30,000.[63] Survivors of Radagaisus' defeat thus probably increased Alaric's following by about 50 per cent in the summer of 408, and *c.* 10,000 slaves later brought the total to *c.* 40,000.

Much has recently been made of these slaves, who have become a prime piece of evidence for the argument that many, perhaps most, of Alaric's followers were not really Goths.[64] This question will be pursued below (see the Conclusion), but it is worth noting that most of these slaves are also likely to have been ex-followers of Radagaisus. Apart from those drafted into the army, so many of Radagaisus' followers were sold into slavery that the bottom fell out of the market (Orosius 7. 37. 13 ff.). It was not unknown for prisoners to be released *en masse* at low prices on to the slave-market in the late Empire, actions which stimulated a trade that was otherwise sluggish in comparison with the great days of imperial expansion.[65] It is likely, therefore, that the very large numbers of slaves who joined Alaric were mostly those followers of Radagaisus sold into slavery only some four years before, now able to exploit the anarchy caused by Stilicho's fall and the Goths' advance to escape from bondage.[66]

This general context also explains why Alaric continued to look towards the west for a negotiated settlement in 408, even though Olympius' regime was refusing to negotiate with him. Stilicho's fall had set in motion a fierce power-struggle, with Olympius purging Stilicho's supporters, and instituting treason-trials to prove that Stilicho had aspired to the imperial throne (Zosimus 5.

[63] Maenchen-Helfen, 459 takes a gloomy view of Olympiodorus, but everything suggests he produced a precise narrative; mistakes are more likely in those reusing his work at a later date.

[64] Liebeschuetz, *Barbarians and Bishops*, 75 ff.

[65] De Ste. Croix, *Class Struggle*, 226 ff. Apart from those turned into *coloni* (cf. p. 123), large numbers of Sciri were also sold into slavery in 409: Sozomen, *HE* 9. 5.

[66] Greuthungi sold as slaves and distributed as *coloni* seem, similarly, to have swollen Tribigild's revolt in 399; cf. Heather, 'Anti-Scythian Tirade', 156–7.

35. 1–4). The situation was further destabilized by the invaders who had crossed the Rhine in 406, and the usurper Constantine, who by 408 was even threatening Spain.[67] Circumstances must have seemed ripe for the Goths to extract a favourable agreement. At this point, they move outside the main geographical focus of this study, but events will be followed, if in less detail, down to 418, when stability finally returned to Gotho-Roman relations.

Alaric's first approach to Honorius from Noricum was conciliatory, offering peace in return for a 'small' sum of money and a hostage exchange, after which the Goths would retreat to Pannonia. Honorius, however, prepared for war (Zosimus 5. 36. 1–3). Alaric then gathered his forces, ordering his brother-in-law Athaulf to join him with the Goths and Huns he commanded in Pannonia. Athaulf's group seems to have been guarding Alaric's line of retreat, and was already, in all probability, an integral part of his force (App. B). Without waiting for Athaulf, Alaric advanced to Rome, and besieged the city in winter 408/9 to pressurize the imperial government into negotiations. Its inhabitants were reduced to such dire straits that they came to terms. The Goths were promised gifts, and leading Romans went to Ravenna to persuade Honorius to negotiate. The emperor vacillated.[68]

This pattern repeated itself throughout the next year and a half. Alaric used the imperial capital as a bargaining counter; at different points the two sides came close to agreement. The fall of Olympius in April 409, for instance, led to a truce with the new regime headed by that Jovius, now praetorian prefect of Italy, who had been Stilicho's prefect in Illyricum. He had already co-operated with Alaric once, and, not surprisingly, was more open to compromise. The two worked out a detailed agreement, but it was destroyed by Honorius' intransigence. At the moment of ratification, he declared that he would never appoint one of Alaric's race *magister militum*. The emperor also rejected a more moderate offer which, much to everyone's surprise, Alaric made immediately

---

[67] Matthews, *Western Aristocracies*, 307 ff.; Demougeot, *De l'unité*, 376 ff.

[68] Zosimus 5. 36. 1–44; Sozomen, *HE* 9. 6. Good accounts of Alaric in Italy are Matthews, *Western Aristocracies*, 286 ff. and 'Olympiodorus of Thebes', 79–97; Demougeot, *De l'unité*, 432 ff.

afterwards (Zosimus 5. 45–51; Sozomen, *HE* 9. 7). This provoked an audacious response. With the co-operation of the Senate, Alaric made his own candidate, Attalus, emperor in December 409. Again, his main aim was to pressurize Honorius, for in the following summer, he readily deposed Attalus in return for peace (Zosimus 6. 6–12; Sozomen, *HE* 9. 8). Just, however, as Alaric was advancing on Ravenna to confirm the agreement, he was attacked by his old rival Sarus, seemingly acting on personal initiative. In frustration, Alaric turned his forces around, and sacked Rome; the date was 24 August 410 (Zosimus 6. 13 (incomplete); Sozomen, *HE* 9. 9). The sack, then, was incidental; the Goths wanted to force Honorius into a formal peace-agreement, and besieging Rome was a means to that end. The fall of the Empire's capital city actually represents a Gothic failure.

Although they were in the end denied, some of Alaric's aims emerge clearly from his various negotiations with Honorius. Above all, he wanted a fully recognized position for his people within the western Empire. This is demonstrated by the moderate offer made after Honorius had destroyed the settlement worked out with Jovius. Alaric then dropped all demands for a general-ship, an annual subsidy in gold, and lands close to Ravenna (Zosimus 5. 48. 3). These were the kind of demands he had been making of different imperial regimes since 395. The subsidy would have enriched his followers, the generalship would have entrenched him at court, and his followers would have been to hand around Ravenna to reinforce their leader's position. Yet he was willing to forgo all this, at a moment when he was militarily dominant in Italy, for no more than recognition of the Goths' right to exist as part of the western Empire and an unspecified amount of corn per year (Zosimus 5. 50. 3). This strikingly illustrates where Alaric felt that the balance of power ultimately lay. At this particular moment his Goths had the *de facto* power to establish themselves somewhere in the western Empire, but this was not sufficient. Alaric wanted Ravenna's sanction, and was willing to trade present advantage for full recognition. This suggests that he felt that imperial power would revive, and wanted a fully legal settlement against that eventuality. Given its antiquity, probably no contemporary, early in the fifth century, could have envisaged the western Empire's permanent collapse. It still controlled the revenues of North Africa, and enough of Italy and Spain to fuel a recovery.

Otherwise, Alaric attempted to extract what concessions he could. High on the list was a generalship: a symbol and practical guarantee of long-term security. When he felt himself to hold the initiative, he pressed in addition for an annual subsidy in gold, and larger corn-supplies; both would have strengthened his hold on the loyalties of his followers. The proposed site of a Gothic settlement similarly varied. From Jovius, Alaric demanded lands in a strategic position on either side of the Alps in Venetia, Noricum, and Dalmatia. The Goths would then have controlled vital communication routes, and could have intervened quickly at Ravenna.

Less clear, however, is the form that any settlement would have taken; were the Goths to return to farming? Alaric made two territorial demands and it has recently been argued that the demand in each case was not for land to farm, but for an area in which Alaric's force could be billeted. The fact that Alaric demanded corn-supplies is taken to show that he did not envisage farming. The language used by the sources is inconclusive; Zosimus tells us merely that the Goths wanted areas to 'live in' (οἰκεῖν, 5. 48. 3; πρὸς οἴκησιν, 5. 50. 3). This could represent a demand for agricultural land or for billets, but, overall, the evidence in favour of billeting is less than convincing. As we have seen, Alaric's followers were very much a people; he had gathered most of the treaty Goths behind him in 395, and Roman sources perceived him as the leader of the Goths who crossed the Danube in 376. It is a priori likely that such a group would have wanted, from any negotiated agreement with the Roman state, secure entitlement to agricultural land and its income. This was certainly the case in 418 when the wanderings of Alaric's Goths finally came to an end (see below). Some confirmation of this is provided by Orosius, who reports that Alaric had 'humbly sought somewhere to settle' from Stilicho (7. 38).

Aims could have changed between 408–10 and 418, but there is no good evidence for this. In particular, the demand for annual corn-supplies does not tell decisively against farming. We need to know whether the supplies were to feed all Alaric's followers, or a part; whether they were a supplement, or the Goths' entire income. What evidence there is suggests that they were merely a supplement. In 416 the Goths were given 600,000 modii of wheat. This was perhaps not meant as an annual grant, but it brings the problem of feeding Alaric's force by corn-supplies clearly into perspective. At official rates, this represents a year's ration for some 15,000 men (or perhaps 20,000).[69] Alaric's Goths, however, consisted of rather more than 15,000 (even allowing for losses between 410 and 416), and there were also women and children, who would have taken the total well past 100,000. At official rates, the corn supplied in 416 would have lasted the Goths about two months.

This makes it seem doubtful that the Roman state would have wanted to take on the responsibility of feeding such a large group from its own stores. Food rations, though often commuted to cash payments, were an important part of military pay,[70] and this suggests an alternative explanation of the corn-supplies discussed in the negotiations. Military alliance was part of every contemplated agreement between Goths and Romans, and corn-supplies may have been viewed as a return for military service, their size calculated according to the number of troops notionally held ready for action. It is impossible to prove that Alaric's Goths already wanted agricultural land in 409/10, but it does seem unlikely that the Empire would have wanted to supply them. Supplies are thus more likely to have been merely a part of the Goths' income. A good final indication of this is that, in his moderate mood, Alaric was willing to settle for as much corn each year as the Empire thought sufficient (Zosimus 5. 50. 3). If such supplies were really to be the Goths' entire income, he could hardly have left the determination of their size to the Romans. The Goths may also have received supplies even after taking up lands in southern Gaul, which would confirm their supplementary role.[71] Room for doubt remains, but a land settlement was probably the only reasonable way of providing for so many Goths.

---

[69] Jones, iii. 39 n. 65; 191 n. 44; 217 n. 23; cf. Liebeschuetz, *Barbarians and Bishops*, 73.

[70] Jones, 623 ff. (esp. 626 ff.).

[71] Philostorgius, *HE* 12. 4–5 (= Olympiodorus fr. 26. 2) records that supplies and land for farming were granted to the Goths in 416/18, but this is only Photius' summary; perhaps the supplies were to tide them over until lands were allocated; cf. p. 245 for similar arrangements.

E. *Italy to Gaul*

After the sacking of Rome, the amount of detailed information available to us declines dramatically. Of the rest of Alaric's reign, we know only that he marched south, contemplated an attack on Sicily which was frustrated by the weather, and then died of disease. His brother-in-law Athaulf succeeded him and ruled for five years.[72] No more than a sketchy account of Athaulf's reign can be reconstructed, but he seems to have followed similar policies to Alaric. As Alaric's second in command, he must have already made a substantial contribution to them. During the first year of Athaulf's reign, the Goths remained in Italy, but moved to Gaul in 412. Once there, Athaulf swung Gothic support behind the usurper Jovinus, whose rebellion had broken out in 411. Supporting a usurper was a good lever to force Honorius into an agreement, as Alaric had found with Attalus, and Athaulf's main interest remained an accord with Ravenna. When Jovinus proved difficult, the Goths swapped sides, forcing the usurper to surrender to Honorius, a change of policy instigated by the praetorian prefect Dardanus. At this point, Athaulf must have felt that a settlement was close. We know only that it was to involve grain-supplies;[73] food was hard to come by in war-torn Gaul.

A full agreement did not follow, however, since Athaulf refused to return the emperor's sister Galla Placidia, who had been captured in Rome (Olympiodorus frr. 22. 1–3). Instead, Athaulf married her in January 414 at Narbonne, celebrating the event in Roman fashion at the urban villa of one Ingenuus, a leading Gallo-Roman aristocrat.[74] This act expressed Athaulf's determination to be part of the Empire, a leader of troops who had married into the imperial family. Such was also the tone of his celebrated remark that, after some hesitation, he had decided to use Gothic military power in defence of 'Romania', rather than replace it with 'Gothia'.[75] His plans received a further boost when Placidia bore him a son, after which he became 'even more friendly towards the

[72] Refs. as *PLRE* i. 48; cf. Schmidt, 452 ff.; Demougeot, ii. 464 ff.; Wolfram, 161 ff.

[73] Olympiodorus frr. 18, 20. See generally Matthews, *Western Aristocracies*, 313 ff.

[74] Philostorgius, *HE* 12. 4 = Olympiodorus fr. 24.

[75] Orosius 7. 43. 2–3; cf. Thompson, 'Fritigern to Euric', 113–14; Wallace-Hadrill, 'Gothia and Romania', 25 ff.

Romans' (Olympiodorus fr. 26). The reason for this is easily understood. The son was named Theodosius: grandson of one emperor by that name and first cousin to another. The ruling western emperor, Honorius, was the child's uncle, and himself childless. Athaulf was thus the father of a child with some claim to be Honorius' heir, and had every interest in rebuilding relations.

As events turned out, no agreement was reached between Goths and Empire in Athaulf's lifetime. His son died shortly after birth, and the Goths came under increasing pressure from Constantius, *magister militum* and the main power behind Honorius' throne, who restored stability to the western Empire. Having defeated the usurper Constantine in 411, he had organized, with Dardanus, Athaulf's change of sides which defeated Jovinus in 413. He then turned his attention to the third great source of Gallic instability: the Goths. When Athaulf refused to return Galla Placidia, war began in earnest in 414. Constantius drove the Goths into Spain, using an economic blockade imposed by land and sea. In response, Athaulf raised Attalus to the purple again, and made himself *magister militum.*[76]

The Goths' lack of food became more pressing, however, and discontent grew. Dissent surfaced in the person of the unlikely-named Dubius, a groom with a grudge, who mortally wounded Athaulf in summer 415. Athaulf had killed Dubius' former lord, who is unnamed, but described as 'a king of part of the Goths'. On his death-bed, Athaulf passed the leadership to his brother, but dynastic continuity was destroyed by Sergeric, brother of that Sarus who had previously fought Alaric. Sergeric took over, 'by conspiracy and coup rather than by the Gothic law of succession' (Olympiodorus fr. 26. 1). This involved the slaughter of Athaulf's children, and probably also of the brother who was supposed to succeed, since nothing more is heard of him. If, as seems likely, the groom's anonymous former master killed by Athaulf had been Sarus, Sergeric might even have been behind the assassination.[77] Sergeric's rule lasted only seven days before he too was killed; Orosius tells us that he was 'inclined to peace' (7. 43. 8–9). Succession next fell on Vallia, who had no recorded family ties with previous rulers. Orosius reports that he was elected to carry on the war (7. 43. 10), but it did not go well for the Goths. In 416

[76] Schmidt, 457–8; Demougeot, ii. 466 ff.; Wolfram, 163–4.
[77] Cf. p. 197.

Vallia tried to transfer them to North Africa, but a number of ships were wrecked. In the face of Constantius' pressure, and lacking a viable alternative, Vallia finally made peace in the same year. Placidia was sent back to Honorius in return for food, and Gothic military power swung behind the Empire.[78] For two years, the Goths attacked Vandals and Alans in northern Spain,[79] before being settled in southern Gaul in 418.

We have no detailed information about the agreements of 416 and 418; their terms must be reconstructed from chronicle references and subsequent Gothic activity. Orosius alleges that the peace was very favourable to the Romans; the Goths handed over hostages of the highest rank, and agreed to fight for the Empire (7. 43. 12–13). This is confirmed by the Goths' activities in Spain, and we again find them fighting there for the Empire in the 420s.[80] The agreement would not appear, however, to have been a *foedus* where a large body of Goths became a permanent part of the Roman army, receiving large sums of money annually for their upkeep. We have no record of such payments after 418, and, perhaps more significantly, given our lack of sources, no Gallic Gothic leader ever became a *magister militum*, unlike those in the Balkans in the 470s and 480s (see Part III). We can perhaps guess, therefore, that, as at other points, the Goths received payment only when military service was required, and that terms had to be negotiated on each occasion. As in the past, the overall form of the agreement may have been a *foedus* after *deditio* (cf. p. 158). Of other arrangements, such as annual gifts, we have no reliable information, but these are likely to have been used to maintain the relationship, along, perhaps, with an annual grain-ration.

The Goths themselves were settled in the Garonne valley from Toulouse to Bordeaux.[81] It used to be accepted that the system governing army-billeting (*hospitalitas*) was adapted to make land available, which the Goths then farmed. This vision of barbarian settlement was applied quite generally to all tribal groups who took land in the western Empire in the fifth century. More recently, it has been argued, largely on the basis of evidence from Ostrogothic

---

[78] Olympiodorus frr. 29. 1, 30; Philostorgius, *HE* 12. 4–5 (= Olympiodorus fr. 26. 2); Orosius 7. 43. 10 ff.

[79] Refs. as *PLRE* ii. 1148.

[80] e.g. Hyd. 77, s.a. 421 (*CM* ii. 20).

[81] Hyd. 69, s.a. 418 (*CM* ii. 19); Prosp. 1271, s.a. 419 (*CM* i. 469).

Italy, that tax-revenues rather than landed estates were divided with the barbarians: one-third going to the king, one-third to his followers, and the rest retained by the local Roman authorities. The argument is in part convincing. Billeting rules have been shown to have nothing to do with land-allocations, and much of the evidence from later barbarian kingdoms is concerned with tax-revenues.[82] Nevertheless, the texts do indicate that land itself was at stake in 418, and there seems no reason not to accept this evidence.[83] Inferences from later Italian circumstances (and those of other barbarian kingdoms) are not directly relevant, and it is very dangerous to apply a single model to all barbarian settlements. The 418 settlement followed Roman military successes, which forced the Goths to make peace from a relatively unfavourable position. Conditions were thus quite different from those of Italy after 493, where the Ostrogoths were dominant and the western Empire no longer in existence.[84] In 418, then, the Goths probably returned to the land, and such a settlement may always have been envisaged as part of a lasting solution to Gotho-Roman relations. If not, the Goths' experience of hunger between 410 and 416 will have taught them that it was better to have real power over their economic position by controlling the lands that fed them, rather than to be dependent on food-supplies and at the mercy of the Roman state.

In many ways, then, the 418 settlement is a measure of the extent to which the western Empire had recovered under Constantius. At the height of his ambitions, Alaric had demanded a military alliance, a land-grant close to the political heart of the Empire, the post of *magister militum*, annual payments in gold, and a large quantity of corn per year (Zosimus 5. 48. 3). Similar, if not greater pretensions had been shown by Athaulf in marrying a

---

[82] Goffart, *Barbarians and Romans*, esp. 103 ff. (followed e.g. by Wolfram, 222 ff.). See also Durliat, 'Le salaire de la paix', esp. 55–60.

[83] Esp. Philostorgius, *HE* 12. 4–5 (= Olympiodorus fr. 26. 2) reporting that the Goths were given 'land for farming' (χώρας εἰς γεωργίαν). The other texts are collected by Burns, 'The Settlement of 418'; cf. Liebeschuetz, *Barbarians and Bishops*, 73–4; Claude, 'Zur Ansiedlung'. Goffart's attempt, *Barbarians and Romans*, 104 n. 2 to undermine Philostorgius' evidence is unconvincing.

[84] *Contra* Goffart, *Barbarians and Romans*, 103. The extent to which tax was taken rather than land is likely to have increased as the Roman state weakened, these revenues being its lifeblood. Even in Ostrogothic Italy, the Goths probably wanted land as well: Barnish, 'Barbarian Settlement', 174 ff.

princess of the purple and naming his son Theodosius. The remark that he would henceforth use Gothic military power to uphold the Roman state displays a similar arrogance, as though it were Athaulf's decision whether the Empire should continue or not. Constantius successfully resisted such attempts by the Goths to thrust themselves centre-stage into imperial politics. The final settlement of 418 is, in fact, much closer to Alaric's most modest set of demands: a military alliance, a land-grant somewhere on the frontier (specifically Noricum), and as much corn as the Romans determined his followers should have (no gold payments and no generalship: Zosimus 5. 50. 3). In 409, these had surprised everyone with their moderation, but Alaric's estimate of the latent strength of the western Empire seems to have been largely correct. After 418, Vallia and Theoderic I remained without generalships, perched on the edge of Roman territory beside the Atlantic ocean.

This is not to say that the Goths' efforts over a generation had achieved nothing. In 395, the Romans could still contemplate revising the treaty of 382. Theodosius seems to have been happy to watch Gothic nobles killing one another, and, perhaps deliberately, managed to make the Goths bear the brunt of the fighting at the Frigidus. Such measures could have prepared the ground for enforcing detribalization upon the Goths, either by military action, or perhaps more likely, by wearing the Goths down over a longer period. Any fighting eroded Gothic numbers, and dissensions among their leaders disrupted unity, so that such policies promoted a creeping detribalization without exposing Roman forces to the dangers of battle. By 418 the issues had changed. Gotho-Roman relations were no longer concerned with whether the Goths should exist or not as an autonomous entity on Roman soil, but with how precisely this entity should be integrated into the Empire: should the Goths be totally immersed in imperial political life, or kept to the periphery? A generation of struggle had shown it was no longer possible to contemplate the total defeat of the Goths.

The change of policy incorporated in the 382 treaty had been in part dictated by temporary imperial weakness after Hadrianople, but, by 418, the formation of a new Gothic political unit had altered the balance of power between Goth and Roman more fundamentally. Alaric first united the Tervingi and Greuthungi; he then added another 10,000 or so recruits from barbarian contingents in the Roman army, who were probably survivors of Radagaisus' force, and large numbers of runaway slaves (again probably survivors from Radagaisus) brought the total to *c.* 40,000 fighting men. There may well have been losses by 418, but this unprecedentedly large force changed the political agenda; it was now impossible for the Goths to be destroyed.

Alaric's success was also responsible for the other major change between 382 and 418. In 382 the Empire had refused to recognize any Gothic leaders as pre-eminent; the ousting of Fritigern, Alatheus, and Saphrax may even have been a condition of the peace (Ch. 3). The reign of Alaric, its achievement consolidated by Athaulf, forced the Empire to modify this approach. From 397 at the latest, the imperial authorities of east and west had to negotiate with a single Gothic ruler, and this continued after Alaric's death. Even if no generalship was forthcoming, one leader represented all the Goths, and the agreements of 416 and 418 were made with him. Important Romans even had to serve as hostages at the court of Gothic kings (Sid. Ap. *Carm.* 7. 213 ff.). By 418 the Goths had won full recognition of their independence from the Roman state.

There is, of course, a Roman side to the treaty as well, but the *concilium* of the Gallic provinces has been explored elsewhere,[85] and we have already strayed some way from the Balkans. Suffice it to say that the treaty of 418 was in many ways a fair measure of the balance of power at this date. A resurgent Empire had restrained the Goths' most extravagant ambitions, but the Goths were now firmly entrenched on Roman soil under a recognized king. A temporary break with traditional policies of detribalization had become permanent coexistence. In 418 it was impossible to say how matters would develop. The emergence of a separate Gothic kingdom in Gaul was no certainty,[86] but that story lies beyond the scope of this study.

[85] See Matthews, *Western Aristocracies*, 333 ff. with refs.: cf. Heather, 'Visigothic Kingdom'.

[86] Heather, 'Visigothic Kingdom'.

PART III

THE FORMATION OF THE OSTROGOTHS
GOTHS IN THE BALKANS, 450–489

INTRODUCTION TO PART III

Our first wave of Goths left the Balkans in 408 under the leadership of Alaric. The next two or three generations saw the rise and dramatic fall of a new power in the Balkans landscape: the Huns. Much of the history of the first half of the fifth century is very obscure, in large part owing to the loss of the histories of Olympiodorus and Priscus. Olympiodorus' work ran down to 425, and dealt to some extent with events north of the Danube, but little now survives from the period after *c*.410. Priscus' account began in the 430s at the latest, but surviving fragments concentrate on the Huns. Many of the Goths who made up the second wave of Gothic immigration into the Balkans, the focus of our attention in the third part of this study, were subject to Hunnic dominion up to *c*.450, and find no independent mention (much as peoples subject to the Goths are not mentioned in fourth-century sources: p. 90).

Archaeological evidence is, in a sense, more helpful. Modern methods, for instance, are making Sîntana de Mureş–Černjachov sites yield more information, and it has become apparent that they were not all suddenly abandoned. A much more differentiated picture of the westward movement, through the Carpathians and into the middle Danube region, of a number of distinct Germanic groups between *c*.375 and 450, is beginning to fill in the period for which we lack literary evidence.[1] This also corresponds to what literary evidence there is. For instance, two groups of Greuthungi came to the Danube at ten-year intervals (376 and 386: p. 13), and it was then another twenty years before Radagaisus' Goths crossed the river in 405/6, perhaps forcing an entry over the middle rather than the lower Danube.[2] Some rich burials also bear witness to the growth of a wealthy class who administered and

---

[1] Bierbrauer, 'Zur Gliederung des ostgermanischen Fundstoffs des 5. Jahrhunderts in Sudosteuropa', 131 ff. with refs.; cf. Horedt, 'Wandervölker und Romanen', 117 ff.; Wolfram, 254–5. Compare previous suggestions of a sudden break: e.g. Zasetskaja, 'The Role of the Huns', 130–1.

[2] Zosimus 5. 26. 3 mentions both the Rhine and Danube, suggesting that Radagaisus came from the middle Danube rather than further east.

benefited from the Hunnic empire.[3] But archaeological evidence is not specific enough to illuminate the history of particular Gothic political units, and can be of only marginal assistance to us here. Even more important, Gothic graves have not been identified within the Roman Balkans. What follows, therefore, can be no more than an introductory sketch of the history of the Goths who stayed north of the Danube after 376.

As we have seen, the Huns did not suddenly conquer everything north of the Danube in 376. Several Gothic groups maintained their independence there for at least a decade, and it is not until *c*.400 that a Hunnic group, that of Uldin, is attested as the major power facing the Empire across the Danube frontier (p. 135). The situation in the late fourth century was thus a far cry from the 440s, when Attila's empire held most of the tribes north of both the lower and middle Danube in its sway. Of the events leading to the creation of this empire, we are woefully ignorant. It does seem, however, to have involved two processes. On the one hand, increasing numbers of tribal groups (Goths, Gepids, Rugi, Heruli, Sarmatians, etc.) were brought under Hunnic dominion. I am inclined to believe, for instance, that the mass exodus of groups from the middle Danube region in 405/6 (both Radagaisus' Goths and the tribes who made the Rhine crossing in December 406 seem to have come from this region) represents another stage in the assertion of Hunnic power.[4] The Huns may have been pressing upon them directly or through intermediaries, as in 376 when the exodus of the Tervingi was caused as much by a knock-on effect, the westward movement of the Greuthungi, as by direct Hunnic action. At the same time, the Hunnic tribes themselves seem to have become increasingly united, until, under Attila, they formed a single body. In the previous generation, they had been divided

[3] Horedt, 'Apahida II', 366–7; Horedt–Protase, 'Das zweite Fürstengrab', 174 ff.; Harhoiu, *The Treasure from Pietroasa*, 23 ff. Such finds might be associated with the aristocrats (Hunnic and other), whom Priscus encountered at Attila's court; on these, see Maenchen-Helfen, 192–5, 198–9.

[4] On Radagaisus, see n. 2. The Rhine crossing of 406 included Vandals, Alans, and Sueves, of whom at least the Vandals had previously been in the middle Danube region, opposite Noricum and Raetia in 402: Claudian, *Get.* 363–5, 414–15. Cf. also Jerome, *ep.* 123. 16 mentioning Quadi and *hostes Pannonii*. Maenchen-Helfen, 60–1 argues against such a characterization of these events, but there is no reason to suppose that the model Ammianus gives us for the movements of 376 does not apply here too.

between two of Attila's uncles, and it was only Attila's murder of his brother Bleda which transformed the situation.[5]

We must see the history of Gothic tribes north of the Danube against this general background. There is no specific information about when precisely different Gothic groups were conquered, but probably not all Goths fell to the Huns at the same time. At least, we encounter a number of Gothic groups in later sources, whose relations with the Huns had been far from identical. One group under the leadership of the Amal family, about whom we shall have much more to say, had reasserted its independence by 455, for instance, very shortly after Attila's death (see Ch. 7), while other Goths continued to be ruled by the sons of Attila into the late 460s.[6] More Goths in the Crimea, on the other hand, seem to have used the geographical advantages of the area to maintain their independence throughout the period of Hunnic domination (Procopius, *Wars* 8. 5. 15 ff.); another group may have been rescued from the Huns by the eastern Empire in the 420s (p. 262). As we might expect from our survey of the Gothic tribes of the south-western USSR and Romania before the Huns, a number of separate Gothic political units experienced quite different histories as Hunnic power rose and fell north of the Danube between *c*.375 and 450.

Of the various Gothic groups who appear—some very fleetingly—in the sources, we shall be concerned with essentially two. First, the Amal-led Goths who come to our attention in the middle Danube region some time in the 450s, and had certainly been part of Attila's empire. Jordanes devotes some space to their experience of Hunnic dominion, but this information is highly problematic. Much better evidence of their subjection is their participation in the battle of the Catalaunian Plains (*Getica* 38. 197 ff.; esp. the detail at 40. 209), and the more convincing account of how they regained independence (p. 249). It is unclear when the Huns had first conquered them. Our second Goth group were already established in the Thracian diocese of the Roman Empire by the

[5] See Maenchen-Helfen, 81 ff.; this should be compared with Ammianus' famous description (seemingly borne out by events) of the Huns' political disunity in 376 (31. 2. 7).

[6] Priscus fr. 49. The Goths mentioned here may have something to do with the Gothic king Bigelis who was killed in Thrace in the late 460s (Jordanes, *Romana* 336); cf. *PLRE* ii. 229.

late 460s. As we shall see, they enjoyed a special relationship with Constantinople, which, together with other evidence, might suggest that they had entered the Empire some time previously. It is also likely that some of them, at least, had again suffered Hunnic domination for a time. As the Amal-led Goths threw off Hunnic hegemony and asserted their power in the middle Danube region, they became aware of the favour enjoyed by this second group. Our main concern, indeed, will be the effects of the rivalry that developed between them, both for imperial honours and for primacy in the Gothic tribal world. It came to a head after 473, when the Pannonian Goths moved into lands directly controlled by the eastern Empire, initiating a decade of direct competition. As the necessary backdrop to our study of this conflict, it is important first briefly to survey the major sources from which the creation of the Ostrogoths must be reconstructed.

Jordanes

The third main subsection of Jordanes' *Getica* is devoted to the independent 'Ostrogoths', describing the Amal-led Goths from the time of the Hunnic invasions to the overthrow of their kingdom in Italy. A not insubstantial part of this (48. 246–57. 297) deals with the matter that chiefly concerns us here, their time in the Balkans. It has been thought that Priscus was the source for this material, as far, at least, as the Goths' move into Macedonia (56. 283). Priscus being a reliable contemporary source, Jordanes' account could be considered trustworthy by association.[7] Priscus is occasionally cited in the *Getica*, including once in this section (49. 254–5),[8] but his work does not seem to underlie the bulk of Jordanes' narrative. At 53. 272–3, for instance, Jordanes describes the second war between the Pannonian Goths and the Huns led by Attila's son 'Dintzic'. The son also appears in Priscus, but the name is consistently spelt 'Dengizich', suggesting that Jordanes used a non-Priscian tradition.[9] Likewise, a list of refugee peoples who settled in the eastern Empire after Attila's death would seem to come from Jordanes' personal knowledge. Before his *conversio*, he had been secretary to a commander of allied troops (50. 265–6),

---

[7] e.g. Mommsen, pp. xxxiv ff.

[8] Priscus is also cited at *Getica* 24. 123, 34. 178, 35. 183, 42. 222.

[9] Priscus frr. 46, 48. 1; Blockley, i. 113–14.

which combines with references in the passage to his own day to suggest that he himself was the source.[10] More generally, the *Getica* is Goth-centred; other tribal groups and the Empire itself appear only as they affect the Goths. In the surviving fragments of Priscus, by contrast, foreign peoples (including Goths) appear only when they come into contact with the Empire. The difference is underlined by the one event common to them both. Priscus mentions a war between the Goths and the Sciri because both sides appealed to the emperor Leo (fr. 45), Jordanes refers to the war, but ignores any imperial involvement (53. 275 ff.).[11] The *Getica*'s account is also marred by omissions and distortions of a kind which are unlikely to have originated with Priscus.

Its whole account of the Pannonian Goths' early history, for instance, is unconvincing, thoroughly distorting Valamer's career. Purely Gothic events of *c.*450 have been transformed into an account of Hunno-Gothic relations after 375, and the *Getica* does not realize that it was Valamer who initially united the Pannonian Goths, defeating Amal and non-Amal rivals (p. 240). Its account of how these Goths settled in Pannonia (on the middle Danube) also fails to inspire confidence. According to the *Getica*, the Goths remained in south Russia (the Scythian Pontus) until after the Gepids defeated the Huns at the battle of the river Nedao (*c.*454). This forced the Huns to abandon Dacia to the Gepids and return to their old homes in Scythia (i.e. the south-western USSR). Rather than confront the Huns, the Goths asked for and received Pannonia from the eastern Empire. According to the *Getica*, therefore, the Goths moved to the middle Danube only after *c.*450 (50. 263 ff.).[12] But archaeological evidence suggests that at least some Goths had moved westwards from the south-western USSR long before this (p. 227), and the Huns were to remain a force around the Danube into the 460s.[13] The *Getica*'s account of how the Amal-led Goths came to take Pannonia is thus far from convincing.

Other problems in this part of the *Getica* are the result of more deliberate distortion. Theoderic the Amal's struggle with the

[10] Cf. Macartney, 'The End of the Huns', 112–13; Blockley, ii. 392 n. 119.

[11] Cf. Pohl, 'Die Gepiden', 264. See also Blockley, i. 113–14.

[12] *Getica* 48. 246 confirms that Jordanes sees the Ostrogoths as living in the south-western USSR while under Hunnic domination.

[13] Maenchen-Helfen, 108 ff.

Thracian Goths and their leader Theoderic the son of Triarius (also known as Strabo, 'the Squinter') has been largely suppressed. This preserves the fiction that the Amals alone had provided legitimate Gothic kings since time immemorial. Likewise, years of conflict between Theoderic the Amal and the emperor Zeno (474–91) are ignored, in order to portray their relationship as one of uninterrupted harmony (57. 289 ff.). The ultimate point of this was to legitimize Theoderic's seizure of power in Italy (p. 56). There is, finally, a suspicion of pro-Gothic bias in the account of the wars of the Pannonian Goths. After Valamer's death in battle against the Sciri, for instance, his Goths virtually annihilate them in revenge (53. 276). Jordanes may well overstate the Gothic vengeance, since Valamer's followers were left in disarray and fled (*confugerunt*) to his brother Thiudimer (54. 278). Priscus records merely that the two sides disengaged after the first encounter to look for allies (fr. 45). This should perhaps make us suspicious of other unconfirmed reports of Gothic success.

Nevertheless, Jordanes does provide much information on the Pannonian Goths, some of which is confirmed elsewhere. Priscus confirms that a treaty existed between them and the emperor Marcian (fr. 37), and that they warred with the Sciri (fr. 45); John of Antioch confirms that they were settled in Pannonia and that succession passed from Valamer to Thiudimer to Theoderic (fr. 206. 2). A second account of Theoderic's time as a hostage can be found in Theophanes AM 5977 (130–1 de Boor). The *Getica* also preserves a fairly detailed biography of Theoderic, allowing the chronology of his early life to be reconstructed. Alongside this, the cities and routes mentioned in the course of Thiudimer's march into Illyricum in 473 correspond with what existed on the ground (56. 285 ff.).

Making due allowance for distortion, there remains much of value in Jordanes' account. And in general, the characteristics of this section correspond very much to what we might expect from Cassiodorus' lost *Gothic History*. Detailed knowledge of aspects of the period in the Balkans and of Theoderic's life is combined with deliberate omissions and distortions, which strengthen Amal claims to unique pre-eminence, and legitimize the seizure of Italy. Cassiodorus should still have been able to collect quite full information on these events in *c*.525.[14] At the same time, some

[14] Cf. Heather, 'Cassiodorus', 125–6.

matters, such as the invasion of Italy, remained politically sensitive, requiring careful handling.

Priscus of Panium

Had it survived, Priscus' history would have been a major source for the mid-fifth century. Neither its starting nor finishing date has been firmly established, but Priscus is known to have covered events from the 430s to the 470s. The surviving fragments provide invaluable information about relations between the eastern Empire and Attila, and record, in part, the collapse of Hunnic power and emergence of Germanic successor states in the 450s and 460s. There was perhaps some variation in the scale of treatment of these subjects, with proportionately more space being devoted to Attila's empire, but the surviving fragments show that the narrative was in general informative and precise. Perhaps three-quarters of the extant material deals with the 440s, fragments becoming sparse after Attila's death.[15] They confirm and amplify Jordanes at certain points, but do not amount to an independent narrative.

Malchus of Philadelphia

The *Suda* (M 120) and Photius (*Bibliotheca* 78) provide a little information about Malchus; otherwise we have to rely on deductions from the text of his history. He is known to have come from Philadelphia, which because his name is Semitic has been identified with what is now Amman in Jordan. The *Suda*, however, calls him 'Byzantine', suggesting that he was resident in Constantinople. The *Suda* and Photius both describe him as a 'sophist', so that he was clearly highly educated, if not necessarily an academic; such men often held public office in the late Empire.[16] Nothing specifically dates the work's composition or its author's life, but such a hostile account of Zeno probably could not have been published openly during his reign (that is, before 491). At the heart of all the other classicizing histories of late

[15] The relevant fragments are 37, 40. 1–2, 45, 46, 48. 1, 49; cf. Blockley, i. 48 ff.

[16] See the study and notes accompanying Cresci's edition (with Italian translation); cf. Blockley, i. 71 ff.; Baldwin, 'Malchus', 91–107; Laqueur, 'Malchos (2)', 851–7.

antiquity, however, is a narrative of recent events. This is hardly surprising, since it was easier for authors to gather such information, and more contemporary matters would be of the greatest interest to any audience. If Malchus' history was not published before 491, then, it is likely to have appeared soon afterwards.[17]

Both the *Excerpta* and Photius call the work Βυζαντιακά or 'Byzantine History'. As far as the extant fragments allow us to judge, it dealt mainly with Constantinople, the Balkans, and Asia Minor. Some western affairs were covered, particularly those of Africa and Italy, which were still of major concern to the eastern Empire in *c*.500. 'Byzantine History' would have been an appropriate title.[18] The work's chronological scope is more problematic. The *Suda* reports that it ran from the emperor Constantine (presumably the first) to the succession of Anastasius (*c*.325–491), but Photius' copy dealt only with the years 473 to 480 in seven books. The extant fragments tend to confirm the possible inference from Photius, that its overall structure was annalistic, with a book devoted to each year.[19] Photius also reports that his text showed that the author had composed other books dealing with years before 473, and would have written more after 480 had not death intervened. An introduction to the main part of the text may well have covered the period between Constantine and 473, then, presumably in some kind of epitome.[20] It seems less likely, however, that Malchus wrote about events after 480, since like Photius' copy of the text, none of the extant fragments postdates that year. The *Excerpta* series stops abruptly in the middle of an extended sequence of events in which it had shown consistent interest, suggesting that the series ends because the work did. Photius' comment that the author would have written more might explain why the *Suda* thought it went as far as Anastasius; Malchus perhaps expressed this intention without fulfilling it.[21]

---

[17] The reference to the 'Long Walls' (fr. 18. 3, p. 432. 41) has been thought to date the work after 507–12, when Anastasius had them built: Martin, *Theoderich der Große*, 11, 39 n. 1; cf. Baldwin, 'Malchus', 106; Cresci, *Malco*, 22. But Anastasius seems only to have restored a work of Theodosius II (Whitby, 'The Long Walls').

[18] Blockley, i. 73–4; Cresci, *Malco*, 24.

[19] Blockley, i. 72–3; cf. p. 279.

[20] Cf. Cresci, *Malco*, 25.

[21] Ibid. 24 ff.; Blockley, i. 72 follows the *Suda*.

Even of its account of the years 473–80 no full text survives. Apart from Photius' summary, the work has been preserved in fragmentary excerpts, of which the vast majority (including those of most historical importance) were made in the tenth century for the *Excerpta de Legationibus* of the emperor Constantine VII Porphyrogenitus. Separate series of excerpts deal with embassies to and from foreign peoples, and are usually entitled: *Romanorum ad Gentes* and *Gentium ad Romanos*. Of Malchus' work, there are nine fragments in the *RaG* series and six in the *GaR*. Before they can be used, the internal order of each series must be established and the two series integrated. This task is fairly straightforward, however, since the excerptors normally preserve the order of the original work.[22] For Malchus, this is true of the *GaR* fragments, but the *RaG* series provides one of few examples where the excerptors have misplaced material. Events discussed by Theoderic the Amal and Adamantius in *RaG* 1 are actually recounted in *RaG* 8. In Malchus' original, the discussion would surely not have preceded the events. Since the nineteenth century the difficulty has been resolved by moving the first two excerpts to the end of the sequence. The neatness of this solution suggests that the misplacement had a simple cause; a page perhaps fell out of a manuscript and was replaced incorrectly.[23] Internal indications and the order of the fragments in the two sequences can then date their contents with some security.

About three-quarters of the surviving material concentrates on relations between the Pannonian and Thracian Goths and the eastern Empire after 473. Whether this reflects chance or the proportions of the original work is unknowable, but it does mean that the surviving fragments make two major contributions to historical knowledge. First, without Malchus there would be little comparative material with which to evaluate the true importance of Theoderic Strabo, and it would be much harder to get the

---

[22] Cf. Blockley, i. 71, 124 ff.; Cresci, *Malco*, 49 ff. See generally, Moore, *Polybius*, 129.

[23] First adopted by Müller in *FHG* iv, followed by Blockley and Cresci. Errington, 'Malchos von Philadelphia', 82–110, argues that while *RaG* 1 (fr. 20) must be moved, no such necessity applies to *RaG* 2 (fr. 22). The latter dates to late 479, so that, in his view, the action of the other *RaG* fragments falls after this date. This creates so many problems that the traditional solution must be preferred; cf. Blockley, 'The fragments of Malchus' History', 152–3.

Getica's misleading account of unique Amal royalty into perspective. Second, the fragments also describe relations between the Goths and the eastern Empire in great detail. Given the excerptors' interests, much of the information concerns diplomacy, providing accounts not only of important agreements, but also details of bargaining positions adopted by Goths and Empire at different moments. The exchanges are covered in enormous detail, and it is the quality of Malchus' narrative which allows the history of our second Gothic wave of occupation in the Balkans to be reconstructed. Even the Gothic point of view receives considerable coverage.[24] There is no space to deal with the question here, but it seems likely that the quality of the account reflects the fact that Malchus drew on original treaties and diplomatic correspondence.[25]

Several other features of the work also require comment. As was expected of a classicizing historian, Malchus wrote in an elevated style, using many Atticisms. But his interpretation of the genre is less rigid than some. Circumlocutions and explanatory formulae are occasionally used, but common Latin administrative terms appear in simple Greek transcription. Malchus also had no aversion to precise numbers, which allows us, for instance, to calculate the approximate size of the Gothic groups. Nor did he feel it necessary to use classical equations instead of contemporary names, so that Goths, Persians, Italians, and Arabs all appear as themselves, rather than as Scythians or Colchians. As *RaG* I shows, he was capable of recounting complicated events in clear language, and Photius' judgement is not misplaced; 'in short, the work is a paradigm of historical writing'.[26]

There are, of course, problems. The narrative displays the concentration on individuals which was demanded generally by the genre, but which can often distort causation. For instance, Malchus blames Zeno for showing his usual cowardice when he did not lead the praesental armies against Theoderic the Amal in 478. But dissent was already evident among these troops and caused their dispersal to winter quarters (cf. p. 281); a desire not to lose one's throne is not in itself cowardice. Zeno's actions otherwise display much personal vigour, not to say brutality, which

---

[24] Cf. Laqueur, 'Malchos', 853.

[25] I intend to deal with this question in a separate paper.

[26] Cresci, *Malco*, 41 ff.; Blockley, i. 74–5.

seems to rebut the charge Malchus levels generally against him. Likewise, the emperor Leo is painted in the blackest terms, and there are hints that his wife Verina was also portrayed as a sinister figure.[27] These individuals may have had vices, but the concentration on their personalities as the motive force behind important events is somewhat misleading.

Malchus also uses the rhetorical set piece on occasions such as the confrontation between the two Theoderics at Mount Sondis in 478 (fr. 18. 2). Instead of sending promised troops, Zeno had left the Amal to face Strabo by himself, and the Goths eventually decided not to fight one another. Malchus' account of how this came about is unconvincing. The Amal is portrayed as grasping Zeno's betrayal only after two highly rhetorical speeches from Strabo, and after his own people had come to him demanding that there should be no fighting (ibid., p. 428. 30 ff.). The speeches and colourful drama of the confrontation undermine confidence in the passage. The Amal was already suspicious of Zeno, having refused to agree to the joint operation until the emperor and his chief ministers swore not to treat with Strabo (ibid. p. 426. 5 ff.). It seems unlikely that he would have required Strabo's rhetorical promptings to realize that he had been betrayed. This is confirmed by the many Atticisms in the speeches, which also include an imitation of Thucydides and a classical reference to a Cadmean victory, somewhat out of place in a purely Gothic confrontation.[28] Malchus' reconstruction of the Sondis incident satisfied the demands of his genre, but seems unhistorical, much of it probably originating in the author's imagination. As we might expect, not all of Malchus' text is of equal value.

John of Antioch

The fragments of John of Antioch cover Zeno's entire reign, and allow events to be followed after Malchus' account ends in 479/80. In particular, John describes the unification of the Goths and the later stages of relations between Zeno and Theoderic the Amal, including the latter's move to Italy. There is a gap, however, where the fragments might originally have described the terms under which this took place. John also supplements Malchus by

[27] Cf. Blockley, i. 78 ff.; Baldwin, 'Malchus', 102 ff.

[28] Cf. the commentary of Cresci, *Malco*, 215 ff. More generally, Blockley, i. 76–7; Cresci, *Malco*, 38 ff.

concentrating on a different aspect of events. Where Malchus (or what survives) describes relations between Zeno and the Goths, John of Antioch concentrates on quarrels at court.

In the earlier parts of his work, the extant fragments suggest that John reused existing narratives, barely altering them. For the reigns of Marcian and Leo, he seems to have used Priscus,[29] but since Priscus ended in the early 470s, his account of Zeno must have come from another source. This was not Malchus. Where the two overlap, there are differences in content, style, and usage. They give different accounts of the death of Heraclius,[30] and of the whereabouts of Theoderic Strabo during Marcian's coup.[31] Where Malchus wrote 'Byzantium' and 'Epidamnus', John used 'Constantinople' and 'Dyrrhachium'. Unlike Malchus, John also made great use of the λεγόμενος ('so-called') formula for introducing non-classical terms.[32] Where they can be compared, the general styles of the narratives are also quite distinct. John of Antioch is more anecdotal, for instance, in his account of Gothic affairs. This suggests that when the two very occasionally differ, Malchus should be preferred.

John's source for Zeno's reign may well have been the lost history of the Isaurian Candidus. All that survives of this work is Photius' summary description (*Bibliotheca* 79), which records that it ran from the proclamation of Leo as emperor to that of Anastasius (457–91). As described by Photius, its other characteristics correspond to those displayed by the relevant fragments of John of Antioch. Candidus' main focus of interest was the involvement of Isaurians, particularly Zeno and Illus, in imperial politics. This matches the fragments of John, which concentrate on the court struggles of Zeno's day, and his stormy relationship with Illus. In particular, Photius' summary of Candidus and the fragments of John of Antioch provide very similar accounts of the usurpation of Basiliscus (p. 272). Photius also mentions that the deeds of Odovacar and Theoderic Strabo were among the subjects covered by Candidus, both of whom appear in John. The evidence is thus suggestive, if not conclusive, that John preserves the substance of Candidus' account.

---

[29] Thompson, *Attila*, 13–14; Blockley, i. 114.
[30] John of Antioch fr. 210; Malchus fr. 6. 2.
[31] John of Antioch fr. 211. 3; Malchus fr. 22.
[32] Cf. Blockley, i. 125.

Other Sources

A variety of sources, particularly chronicles, provide supplementary information. The most consistently useful are the Latin work of Marcellinus Comes and the Greek text of Malalas. Although writing in Latin, Marcellinus worked in Constantinople in the mid-sixth century. His chronicle is particularly valuable because he came from Illyricum and had a strong interest in the region and some of its personalities, notably the general Sabinianus. He is also our sole authority for some important events, including the attack on the south-east Balkans, which led to Theoderic the Amal being appointed consul for 484.[33] The only complete Greek manuscript of Malalas is clearly an abridgement; Slavonic versions and extracts preserved in the *Excerpta de Insidiis* often provide fuller accounts of individual incidents.[34] One *de Insidiis* extract, for instance, adds greatly to our understanding of the relationship between Aspar and the Thracian Goths, where the complete Greek text is silent (Ch. 7).

A second Greek tradition has been preserved by Theophanes, a ninth-century compiler, using earlier materials (including Malalas). For the reigns of Leo and Zeno, he occasionally provides useful information, and with regard to the Goths, reports in particular the marriage alliance between Aspar and the family of Strabo. For the 480s, Theophanes is often paralleled by the *Ecclesiastical History* of Evagrius, and both would seem to be following the historical epitome of Eustathius of Antioch. They differ on occasion from John of Antioch, and the mistakes in their account suggest that it is better to follow the latter in such cases.[35] Occasional references in panegyrics and other sources add a few further points.

[33] See generally Croke, *Marcellinus Comes*.
[34] Cf. Bury, 'Krumbacher's Byzantine Literature', 207 ff. The strands are brought together in the recent translation by Jeffreys *et al.*
[35] Allen, *Evagrius Scholasticus*, 154 ff.

7

PANNONIANS AND THRACIANS
THE ORIGINS OF CONFLICT
453–473

A. *Amal-Led Goths in Pannonia*

The *Getica* identifies these Goths as the 'Ostrogoths', the second of two ancient subdivisions of the Gothic people, describing how these descendants of the fourth-century Ostrogoths re-emerged after the fall of the Hunnic Empire still ruled by the Amal dynasty, which had always guided their fate (58. 246 ff.). But there is no evidence that the Amals had ruled a substantial portion of the Goths before the Hunnic invasions, and after *c*.450 many of the Goths then in eastern Europe did not owe them allegiance (Ch. 1). The history of the Amals and of the Goths they ruled must be approached afresh.

The Origins of Amal Rule

Valamer did not inherit unchallenged Amal supremacy over even those Goths who came to be settled in Pannonia. What the *Getica* presents as an account of Ermenaric's successors in fact seems to describe Valamer's defeat of a rival Gothic leader, Vinitharius, and his attempt to conciliate that leader's followers by marrying his granddaughter, Vadamerca. Several branches of a third ruling dynasty, that of Hunimund, can also be identified. Hunimund and his son Thorismud both ruled quite independently, while Gensemund, a second son of Hunimund, accepted Valamer's hegemony. Thorismud's son Beremud probably chose to flee rather than resist growing Amal domination.[1] Instead of an Amal family with unique prestige in *c*.450, we must envisage a series of competing noble lines. Valamer united the Pannonian Goths, partly by

---

[1] *Getica* 48. 246–52; cf. Heather, 'Cassiodorus', 116 ff.

military action (Vinitharius was killed, Beremud forced to flee) and partly by conciliation (Gensemund accepted Amal rule, Vadamerca an Amal marriage). Hence Valamer's role in the history of these Goths resembles that of Clovis among the Salian Franks (Gregory of Tours, *HF* 2. 40 ff.): both were leaders who united their peoples by extinguishing rival ruling lines.

Even after Valamer's successes, the Pannonian Goths were not fully united. The *Getica* stresses that his two brothers, Thiudimer and Vidimer, accepted his pre-eminence with all good will (48. 253), but the three were separate in the normal course of events. They settled their followers in distinct areas of Pannonia, probably in an arc south-eastwards from Lake Balaton,[2] and often acted independently: Valamer was attacked by the Huns and Sciri without his brothers being involved (52. 268–9, 53. 275–6), Thiudimer alone attacked the Suevi (53. 274), and Vidimer did not follow Thiudimer in 473 (56. 283). This devolution of power probably reflects the fact that the Pannonian Goths were used to acting in independent groups; a legacy from the past which Valamer's aggregation of power did not change overnight.

It is unclear when exactly Valamer united these Goths. It must have been *c*.450, but an obvious question is whether it preceded or followed Attila's death (453) and the collapse of the Hunnic empire. Two sources suggest that Valamer was pre-eminent before Attila's death, but neither inspires much confidence. The first mentions his special relationship with Attila incidentally, in a passage devoted to the light which Valamer's body used to emit.[3] The second is Jordanes (*Getica* 38. 199–200, 48. 252–3; cf. *Romana* 331), but his word on matters to do with the Amal dynasty cannot be conclusive. Of more disinterested sources, Priscus seems to mention Goths in important positions under Attila: Onegesius, Edeco, Berichus, and Scottas, all perhaps with Gothic names.[4] None is recognizable as a member of the Amal family, however,

---

[2] *Getica* 52. 268 is difficult to interpret. On the basis of it, the brothers have been arranged both north–south (Schmidt, 269; Ensslin, 'Die Ostgoten', 155 ff.) and, perhaps preferably, east–west around Lake Balaton (Wolfram, 260; Mirković, 'Ostgoten in Pannonien', 127. Kiss, 'Siedlungsgebiet der Ostgoten', 329–39 adduces archaeological evidence, but cannot prove that particular objects reflect Pannonian Goths.

[3] Damascius = Photius, *Bibliotheca* 242. 64.

[4] Fr. 11. 2; cf. Wolfram, 256. On the names, see Maenchen-Helfen, 192–3 and (for Berichus) Schönfeld, *Wörterbuch*, 50. The etymologies are not undisputed.

and Theophanes gives Valamer a leading role only in the time of Attila's sons: AM 5977 (131 de Boor).

A number of small groups under their own leader would have been easier for the Huns to control. Relevant evidence is limited, but the Huns seem to have been suspicious of leaders with too great a following. When Attila conquered the Akatziri, for instance, the existing overall leader was deposed and Attila's son set up in his place (Priscus fr. 11. 2). Rulers of subunits retained authority, but the Huns broke down the central leadership structure which might have united the Akatziri against them. Likewise, Goths in a Hun-led force of the 460s retained only their own lower-level leaders (Priscus fr. 49). From this perspective, it might be surprising for Attila to have trusted Valamer to lead a united people, but the argument cannot be pressed. There was no regular mechanism of government in the Hunnic empire, and the exercise of power was dependent on the exertions of particular rulers. In such circumstances, control over subject peoples probably ebbed and flowed, and it would have been possible for dangerous confederations to build up among them.[5] Arderic, for instance, seems to have led the Gepids as a united force at the time of the Nedao in *c*.454 (*Getica* 50. 260 ff.; cf. 38. 199). Unification is perhaps more likely to have followed Attila's death and the disintegration of the Hunnic empire, but the evidence is not conclusive.

The Pannonian Goths c.450–473

According to the *Getica*, the Amal-led Goths received Pannonia from the emperor Marcian (451–7) after the battle of the Nedao; it was only at this point that they moved west from south Russia (*Getica* 50. 262 ff.). But the Huns remained in the Danubian region until the mid-460s, and many Goths had moved out of Russia long before *c*.450 (p. 227). We also know that Attila had forced both halves of the Empire to cede parts of Pannonia to him in the 440s.[6] It seems quite likely, therefore, that the Goths were originally settled there by the Huns themselves, and that their negotiations with Marcian were concerned with no more than Roman recognition for land already held.

[5] Cf. Avar control of the Slavs: Whitby, *The Emperor Maurice*, 169 ff.
[6] Maenchen-Helfen, 108 ff.

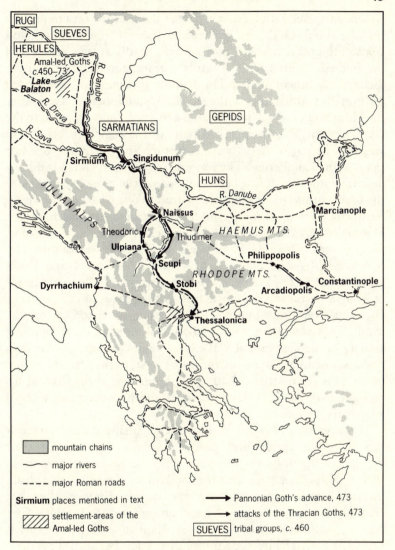

FIG. 6. The Pannonian Goths, *c*.450–73

If so, attempts to reconstruct Marcian's motives for settling the Goths in Pannonia, supposing it a sign of a close relationship,[7] may

---

[7] e.g. Wolfram, 259; Burns, *History of the Ostrogoths*, 60 ff.

well be misplaced. Indeed, it is part of the *Getica*'s bias to present the Amal-led Goths as particular allies of the Empire, and Constantinople's strategic position was hardly strong enough, in the immediate aftermath of Attila's death, for Marcian to have dictated Danubian affairs. The Hunnic invasions, in fact, ended for ever Roman control of the middle Danube region. Even after the Huns and Goths left in the 460s and 470s, control passed to the Gepids, until Theoderic added parts of the region to his Italian kingdom in 505/6. Areas were recaptured by Justinian, but lost again to the Lombards.[8] The Empire was thus forced to abandon a defensive line which had been founded on the river Danube since the first century AD. It retreated instead to one based on the rivers Sava and Drava, although in the immediate aftermath of the Hunnic empire this was by no means secure. In *c.*470, for instance, Singidunum, where the Sava meets the Danube, was captured by Sarmatians (*Getica* 55. 282), while life in Moesia I and Dacia Ripensis seems to have been severely disrupted.[9] The curtailment of Roman power was acknowledged in the retreat of the capital of Illyricum from Sirmium to Thessalonica, over 500 km. to the south. This took place in the 440s, and stimulated much building activity in the new capital.[10] We know that Marcian sent the then *comes* Anthemius, later emperor in the west, to the Danube region in the 450s after Attila's death (Sid. Ap. *Carm.* 2. 199 ff.), but his mission may have been more to establish contact with tribal groups than to dictate to them.

However they obtained Pannonia, the Amal-led Goths were at this point an agricultural people. Jordanes' account of their Pannonian period never mentions this, and his concentration on their wars might suggest that the spoils of war provided their main income. But negotiations with the eastern Empire after 473 centred on the possession of good agricultural land, which they were to settle and farm themselves. Explicit evidence of this is provided by Malchus' record of a discussion between Theoderic

---

[8] Lakatos, *Quellenbuch*, 63 ff.; Radan–Lengyel, *Roman Pannonia*, 404 ff.

[9] Attila had ordered their evacuation in the treaty of 447 (Priscus fr. 11. 1, p. 242. 9 ff.); in 457 this was the only area not to receive the emperor Leo's circular letter (Maenchen-Helfen, 59), although this might be coincidence.

[10] Cf. the works of Vickers, 'The Late Roman Walls'; 'A Note on the Byzantine Palace'; 'Observations on the Octagon', with further refs.

the Amal and Zeno's representative Adamantius outside Dyrrhachium in late 479.[11] He was attempting to persuade Theoderic to
move from Epirus to Pautalia in Dardania, and describes the
latter's virtues in a striking manner (fr. 20, p. 446. 199ff.),

(Theoderic) should leave Epirus and the cities there since it was
intolerable to all that such great cities should be occupied by him, their
inhabitants having been ejected, and go to Dardania, where, compared
with their current homes [i.e. Epirus], there was much land, beautiful,
fertile and depopulated. This he could farm and support his army with an
abundance of everything.

Adamantius is quite specific that the attraction for the Goths is not
only the fertile land, but also the lack of inhabitants (ἐνδεᾶ δὲ
οἰκητόρων). There can be no confusion here between actual land
and its produce, tax revenues in money or kind.[12] Since the local
population was small, the land could only support the Goths if
they themselves farmed it.

Similarly, when sending Adamantius to negotiate, Zeno specifically noted that the Goths had sown no seed for the year and had
no hope of a harvest. He consequently gave Adamantius 200 lb. of
gold to buy food for them until they could grow their own (ibid., p.
438. 55 ff.). The evidence seems unambiguous that the Goths
usually produced their own food. Likewise, Malchus reports that
in 478 Theoderic the Amal 'demanded that he be given land upon
which to settle and sufficient grain to support his army until the
next harvest' (fr. 18. 3, p. 430. 5 ff.). The Amal-led Goths thus
negotiated after 473 for land which they were to farm themselves;
they would surely have had no interest in this had they not been
farmers during the Pannonian period. We also know from Priscus
that the Huns confiscated the surplus food of their other Gothic
subjects (fr. 49), and this is likely to have been the fate of the
Amal-led Goths until they reasserted their independence.[13]

[11] Malchus has probably based himself on the written account of the meeting
Adamantius sent to Zeno (fr. 20, p. 448. 257–8).

[12] Cf. Goffart, *Barbarians and Romans*, esp. 210 ff., who greatly exploits the
possibility of such a confusion.

[13] Liebeschuetz, *Barbarians and Bishops*, 81 ff. is right to stress that they
moved around a great deal in these years, and this surely disrupted their ability to
farm. Nevertheless, Malchus shows that agricultural land was a central concern,
and, as will emerge, the instability was largely the result of political conflicts
rather than a sign that the Goths were nomadic.

How precisely they overthrew Hunnic dominion is problematic. The *Getica* refers to Goths (not specifically the Pannonian Goths) fighting at the Nedao (453/4), giving no further details, and does not hide the fact that the Gepids were largely responsible for the Huns' defeat. The Pannonian Goths, it seems, did not fight at all, or sided with the Huns.[14] Valamer's subsequent war with the sons of Attila thus becomes the most likely point at which Gothic independence was asserted. In this campaign, probably of 453/4,[15] Attila's sons failed to re-establish their control over Valamer's Goths (*Getica* 52. 268–9). Valamer's unification of the Pannonian Goths was probably a prerequisite for success, since it created a Gothic force strong enough to resist the Huns. Other Goths, who did not unite, remained subjects of the Huns into the 460s (Priscus fr. 49). In addition, civil war between Attila's sons (*Getica* 50. 259) and the success of the Gepids had both weakened Hunnic power. Gothic independence should thus be seen as the result of a process rather than a single event. Divisions among the Huns, defeat by the Gepids, and Gothic unification altered the balance of power, so that when it came to a specific test of strength between Valamer and Attila's sons, the Goths prevailed.

[14] *Getica* 50. 259 ff.; cf. Wolfram, 258–9 for the date. That they did not fight has been argued by Alföldi, *Untergang*, ii. 97 ff; Maenchen-Helfen, 144; Ensslin, 'Die Ostgoten', 151–2; Burns, *History of the Ostrogoths*, 52. Schmidt, 268–9; Wolfram, 258–9 consider that they fought for the Huns.

[15] It is said to have been fought in the year of Theoderic's birth, and chronology can be reconstructed from 500, when Theoderic celebrated his Tricennalia. He thus became king in *c*.471, but this cannot be associated with his succession to sole power after Thiudimer's death (*Getica* 56. 288) because that took place after 473 (p. 275). Rather, it must be associated with *Getica* 55. 282 when Theoderic first gathered his own following at the age of 18: cf. Wolfram, 267; Ensslin, *Theoderich der Große*, 40 n. 13; Claude, 'Die ostgotischen Königserhebungen', 153–4 and 'Zur Königserhebung', 1 ff. From this it follows that Theoderic was born *c*.453/4, and that it was *c*.460/1 when, aged 7, he went to Constantinople as a hostage (*Getica* 52. 271). Wolfram, 261 ff. makes Theoderic 15 on his return from Constantinople, but *Getica* 55. 282 is explicit that he was 18; cf. Claude, 'Zur Königserhebung', 1–2 and 'Die ostgotischen Königserhebungen', 153 ff. Wolfram, 262 also supposes that Theoderic went to Constantinople in 459 (implying that he had been born 451/2) because a continuation of Prosper indicates that the campaign preceding this event was under way in 459. But this does not date the actual treaty, and may also be a confused reference to events of 479: see below, n. 18.

The rest of Jordanes' account of the years before 473 is straightforward, and has been well studied,[16] so that we can concentrate here on the Pannonian Goths' rise to prominence. Priscus confirms that they made diplomatic contact with the eastern Empire in the reign of Marcian, because Valamer was acting 'in breach of a treaty' when he attacked Illyricum early in the reign of Marcian's successor Leo ($\pi\alpha\rho\alpha\sigma\pi o\nu\delta\eta\sigma\alpha\nu\tau os$, fr. 37). The nature of this agreement is not entirely clear. Jordanes maintains that the Empire had agreed to pay an annual subsidy and that the Goths attacked because it was withheld (*Getica* 52. 270–1).[17] But this is the cause of all conflict between Romans and Goths in the *Getica* (p. 108), and Priscus refers to no Gothic complaints of a subsidy having been stopped, nor to any arrears being claimed (fr. 37). The *Getica* may thus have misinterpreted the Goths' contacts with Marcian. In Leo's reign, however, the Goths did force the eastern Empire to grant them a subsidy (*Getica* 52. 271).[18] Under the terms of a second treaty, they received 300 lb. of gold annually, to combat the starvation which had, they claimed, forced them to attack Illyricum (Priscus fr. 37). In return, Leo extracted guarantees of good behaviour, as part of which Valamer's nephew Theoderic went to Constantinople as a hostage, probably in *c*.461. He remained there for ten years.[19]

A number of related motives underlay the Goths' desire for closer relations with Constantinople. From Priscus (fr. 37) and Jordanes (*Getica* 56. 287), it might appear that the Goths were moved by economic distress. Priscus reports the Goths' claim that they required a subsidy to stave off starvation, and Jordanes that they moved into the Empire in 473 because they had exhausted the middle Danube region. But Priscus is merely passing on the Goths' excuses for attacking the Empire, and Jordanes, as we shall see, provides a less than full account of the move of 473. No doubt

[16] e.g. Schmidt, 268 ff.; Wolfram, 258 ff.; Ensslin, *Theoderich der Große*, 9–16, 34 ff. with refs.

[17] Followed e.g. by Schmidt, 272; Wolfram, 260 ff.; Pohl, 'Die Gepiden', 263–4.

[18] Prosp. Cont. 11 (*CM* i. 492) reports that the Goths seized Dyrrhachium in 459, but it seems unlikely that such a feat would have gone unnoticed in our other sources (especially Jordanes). The Goths did take the city in 479, so that this may well be a confusion.

[19] Cf. n. 15; on his stay there, see Ensslin, *Theoderich der Große*, 23 ff.

an economic motive did underlie the Goths' desire for closer relations, but they may have been moved more by the desire for plunder than by hunger. An annual subsidy also increased the powers of patronage available to Valamer, and hence his ability to attract a following.[20] In similar vein, Jordanes records that Valamer's attack on Illyricum was partly inspired by jealousy of Theoderic Strabo (*Getica* 52. 270–1). This perhaps backdates a rivalry played out after 473 (see below), but illustrates an important point. Imperial honours were a mark of a leader's prestige, which, especially since economic benefits usually accompanied them, could prompt the Goths, or at least their leaders, into ambitious campaigns.

The Empire's reciprocal interest in the Pannonian Goths is only natural. Militarily powerful, they controlled strategic routes from Constantinople to Italy. After their attack on Illyricum, Leo's attitude towards them seems to have been somewhat ambivalent; he supported, for instance, the Sciri in their war against them (Priscus fr. 45). Some idea of the Pannonian Goths' numbers can be reconstructed. In 479, Theoderic the Amal offered to combine 6,000 of his best troops with imperial forces (Malchus fr. 20, p. 446. 215 ff.); this gives us a minimum figure for the number of fighting men in his following. As part of the same offer, baggage and non-combatants were to be placed in a city of the emperor's choice; Theoderic also needed to guard them. A minimum of 2,000 men was required to hold a large city such as Dyrrhachium (ibid., p. 440. 83 ff.), where they then were, which would suggest, allowing some margin for security, that fighting men numbered *c.* 10,000 in 479, and the total, including women and children, *c.* 50,000.[21] Similarly, Theoderic's personal following in 471 is said to have numbered 6,000 men (*Getica* 55. 282); at this point Thiudimer and Vidimer each had their own men as well.[22] If the three sets of followers were approximately the same size, this might imply a figure of *c.* 15,000 rather than 10,000, but the figures are similar enough to define an order of magnitude. In any

---

[20] For an alternative view, see Wolfram, 261 ff.

[21] Cf. Schmidt, 286, 293: the normal ratio of fighting men to total population in such societies is about 1:5.

[22] Theoderic perhaps inherited the followers of Valamer (Wolfram, 267).

case, by 479 Vidimer had left the group, and Theoderic had lost some followers to Theoderic Strabo (see below).[23]

Apart from attacking the Empire, the Pannonian Goths also warred against other powers. First, they defeated the attempts of Attila's sons to reassert Hunnic control; Jordanes nicely illustrates how conditions changed. In the 450s, Attila's sons attacked the Goths as 'fugitive slaves' (*Getica* 52. 268–9), showing that they were then accustomed to dominating the Goths. In a second war of the 460s, however, Attila's son Dengizich was responding defensively to Gothic aggression (*Getica* 53. 272–3). Divided between his various sons, Attila's Huns were no longer able to dominate the Pannonian Goths whom Valamer had united, together perhaps with groups from other peoples. Bittigur Huns, for instance, once part of the Hun Empire (*Getica* 53. 272), appear among the Goths in Italy (Agathias 2. 13. 1 ff.).[24] The Goths' success was mirrored by other groups (Gepids, Suevi, Rugi, etc.) who all threw off Hunnic domination in this period. Cumulatively, these tribes had destroyed the Huns' independence by the late 460s.[25]

The eclipse of Hunnic power let loose rivalry between the Pannonian Goths and other former subjects of Attila. According to Jordanes, conflict started when Thiudimer intercepted a Suevic raiding party, escalated into a war with the Sciri in which Valamer was killed, and culminated in battle on the River Bolia in the late 460s, where the Goths triumphed over a hostile coalition of Suevi, Sciri, Sarmatians, Gepids, and Rugi (*Getica* 53. 274 ff.). Other successful campaigns followed, against the Suevi and Sarmatians,[26] but, despite their victories, it was not long before the Goths abandoned the middle Danube region entirely, invading the eastern Empire in 473. According to the *Getica*, they moved because they had exhausted the area of spoils (56. 283), but it is surprising that the Goths did not stay to enjoy their supremacy:

---

[23] Burns, 'Ostrogothic Population', 460, *The Ostrogoths*, 72 estimates total numbers at *c*. 20,000. Theoderic's third group in 479 numbered 5,000 (Malchus fr. 20, p. 448. 244 ff.), and Burns asserts that the relative strength of the three groups was 1:2:1. This is an arbitrary assertion.

[24] Cf. Burns, *History of the Ostrogoths*, 54.

[25] See generally Maenchen-Helfen, 165 ff.

[26] Theoderic returned from Constantinople before the attack on the Sarmatians, so that this can probably be dated 470/1 (n. 15).

the Gepids, for instance, found the middle Danube perfectly satisfactory for the next century. There were also very specific reasons for the Goths to invade the eastern Empire at that moment (p. 265). The Goths are unlikely to have been forced to leave, but neither perhaps did they overcome their enemies so completely as the *Getica* would have us believe. Increasing competition between the Huns' former subjects may have made the region progressively less attractive as a homeland.

During their stay in Pannonia, finally, the exercise of power among these Goths became more centralized. Even after Valamer had united them, they had continued to operate in three distinct groups, but by 473 this was no longer the case. Valamer, first of all, was killed in battle, and Thiudimer inherited his followers (*Getica* 53. 276 ff.). The early 470s, however, saw more deliberate moves to concentrate authority. In 470/1 Thiudimer promoted his son Theoderic to some form of kingship (*Getica* 56. 282), perhaps giving him the group inherited from Valamer. This seems indicative of dynastic ambition; overall leadership had previously passed from the eldest to the middle brother (*Getica* 54. 278), but Thiudimer's promotion of his son threatened the chances of the third brother, Vidimer, of succeeding in turn.[27] Matters came to a head two years later when a majority of the Goths followed Thiudimer into the eastern Empire, and Vidimer went instead to Italy. Jordanes reports that an amicable casting of lots indicated which way each brother should move (*Getica* 56. 283), but this is unconvincing. Having decided to invade the eastern Empire, Thiudimer would not lightly have countenanced his brother's withholding a portion of Gothic military power. In deciding to march west instead, Vidimer probably occasioned, or reacted to, a major quarrel, and certainly was left with insufficient followers to maintain his independence. He first offered his services to the emperor Glycerius, and then joined the Visigoths (*Getica* 56. 284).[28] Indeed, having already promoted his son to kingship, Thiudimer may well have been happy to bring things to a head this way with his brother, since it established for his own direct

---

[27] Cf. Wolfram, 267–8.

[28] Vidimer's decision probably parallels that of Beremud to flee rather than resist Amal ambitions: Heather, 'Cassiodorus', 122 ff.

line a monopoly of power over the majority of the Pannonian Goths.[29]

B. *The Thracian Goths and Theoderic Triarius*

The Family Ties of Theoderic Strabo

Modern responses to Theoderic Strabo have been conditioned by the Amal propaganda of the *Getica* and Cassiodorus' *Variae*, prompting two alternative positions. The first follows Jordanes' explicit word that Strabo was not an Amal (*Getica* 52. 270), to argue that, since the Amals were the true Gothic royal family, Strabo could not have been a proper Gothic leader. He led merely an offshoot of the Ostrogoths, his position sustained by imperial funds.[30] This is insufficient. Theoderic Strabo was an effective tribal leader, who, as we shall see, even attracted support away from his Amal namesake (Ch. 8). The second position accepts these points, but nevertheless takes it as axiomatic that the Amals had unique prestige. Thus, because Theoderic Strabo was clearly a powerful Gothic king, he must have been an Amal.[31]

Two arguments have been advanced to support this contention. First, Aspar, whose wife was Theoderic Strabo's aunt (p. 255), had a son called Ermenaric. This shows that the Triarii were Amals because an Amal name has been reused. But, as we have seen, the Ermenaric of the *Getica* is taken directly from Ammianus and there is no reason to suppose that he was actually an Amal (Ch. 1). More generally, while it was later common for Franks to name children after ancestors, particularly famous ones, there is no evidence that the Amal family (or, indeed, Goths more generally) followed this practice.[32] Second, John of Antioch (fr. 214. 3) records that Theoderic Strabo's son Recitach was the ἀνεψιός of Theoderic the Amal in 483/4. This has been taken to mean that they were blood relatives, but is much too strong a conclusion.

---

[29] Other Amals left the tribal group for the eastern Empire: Andag (*Getica* 40, 209, 50. 266), and Sidimund (Malchus fr. 20). They were perhaps forced out: Wolfram, 260.

[30] e.g. Schmidt, 271–2; Ensslin, *Theoderich der Große*, 14–15; Burns, *History of the Ostrogoths*, 66–7.

[31] Wolfram, esp. 29 ff., 260, 268 ff.

[32] Heather, 'Cassiodorus', 106.

ἀνεψιός in late Greek can mean 'nephew', 'first cousin', or 'cousin' more generally. John of Antioch otherwise uses it to mean 'nephew',[33] but this does not seem possible here, since it would make Theoderic the Amal the brother of Theoderic Strabo or of his wife. If the first is impossible, the second is very unlikely. 'First cousin' also seems unlikely, for this would make either Theoderic Strabo a fourth brother for Valamer, Thiudimer, and Vidimer (impossible), or Strabo's wife their sister. This illustrates an important point; the only way in which ἀνεψιός can have either of its precise meanings is for a female Amal to have married into the Triarius line. This would give Recitach some Amal blood, but does not turn the Triarii into Amals. If the term has an imprecise meaning, the number of ways in which the link could have been formed increases dramatically, and, as the relationship becomes more vague, there is ever less necessity for it to imply that Theoderic Strabo belonged to the Amal line. We should perhaps return to the old suggestion, then, that a marriage-alliance linked Theoderic and Recitach this could have been negotiated in 478, when the two Theoderics agreed a non-aggression pact, or after 480 when both were in conflict with the Empire simultaneously.[34] Alternatively, since John of Antioch was a compiler reworking older material, and ἀνεψιός cannot here mean 'nephew' as it usually does in his work, he may simply have become confused. The fact that γένος means 'race' or 'family' often causes difficulty, for instance, and a racial relation could have been confused for a family tie.

We should therefore accept as probable Jordanes' explicit statement that Theoderic Strabo was not an Amal. This is also in line with the broader historical context. Gothic tribal divisions changed dramatically in the course of the Hunnic invasions. The 'Ostrogoths', meaning the Goths whom Theoderic the Amal led to Italy, came into existence only between c.450 and 489, and there is no good evidence that these Goths had ever previously been united

---

[33] Cf. John of Antioch frr. 209. 2, 217*b*: the first of Gundobad and Recimer, the second of the emperors Justin II and Justinian. Fr. 209. 2 does also say, mistakenly, that Gundobad was Recimer's brother (τοῦ ʿΡεκίμερος ἀδελφοῦ), but this is obviously a corruption of the phrase that Malalas, Bonn 374–5, uses of them τὸν υἱὸν τῆς ἀδελφῆς αὐτοῦ ('the son of his sister'): 'son of' has simply dropped out of the description; cf. n. 40 on Aspar and Theoderic Strabo.

[34] Martin, *Theoderich der Große*, 24–5.

before the Hunnic invasions. The Pannonian and Thracian Goths had been separate since at least the 450s, and probably for much longer, making it very unlikely that they would both have been ruled by a single dynasty, especially since Valamer, as we have seen, had even had to defeat rivals from other families to assert Amal rule in Pannonia. John of Antioch's report remains intriguing, but, as the broader historical context would suggest, the line of Theoderic Strabo should be viewed as a perfectly genuine, non-Amal, Gothic ruling dynasty.

The Thracian Goths as Imperial Foederati

Probably in 477, envoys came from Theoderic Strabo to the Emperor Zeno in Constantinople; Malchus characterizes the senders of this embassy as 'the allied Goths in Thrace, whom the Romans call *foederati*' (φοιδεράτους, fr. 15, p. 420. 1–2). A fragment of Malalas in the *de Insidiis* collection (fr. 31), similarly, refers to the Goths who rebelled after the murder of Aspar as *foederati*; these can again be identified with the Thracian Goths (see below). Two reliable sources thus confirm that Strabo's followers were *foederati*, but what did this term signify in the eastern Empire in *c*.470?

As part of a treaty made with Zeno in 478, it was agreed that the Empire would supply 'pay and food' (συντάξεις τε καὶ τροφήν), for 13,000 men whom Strabo was to choose (Malchus fr. 18. 4, p. 434. 12 ff.). Thus, in 478 at least, the Thracian *foederati* would seem to have been paid as regular soldiers of the imperial army. συντάξεις is the technical term in the papyri for the monetary component of military pay,[35] and the treaty made the Thracians' leader, Theoderic Strabo, *MVM praesentalis* and commander of two Scholae (p. 434. 14 ff.), tending to confirm the inference. What evidence there is suggests that the terms agreed in 478 are quite representative of the way in which the eastern Empire had treated these Gothic *foederati*.

As we shall see, they seem to have served with the imperial army in Thrace for a considerable period before 470 (see below), and Malalas confirms that they were a military force by the 460s at the latest, when they supported Aspar, and some of them were stationed in Constantinople (*De Insidiis* 31 = Bonn 371–2). In a treaty of 473, similarly, it was agreed between the emperor Leo

[35] Preisigke, *Wörterbuch*, ii. 548–9.

and Theoderic Strabo that the latter's followers should receive
2,000 lb. of gold per annum (Malchus fr. 2, p. 408. 22 ff.). It is not
explicitly stated here, as in 478, that the money represented pay
and supplies for a body of Roman troops, but Strabo was also
made *MVM praesentalis* in 473, so that this does seem likely. Two
thousand pounds of gold per annum is also a vast sum, differing
hugely in order of magnitude (by a factor of about ten) from other
amounts known to have been paid simply for the relief of economic
distress.[36] We have no exact figures for the annual value of military
pay in the second half of the fifth century, but estimates vary from
about eight to twelve solidi.[37] At these rates, 2,000 lb. of gold
would pay 18,000 or 12,000 men, so that Zeno would have granted
a comparable sum in 478 for 13,000 men,[38] and money was
probably paid on a similar basis in both cases.

The main feature of the relationship between Thracian *foederati*
and the east Roman state was thus the fact that a large body of
Goths owed military service, in return for which they were paid as
regular Roman troops. Their numbers perhaps varied, but we do
seem to be dealing with a force that was over 10,000 strong (see
below). To this extent, then, the position of the Thracian Goths
corresponds closely to the definition of *foederati* given by Jordanes
and Procopius; that is, a large body of foreigners serving as regular
troops alongside the imperial army (p. 110). Fifth-century sources
say nothing about recognized legal equality, the other feature of
foederati stressed by Procopius, but the Thracian Goths were
intimately involved in imperial politics, suggesting that they did
generally enjoy a special relationship with the Roman state.

In the 460s, they were close allies of the *MVM praesentalis* and
Patrician Aspar. Consul for 434, he had been a dominant figure at

[36] Three hundred pounds of gold per year relieved the starvation of the
Pannonian Goths in *c*.460 (Priscus fr. 37), as did 200 lb. in 479 (Malchus fr. 20, p.
438. 56 ff.).

[37] On the basis of 6th-c. papyri, Johnson and West calculate the actual value of
rations at about 12 solidi (*Byzantine Egypt*, 225 ff.). The military *annona* had an
official value of 4 solidi, but cavalrymen also received a fodder allowance (*capitus*)
valued at 4 solidi (Jones 459 ff.); these sums were supplemented by donatives and
other allowances (Jones, 624 ff.).

[38] Though the treaty distinguishes 'pay and food', a single lump sum may have
been paid to the Goths in 478 as well as in 473. An administrative distinction
continued to be made between *annonae* in cash and *annonae* in kind, but both
were commuted into gold from the mid-5th c.: Jones, 460–1.

court since the 420s, and with his son Ardaburius (consul in 447) exercised considerable influence over imperial affairs: particularly in the elections of the emperors Marcian and Leo. After *c.*460, however, Leo steadily promoted Isaurians, especially Zeno, to counter Aspar's influence. Zeno was responsible for the dismissal of Ardaburius from his generalship in 466; the Isaurian then married one of Leo's daughters, and was appointed consul for 469.[39] In response, Aspar cultivated closer links with the Thracian Goths. A fragment of Malalas tells us that 'Aspar the Patrician troubled the emperor greatly, relying on the force of Goths at his disposal' (*De Insidiis* 31). Individual contacts are also recorded between Aspar and a number of Gothic leaders. Aspar's son Ardaburius attempted to use one Anagastes, a Gothic *MVM per Thracias*, to kill Zeno at one point (John of Antioch fr. 206. 2). Ostrys was a second Gothic associate of Aspar, commander of the Goths in Constantinople (Malalas, Bonn 371–2). And with Theoderic Strabo, there was even a marriage-alliance; he was probably the nephew of Aspar's wife.[40]

These close relations with Aspar dictated the stance taken by Strabo and the Thracian Goths in court politics. In 470/1 Leo was forced to marry a second daughter to Aspar's son Patricius, who was made Caesar and Leo's heir. Aspar was surely looking to limit Zeno's increasing prestige, but Leo responded by having Aspar and Ardaburius murdered in 471. Gothic forces in Constantinople, led by Ostrys, immediately revolted, attempting to storm the palace. Forced back, they fled to Thrace where Ostrys was supported by a general Gothic rising. Malalas particularly mentions the involvement in this of the 'federates', so that the participation of the Thracian Goths seems certain.[41] The motivation behind their rebellion seems straightforward. Apart from a simple desire for revenge, Aspar's murder removed the Thracian Goths' principal guarantee of court patronage, and threatened their special status.

[39] Brooks, 'Zenon and the Isaurians', 211 ff.; Scott, 'Aspar', 59 ff.

[40] Theophanes AM 5964 (117 de Boor) makes Strabo the brother of Aspar's wife (τῆς δε Ἀσπαρος γαμετῆς ἀδελφός), AM 5970 (126 de Boor) her nephew ἀδελφόπαις τῆς γαμετῆς Ἀσπαρος). The latter is probably to be preferred since a slight error turns nephew into brother (ἀδελφόπαις into ἀδελφός), but the reverse error is more difficult; cf. *PLRE* ii. 1073.

[41] Malalas, Bonn 371–2; *De Insidiis* 31; cf. Brooks, 'Zenon and the Isaurians', 211–12.

By *c.*470, the Thracian Goths thus occupied an important position in the Empire. Favoured *foederati*, they had been allies of Aspar, perhaps the most significant figure at court apart from the emperor himself, and supplied part of the palace guard which constituted Constantinople's garrison. Theoderic Strabo himself owned property in the city (Malchus fr. 18. 4), was linked by marriage to Aspar (and hence to the imperial family), and seems to have cultivated his own supporters among the imperial bureaucracy. In 477, certain individuals supplied him with detailed information about events inside the capital (id. fr. 15). The Thracian Goths and their leaders had played a much more central role in the Empire than the Amal-led parvenus from Pannonia.

The Thracian Goths as Tribal People

As we have seen, the treaty of 478 declared that the Empire would supply pay and food for 13,000 men, and the 2,000 lb. of gold paid annually after 473 would have supplied salaries for a similar number of men. The Goths' actual numbers are unlikely to have been exactly the same as those notionally provided for by these treaties. As we shall see, numbers ebbed and flowed, and it was in Theoderic Strabo's interest to extract as large a sum as possible from the Empire, whatever the size of his following. Moreover, as we shall see, Strabo was in a particularly strong position in 478 (Ch. 8). Nevertheless, having paid them for some time previously, the Empire no doubt knew approximately how many Thracian Goths there were. The figures in the treaties are the result of bargaining, in which Strabo would not have been able to pitch his demands too high, and can probably be taken as a rough guide to the size of his following. He had a minimum of 10,000 warriors in the 470s, implying a total, including women and children, of at least 50,000. The Thracian Goths were thus similar in order of magnitude to the Pannonian Goths, and in terms of the number of Goths they led the two Theoderics were of equal standing. This is what we might expect. If one or other had had a preponderance of strength, an extended struggle could never have developed; the stronger would have quickly defeated the weaker.[42]

---

[42] Burns, 'Calculating Ostrogothic Population', 459–60 takes instead John of Antioch's figure of 30,000 (fr. 211. 5, referring to 481). Figures based on the treaties seem more reliable, but see further p. 298.

As their name suggests, Theoderic Strabo's followers were settled in Thrace, perhaps on the Plain itself. The diocese also included Moesia Inferior and Scythia Minor north of the Haemus mountains, but the plains nearer Constantinople seem to have been the centre of the Goths' activities. In 473, they attacked Philippopolis and Arcadiopolis (Malchus fr. 2), and in 479/480 (ibid. fr. 22) and 481 (p. 245) there was no major barrier between their lands and the imperial capital. Likewise, although they had taken refuge in the Haemus in 478, Theoderic the Amal clearly expected to find them on the Thracian Plain. The joint Amal–imperial force attacking them was to reach maximum strength only on the Hebrus river near Hadrianople (Malchus fr. 18. 2). Military operations need not coincide with their area of settlement, but this is perhaps likely. Besides, other allied groups seem to have occupied Moesia Inferior and Scythia Minor. Between 474 and 476 the Pannonian Goths moved from Macedonia to Moesia Inferior (Ch. 8), and Scythia Minor was already held by the Huns of Hernac (*Getica* 50. 266).[43]

It is worth stressing that such treatment would have been quite exceptional; other foreign settlers were kept north of the Haemus mountains. The Amal-led Goths, for instance, were not even settled on the Plain when their leader was consul and *MVM praesentalis* (p. 301). Similarly, of six foreign settlements allowed after the collapse of the Hun Empire, only one (although a second is unidentifiable) was placed on the Thracian Plain. A mixed group of Rugi and other peoples was settled around Bizye and Arcadiopolis, but the others were stationed primarily in Dacia Ripensis, the two Moesias, and Scythia Minor.[44] If tens of thousands of Thracian Goths were settled on the plain, this would be a further indication of the special relationship they enjoyed with Constantinople.

The evidence also suggests that they farmed at least some of the land they held. We have no explicit statement to that effect, but this lack is not in itself surprising. By *c*.470, the Thracian Goths held an established position in the Empire, and the basic pattern of their integration into it had already been set, long before Malchus provides us with detailed evidence on their dealings with the

---

[43] Surely to be identified with the son of Attila who refused to attack the Empire in the 460s (Priscus fr. 49; cf. *PLRE* ii. 400–1).

[44] *Getica* 50. 265–6: the Sacromontisi and Fossatisii cannot be placed.

Roman state (Malchus' evidence, for instance, proves that the Pannonian Goths were interested in farmland: see above). Any settlement on Thracian farmland would have been organized when the Goths first entered the Empire. It was not at issue in the 470s, when disputes centred on political solutions to relations between their leaders and the imperial authorities. We should expect, therefore, evidence only of a more incidental kind.

The fact that the Pannonian Goths received farmland is in itself a first indication that the same might be true of the Thracian Goths. The Empire is likely to have adopted the same approach to Gothic groups posing similar problems. Other evidence points in the same direction. In an embassy of 477, Theoderic Strabo asked to be allowed to live as a private citizen among his own people and enjoy possession of what he had already taken (Malchus fr. 18. 1, p. 426. 5 ff.). In economic terms, he was offering to live without the monetary income which came with the rank of *MVM praesentalis* and his followers' status as imperial troops. Such an offer could only have been made if his group had other means of support. None is specified, but farming is the obvious alternative. Similarly, co-conspirators of Marcian who fled to Strabo after their attempted coup, are picturesquely described farming among the Thracian Goths (Malchus fr. 22). This cannot be taken literally, but suggests strongly that farming was the Goths' normal occupation. Likewise, in another set of negotiations with Zeno, Strabo claimed to be unable to live off his own lands because he had now gathered together too many tribes (fr. 18. 1, p. 426. 12 ff.). Again, this seems to imply that his lands had normally produced enough to support his followers. Like their Pannonian counterparts, the Thracian Goths seem to have derived an income from cultivation in addition to annual payments from the Empire.

Again, this is not really surprising. Large annual payments from imperial treasuries were no doubt welcome, but land itself was always the basic means of accumulating wealth in the ancient world. And the Goths had always been farmers. As we have seen, fourth-century evidence (literary and archaeological) shows that they had then lived in small agricultural communities (Ch. 3), and while the Huns caused great dislocation to their way of life, this feature of it, at least, remained constant. The Goths who fled from the Huns and gathered behind Alaric seem to have continued, at least up to 418, to regard land as their main source of regular income (Ch. 6). Likewise, the Huns exploited the continued agricultural productivity of Goths remaining north of the Danube (Priscus fr. 49). Holding farmland also increased the security of the Goths' position inside the Empire. To have no other source of income but annual payments would have placed them entirely in the hands of the imperial authorities: in any dispute, money just had to be withheld for the Goths to face starvation. Land gave them some economic, and hence political independence; it could not be removed simply at the stroke of an emperor's pen. By *c*.470, as we have seen, the Thracian Goths were fully integrated into the Empire and may have been correspondingly disposed to trust the imperial authorities. This relationship had not sprung into being fully formed, and a land grant is likely to have played a major role in its initial creation.[45]

Of the origins of this relationship and the background history of the Thracian Goths, we have little explicit information. The *Getica* tells us that Theoderic Strabo already enjoyed great favour in Constantinople in the 450s under Marcian (*Getica* 52. 270). It is usually assumed, therefore, that Strabo led a Gothic force who had thrown off Hunnic domination after Attila's death and been accepted into the Empire at this point.[46] Jordanes' report is, however, highly problematic. First, Strabo is unlikely to have been pre-eminent at such an early date. As we have seen, the Gothic revolt sparked off by Aspar's murder was actually led by another of his Gothic associates, Ostrys. Theophanes does also mention Strabo in the attack on the imperial palace, but Malalas makes it clear that Ostrys took the lead not only in the attack on the palace, but also in the whole Thracian revolt. Ostrys' pre-eminent role seems to be reflected in the somewhat enigmatic saying that 'the dead man has no friend but Ostrys'.[47]

In addition, Aspar's marriage-alliance with the Triarius family was probably not made in the first instance with Theoderic Strabo himself. Strabo seems to have been the nephew of Aspar's wife (p. 255), and it is much more likely that the match consolidated links between Aspar and someone actually in the wife's (or even the preceding) generation. The wife's brother, Theoderic Strabo's

---

[45] *Contra* Liebeschuetz, *Barbarians and Bishops*, 80–1.

[46] Ensslin, *Theoderich der Große*, 12; Demandt, 'Magister Militum', 769 ff.; Wolfram, 260; Schmidt, 271, 278 ff.

[47] Malalas, Bonn 371–2; Theophanes AM 5964 (117 de Boor).

father perhaps, was probably the main object of the manœuvre; sisters or daughters, not aunts, are normally used to cement alliances. Jordanes' report that Strabo himself was already prominent in the 450s thus seems mistaken. The *Getica*'s report is designed to hide the fact that the Amals and the Triarius line fought out their rivalry over an entire decade after 473, so that this conclusion poses no great problem. A natural suggestion, indeed, is that the mysterious 'Triarius', father of the Thracian Theoderic, should be identified with the Ostrys so prominent in 470. Triarius is clearly the Latinized form of a Gothic name, of which 'Ostrys' might well be an alternative transcription.[48] Whatever the case, Theoderic Strabo certainly supplanted Ostrys some time between 471 and 473, when we find him (in Malchus) as the unchallenged leader of the Thracian Goths. If Ostrys was his father, he may just have died; if not, Theoderic must have killed and replaced him.

It is also unlikely that the Thracian Goths of the 470s had long been united behind a single leader. Ostrys is not the only Gothic leader associated with Thrace in the 460s, nor the only one with whom Aspar had dealings (cf. p. 255). The sources also mention Ullibos, probably a Goth, who revolted in Thrace and was killed there by a third Goth, Anagastes.[49] *MVM per Thracias*, Anagastes rebelled at about the same time as Ullibos (469/70), and their revolts were probably related; the circumstances of Ullibos' death (Anagastes killed him personally, *Suda Y* 583) suggest that the two had previously been working together, so that Anagastes may well have killed Ullibos as a rival. In 469, Anagastes was also involved in a plot to kill Zeno, later revealing that he had been suborned by Aspar's son Ardaburius (John of Antioch fr. 206. 2). Leaders other than Ostrys and Theoderic Strabo thus commanded Goths in

---

[48] I have sometimes wondered if Ostrys might not be Theoderic the son of Triarius in another guise, the chroniclers having confused *OTPIAPIOY*, for instance, or something similar as a name; in the same way, Photius, *Bibliotheca* 78 calls him Theoderic the son of Otriarius (τὸν τοῦ ᾿Οτριαρίου Θευδέριχον) probably as a misinterpretation of ΘΕΥΔΕΡΙΧΟΣΟΤΡΙΑΡΙΟΥ. But Theophanes' mention of Strabo alongside Ostrys in this attack seems to deny the doublet (cf. n. 47). The fact that Aspar married Strabo's aunt would in any case indicate that Strabo's family had been important in his father's generation. Schönfeld, *Wörterbuch*, offers no suggestion for Gothic names behind either Ostrys or Triarius.

[49] *PLRE* ii. 1180–1 and 75–6 respectively.

Thrace in the 460s (Anagastes had sufficient followers to seize some towns), and were cultivated by Aspar and Ardaburius.

The immediate origins of the Thracian Goths are thus far from simple. Theoderic Strabo led a united group in 473, but to do so must have superseded the other leaders known from the 460s. Ostrys perhaps just died, but the disappearance of Anagastes (not mentioned again after *c*.469) looks more sinister. His own removal of Ullibos perhaps presaged his own fate, and Strabo and the united Goths probably emerged from a struggle for pre-eminence between a number of leaders. The treaty of 473 between Strabo and the emperor Leo, as we shall see in more detail later, confirms the point. Leo was to recognize no other Gothic ruler, nor accept any other Goths into his service, clauses which betray the anxieties of a newly established leader (see below). The Gothic *foederati* of the 460s were thus probably composed of a number of groups settled in different parts of Thrace under individual commanders. Settling Goths in this way would have been more in conformity with traditional Roman policy: a united body would have posed a greater potential threat to the Empire than settlers divided into smaller units.

It is perhaps mistaken, therefore, to search for a single origin for the Thracian Goths. The groups united behind Theoderic Strabo in 473 could have entered the Empire on a number of occasions. The 450s are one likely period, when many peoples, including, as we have seen, the Pannonian Goths, threw off Hunnic dominion. Equally, the final crisis of the Hun Empire brought more Goths into the eastern Empire in the late 460s. Priscus describes the slaughter of one mixed Hun–Goth force at this time, but notes that there were many others (fr. 49). We also hear of a Gothic force led by Bigelis defeated at about this time.[50]

Some Goths, however, may have been in Thrace for a considerably longer period. The evidence is fragmentary, but this is to be expected, since the loss of much of the histories of Olympiodorus and Priscus means that we have no narrative account of the eastern Empire in the first half of the fifth century. What survives largely concerns certain important individuals, but does seem to reflect consistent Gothic involvement in the army, centred on Thrace. Anagastes, *MVM per Thracias* and leader of a revolt in 469/70,

---

[50] Jordanes, *Romana* 336; cf. *PLRE* ii. 229.

had a father Arnegisclus who was himself *MVM per Thracias* in the 440s (*PLRE* ii. 151). Other Germanic-named officers were his contemporaries. Ansila, Arintheus, and Ariobindus (*PLRE* ii. 92–3, 142–3, 145–6 respectively) were commanders of the ill-fated Vandal expedition of 441, which took troops from the Balkans.[51] Of these, Ariobindus was the most distinguished; he held the post of *comes foederatorum* in 422, before being appointed *MVM praesentalis* in 434, the same year that he was granted the consulate. Similarly, Fl. Plintha, a Goth and perhaps Aspar's father-in-law, was *comes* in 418 and *MVM praesentalis* between 419 and 438 (*PLRE* ii. 892–3).

The involvement of Gothic troops *en masse* in imperial armies of the 440s and before is harder to document, but the appearance of Gothic officers is perhaps an indication that they were present. It is particularly striking that Ariobindus was already *comes foederatorum* in 422,[52] for, as we have seen, the Thracian Goths were specifically designated *foederati*. In addition, Theophanes describes an early settlement of Goths in Thrace. The passage is largely taken from Procopius, but Theophanes adds a note, clearly dated to the 420s, that Goths were at that time moved from Pannonia to Thrace. The report is not conclusive,[53] but such a settlement would be consistent with the appearance of Gothic officers, including a *comes foederatorum*, associated in part with Thrace from the 420s onwards. And if at least some of the Thracian Goths had been part of the Empire for such a period, their special relationship with Aspar is readily explicable.

The full details are beyond recovery, but it seems clear that in the 460s the Thracian *foederati* consisted of a number of units, under several leaders, who had to be balanced against one another. Natural rivalries would otherwise have tended to violence, as they

---

[51] Cf. Maenchen-Helfen, 108–9.

[52] Malalas, Bonn 364; cf. Cedrenus, Bonn i. 599.

[53] Theophanes AM 5931 (94 de Boor); cf. Procopius, *Wars* 3. 2. 39–40 with Croke, 'The Hun Invasion of Thrace', 360. The Goths were resettled in the 19th year of Theodosius II: 421 (counting from 402 when he was first Augustus) or 427 (from 408, when he became sole emperor). As Croke shows, Theophanes uses both methods in different places. The main problem is that the Goths are said to have stayed in Thrace for 58 years, but no Gothic exodus is known in 479 or 485. An emendation to 68 years would solve the problem.

did in the 460s. Thus, whereas Aspar allied himself through marriage to Ostrys and gave him a command around the palace, Anagastes succeeded his father Arnegisclus as *MVM per Thracias*, Ariobindus was *comes foederatorum*, and others such as Ansila and Arintheus received lesser commands. This must always have been a delicate balancing act, and the rise of Zeno made it much more difficult. The Isaurian, it would seem, managed to win over to his camp Anagastes at least, persuading him to implicate Aspar's son Ardaburius (p. 255). Conflict at court between Aspar and the Isaurians probably gave greater scope to personal ambition among the Thracians, perhaps prompting the revolts of Ullibos and Anagastes in the late 460s. The murder of Aspar certainly provoked the more general Thracian revolt, in the course of which Theoderic Strabo eliminated all rivals to unite the Thracian *foederati*. Anarchy in court politics had allowed an over-mighty Gothic leader to establish himself in Thrace.

None of this would deny that Theoderic Strabo was a genuine Gothic leader. As we have seen, despite being in receipt of regular pay, the Thracian Goths probably still maintained part of their traditional agricultural way of life. The way in which they united behind Strabo's leadership in the 470s also suggests that much of their independent Gothic identity had survived their stay in the Empire (however long that may have been). While leaders such as Ostrys and Anagastes moved in court circles at the top end of imperial military hierarchies, absorbing much of imperial culture, there was little need for the rank and file to have been greatly affected by it. A crucial question is whether imperial subsidies were paid to each individual, or whether in lump sums to leaders who then distributed them to their followers. Our one piece of evidence suggests the latter. In 478, Zeno agreed to supply pay and food to 13,000 men 'chosen by Theoderic' (Malchus fr. 18. 4, p. 434. 13). Roman money thus reinforced rather than dismantled existing Gothic social hierarchies. The actions of Theoderic Strabo between 471 and 473 probably resembled those of Alaric before 395 (not to mention Valamer's in *c*.450), in uniting behind a single leader groups kept divided by the Romans or Huns. Strabo was also an imperial politician, but, as Alaric had found, once Goths were established on Roman land, this was simply another attribute of any successful Gothic leader.

C. The Year 473

In 473, the Pannonian Goths under Thiudimer advanced into Illyricum (*Getica* 56. 283 ff.).[54] This inaugurated direct competition with the Thracian Goths, who had previously been separated from them by several hundred kilometres and an imperial frontier. It has sometimes been argued that the emperor Leo actually invited the Pannonian Goths into the Empire to control the Thracian Goths, who were still in revolt.[55] No explicit evidence supports such an idea, however, and it rests largely on the assumption, derived from Jordanes, that the Amal-led Goths were especially favoured allies of the Empire. As we have seen, this is misleading (p. 56). Leo had preferred to support the Pannonian Goths' enemies on at least one occasion in the 460s, and it is hard to believe that he would introduce this large and independent force into imperial lands, where they would be difficult to control, and able to inflict costly damage.[56] Even Jordanes makes no claim that Thiudimer's Goths came at Leo's invitation. In the *Getica*, Gothic tribesmen demand to move because they faced economic hardship in Pannonia. After casting lots, Thiudimer tells Vidimer to go west, and himself undertakes what is explicitly a military expedition into Illyricum. The move was preceded by a successful attack on Singidunum, after which the Goths refused to return the city to the Empire; a further sign that they were not imperial allies (55. 282 ff.). The move from Pannonia was thus an attack on the Empire, and, as we have seen, the casting of lots probably hides a split between Thiudimer and his brother.

The decision to move had important consequences for the Goths, and could not have been taken lightly. To its Germanic neighbours, the eastern Empire would still have seemed very powerful, having just survived Attila's onslaughts. In part, the Goths were surely motivated by economic considerations, as

[54] Going west at the same time, Vidimer encountered the emperor Glycerius, who ruled from Mar. 473 to June 474: *PLRE* ii. 1069–70. Schmidt, 278–9 (cf. Burns, *History of the Ostrogoths*, 64–5) dates the move to 471 because he mistakenly dates Theoderic's kingship from Thiudimer's death: n. 15.

[55] e.g. Martin, *Theoderich der Große*, 24 ff.; Burns, *History of the Ostrogoths*, 67–8; Wolfram, 268.

[56] In 479 Zeno wanted to use the Thracian and Pannonian Goths to balance one another (Malchus fr. 20), but this was making the best of a bad situation, when the Goths were already established on imperial territory.

Jordanes reports. The eastern Empire offered much richer pickings than the middle Danube region. Malchus, for instance, has Theoderic Strabo say to the Amal-led Goths that they had entered the Empire to be able 'to measure gold by the bushel' (fr. 18. 2). But Thiudimer must also have taken account of the Empire's political situation. By 473, the Thracian Goths had been in revolt for two years, and imperial forces already faced one enemy in the Balkans. This gave the Pannonian Goths the perfect opportunity to invade, having perhaps prepared for the move by capturing Singidunum in the previous year.[57]

More specifically, Thiudimer probably also had it in mind to attempt to usurp the privileged position of Theoderic Strabo and his followers. The Thracian *foederati* received annual payments on a very large scale, seven times the size of the subsidy accorded the Pannonian Goths by Leo,[58] and their leaders enjoyed high court honours. Thiudimer surely had it in mind to share in these benefits, and the extended revolt of the Thracian Goths prompted him at least to attempt to persuade Leo that his followers might make better allies. It is perhaps not coincidental that Theoderic the Amal returned to his father in 471 (*Getica* 55. 281–2; cf. p. 246). He no doubt brought news of the Thracians' revolt, and, more important, after ten years at court, was fully aware of the benefits usually enjoyed by the Thracian Goths. Jordanes reports that jealousy of Theoderic Strabo underlay Valamer's attack on Illyricum in the 450s (*Getica* 52. 270–1), but Strabo was not then undisputed leader in Thrace, and this observation seems much more relevant to Thiudimer's attack of 473.[59]

His Goths advanced along the main road south from Pannonia as far as Naissus, where they divided their forces. One group under Theoderic advanced by way of Ulpiana to Stobi, while Thiudimer took the other main route south, leaving garrisons in his wake. Serious opposition was first encountered outside Thessalonica—an army led by the Patrician Hilarianus—and a truce

---

[57] Jordanes portrays Theoderic's attack on the Sarmatians and capture of Singidunum (*c.*472) as an independent action, but it laid open the main road to Naissus; cf. Wolfram, 267.

[58] In 473, the Thracian Goths were granted 2,000 lb. of gold by Leo (p. 267), the Pannonian Goths extracted 300 lb. of gold per annum in *c.*460 (p. 247).

[59] For an alternative view, see Wolfram, 269.

followed. Land in the Macedonian canton of Eordaia (encompassing the cities of Cyrrhus, Pella, Europus, Methone, Pydna, Beroea,
and Dium) was granted the Goths in return for peace (*Getica* 56.
285–7). This was a fertile area, through which a number of major
routes passed. The Via Egnatia ran east–west from Dyrrhachium
to Constantinople, while other routes led north from Thessalonica
to the Danube via Scupi, and south into Thessaly and Greece.[60]

We are not told whether the Pannonian Goths at this point
received a subsidy greater than the 300 lb. of gold granted by Leo,
but it is perhaps unlikely. In 476 the Senate reported to Zeno that
the Empire could not afford such sums for both sets of Goths at
once (Malchus fr. 15, p. 420. 10 ff.), and in 473 the Empire finally
made peace with the Thracian Goths, agreeing to pay them a large
sum (see below). The Pannonian Goths, therefore, probably did
not win a large subsidy as well, but did receive good agricultural
land, guaranteeing them a basic income (cf. p. 244). No account
survives of the Goths' resettlement in Eordaia. The negative
reactions of the citizens of nearby Thessalonica and Dyrrhachium
to rumours that the same Goths were returning to the area in 479
suggest, however, that it caused considerable disruption.[61] But
even if the Pannonian Goths merely swapped one parcel of
agricultural land for another (and Jordanes claims no imperial
honours for Thiudimer), they had begun to make an impact on the
minds of imperial politicians. Previously an important neighbour,
they were now a powerful independent force within the Empire's
borders.

The imperial authorities seem to have wanted to deal with the
Pannonian Goths largely by diplomacy. Battle was expensive and
dangerous, and Theoderic Strabo was still in revolt further east. It
is perhaps not surprising, therefore, that the Empire confronted
the Pannonian Goths, initially at least, only to force them to come
to terms. The official sent to deal with them, Hilarianus, was Leo's
magister officiorum. A civilian administrator, he perhaps did not

---

[60] Bury, i. 412 n. 14 argued that Thiudimer reached only Naissus in 473, but
the Goths were then settled near Thessalonica: Hammond, *Macedonia*, i. 106 ff.
They would have remembered Cyrrhus, near Thessalonica, where Thiudimer
died shortly afterwards: *Getica* 56. 288.

[61] Malchus fr. 20; cf. Wolfram, 273.

actually command the army, but was empowered, like Adamantius in 479, to conduct negotiations and supervise a settlement.[62] The area chosen to receive the Goths reflects imperial interests. It did not contain large cities, so that the settlement threatened none of the main centres of imperial administration and culture. The Goths were kept at a safe distance from Constantinople, and the road-network made it possible both to use the newcomers and to concentrate forces against them swiftly in any emergency.

Events in Thrace in the same year make sense when it is realized that the Empire faced this simultaneous threat in Macedonia. Theoderic Strabo was able to attack two major cities, Arcadiopolis and Philippopolis,[63] without having to fight an imperial army. The former was starved into submission, while buildings outside the walls were burnt at Philippopolis.[64] This total freedom of action probably reflects the transfer of much of the imperial army to Thessalonica; the two Gothic groups had overstretched imperial military resources. Nevertheless, the Thracian Goths also found it expedient to compromise. The Empire was constrained by the damage they inflicted on its cities, but the Goths were themselves suffering from famine.

The aims of the Thracian Goths can be reconstructed because Malchus summarizes both the final treaty with Leo in 473 and Theoderic Strabo's initial demands. Regarding financial matters, he originally demanded that his people should 'possess Thrace' (νέμεσθαι τὴν Θράκην συγχωρηθῆναι αὐτῷ). The exact significance of this phrase is unclear, but it seems similar to Fritigern's open demand in 378 (p. 175), suggesting that he had it in mind to turn Thrace into a semi-independent domain, where he would exercise unfettered authority and control revenues. In the final treaty, however, he was forced to moderate his demands, securing instead an annual income of 2,000 lb. of gold, probably in the form

---

[62] *PLRE* ii. 561–2; on Adamantius, see Malchus fr. 20. On the other hand, Illus was to command praesental forces as *magister officiorum* in 478 (Ch. 8).

[63] 'Philippi' (Malchus fr. 2, p. 408. 13) is probably Philippopolis. Malchus is explicit that Strabo's two attacks were made in Thrace, and the name has this meaning in Priscus fr. 14, p. 292. 78; *contra* Cesci, *Malco*, 166.

[64] Malchus fr. 2 Malchus fr. 1. refers to the 17th and last year of the emperor Leo—7 Feb. 473 onwards—so that fr. 2, where Leo is still alive, must again refer to 473; cf. Cresci, *Malco*, 164.

of salaries for military service.[65] Winning an annual income in gold was probably Strabo's first concern; it gave him considerable and regular powers of patronage which no doubt strengthened the loyalties of his followers. These powers are emphasized by the wording of his second treaty with the eastern Empire in 478, where pay and rations were to be distributed to 13,000 men 'whom Theoderic [Strabo] chose' (Malchus fr. 18. 4, p. 434. 13).

Strabo's ambitions for a career at court also find expression. He demanded to succeed to Aspar's titles, and in the actual treaty was appointed to an imperial command: στρατηγὸν δύο στρατηγιῶν τῶν ἀμφὶ βασιλέα, αἵπερ εἰσὶ μέγισται εἰς τὴν ἑτέραν γῆν.[66] The first part of this is simply a Greek form of *magister utriusque militiae praesentalis*. The mention of 'two forces' refers to the cavalry and infantry of which each praesental army was in theory composed; *magister utriusque militiae* is a later form of *magister equitum et peditum*, which makes the point clear.[67] τῶν ἀμφὶ βασιλέα speaks for itself.[68] The second part of Malchus' description is harder to interpret, but seems to be making the point that Strabo commanded the senior of the praesental armies. The two praesental armies appear in the *Notitia Dignitatum* as equal, and even parallel,[69] but in the second half of the fifth century, one was known as the 'the Great Praesental Army'. According to Malalas, Armatus in *c*.475 (Bonn 378), Longinus in 486 (*De Insidiis* 164), and Patricius in 503 (Bonn 398; cf. Zacharias of Mytilene, *HE* 7. 4) all commanded this senior force.[70] αἵπερ εἰσὶ μέγισται is thus

---

[65] Wolfram, 269 argues that Triarius was demanding settlement in Thrace, but this does not seem strong enough. He also fails to notice that the final agreement was a compromise.

[66] Malchus fr. 2. Blockley, ii. 408. 23–5 follows the suggestion of Valesius in emending εἰς τὴν ἑτέραν γῆν to εἰς τὴν σφετέραν γῆν and moving the phrase after ἀποστῆναι (ibid. 26). As we shall see, the phrase is difficult to interpret, but this escape does not seem legitimate; cf. Cresci, *Malco*, 167: who points out, amongst other things, that μέγισται seems to require some kind of qualification.

[67] Jones, esp. 124–5, 174 ff., 341 ff., 375–6, 608 ff.

[68] John of Antioch fr. 210 calls Triarius *MVM per Thracias*, but an emendation from διέπων to διέποντα would make Heraclius, and not the Goth, commander in Thrace: cf. *PLRE* ii. 542; Blockley, ii. 457 n. 8.

[69] *Not. Dig.*, Or. 5, 6; cf. Hoffmann, *Bewegungsheer*, 409 ff.

[70] Cf. Stein, ii. 431 n. 4. Command of the first praesental army (the *Notitia* distinguishes them as 'first' and 'second') was perhaps always senior. In 399, one *MVM praesentalis*, Gainas, was already senior to the other (Zosimus 5. 15. 5; cf. Demandt, 'Magister militum', 734–5.

making the point that the two praesental forces commanded by
Strabo (one of cavalry and one of infantry) were larger than the
two commanded by the other *MVM praesentalis*. εἰς τὴν ἐτέραν
γῆν remains problematic, but Malchus is perhaps giving a geographical indication of where the senior army was stationed.[71]
Alternatively, ἐτέραν could be emended to ἡμετέραν, so that
Malchus is commenting that Strabo was appointed to the two
forces 'which are the greatest in our (sc. Roman) land'. This kind
of comment is paralleled elsewhere in Malchus.[72]

Leo thus appointed Theoderic Strabo to the most senior
command in the eastern army. This pre-eminent position had
many benefits. Amongst other things, it made him an *illustris* with
ready access to the emperor and court. Where such benefits may
have remained largely potential for Alaric after 397 (Ch. 6),
Strabo, as we have seen, already had many contacts in Constantinople from his days in Aspar's entourage, and was probably
genuinely interested in the prospect of exercising influence at the
heart of the Empire. At the same time, the post was important to
him as Gothic leader. His acceptance at court guaranteed the long
term security of his followers as allied troops of the Empire. This
must have strengthened their confidence in this newly established
leader.

The other clauses of the treaty acknowledged Theoderic Strabo's place in the Gothic world. Leo recognized him as 'sole ruler of
the Goths' (τῶν Γότθων αὐτοκράτορα[73]), and promised not to
receive any of 'them' (meaning Goths: αὐτῶν referring to Γότθων)
who wished to serve him. Unlike the other clauses, these are not
separated by δέ but united by καί, and refer to the same subject:
Gothic affairs.[74] Strabo had been only one of several important

---

[71] Haldon, *Byzantine Praetorians*, 447 n. 363 assumes that the two armies
were billeted either side of the Bosporos. Incidental references do suggest such a
geographical distinction. Gainas and Leo commanded on either side of the
Bosporos in 399 (Zosimus 5. 14. 1 ff.), Armatus' praesental troops were stationed
on the European side (Malalas, Bonn 379), and Illus in 478 mobilized an army
from Asia which can only be a praesental force (Malchus fr. 18. 1).

[72] e.g. fr. 20, p. 436. 24–6.

[73] Schmidt, 271, translates it 'Gothic king', which misses the significance.

[74] Malchus fr. 2. Blockley, ii. 408. 25–7 inserts εἰς τὴν σφετέραν γῆν at this
point (cf. n. 66). But the text is best read αὐτὸν δὲ τῶν Γότθων αὐτοκράτορα εἶναι,
καὶ μηδένας ἐξ αὐτῶν ἀποστῆναι θέλοντας τὸν βασιλέα δέχεσθαι; cf. Cresci,
Malco, 167.

Goths in Aspar's entourage in the 460s, and, as we have seen, between Aspar's murder in 471 and 473 had established his pre-eminence among the Thracian *foederati*. In this context, the clauses have an obvious significance. Strabo was extracting imperial recognition for his newly established position in Thrace; he was 'sole ruler' there and no negotiations should take place with anyone else.[75] The second provision was probably designed to prevent the Empire from harbouring any fugitive rivals, whose cause might be revived at a critical moment to undermine his authority.[76]

The clauses may also have had a wider significance, responding to the direct challenge posed to Strabo's position by the Amal-led Goths in 473. His claim to be 'sole ruler' of the Goths also subordinated to himself the Amal leaders of the Pannonian Goths, as much as any Thracian rivals. The second clause, similarly, could be interpreted as an attempt to limit Leo's dealings with the Pannonian newcomers. Leo promised not to receive any Goths, not just Thracian deserters, and the second clause may mirror a concern that the Pannonian Goths should not replace the Thracians as imperial *foederati*.

From the Empire's point of view, the arrival of the Pannonian Goths overstretched military capacity, so that Leo was forced to make concessions to both Gothic groups. But direct rule was maintained over Thrace; in 473, the Thracian Goths failed to turn it into an independent kingdom. And, despite his new dignities, Theoderic Strabo was not yet in a position to take up the mantle of Aspar, so that Leo did not lose his political independence. Strabo had prestige, but Aspar's ability to influence imperial affairs had been built up from the 420s by the constant exercise of patronage; Theoderic Strabo's men did not fill all the important posts at court. Equally important, the Isaurians, and particularly Zeno (perhaps the other *MVM praesentalis*), still remained to balance the Goths. The Goths' return to court may even have provided Leo with a useful counter to the Isaurians, whose undisputed influence was probably no more welcome to him than that of Aspar.

[75] Cf. Bury, i. 413 n. 3; Cresci, *Malco*, 167–8. It has usually been thought that Strabo wanted this recognition because he was not a proper Gothic leader, but this is mistaken (cf. p. 263).
[76] Cf. Wolfram, 269.

The Pannonian Goths created a new strategic situation in 473. Two Gothic groups now faced each other in the Balkan provinces of the Empire, in response to which two agreements established a balance of power. Theoderic Strabo returned to court politics and gained financial rewards for his followers, while the Pannonian Goths, if more on the periphery, took over good agricultural land and increased their potential as a force in imperial politics. Natural rivalry between the two Gothic groups made for tensions which this compromise did nothing to ease, however, and the balance of power was shattered after less than twelve months by the death of the emperor Leo.

8

ZENO AND THE GOTHS, 474–479

On 18 January 474 the emperor Leo I died (Theophanes AM 5966 (120 de Boor)), to be succeeded by his 7-year-old grandson Leo II, the son of his daughter Ariadne and, more significantly, of Zeno, the Isaurian Patrician and *MVM praesentalis*. Power was in fact wielded by Zeno, proclaimed co-emperor on 9 February 474. When Leo II died in November 474 Zeno became sole Augustus.[1] Power had passed to an Isaurian generalissimo, and the balance between Goths and Isaurians established in 473 was overturned.

A. *The Usurpation of Basiliscus, 474–476*

Late in 474, a conspiracy was hatched against Zeno, initially at court. It involved the empress Verina, wife of Leo I, her brother the Patrician Basiliscus, their nephew Armatus, *MVM per Thracias*, and the former *magister officiorum* Patricius. They also won support from the Isaurian general Illus and Theoderic Strabo. Fearful of assassination, Zeno was tricked into leaving Constantinople, and fled to Isauria. His supporters in the city were massacred. Basiliscus took the throne (although Verina seems to have intended her lover Patricius to rule) and reigned from January 475 to August 476.[2]

Zeno, however, was an Isaurian chieftain with sources of support in his own country, so that Basiliscus sent Illus and his brother Trocundes against him with an army. Away from Constantinople, they decided, after capturing Zeno's brother Longinus, that more was to be gained from Zeno than Basiliscus. Presumably, they thought to use Longinus as a hostage.[3] When the

---

[1] Brooks, 'Zenon and the Isaurians', 211 ff.

[2] John of Antioch fr. 210; Candidus in Photius, *Bibliotheca* 79; Malalas, Bonn 368; *Chronicon Paschale*, s.a. 478; cf. Brooks, 'Zenon and the Isaurians', 216–17.

[3] Marcellinus Comes s.a. 485 (*CM* ii. 93) records that Illus released Longinus in 485 after ten years' captivity; cf. Brooks, 'Zenon and the Isaurians', 217 ff.

MVM praesentalis Armatus, leading Basiliscus' troops around Constantinople, also changed sides (Malalas, Bonn 379), the usurper's fate was sealed. In August 476 Zeno returned to the capital in triumph. Between January 474 and August 476 there were thus three imperial administrations, a political instability which offered great opportunities to the Goths. Both groups were militarily powerful, and in great demand among claimants to the throne.

The Thracian Goths

The actions of Theoderic Strabo were largely dictated by past quarrels. Before 471, his alliance with Aspar had brought him into conflict with Zeno, and relations between them quickly deteriorated again in 474. Zeno now controlled the imperial treasuries from which Strabo was accustomed to pay his followers. This, of course, was a potential threat to his whole position. On the other hand, Zeno had himself only recently acquired the throne and was far from secure. He in turn could not but be suspicious of Strabo as the leader of a powerful force with whom he had previously competed.

Hostilities do not seem to have broken out immediately. Strabo had captured one of Zeno's supporters, the *MVM per Thracias* Heraclius (cf. p. 268); an exchange of messages arranged a ransom which secured his release. According to John of Antioch (fr. 210), Heraclius' murder preceded the Thracian Goths' revolt, so that his capture must be placed before the start of open warfare. Perhaps Strabo seized him in a preventive move, or in response to Zeno cutting off funds from the Thracian Goths. Heraclius, however, was murdered shortly after his release in Arcadiopolis, by some Goths who were perhaps acting on Strabo's orders,[4] and war soon followed. The nature of the fighting is not recorded, but the Goths probably again attacked Thracian cities; we hear only that Illus brought them relief (ibid.). Unlike 473, imperial forces were not distracted by attacks elsewhere in the Balkans, and Theoderic Strabo seems to have achieved nothing significant.

This mattered little, because Basiliscus' successful coup allowed him to return to court. Between January 475 and August 476 Strabo was again *MVM praesentalis*, receiving other unspecified

---

[4] Malchus fr. 6. 1. 2; cf. p. 238.

honours, and owning wealth and property in Constantinople.[5] On
his promotion, annual payments were presumably restored to his
followers; the Thracian Goths were once more soldiers of the
Empire (cf. p. 258). Some of his wider ambitions, however, were
resisted. Unlike Leo in 473, Basiliscus appointed Strabo only to
the junior praesental command. Malalas reports that Armatus
commanded the 'Great Praesental Army' under Basiliscus (Bonn
378), which is confirmed by an entry in the *Suda* which tells us
that Armatus was the most powerful man in the state, and that
Strabo 'took it hard . . . that he was surpassed in honour by a
young man who thought only of his hair and attending to his
body'.[6] As his previous demands to inherit Aspar's titles confirm
(p. 268), Strabo wanted a career of similar stature to that of his
former patron, but Basiliscus may have feared to fall too much
under the influence of his Gothic general.

The Thracian leader seems to have succeeded, however, in
establishing his influence at court in a second way. In a speech to
the army after his return from exile, Zeno made several accusa-
tions against Strabo, amongst which he claimed that the Goth had
persuaded Basiliscus to disband the army on the grounds that the
Goths were sufficient by themselves (Malchus fr. 15, p. 422. 21–2).
Zeno had reason to exaggerate, since he was preparing his
audience for a possible war against the Thracian Goths, but we do
hear of Goths among Basiliscus' palace guard (*Life of Daniel the
Stylite* 75). These words perhaps mean, therefore, that Strabo
reintroduced Gothic troops to Constantinople, replacing with
them the Scholae and palace guards.[7] No regular troops were
stationed in the city,[8] and the desire to maintain troops in the
capital was common to all who sought power in this period. Aspar
kept many Goths among the palace troops, and Zeno kept
Isaurians nearby at Chalcedon.[9]

Theoderic Strabo thus used Basiliscus' usurpation to further his
political ambitions and strengthen his position as Gothic leader.
The return of Zeno, however, negated all his gains, for the Goth

[5] Theophanes AM 5970 (126 de Boor); Malchus fr. 18. 4; cf. *PLRE* ii. 1074–5.
[6] *Suda* A 3970 translated in Blockley, ii. 477.
[7] Schmidt, 279–80 (and others) consider Strabo to have planned a usurpation,
but this goes beyond the evidence; cf. Cresci, *Malco*, 201–2.
[8] Cf. Dagron, *Naissance*, 108 ff.
[9] Aspar: p. 255; Zeno: John of Antioch frr. 210, 211. 3; Theophanes AM 5964
(117–18 de Boor).

lost his honours and his followers their subsidies. The Thracian Goths did not actually defend Basiliscus in summer 476, and this has been taken as a sign that Strabo had become disaffected with the usurper's regime because of Armatus. But the Thracian Goths could expect no favours from Zeno, and it seems much more likely that they were preoccupied with the Amal-led Goths, who, by summer 476, were allies of Zeno and established just north of the Haemus (see below). On Zeno's return, the overall position of the Thracian Goths' was considerably more precarious than it had been even after Aspar's murder or Zeno's accession. By 476, the Pannonian Goths were fully-fledged rivals for the privileges which had previously been the preserve of the Thracian *foederati*.

The Amal-Led Goths

Unless they were destroyed or expelled, it was inevitable that the Pannonian Goths would eventually increase their involvement in imperial affairs: a powerful military force could not move into imperial lands without materially affecting the political balance of power. The nature of their involvement was dictated by the relationship which grew up between the emperor Zeno and Theoderic the son of Thiudimer. Zeno used the Pannonian Goths to neutralize the power of the Thracians, and, in return, Theoderic the Amal received imperial honours, money, and recognition.

It is not clear when Zeno first made contact with the Pannonian Goths. Probably in 474, Thiudimer died while they were still settled in Macedonia (*Getica* 56. 288),[10] but by 476 they had established themselves some 400 km. to the north at Novae in Moesia Inferior (Anon. Val. 9. 42). Nothing is heard of them between, but their most direct route would have been along the main roads via Stobi, Serdica, and Oescus (Fig. 7). Once again, the move seems to have involved the whole group, since the return journey in 478/9 involved women, herds, and a substantial baggage-train (Malchus frr. 18. 2, pp. 428. 28 ff., 430. 55–6; 20, p. 446. 228 ff.). It is in any case unlikely that the non–combatants would have been left behind without protection.[11] Once established at Novae, the Amal-led Goths were astride numerous

[10] Cf. *PLRE* ii. 1078; Wolfram, 269–70; Ensslin, *Theoderich der Große*, 40.

[11] Burns, *History of the Ostrogoths*, 59–60 seems to have been confused by Theoderic's later offer (Malchus fr. 20, p. 446. 215 ff.) into thinking that he took with him only picked warriors in 476.

north–south routes through the Haemus, and the passes through
the eastern Haemus are too gentle to be blocked against an
invader. They could thus intervene quickly in Thrace.

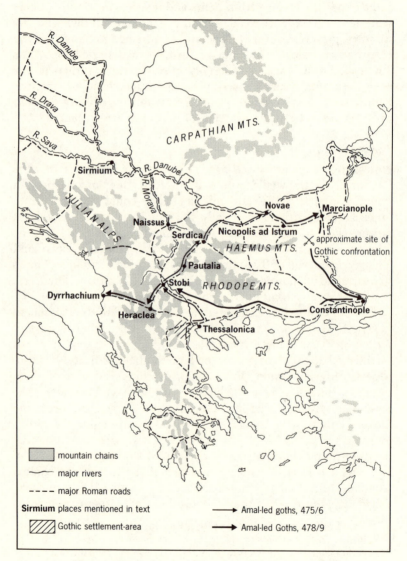

FIG. 7. Campaigns of Theoderic the Amal, 476–9

The few indications we have agree that the move to Novae had not been agreed beforehand with Zeno. In conversation with Adamantius outside Dyrrhachium in late 479, the Goth described it in these words, 'I chose to live completely outside Thrace, far away towards Scythia' (Malchus fr. 20, p. 444. 171–2). This strongly suggests that Theoderic had himself decided to move to Novae (which was, as he put it, 'outside Thrace and near Scythia Minor'). The Anonymous Valesianus seems to confirm this, recording that the first contact between Zeno and Theoderic occurred while Zeno was still in Isauria, but after the Goths had already reached Novae (9. 42).[12]

No explicit record of the Amal's motives survives, but the general context is suggestive. In 473, the Pannonian Goths had deliberately sought to exploit the Empire's difficulties for economic and political gain. Hilarianus, however, confined them to Macedonia, and there is no sign that Thiudimer received imperial honours or a substantial subsidy (Ch. 7). In other words, the Goths had failed to win the hoped-for benefits. In similarly aggressive vein, their leaders probably used the chaos engendered by Basiliscus' usurpation to move their followers to Novae precisely to offer Zeno the opportunity of using them against Basiliscus. Taking over a major military base on the Danube,[13] they put themselves in a position to intervene in the Thracian Plain. That attracting Zeno's attention was a conscious aim is also suggested by the Amal's own account of his motives, 'staying [in Novae] I thought that I should trouble no one, yet from there I should be ready to obey whatever the emperor commanded' (Malchus fr. 20, p. 444. 172 ff.). The Amal's aims were the same as his father's in 473; he wanted to involve his Goths more fully in imperial affairs, and win a share of the financial and other benefits that would naturally follow.[14]

When Zeno returned from exile in 476, the terms of his relationship with the Amal had been settled. He had negotiated with the Goths while still in Isauria, and although the sources

[12] Wolfram, 270; Schmidt, 280–1; Bury, i. 412 consider the move unofficial, Burns, *The Ostrogoths*, 68–9 as a sign of an early alliance.

[13] Novae controlled an easy Danube crossing, and was heavily fortified: Hoddinott, *Bulgaria in Antiquity*, 128; Poulter, 'Town and Country', 101; Chichikova, 'Novae', 11 ff.

[14] Wolfram, 270 suggests that the move also gave Theoderic the chance to attract further followers from barbarian kingdoms to the north.

record no Pannonian Gothic involvement in Zeno's return, the threat they posed from north of the Haemus may well have attracted Theoderic Strabo away from Constantinople in summer 476. Zeno granted a generalship and other honours to the Amal precisely on condition that he attack Strabo (fr. 18. 2, p. 426. 4–5), and the Amal originally promised to fight his Gothic rival by himself (fr. 18. 3, p. 432. 18–19). There is every reason to suppose that this *quid pro quo* already applied in 476, since it is hard otherwise to envisage why the Thracian Goths did not defend Basiliscus. The struggle for the imperial throne thus incidentally intensified Gothic rivalries; the two groups now faced each other across the Haemus mountains.

For the Amal-led Goths, Zeno's triumphant return from exile brought great rewards. Theoderic the Amal replaced Strabo as *MVM praesentalis*, and we know that his followers received the moneys that usually went to the Thracian *foederati*. In 477, Zeno rejected an approach from the Thracian Goths on the grounds that the Empire could not afford to pay both Gothic groups at once (Malchus fr. 15). The Amal was also designated Patrician and 'friend', adopted as son-at-arms, and apparently given large personal gifts.[15] He had fulfilled many of the personal aims which had prompted the move from the middle Danube region, and strengthened himself as Gothic leader in the process. A large annual income had been secured (or, at least, the promise of it; the sums were perhaps never paid[16]), and, together with imperial honours, this must have increased his prestige and his hold on his followers' loyalties. In summer 476, a new Gothic leader seemed to have been rewarded for audacity with the prospect of a prosperous future in the eastern Empire.

B. *The Empire Strikes Back, 476–479*

By late summer 476, Zeno had regained the throne, but only by bargaining with Illus who held his brother Longinus hostage. Concessions had also been made to another of Basiliscus' supporters, Armatus, who was appointed *MVM praesentalis* for life,

[15] Malchus fr. 20, p. 444. 186 ff.; cf. e.g. *PLRE* ii. 1079; Wolfram, 270–1; Schmidt, 279 ff.; Ensslin, *Theoderich der Große*, 44.

[16] Theoderic complained in 479 that he had never seen his paymaster (Malchus fr. 20, p. 444. 176 ff.). This seems to refer to the whole period after 476.

Patrician, and consul for 476, his son Patricius receiving the dignity of Caesar.[17] Zeno had reason to feel insecure, but the situation was more stable than it had been in 474, and Zeno was able to begin tackling the overall strategic problem posed by the Goths.

For 477 we have no narrative outline, but Malchus records diplomatic contacts which illuminate the ebb and flow of fortunes. Early in the year, the Thracian Goths sent a first embassy to Zeno stating that Strabo 'wished to live a life of peace and not to be at war with the state'.[18] A later message of Zeno also recalls this embassy, describing its proposals in more detail. Strabo offered to live as a private citizen, renouncing all imperial honours—and hence the subsidy which came to his followers when he was a recognized imperial general—and was willing for his son to become a hostage.[19] Early in 477, therefore, Strabo felt sufficiently threatened to offer Zeno peace on terms which, on the surface at least, were quite unfavourable to himself.

The nature of the threat is unspecified, but probably centred around some kind of confrontation with the Amal-led Goths. Early in 478, Zeno urged the Amal-led Goths to delay battle with Strabo no longer (Malchus fr. 18. 2, p. 426. 3–5), so that 477 cannot have seen fighting between them on a large scale, but there may well have been some raiding or skirmishing. Theoderic the Amal had not just remained at Novae, but by winter 477/8 was encamped at Marcianople (ibid., p. 428. 12 ff.), much closer to the Thracian Goths. In 478, Strabo could also accuse the Amal of creating Gothic widows (ibid. p. 430. 49–50), so that some fighting

---

[17] Malalas, Bonn 379; *Chron. Pasch.*, s.a. 478, 484; cf. *PLRE* ii. 149.

[18] Malchus fr. 15; dated by the *Gentium ad Romanos* fragments, where it is no. 4: no. 3 (fr. 14) records embassies congratulating Zeno on regaining the throne, which must be dated late 476; no. 4 opens 'in the next year', suggesting that it belongs to the year after no. 3, i.e. 477 (cf. Cresci, *Malco*, 197–8). This is confirmed by no. 5 (fr. 17) beginning 'in the same year' which records an embassy from the Vandal Huneric whose contents suggest strongly that it was sent early in the king's reign; Huneric was crowned in Jan. 477. Cf. Cresci, 197–8: the anti-Armatus polemic of Zeno's speech also dates the fragment; Zeno had him assassinated in 477.

[19] Malchus fr. 18. 1, p. 426. 5–9; cf. Wolfram, 271; Blockley, ii. 459 n. 32; Cresci, *Malco*, 207–8.

had taken place: perhaps in 477, as well as in 478. Whatever form fighting took in 477, Strabo emerged from it in the ascendant, having attracted rank-and-file Gothic support away from his Amal rival. By early 478, we are told, the former had become stronger and the latter weaker, and the reason the Thracian leader now gave for rejecting the unfavourable terms he had previously offered was that he had more people to feed (fr. 18. 1, p. 426. 1–4, 12–15). The indications seem unequivocal; in 477 Strabo improved his position by winning over some of his rival's followers. This gave him confidence to press Zeno for a more favourable settlement.

For the next two years, we have more information.[20] When Strabo rejected Zeno's offer, the emperor turned back to Theoderic the Amal, ostensibly agreeing to mount a joint campaign with him against the Thracian Goths (see below). The Amal moved south towards Hadrianople, where the combined force was to reach maximum strength on the River Hebrus. He found, however, only the Thracian Goths, encamped on Mount Sondis. This has never been identified, but was a high point, difficult to attack, which dominated the Amal's route through the Haemus (fr. 18. 2, p. 428. 23 ff.). Malchus mentions that neither Thracian nor praesental troops had met the Amal, but this must not confuse the geography; the Amal had just reached the 'Gates of the Haemus', and the confrontation took place in a 'wilderness' ($\dot{\epsilon}\rho\eta\mu\dot{\iota}a$), which must refer to the Haemus mountains rather than the Thracian Plain (Malchus uses 'wilderness' of another Balkan mountain range at fr. 20, p. 440. 110).[21] Instead of fighting, the two Theoderics concluded a non-aggression pact, and both sent embassies to Zeno.

Feeling himself betrayed, the Amal also advanced his troops towards Constantinople, demanding recompense. Zeno tried to bribe him into breaking the non-aggression pact, but without success. Skirmishing took place when the Amal's advance guard

---

[20] Other accounts: Schmidt, 280 ff.; Martin, *Theoderich der Große*, 36 ff.; Wolfram, 271 ff.; Ensslin, *Theoderich der Große*, 47 ff.; Bury, i. 415 ff.; Stein, ii. 12 ff. Burns, *History of the Ostrogoths*, 57 ff. misleadingly places the action during Zeno's exile.

[21] The solution usually preferred is that of Jirecek, *Die Heerstraße*, 147, who suggested the area between Provadija and Ajtos; cf. Cresci, *Malco*, 214.

reached the Long Walls,[22] but they were repulsed, and he retreated towards Rhodope. Before Zeno could capitalize on this success, mutinous talk among his troops forced their dispersal to winter quarters, and he made peace with the Thracian Goths. As these events unfolded late in 478, the Amal-led Goths seem to have been trapped on the Thracian Plain by imperial troops blocking adjacent mountain passes (Malchus fr. 18. 3–4).

The Amal-led Goths are next encountered in Macedonia. The year would seem to be 479; at least, the relevant fragment of Malchus (fr. 20) describes a continuous sequence of events, the last of which is dated to the end of that year.[23] In winter 478/9, therefore, Theoderic had probably traversed the passes between Thrace and Macedonia, where his sacking of Stobi convinced Zeno that peace had to be made (ibid., p. 436. 20 ff.). The Goths moved to Heraclea Lyncestis on the Pelagonian Plain, where supplies were provided while negotiations proceeded. Zeno offered them land around Pautalia (ibid., p. 438. 46 ff.), but Theoderic took what seemed to him a better opportunity. Through Sidimund, a relative who held some land in the vicinity, he spread rumours in Dyrrhachium, the capital of Epirus Nova, that Zeno was about to settle his Goths in the area. The garrison and leading citizens fled, and Theoderic occupied the city with his more mobile forces (ibid., p. 440. 100 ff.).

In response, Zeno's representative Adamantius rushed to Dyrrhachium, where he negotiated with the Amal in an attempt to make peace. Adamantius, however, had no authority to offer the Goths anything other than Pautalia, so that Theoderic's counter-offers were referred to Zeno (ibid., p. 446. 222 ff.). In the meantime, the newly appointed *MVM per Illyricum* Sabinianus captured the Amal's baggage-train, which was still moving slowly towards Dyrrhachium. This convinced Zeno that he should follow a military policy rather than accept any of Theoderic's offers (ibid., p. 448. 258 ff.). By late 479, therefore, the Amal-led Goths were securely established in Dyrrhachium, but at war with the Empire; the treaty between Zeno and Theoderic Strabo had held firm since 478.

[22] Croke, 'Anastasian Long Walls' argues that the walls are those of the Chersonese, but this seems mistaken: Whitby, 'The Long Walls'.

[23] John of Antioch fr. 211. 3–4 dates the seizure of Dyrrhachium to late 479; cf. Cresci, *Malco*, 226–7.

Zeno's Gothic Policy

At first sight, Zeno seems to have offered complete support to Theoderic the Amal after returning from exile in 476.[24] He granted his group the honours and financial benefits which had previously belonged to the Thracian Goths, and, ostensibly at least, wanted the Amal-led Goths to fight the Thracian Goths and neutralize their power. Early in 478, for instance, 'Zeno . . . sent men to [the Amal], saying that he should put off battle [with Strabo] no longer, but take action now and fulfil the hopes for which he had been judged worthy of a Roman generalship' (Malchus fr. 18. 2, p. 426. 2–5). The Amal was thus made a general precisely to fight the Thracian Goths.

But Zeno was very cautious in his support for the Amal. Early in 477, for example, Zeno responded to the embassy of Strabo which offered peace on minimal terms (p. 279) in two ways. On the one hand, he stirred up the praesental troops against the Thracian Goths and arrested their supporters in the city. He did not actually reject the embassy, however, until he had heard more of what was happening outside the city (Malchus fr. 15, p. 422. 30–1). His answer must eventually have been negative (Zeno had made no treaty with Strabo by early 478: fr. 18. 1), but this episode shows that his support for the Amal was less than absolute; he did not simply dismiss Strabo's envoys out of hand. Before 478, Zeno was also unwilling to assist the Amal with imperial troops; the agreement of 476 stipulated that the Amal was to fight Strabo by himself. In winter 477/8, finally, Zeno, as we have seen, even attempted to come to terms with Theoderic Strabo when he realized the extent to which the Thracian leader had gained from his Amal rival. Strabo rejected the offer, but the exchange confirms that Zeno had never unquestioningly supported the Amal.

The real thrust of the emperor's scheming emerges from the events of 478. When Strabo rebuffed his embassy in winter 477/8, Zeno seemed to return to a policy of supporting the Amal, negotiating with him for a joint campaign against the Thracian Goths. Its ostensible aim was the complete destruction of the power of Theoderic Strabo. In addition to the 10,000 or so men who followed the Amal (p. 248), the joint force was to be composed of 2,000 cavalry and 10,000 infantry under the *MVM*

---

[24] Cf. Schmidt, 280; Burns, *The Ostrogoths*, 67–8; Ensslin, *Theoderich der Große*, 44–5; Martin, *Theoderich der Große*, 32.

per Thracias and a further 6,000 cavalry and 20,000 infantry from around Constantinople, presumably from the praesental armies (Malchus fr. 18. 2, p. 428. 14 ff.). A combined force of nearly 50,000 was thus to fight the *c.* 10,000 soldiers of Theoderic Strabo (p. 253). In the event, no imperial troops actually appeared.

This has sometimes been explained as the gap between Zeno's view of his troops' efficiency and their actual performance. And Malchus does tell us that 'when Zeno appointed Martinianus general, the army fell into disorder' (fr. 18. 2, p. 426. 1–2).[25] Further thought makes it clear, however, that Zeno must have issued orders that the Amal should be left without assistance.[26] To start with, mutinous talk caused the praesental troops to be dispersed to winter quarters only during the Amal's advance on Constantinople (fr. 18. 3, p. 432. 44 ff.). This was long after the two Theoderics had met and agreed not to fight, so that Zeno's troops had failed to appear (fr. 18. 2, p. 428. 23 ff.) before military unrest surfaced among them. Moreover, the Thracian field-army, also due to contribute to the operation, seems to have functioned properly in 478. When the Amal retreated towards Rhodope, he found the mountain-passes blocked by imperial troops (fr. 20, p. 446. 193–4; cf. p. 434. 1–2). These did not belong to the praesental forces, which Zeno had just dispersed, nor to the army of Illyricum.[27] The passes must have been blocked, therefore, by units of the Thracian field-army—some of the troops supposed to be assisting the Amal. As with the praesental troops, it cannot have been indiscipline which caused them to fail to act according to plan.[28]

Theoderic the Amal, at least, had no doubt that the real reason for the non-appearance of these troops was an imperial order (fr. 18. 3, p. 430. 3 ff.). Such an order would have been in keeping with the diplomacy of winter 477/8, when Zeno had attempted to make peace with Strabo, before drawing up plans for the joint campaign. The Amal had clearly suspected that a change of policy was being

[25] Burns, *The Ostrogoths*, 68–9, *History of the Ostrogoths*, 57–8; following Ensslin, *Theoderich der Große*, 46 ff.

[26] Cf. Martin, *Theoderich der Große*, 36 ff.; Wolfram, 271; Schmidt, 282.

[27] When Sabinianus was made its commander in 479, part was elsewhere with Onulf and the rest dispersed among the cities (Malchus fr. 20, p. 442. 131 ff.).

[28] Zeno claimed that the Thracian troops had been frightened away by secret negotiations between the two Theoderics (Malchus fr. 18. 3, p. 432. 20), but it was Zeno who had made secret overtures to the Thracian Goths (fr. 18. 1).

debated, because he insisted that the emperor and his officials should swear not to make peace with his rival before he would commit himself to the campaign (fr. 18. 2, p. 426. 5 ff.). It is also hard to escape the conclusion that Zeno deliberately misled the Amal over the location of the Thracian Goths. The plan seems to have envisaged no military action before the combined force reached full strength in the vicinity of Hadrianople. The two Theoderics actually met, however, much further north, in the eastern Haemus. Zeno must have known of Strabo's whereabouts, because he had just sent an embassy to him (p. 280). Hence, although Zeno knew the Thracian Goths to be in the Haemus, the joint operation worked on the assumption that they were near Hadrianople. In confirmation of the point, the Amal also later made the specific allegation that guides supplied by Zeno in 478 had taken him along obscure routes, which led straight to Mount Sondis and the Thracian Goths (Malchus fr. 20, p. 444. 178 ff.). The conclusion that Zeno drew up the whole plan in bad faith seems inescapable.

The emperor thus had his own plans for solving the Gothic problem. By withholding aid and concealing the true whereabouts of the Thracian Goths, he attempted to induce a head-on clash between the two Gothic groups. As Malchus makes Strabo comment, 'while remaining at peace [the Romans] wish the Goths to wear each other down. Whichever of us falls, they will be the winners with none of the effort, and whichever of us destroys the other side will . . . be left in diminished numbers to face Roman treachery' (Malchus fr. 18. 2, p. 428. 34 ff.). After the Goths had fought, the imperial forces, which Zeno had mobilized, were probably to intervene. Zeno perhaps hoped either to expel the Goths, or to break them down into less threatening groups and resettle them in safe areas, a policy more in line with the Empire's normal approach to foreign immigrants (cf. p. 123). He was calculating that mutual rivalry would force the Theoderics to fight. As it was, if perhaps not quite in the way Malchus presents it (p. 237), they recognized that fighting would benefit only Zeno, and forged a non-aggression pact (ibid. p. 428 ff. 30 ff.).

Zeno's strategic gamble was not so great, however, as it might at first seem. He would not have engineered such a confrontation without having a fall-back plan in case the Goths failed to fight. Although they were rivals, both Theoderics were suspicious of

Zeno; Strabo had refused a treaty with Zeno in winter 477/8, and the Amal had demanded oaths before agreeing to the joint attack. There must always have been a chance that they would see through Zeno's deceptions. The emperor's fall-back plan emerges, perhaps, from the actions of the Thracian and the praesental armies. In 478, the Thracian army blocked the Rhodope passes, while praesental troops skirmished with the Amal's advance guard on the Long Walls (p. 283). Zeno envisaged, perhaps, that the Thracian army would block the passes to keep the Goths in the open country of the Thracian Plain (as they did), while praesental forces advanced from Constantinople. The Goths would then have been trapped between the two, allowing Zeno to crush them or dictate severe terms. The real blow to Zeno, then, was probably not so much the non-aggression pact, but the threatened mutiny of the praesental troops. He was forced to disperse them to winter quarters rather than risk losing his throne. This left two hostile Gothic groups free on the Thracian Plain.

Malchus blames the troops' discontent on Zeno's cowardice (fr. 18. 3, p. 432. 43 ff.). But Malchus levelled the charge of cowardice generally at Zeno (p. 236), and it was probably a political dispute at court which ruined the emperor's plans. In 478, relations between himself and Illus, his fellow Isaurian and *magister officiorum*, deteriorated badly. Illus had survived an assassination attempt in 477, which may have been organized by Zeno, since one of his slaves, Paulus, was responsible. Zeno conciliated Illus by handing the slave over to him. A year later, Zeno was implicated in a second attempt on Illus' life, organized this time by the praetorian prefect Epinicus. Zeno was forced to surrender Epinicus to Illus, who sent him to Isauria under guard, and soon left for Isauria himself (John of Antioch fr. 211. 1–3). This split in the Empire's ruling coalition lasted until the very end of 478, when Zeno persuaded Illus to return to court by handing over to him the Empress Verina, who was blamed for the attack.[29] For Illus to have left court shows that relations were severely strained. In this case the rift was eventually healed, but after 481 the same sequence of events led to the final showdown between the two Isaurians (Ch. 9).

The discontent of the praesental troops in 478 is connected to this court dispute, because, when they were mobilized early in the

[29] Stein, ii. Excursus B, 787; cf. *PLRE* ii. 587–8.

year, Illus was their commander (Malchus fr. 18. 1, p. 426. 21–2). By the time they confronted the Amal on the Long Walls, however, they were led by Martinianus. Between their mobilization and the arrival of the Goths, therefore, the dispute had come to a head and Illus departed for Isauria. Malchus specifically associates military discontent with Martinianus' appointment and hence with Illus' departure (fr. 18. 2, p. 426. 1–2). Zeno's quarrel with Illus had either affected army discipline directly (causing unrest when their commander left the city), or forced Zeno to stay in Constantinople rather than campaign personally against the Goths, a move which aroused the troops' anger.

Once the troops had been dispersed, Zeno could no longer dictate events, and improvised policy as best he could. Peace had to be made with one or both Gothic groups to limit damage to Thrace; having failed to conciliate the Amal, Zeno turned to Theoderic Strabo. Zeno could afford to disband the mutinous troops only because peace was to be made with the Thracian Goths, and, since Strabo was offering the Emperor a way out of his difficulties, he was able to name his own terms (Malchus frr. 18.3, p. 432. 51 ff.; 18. 4, p. 434. 1 ff.). The subsequent peace relieved some of Zeno's anxiety, and his policy towards the Amal-led Goths in 478/9 shows less urgency. No settlement was achieved, and, as we shall see, a number of military and diplomatic manœuvres followed, in which no definite advantage was gained by either side. Both Zeno and Theoderic the Amal kept seeking opportunities for obtaining better terms, so that final agreement was never reached.

The Thracian Goths

Immediately after Zeno's return in 476, Strabo did what he could to come to terms with the new regime. Sending an embassy to request peace, he suggested that the Empire had backed the wrong Gothic leader. In particular, his envoys 'asked the Emperor to consider how little harm the son of Strabo, though an enemy, had done to the Romans and how much damage Theoderic the son of Valamer (*sic*), though a general and a friend, had done to the cities. Zeno ought not now to look to old hatreds rather than how he might most advance the common good' (Malchus fr. 15, p. 420. 1–9). The message is striking for the terms in which it was couched. Rivalry with the Amal, perhaps already implicit in

Strabo's agreement with Leo in 473 (Ch. 7), is now explicit. The Thracian leader knew that to win back his position he had to make his case in terms of why Zeno should prefer him to his Amal rival. The Goths and their leaders were competing for the same honours and financial rewards.

In this embassy, Strabo offered to hand over his son as hostage, and to live as a private citizen among his people, retaining peaceful possession of what he had already seized. By offering to live as a private citizen (ἰδιώτην ὄντα), he renounced all claim to imperial honours, and in particular to the post of *magister militum*, although not to leadership of the Thracian Goths.[30] The third clause proposed that his Goths should live without an annual subsidy, so that they would have presumably existed solely on the produce of their land (cf. p. 258). These terms surrendered everything for which Strabo had fought since the murder of Aspar, and, in the long run, would surely have undermined his position in the Gothic world. The Thracian Goths were to live by their own labours under a titleless leader, while those of his Amal rival would have received imperial salaries as the soldiers of a *MVM praesentalis*. In such circumstances, support must have shifted towards the Amal.

This makes it doubtful that the terms can really be taken at face value. It is just possible that Strabo perceived an overwhelming immediate threat and was willing to make these concessions for peace in the short term, but the rhetoric in which the message was couched suggests that he was simultaneously proposing a different kind of agreement. As we have seen, the message articulates his case in terms of Zeno's having to choose between rival Gothic leaders. Whereas the precise terms he offered indicate that Strabo was ready to surrender, his rhetoric strikes a different note, attempting to persuade the emperor that he should transfer his favour to Strabo; presumably all the Amal's other benefits were to be transferred too. Strabo's embassy was thus not quite so humble as his explicit proposals might suggest, and Zeno had some reason for telling his assembled troops that the Goth did not want peace so much as a generalship (Malchus fr. 15). We are also told that letters from high officials had been forged to give Strabo the impression that he had important sympathizers at court (ibid.); this might help to explain the bold subtext of his embassy. Zeno

[30] Malchus fr. 18. 1, p. 426. 5–9; cf. Cresci, *Malco*, 209.

responded to the rhetoric, rather than Strabo's specific offers, and refused an alliance.

By early 478, however, the Thracian leader had strengthened his position by attracting support away from his Amal rival (see above). His success might seem strange, given the Amal's enormous reputation as a successful Gothic king. This reputation is really based, however, on the skilful way he created a kingdom in Italy; in 477 he had yet to achieve any major success, even if his prestige had been bolstered by imperial honours and the promise of a subsidy. The sources do not specify how Strabo undermined his rival's support, but he may have shown superior military ability in any skirmishing, and he in any case was the more experienced leader. He had been intimately involved in court politics, and, if not with complete success, had led his group through the faction disputes of three reigns (Leo, Zeno, and Basiliscus). The Amal was much less familiar with the imperial court, having spent time there only as a hostage. In addition, Zeno does not seem to have paid the Amal-led Goths their promised salaries (p. 278), which may well have stimulated discontent among Goths who had made two great treks in five years in search of greater wealth. The transfer of support also underlines how fundamentally the two Theoderics threatened one another's position. Their power depended absolutely on their ability to attract followers, who swapped allegiance according to which leader seemed to offer the better prospect of success. Retaining followers' loyalty was of crucial importance, and their support could not simply be taken for granted. In 478, for instance, Malchus has the Amal's followers say that they will desert him unless he makes peace with Strabo (fr. 18. 2, p. 430. 55 ff.).

Buoyed up by his new recruits, Strabo started 478 in a position of renewed strength, which is reflected in his rejection of the terms which he himself had previously offered. He may not even have meant them seriously in 477, and now that his position had improved they were quite unacceptable. Despite some aggressive rhetoric, he was still, however, seeking better terms, rather than a fight to the finish, and carefully left open an alternative to fighting. Malchus records his message: 'since [the Romans] had brought him to the necessity of gathering the tribes . . . he had either to feed those who had come to him or fight alongside them . . . ' (fr.

18. 1, p. 426. 9–15). Zeno could either fight or provide the Thracian Goths with suitable economic support.

Zeno rejected the opening, attempting instead to force the Goths to fight one another. As we have seen, Strabo managed to avoid a battle which would only have reduced overall Gothic strength to Zeno's gain. Malchus' account gives Strabo credit for making his rival realize that he had been tricked by Zeno, but this is not very convincing. When no imperial forces appeared, and Theoderic the Amal encountered the Thracian Goths several hundred kilometres further north than he was expecting, it would surely not have required speeches from Theoderic Strabo to convince him that he had been betrayed (p. 237). The actual terms of the agreement between the two Theoderics are unclear. They agreed not to fight, but a second clause is incomplete. It has recently been reconstructed '⟨but otherwise to do, ἄλλως δὲ πράττειν⟩ whatever they thought advantageous', implying that they were to act independently. This makes some sense of subsequent events when one marched on Constantinople while the other stayed behind.[31] Other indications suggest, however, a slightly more active alliance. Malchus reports, for instance, that Zeno's ambassadors were unable to persuade the Amal to break with Strabo (ξυρραγῆναι ἐκείνῳ), suggesting that the Theoderics were in some way bound together (fr. 18. 3, p. 432. 29 ff.). And news that Strabo had become *MVM praesentalis* was an important factor in the Amal's later decision to negotiate with Zeno (see below), implying perhaps that, in accepting this promotion, Strabo had broken the agreement. The Goths obviously did not agree to fight a joint campaign, but one was possibly not to make peace to the disadvantage of the other. On either interpretation, however, Theoderic Strabo both avoided losing troops in battle, and detached the Amal from his alliance with Zeno.[32]

He crowned these successes with an advantageous treaty when Zeno's plans were ruined by the threatened mutiny. Once again, Strabo used a diplomatic exchange to stress that he was a much more trustworthy ally than the Amal, emphasizing the degree to which the two Goths were in competition (Malchus fr. 18. 4, p. 434. 1 ff.). Since the emperor desperately needed peace, Strabo

[31] Blockley, ii. 459 n. 34.
[32] Cf. p. 252: a marriage-alliance between the two Theoderics was possibly also concluded at this time.

could name his own terms. He re-established himself in Constantinople as *MVM praesentalis*, regaining all the other honours he had previously held, together with command of the two Scholae. Once again, he was able, at least potentially, to exercise influence at court, and his property in the city was returned. As before, the treaty gave him the ample means to reward his followers, stipulating that pay and food were to be supplied annually for 13,000 men, a first instalment being distributed immediately. The agreement fully met Strabo's needs as both Gothic leader and imperial politician.

The Amal-Led Goths

The former Pannonian Goths lost ground to their Thracian competitors between 476 and 479. Starting the period with full imperial recognition, they ended it in open revolt. This was essentially the result of a contradiction between their aims and those of the emperor Zeno. In 476, they had won his favour by agreeing to fight the Thracian Goths without imperial aid. This, however, was a dangerous task, as the events of 477 showed, when Theoderic the Amal lost support to his Thracian rival. Although it put Zeno's favour in jeopardy, the Amal had little choice, therefore, but to avoid confrontation with Strabo until he had secured imperial assistance. He seemed to achieve this in 478, but Zeno's real aim was to weaken both Gothic groups, and the promised military assistance never appeared. The Amal had done what he could, however, to secure the alliance, making the emperor and his advisers swear oaths. Zeno swore not to break the current agreements unless the Amal did so first, and the others swore not to make any agreement with Strabo unless Zeno ordered it (Malchus fr. 18. 2, p. 426. 5 ff.). These precautions were useless because Zeno was willing to perjure himself, but the Amal had recognized the danger.

When Zeno failed to deliver the promised support, the Amal took the only sensible course open to him, making an agreement with his rival. This left his group homeless and in open revolt. Advancing on Constantinople, he demanded land and immediate economic support, threatening that, unless the Empire came to terms, his Goths would inflict damage upon Roman life in the Balkans. Zeno first tried to disrupt the Gothic alliance by offering the Amal a large bribe, but, when that failed, was ready to fight

(Malchus fr. 18. 3, p. 430. 5 ff.). At this point, Zeno's forces proved unreliable, and the Amal was left free on the Thracian Plain, inflicting serious damage on rich areas of Rhodope (fr. 18. 4, p. 434. 2–7). A gap between fragments creates a lacuna in our knowledge of Theoderic's aims and actions at this point. Before reaching Stobi on the other side of the mountains, however, he suffered significant losses (fr. 20, p. 434. 1 ff.). This, together with Adamantius' comment that Zeno had allowed the Goths to cross the mountains after some conflict (ibid., p. 446. 193 ff.), suggests that the Amal's object had been to force a way off the Thracian Plain. In open country his group was vulnerable to attack, so that, even though there were rich pickings, it was important for the Goths to reach an area of greater security. The damage inflicted on the rich farmland of Rhodope perhaps forced Zeno to allow their escape.

Once out of immediate danger, the Amal was concerned to negotiate a settlement with the Empire which offered some hope of long-term security. Tactics shifted from day to day, but his overall aim seems clear enough. He first sacked the city of Stobi, which offered little resistance (ibid., p. 434. 1ff.). At this point, 'Zeno . . . realised that since no one was willing to fight, it would be best to keep the barbarian from destroying the cities by offering moderate terms' (ibid., p. 436. 20 ff.). This had probably been Theoderic's main aim in taking the city anyway. Zeno had at least a diplomatic counter available. Because Strabo had by now made peace, the Amal was isolated. As we have seen, the news that Strabo had become *MVM praesentalis* prompted the Amal to negotiate, and diplomatic exchanges followed.

While these were under way, the Goths moved west to Heraclea, where they were provided with supplies. These were probably made available on imperial orders, since Theoderic had agreed not to inflict damage even though his forces were destitute (ibid., p. 436. 38 ff.). He had received no payments (p. 278), and his group had been in no position to grow food, so that economic aid must have been an important element in the truce. For an unspecified period, the arrangements at Heraclea functioned smoothly. Zeno eventually decided to offer the Goths land around Pautalia (ibid., p. 438. 48 ff.). The Amal, however, wanted to strengthen his bargaining position. Having travelled hundreds of kilometres from the Danube since 477, he had his eyes on

Dyrrhachium, which could function both as a fortified base and an effective bargaining counter. As he put it in a message to a certain Sidimund, 'settling himself in a city with fortifications, [he could] face whatever chance might bring'. Sidimund proved the vital link in an extraordinary chain of events which enabled the Amal to capture the city. Holding estates in the area, Sidimund seems to have been well known: at least, when he reported that Zeno was going to settle the Goths in Dyrrhachium, its leading citizens and garrison believed him. The citizens left to sort out their financial affairs, the soldiers departed rather than risk imperial wrath by fighting the Goths.[33]

The Amal duly took the city, having burnt most of Heraclea when the inhabitants, safe in their refuge, would supply him with no more food. The citizens said that they had no more food to give (p. 440. 94 ff.), but this sounds like an excuse. They perhaps had orders to supply the Goths only while they remained in the area and at peace. The Amal rushed to Dyrrhachium with most of his followers while the baggage-train followed more slowly (ibid. p. 440. 89 ff.). He had won a secure base from which to bargain for good terms, and his renewed confidence is evident in the offers he made to Zeno's ambassador Adamantius when they met soon after the capture of the city. The Goth said he was willing to move to Pautalia in the spring, but was determined to spend winter 479/80 in Dyrrhachium. In the meantime, he offered 6,000 of his best men to join imperial troops in destroying the Thracian Goths, on condition that he became *MVM praesentalis* in Strabo's place. His mother and sister would be hostages for his good behaviour, and he was willing to leave non-combatants and baggage in the city of Zeno's choice. Alternatively, he would go to Dalmatia to restore Julius Nepos to the western throne.[34] Secure in his new base, Theoderic was able to take the diplomatic initiative, and his first concern was again to destroy his arch-rival. Purely inter-Gothic conflict was self-defeating, but, if he could get imperial support, the Amal was quite ready to attack his Thracian namesake.

[33] Malchus fr. 20, p. 438. 75 ff. records that Sidimund went to every citizen; presumably this means every significant citizen.

[34] Malchus fr. 20, p. 446. 205 ff. Wolfram, 275 suggests that only 6,000 Gothic soldiers were available to him in 479, so that he had lost about half his following (cf. p. 248). But Malchus is explicit that he offered 6,000 'of his best men', implying that there were others. The non-combatants would not have been left unguarded in Roman hands.

His calculations were upset by Sabinianus, the newly appointed *MVM per Illyricum*, who captured the Gothic baggage-train. The effects of this are hard to estimate. With the baggage, the Goths presumably lost many of their larger personal possessions, and the capture of over 5,000 prisoners was a significant proportion, perhaps a tenth, of their total strength (cf. p. 248). But most of the Goths, and particularly of the fighting men, had reached Dyrrha-chium safely, and Theoderic had anyway been willing to leave the baggage in the city of Zeno's choice. It would seem, therefore, that his group could function without it. Nevertheless, Sabinianus had balanced out the Amal's success at Dyrrhachium, and given Zeno hope that further military action might force the Goths to accept a less favourable peace settlement. He decided, therefore, to reject Theoderic's offers (ibid., p. 446. 228 ff.).

Although he eventually failed to consolidate his previous gains, the Amal showed considerable leadership ability between 476 and 479. Realizing that he could not safely confront the Thracian Goths without help, he first won the promise of imperial aid, and then made peace with Strabo as necessity demanded. Indiscipline among the praesental troops allowed him to extract his group from a potential trap, and he eventually secured a fortified base from which to force Zeno to negotiate in good faith. From all this, the Amal had learnt much of Zeno's duplicity, but his own move into the Empire in 473 had itself been carefully calculated, and he could have been expecting no favours.

By the end of 479, Zeno was more or less back to where he had started in 476. One Gothic group was allied to him, one in revolt. Theoderic Strabo had merely replaced Theoderic the Amal as *MVM praesentalis*, and the Gothic problem was no nearer solu-tion. The Empire was either unwilling, or, perhaps more likely, as the Senate had reported to Zeno in 477 (p. 287), unable to find sufficient funds to pay both Gothic groups to keep the peace at once. In any case, such was the rivalry between the two Gothic leaders that any peace on this basis could only be fragile. Zeno could do no more at this point than buy peace from Theoderic Strabo, his erstwhile enemy, and await the outcome of Sabinianus' manœuvres in Epirus.

9

SOLVING THE GOTHIC PROBLEM

A. *Gothic Unification, 479–484*

Late in 479 political calm in Constantinople was shattered by the attempted coup of Marcian.[1] He was a grandson of the emperor Marcian of the 450s, son of the western emperor Anthemius, consul for 469 and 472, and husband of Leontia, younger daughter of the emperor Leo (*PLRE* ii. 717). Theoderic Strabo was with his followers in Thrace, and, on hearing of the coup, advanced towards the city (Malchus fr. 22). Given the time needed to mobilize, his prompt arrival suggests that he had been party to the plot, as John of Antioch maintains. Some of the conspirators also sought sanctuary with him, which confirms the point. In the event, the plot was frustrated by Illus' Isaurians, who arrived from across the Bosporos to capture Marcian (John of Antioch fr. 211. 3–4), and, on hearing that Marcian had failed, Strabo claimed that he had come to the city to save Zeno (Malchus fr. 22, p. 450. 5).

Zeno persuaded him to leave by threats, promises, and a large sum of money. Official contact was maintained long enough for messages to pass between them concerning the fugitive conspirators,[2] but Zeno could not tolerate someone who had just tried to unseat him (and who refused to surrender the refugees). Strabo was thus soon replaced as *MVM praesentalis* by Illus' brother Trocundes, and Zeno also persuaded Bulgars to attack the Thracian Goths, probably in 480. Strabo repulsed the assault,[3] and

---

[1] John of Antioch fr. 211. 3 places it 'towards the end of the consulship of Zeno' (late 479). Brief accounts of the following years can be found in Wolfram, 276–7; Schmidt, 286–7; Ensslin, *Theoderich der Große*, 57–8; Burns, *The Ostrogoths*, 72; Martin, *Theoderich der Große*, 50–3.

[2] Candidus fr. 1 says that Marcian's brother Procopius fled to Thrace, but Malchus fr. 22, p. 452. 28 ff. shows that it was only men of lesser importance; cf. Cresci, *Malco*, 251. Procopius fled to Rome: Theophanes, AM 5971 (127 de Boor).

[3] John of Antioch fr. 211. 4. The 'Huns' whom Triarius defeated in 481 were probably Zeno's Bulgars: id. fr. 211. 5.

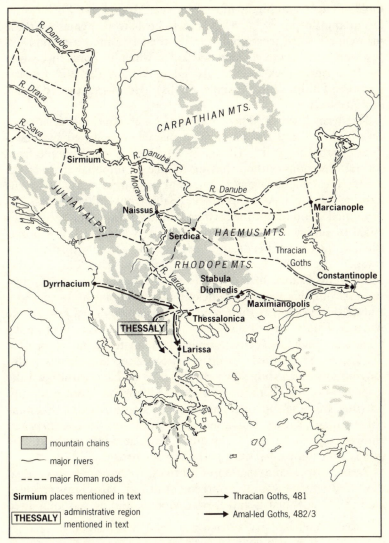

FIG. 8. Gothic campaigns of the early 480s

advanced again on the imperial capital in 481 (Fig. 8). His Goths first attacked the main gates of the city, but were beaten off by Illus' troops, then renewed the assault from Sycae across the

Golden Horn, and finally moved to Near Hestiae and Sosthenium beside the Bosporos, in an attempt to cross to Bithynia. All these manœuvres were frustrated. Strabo then mounted a second expedition towards Greece, but was killed when his horse threw him on to a spear-rack at Stabula Diomedis on the Via Egnatia (between Philippi and Maximianopolis).[4] He was succeeded by his son Recitach.

We hear little of Theoderic the Amal after the seizure of Dyrrhachium, but the freedom of manœuvre enjoyed by Theoderic Strabo in 481 is striking. He attacked Constantinople from several directions without having to face an imperial army in the field.[5] This might suggest that imperial forces were in Epirus fighting the Amal. As we have seen, Sabinianus' initial success had prompted Zeno to opt for further military action, but Sabinianus failed to subjugate the Goths. The task, we are told, was unfinished at the time of his death in 481,[6] and in 482 the Amal's forces ravaged much of the south-west Balkans. Our only source, Marcellinus Comes, blames the death of Sabinianus for the Goths' success, but this seems insufficient. The contrast between 480/1 and 482 suggests that the troops previously deployed against the Amal had been moved elsewhere. Strabo's attack on Constantinople may thus have caused imperial troops to be moved back to Thrace in 482. Mutual hostility between Zeno and Illus was also moving towards a showdown, and Zeno may have withdrawn the troops to prepare them for civil war. 481 saw yet another attempt on Illus' life, the sources blaming Zeno's wife Ariadne. Presumably to allay his fears, Illus was appointed *MVM per Orientem* and allowed to go to Antioch.[7] The quarrel escalated into civil war only in 484, but both sides were preparing for battle.

Perhaps for a combination of motives, therefore, Zeno granted the Amal a very favourable agreement in 483. His Goths received land in Dacia Ripensis and Lower Moesia, and he was appointed

[4] John of Antioch fr. 211. 5 (the best account); Marcellinus Comes s.a. 481 (*CM* ii. 92); Theophanes AM 5970 (126 de Boor); Evagrius, *HE* 3. 25; Jordanes, *Romana* 346; cf. *PLRE* ii. 1076.

[5] Cf. John of Antioch fr. 211. 5: Illus had enough troops to defend the capital, but they never ventured outside the walls.

[6] Marcellinus Comes s.a. 481 (*CM* ii. 92).

[7] Malalas, Bonn 387–8; Theophanes AM 5972 (127–8 de Boor); Marcellinus Comes s.a. 484 (*CM* ii. 92); *Life of Joshua the Stylite* 13; Evagrius *HE* 3. 27. Illus was certainly in Antioch by Feb. 482 (Stein, ii. 19 n. 1).

MVM praesentalis and consul for 484.[8] The emperor also seems to have come to terms with Strabo's son Recitach. The sources do not make this explicit, but Recitach was murdered by agents of the Amal at the instigation of Zeno in Bonophatianae, probably a suburb of Constantinople, on his way from a bath to a feast in late 483 or early 484 (John of Antioch fr. 214. 3).[9] Without an agreement, he would not have been engaged in such pursuits within the capital (or any Roman city). With his death, the line of Strabo ceased to be a political force, and the Thracian Goths never reappear as an independent political unit.

The Thracian Goths

In view of his gains in 478, it might be wondered why Theoderic Strabo jeopardized them only a year later by supporting Marcian. They were, however, far from secure. Zeno had granted Strabo's wishes only in extreme adversity when he had had to make peace (p. 286). Given the history of animosity between Strabo and Zeno, there could be no guarantee that the emperor would uphold the agreement if his situation improved. And once Illus and Zeno had patched up their quarrel (by summer 479),[10] Strabo had reason to doubt the security of his position. Marcian's plot may thus have offered Strabo better hopes for a secure future: like Basiliscus, whom he had also supported, Marcian belonged to the traditional imperial family, with which Strabo had no long-standing conflict. With Marcian as emperor, the Thracian leader could have every hope of coexisting peacefully with imperial power, and of enjoying all the benefits which had traditionally been accorded the Thracian *foederati*.

The coup's failure left the Thracian Goths in a difficult position. Strabo pretended for a while to be Zeno's ally, but conflict between them was inevitable, especially when Strabo refused to surrender the conspirators. The Goth was prevented from taking further action in 480 by the Bulgars (brought in by Zeno perhaps because imperial forces were committed in Epirus), and it was not until 481 that he was free to attack Constantinople.

---

[8] Marcellinus Comes s.a. 483 (*CM* ii. 92).

[9] Usually dated to 484, because it reports Recitach's jealousy of the Amal's consulship (484), e.g. *PLRE* ii. 936. But the nomination would have been announced in autumn 483.

[10] Illus returned in winter 478/9: Stein. ii, Excursus B, 787.

John of Antioch (fr. 211. 5) states that Strabo had 30,000 Scythians with him in 481. This has sometimes been taken as a reliable indication of the size of his army,[11] but is much higher than the better indications Malchus gives, and either is exaggerated, or—perhaps less likely—means that Strabo had some other allies (perhaps the Bulgars sent against him by Zeno in 480, or even imperial forces stationed in Thrace). Even in Italy, the united force of both Theoderics numbered no more than 25,000–30,000 men (p. 302).

Attacking Constantinople was a major escalation in the scale of the Thracian Goths' operations; previously they had attacked only Thracian cities. There is no record of any attempt to open negotiations, and Strabo seems to have been intent on capturing the city. He certainly made two determined attacks, and was attempting to cross to Bithynia, perhaps to mount a third from Chalcedon, when the imperial navy forced him to abandon his designs.[12] We have no explicit account of his aims, but Malchus gives the following account of his motivation for advancing on Constantinople at the time of Marcian's coup: 'he thought that now was the time . . . to attack the city and the Emperor himself' (fr. 22, p. 450. 2 ff.). By 479, then, Strabo was already coming to the conclusion that his only safe course of action was to replace Zeno entirely. It was no longer enough simply to apply military pressure to procure a favourable agreement, since there could be no guarantee of it being kept. By 481, his resolve seems to have hardened. With the bulk of the imperial army perhaps occupied in Epirus, 481 offered Strabo the opportunity to set another emperor on the throne, with whom he could negotiate in good faith. It is unlikely that he wanted the throne for himself, not even Aspar had aspired to such heights.[13]

When the attacks failed, Strabo led his force westwards. His plans at this point are uncertain because he died *en route*. At the

---

[11] e.g. Wolfram, 276. Burns, 'Calculating Ostrogothic Population', 461–2 takes the figure to refer also to women and children. This is possible, but would suggest that Strabo's force had shrunk since 478, when it already consisted of *c*. 10,000 men (implying a total of *c*. 50,000: p. 253), which seems unlikely, and the text does read as though purely military numbers were meant.

[12] John of Antioch fr. 211. 5; other refs. *PLRE* ii. 1076.

[13] Cf. Scott, 'Aspar', 67.

western end of the Via Egnatia, however, lay Dyrrhachium, the base of Theoderic the Amal since 479, so that Strabo may have meant to assist the Amal. Co-operation between the Gothic leaders, of course, would have doubled the Goths' military power, and greatly increased their chances of forcing the Empire to make a favourable settlement. John of Antioch reports, indeed, that, after Marcian's coup, 'the union (συζυγία) of the Theoderics again troubled the Romans, and ravaged the cities of Thrace . . .' (fr. 211. 4). What this means is unclear; it may indicate no more than that both were in revolt at the same time. But the direction of the Thracian leader's march is suggestive, and the Goths had again perhaps submerged their differences, as they did in 478.[14]

Strabo's death undermined whatever plans had been made. Succession first passed to Recitach and his two (anonymous) uncles, but Recitach later murdered them to rule alone (John of Antioch fr. 211. 5). This must have strained loyalties among the Thracian Goths, and certainly diverted some attention away from the question of relations with the Empire. Some have thought that Recitach squandered his father's inheritance, in that these dynastic murders made it easy for the Amal to assassinate Recitach in turn and attach the Thracian Goths to his own following.[15] There is no reason to suppose, however, that the uncles would not have attempted to oust Recitach if they had found the opportunity. Quite a close parallel, in fact, is provided by Theoderic the Amal's relations with his uncle Vidimer, only in that case, as we have seen, his father was alive to help him dispose of the uncle in question (p. 250). Securing one's position at the head of the group had to be the first priority for any new leader. Recitach did not have the prestige of his father, and it is not surprising that his subsequent ambitions were more restrained. He seems to have confined his activities to Thrace, where he 'exercised great authority' (John of Antioch fr. 211. 5). And while he did eventually make a treaty with Zeno, Trocundes (up to 484) was one *MVM praesentalis* (*PLRE* ii. 1127), and (from 483 at least) Theoderic the Amal was the other. Recitach may perhaps have been appointed *MVM per Thracias*,

---

[14] Cf. Schmidt, 286; this is the other possible moment for a marriage-alliance (p. 252).

[15] Cf. Wolfram, 276–7 n. 148; Stein, ii. 17–18.

but the terms of his agreement could not have been very favourable.

The Amal-Led Goths

The Goths of Theoderic the Amal perhaps spent 480 and 481 safe in Dyrrhachium. After losing their baggage-train, they were content (or perhaps forced) to await developments; the reason their leader had seized the city in the first place (p. 292). Some kind of alliance with Theoderic Strabo may have brought more positive action in 481, but this was frustrated by the latter's death, and the sources do not record the Amal's actions in this year. In 482, however, he broke out of Dyrrhachium and ravaged Macedonia and Thessaly, even capturing Larissa, the latter's capital. These successes forced Zeno to send troops to the area in 483 under Moschianus and John the Scythian.[16] Instead of continuing to pursue a military option, however, Zeno offered peace on terms which favoured the Goths. He simultaneously made the split with Illus decisive by demanding the return of his brother Longinus (captured in 475),[17] and it seems reasonable to link the two developments. To fight Illus, Zeno was willing to pay a high price for peace with the Amal-led Goths. This reinforces the suggestion that the agreement with Recitach had involved only relatively minor concessions, since there seems to have been enough money available to pay off the Amal-led Goths, who were clearly treated very generously, at the same time (cf. p. 287).

The Amal consequently regained the post of *MVM praesentalis* and was nominated consul for 484: an unprecedented honour for a barbarian leader. Aspar and some of his family had received the consulship, but, while of foreign origins, they were thoroughly Romanized men who had followed Roman military careers. Never before had the consulship been granted to one who was purely the leader of a tribal group within the Empire. This is a clear sign of Zeno's need to conciliate the Amal, and must have advanced his prestige among Goths and Romans alike. These appointments also brought in their train admission to Constantinople and much closer involvement at court; although *MVM praesentalis* after 476, the Amal had not then been received into the city.

---

[16] Marcellinus Comes s.a. 482 (*CM* ii. 92); John of Antioch fr. 213.
[17] The main source is John of Antioch fr. 214. 7; cf. *PLRE* ii. 588–9 with refs.

His followers received land in Dacia Ripensis and Moesia Secunda.[18] If their demands had remained constant since the 470s, and there is no reason to suppose that they had not, these included farmland to guarantee their economic livelihood (p. 245). It also placed them in a strategic position from which they could intervene in Thrace and Constantinople. Annual payments, as salaries for military service, were probably also restored to them. Such payments had been part of all previous treaties offering the Goths favourable terms, and, as we shall see, Gothic troops did serve against Illus. The events of 482/3 thus followed a familiar pattern. By military action, the Amal forced the Empire to grant him a favourable settlement. The impact of his action was magnified by Zeno's need for a united front against Illus, and he gained unprecedented honours.

In 483 or early 484 the Amal improved his position still further. Ever since his Goths had moved from Pannonia, there had been intense competition between their leadership and that of the Thracian Goths. Differences were occasionally submerged, but the Amals had set out in 473 to win a share of the privileges which had previously belonged to the Thracian *foederati*. The contest was also played out on a more fundamental level. In 477, Strabo had attracted away support from his Amal rival, emphasizing that two ambitious Gothic leaders could not co-exist in close proximity. They drew on the same basis of support, which could and did move between them.

When the opportunity presented itself, therefore, Theoderic the Amal naturally took the chance to destroy the power of the Triarius dynasty. In 483/4 Recitach became jealous of Theoderic's consulship (John of Antioch fr. 214. 3). The details of his own agreement with Zeno have not survived, but Recitach certainly received less generous treatment. On top of his relative inexperience and the fierce succession struggle, his jealousy was based on the very real fear that his power-base would be undermined by desertions to the much more successful Amal. Rivalry between the two dynasties could not be submerged indefinitely; by assassinating possibly the last surviving male of the Triarius line, Theoderic took advantage of the perhaps temporary weakness of his opponent to get his retaliation in first.

[18] Marcellinus Comes s.a. 483 (*CM* ii. 92).

At this point, the majority of the Thracian Goths joined Theoderic the Amal.[19] We have no explicit statement to this effect, and some Thracian Goths preferred to give their allegiance to Zeno. Procopius, for instance, records that Bessas and Godigisclus, who were prominent in the eastern Empire's army in the sixth century, 'had dwelt in Thrace from of old and did not follow Theoderic [the Amal] to Italy' (*Wars* 1. 8. 3; cf. 5. 5. 3; 5. 16. 2). Other individuals with possibly Gothic names also served in the eastern Empire's armies after 500. Procopius mentions Thurimuth (*Wars* 5. 11. 11), Gudilas (7. 30. 6), Indulf (7. 35. 23), and Arimuth (8. 27. 13). John of Antioch refers to Alathar (fr. 214*e*. 6), and Jordanes to the Andag/Andela clan, not to mention his own family (*Getica* 50. 266). They are not necessarily all Thracian Goths who stayed behind, but some of them might be.[20] Nevertheless, no large Gothic group remained in the Balkans after Theoderic left for Italy in 488/9. In the well-documented revolt of Vitalian, for instance, which started among the allied troops in Thrace and Lower Moesia, no reference is made to a large body of Goths, and Vitalian's main supporters would seem to have been Hunnic allies (Evagrius, *HE* 3. 43; John of Antioch fr. 214*e*. 1).[21] The Thracian Gothic *foederati* as such, no longer existed.

The murder of Recitach thus enabled the Amal to unite the majority of Goths in the Balkan peninsula. This must have approximately doubled the military power of his following from about 10,000 to over 20,000 warriors, implying a total population for the united group of over 100,000 (cf. pp. 248, 253). The army of Ostrogothic Italy in the 530s and 540s has been calculated at *c*. 25,000–30,000 men. We should expect some fluctuation between the 480s and the 530s, but the later figure does seem to confirm the order of magnitude of the newly united force.[22] Theoderic the Amal was the unchallenged leader of a very powerful force, with

[19] Cf. Wolfram, 276; Schmidt, 267–8; Burns, *The Ostrogoths*, 72.

[20] Cf. Wolfram, 279 n. 162.

[21] For references and some discussion, *PLRE* ii. 1171 ff. Vitalian was possibly another Goth who did not follow Theoderic. Zacharias of Mytilene, *HE* 7.13, 8. 2 calls him a Goth; cf. Marcellinus Comes s.a. 514, 519 (*Vitalianus Scythus*). His sons, however, were called Buzes, Cutzes, and Venilus, which seem more Hunnic.

[22] Hannestad, 'Les forces militaires', 136 ff. Following his previous estimates, Burns, 'Calculating Ostrogothic Population', 463 has to postulate a doubling of the united group between *c*.490 and 530.

every chance of wielding greater influence at the heart of the Empire.

The unification of the Goths was made possible by the increasing contact that the rank and file of the two groups had experienced with one another. Without this they would not have been willing to follow a single leader. The process began at the latest in 477, when, as we have seen, some of the Amal-led Goths joined Theoderic Strabo. Apart from perceptions of which leader was likely to do better, a further reason for such switches of allegiance can probably be found in the events of 478. The confrontation around Mount Sondis made the Goths aware of the risks which open conflict between them posed to their long-term survival. The thoughts which Malchus gives to Theoderic Strabo must have occurred to all; if the Goths fought, then only the Romans would gain and Gothic independence would be threatened (fr. 18. 2). The logical extension of this thought was that, whereas their leaders were in competition, the Goths as a whole stood to gain more from confronting the Empire as a united force. This may have been confirmed in 480/1 if an alliance, or set of common interests, again united the Goths. Gothic unification must be viewed on two levels. On the one hand it was brought about by leadership rivalries, which produced a single pre-eminent dynasty. But the bulk of the Goths were willing to accept unification as the natural outcome of Recitach's assassination only because they had come to realize that unity rather than conflict best served their interests. For the Goths as a whole, the Empire, rather than any rival leadership line, was the main enemy.

It is worth considering, finally, why Zeno should have instigated Recitach's murder, since it united the Goths under one leader and made them that much more dangerous. The key would seem to lie in the fact that Recitach was becoming disaffected. This undermined the united front Zeno had created, whether Recitach was acting independently or had actually been approached by Illus.[23] Zeno was probably willing to countenance Gothic unification, at least in the short term, to deal with his Isaurian rival. As his generous treatment of Theoderic the Amal also indicates, Illus was Zeno's first priority.

---

[23] Cf. John of Antioch fr. 214. 2: Illus spread his net wide in search of support, to the Persians, the Armenians, and Odovacar in Italy.

B. *The Road to Italy, 484–489*

Two conflicts dominate this period: between Zeno and Illus, and between Zeno and Theoderic the Amal. In the course of them, it became clear that a radical solution was required to break the deadlocked relationship of emperor and Goth. Between 481 and 483/4, Zeno, as we have seen, carefully constructed a united front against Illus, and made unprecedented concessions to the Amal in order to concentrate on defeating his Isaurian rival. In 483 Zeno demanded the return of his brother Longinus, and in 484 dismissed Illus and Trocundes from their respective posts as *MVM per Orientem* and *MVM praesentalis*. This provoked open warfare. Illus set up his own candidates for the throne, Marcian and then Leontius, another Isaurian (*PLRE* ii. 670–1), and sought outside support. Zeno mobilized his forces, drawing in part on Theoderic's Goths. When the armies met near Antioch in September 484, Illus' was so inferior that he disbanded, and retired with picked troops to the fortress of Papiris. The siege lasted four years until Illus was betrayed.[24]

The first signs of renewed tension between Zeno and Theoderic appeared in the course of the campaign. According to John of Antioch, the Goth at first fought against Illus with his Gothic troops, but was recalled when Zeno began to doubt his loyalty. His Gothic troops continued to fight until Illus retired to Papiris (fr. 214. 4–6). Evagrius and Theophanes both report that Theoderic returned only after Illus had fled, but John of Antioch should probably be preferred (cf. p. 239).[25] Lack of trust was already souring relations between Zeno and Theoderic, even if it did not lead to an immediate break; there is no record of any conflict between them in 485.

In 486, however, Theoderic rebelled and ravaged Thrace, perhaps trying to apply pressure on Zeno.[26] In 487 the pressure was increased when he advanced on Constantinople. Encamped at Rhegium, he harried the city's suburbs and even cut a major aqueduct. At this point, Zeno decided that a compromise had to be

[24] John of Antioch fr. 214. 1, 2, 5–10; Brooks, 'Zenon and the Isaurians', 223 ff.

[25] Theophanes AM 5977 (131 de Boor); Evagrius, *HE* 3. 27. On these events, see Stein, ii. 29; Schmidt, 287–8; Burns, *The Ostrogoths*, 72–3; Wolfram, 277.

[26] John of Antioch fr. 214. 7 (dated by the consulship of Longinus); Zacharias of Mytilene, *HE* 6. 6; cf. Wolfram, 277.

reached. Theoderic's sister, who had been living in the city, was sent to her brother with a large sum of money. The surviving sources give no impression of the ebb and flow of subsequent negotiations, and it is not clear whether final agreement came in 487 or slightly later. By 488, however, it had been resolved that Theoderic should take his people to Italy and rule there in the name of Zeno.[27]

The Goths could no longer enjoy an established position in the eastern Empire because of a mutual lack of trust between their leader and the emperor Zeno. The emperor had struggled throughout his reign to retain the throne and his political independence in the face of overbearing subordinates. He had survived coups mounted by members of the imperial family such as Basiliscus and Marcian, and fought off the influence of powerful generals such as Armatus, Illus, and Theoderic Strabo. Once Illus had been dealt with, he could not guarantee that the Amal would not use his expanded power-base to follow in the footsteps of generals who had become the power behind the throne. There were many examples of this, of course, from Stilicho to Illus, including Zeno himself, who had done much the same in the reign of Leo, and Theoderic had shown every inclination to extend his influence within Constantinople. The Amals' bold move in 473 shows that they wished to entrench themselves in the eastern Empire, and in 479 Theoderic had also demanded to be received into Constantinople as a Roman citizen (Malchus fr. 20, p. 446. 219–20). He later achieved this ambition as consul for 484, but Zeno clearly had some reason to perceive Theoderic the Amal as a threat.

At the same time, the Amal had enough experience to know (or at least suspect) that Zeno would not, in the long term, tolerate his independent power. Malalas, in fact, states that Theoderic had in mind Zeno's treatment of Armatus when he rebelled.[28] Armatus defected from Basiliscus to Zeno in 476, and was made *MVM praesentalis* for life. Within a year, however, Zeno had had him assassinated (Ch. 8). The elimination by murder of men who had

---

[27] The main sources are John of Antioch fr. 214. 8–9; Marcellinus Comes s.a. 487 (*CM* ii. 93); Malalas, Bonn 383; Theophanes AM 5977 (131 de Boor); Michael the Syrian 9. 6. See also *PLRE* ii. 1081–2.

[28] Malalas, Bonn 383; *De Insidiis* 34; cf. *PLRE* ii. 149. Theoderic's fear of Zeno is also mentioned by Evagrius, *HE* 3. 27 and Procopius, *Wars* 5. 1. 9 ff.

come to court with high honours was one of Zeno's standard
tactics, deployed not just against Armatus, but also against Illus.
By the mid-480s, therefore, a clash of interests had become
manifest, which there was no obvious way to resolve while the
Goths remained in the eastern Empire. By damaging Thrace or
the outskirts of Constantinople Theoderic could force Zeno to
negotiate, but this would not have solved the underlying problem.
As Theoderic Strabo had concluded by 481 at the latest (see
above), in anything but the short term, Zeno would not allow a
Gothic general the kind of influence that the size of his army and
understandable personal ambition dictated he should possess. The
Amal was too experienced to allow himself to be easily assassinated, and Zeno too secure behind the walls of Constantinople to
be replaced (as Strabo had found in 481). The Amal also faced the
problem that, ultimately, Zeno probably did have sufficient
resources to defeat him. Battle would have been an expensive and
risky option, but if the violence in Thrace had continued for long
enough, Zeno might eventually have taken it.[29] The situation as it
stood gave no satisfaction to either party.

To break the impasse, it was decided that Theoderic should
march on Italy, where he had destroyed the power of Odovacar by
493.[30] We do not know how precisely this solution was reached,
but certain observations can be made. The sources disagree over
whether Zeno or Theoderic played the greater role. Western
sources—Ennodius' *Panegyric on Theoderic* and the *Getica*
(probably following Cassiodorus' *Gothic History*; cf. Ch. 2)—
stress the Goth's initiative and ignore Zeno. Stemming directly or
indirectly from the Ostrogothic court at Ravenna, these works had
every interest in suppressing the emperor's role. This does not
mean, however, that the move was instigated entirely by Zeno.[31]
He must have played an important part, as eastern sources
maintain,[32] but Theoderic needed to break the deadlock too. The

---

[29] Suggested by Procopius, *Wars* 5. 1. 12; cf. Wolfram, 279.

[30] Secondary accounts: Bury, i. 422–3; Stein, ii. 40–1; Martin, *Theoderich der
Große*, 58 ff.; Schmidt, 293 ff.; Ensslin, *Theoderich der Große*, 66 ff.; Burns, *The
Ostrogoths*, 73 ff.; Wolfram, 278 ff.

[31] Ennodius, *Pan.* 14, 25 (cf. *Life of Epiphanius* 109); Jordanes, *Getica* 57.
289 ff.; cf. Moorhead, 'Theoderic, Zeno and Odovacar', 262–3.

[32] Procopius, *Wars* 5. 1. 9–12; Evagrius, *HE* 3. 27; Theophanes AM 5977 (131
de Boor); Jordanes, *Romana* 348; cf. Moorhead, 'Theoderic, Zeno, and Odovacar', 262–3.

Amal had himself suggested in 479 that, in alliance with imperial forces, he might intervene to restore Julius Nepos, the deposed western emperor (Malchus fr. 20, p. 446. 216 ff.). He was not then thinking of moving his whole people (only 6,000 of his best soldiers were to be involved), but to restore Nepos it was necessary to oust Odovacar. Thus Italy did not lie beyond the Goth's vision, and both parties must have considered the agreement of 487/8 a reasonable solution to their problems.

Zeno's relations with Odovacar had never been easy. In 476, for instance, he had made it clear to Odovacar that Julius Nepos was, as far as the East was concerned, the legitimate ruler of Italy. Odovacar was told to seek official recognition from Nepos, and receive him back into Italy (Malchus fr. 14). And Zeno never seems to have accorded Odovacar the dignities which would have acknowledged his right to rule in Italy, although he did confirm consuls nominated in the West.[33] In 486/7, Zeno had also stirred up the Rugi to attack Odovacar, who, according to John of Antioch, was planning an alliance with Illus. This is perhaps unlikely, but may have made good propaganda, and Zeno's conduct in any case illustrates his hostility to Odovacar. As it was, Odovacar launched a pre-emptive strike which crushed the Rugi (some of whom fled to Theoderic), and sent spoils to Zeno.[34] Nothing suggests that there was any love lost between Theoderic and Odovacar either: some sources even report that, in killing Odovacar, Theoderic claimed to be avenging kin.[35] This is perhaps no more than a reflection of Theoderic's propaganda, which had to find a good excuse for murdering Odovacar at a banquet after the two had made peace. Neither Zeno nor Theoderic, then, would have had any qualms about solving his problems at Odovacar's expense.

No authoritative account survives of the terms they agreed, and the sources again differ much as we might expect. Western writers, especially those with some connection to the Ostrogothic court,

[33] Jones, 'Odovacar and Theoderic', 126–7 (= Brunt (ed.), *The Roman Economy*, 365 ff.) shows that consulships were awarded by the East and not Odovacar.

[34] John of Antioch fr. 214. 6; Procopius, *Wars* 7. 2. 1 ff.; Pohl, 'Die Gepiden', 278 ff. Cf. McCormick, 'Odoacer', 212–22; spoils were sent as part of Odovacar's attempt to portray himself as Zeno's loyal subject.

[35] John of Antioch fr. 214*a*; Ennodius, *Pan.* 25; cf. Wolfram, 278 n. 159. See also *PLRE* ii. 793.

stress that Theoderic was to rule Italy in his own right, while their eastern counterparts report that he held authority only as Zeno's deputy. Jones's solution seems to fit the facts most fully. According to the agreement, Theoderic went to Italy as Patrician and *MVM praesentalis*, ruling strictly as Zeno's representative. Once there, however, he declared himself King of Italy, denying that Zeno was the source of his authority. This led to a diplomatic breach, which was healed only when Theoderic reached a compromise with the emperor Anastasius.[36]

In its essentials, however, the agreement of 487/8 satisfied both parties. For Zeno, an over-mighty subject was removed without resort to fighting. With Theoderic's departure for Italy, the last major threat to his independence disappeared. For the Goths, a move to Italy offered them a secure place in the Mediterranean world, something they could no longer find in the Balkans. The way was open for them to establish a realm where they could live and prosper. The alternative, if they remained in the Balkans, was to be broken down into smaller groups, whose leaders would not be too great a threat to Zeno. As we have seen, some were content to stay behind, but the majority wanted to remain a united force. In the autumn and winter of 488/9, Theoderic, as Patrician and *MVM praesentalis*, set out with his followers to create a Gothic kingdom in the rich and famous lands of Italy.

---

[36] 'Odovacar and Theoderic', *passim*; cf. Moorhead, 'Theoderic, Zeno, and Odovacar', 263–4.

CONCLUSION

Several themes have run through this study of the transformation of the Goths in the so-called migration period, a series of population movements stimulated, as far as we can tell, by Hunnic invasions of the later fourth century. It is my aim here briefly to reflect on some of the more important of them: the nature of the Goths' relations with the Roman state, the actual process of transformation, and the part played by royal dynasties in the creation and maintenance of tribal groupings. The discussion is open-ended, and deliberately so, seeking to set what we have observed among the Goths in a broader context defined by current scholarly debate.

Not the least striking aspect of the story has been the enforced retreat of Roman power in the hundred years or so after 375. This can be measured in various ways. Territorially, it is very obvious. Other groups (like Vandals, Burgundians, and Franks) had played a large part, but by c.500, the two Gothic groups who are the main focus of our study had been instrumental in the dismemberment of the western Roman Empire, carving out kingdoms in Italy and in southern Gaul and Spain. Within the Balkans too, the lowland areas of the middle Danube had been definitively lost. The retreat can also be seen diplomatically, in the changing nature of the Empire's relations with the Goths who had held land for a time within the Danubian frontier region.

The first Gothic crossing of the Danube in 376 was itself a break in traditional Roman methods of dealing with tribal groups; tied up on the Persian front, Valens was unable to control the influx in time-tested fashion. Subsequent agreements granted these Goths ever more favourable terms. The peace of 382 sanctioned the Gothic immigrants' semi-autonomy, and a Gothic leader extracted a generalship for the first time in 397. None of these concessions was surrendered lightly by the Roman state, and the treaty of 418 seems to have been a partial stemming of the tide. No generalship was granted to Theoderic I, and the Goths were excluded from the central political role in the western half of the Empire to which Alaric and Athaulf had aspired between 405 and 415. By the time we have detailed information for our second wave of Goths in the Balkans, however, a generalship for the favoured Gothic leader and very large annual payments for his followers are standard features of treaties of alliance. The Roman Empire had previously assimilated tribal peoples conquered in the period of imperial expansion very successfully, and accepted many immigrants, but always on its own terms. Often militarily subdued, tribal groups were settled in ways that curbed their independence and military power. The licensing of Gothic autonomy in 382, and subsequent financial and political concessions, reflect the Empire's increasing inability to deal effectively with tribal immigrants.

There is no reason to think that this weakening in the degree of control exercised over immigrant groups was anything other than involuntary. As we have seen, there is good evidence that success-ive concessions granted to the first wave of Goths, from 376 onwards, were forced upon the various imperial regimes involved (Part II). There is also no doubt that, even though Gothic soldiers could on occasion be useful, large numbers of unassimilated Goths were a disruptive force, quite ready to cause substantial damage in attempting to extract economic and political concessions. The backdrop to much of this study, indeed, is the dramatic change to the strategic balance of power on the Rhine and Danube frontiers in the fourth and fifth centuries which forced the Roman Empire to follow more conciliatory policies towards groups such as the Goths studied here. This, of course, is another subject, requiring study in its own right.[1]

The central focus here has been the effect of migration period phenomena—basically Hunnic attacks and enforced coexistence with Roman power—upon certain Gothic groups. The Huns destroyed one social and political order as they ranged from the south-western USSR to the Rhine over a lengthy period,[2] and a new order eventually emerged from the chaos. The end result was two Gothic groups which were significantly larger than any Gothic political unit previously attested in trustworthy sources (I discount here the empire given to Ermenaric in the *Getica*; cf. p. 88). The

---

[1] I hope to return to this subject more generally in a study for a Cambridge University Press series on Late Antiquity.

[2] Cf. Goffart, *Barbarians and Romans*, 4 ff.: descriptions involving words like 'flood' are misleading; the full nature of the change to the strategic balance of power took some time to make itself apparent.

Visigoths were composed of elements of Tervingi and Greuthungi who crossed the Danube in 376, combined with large numbers of Radagaisus' followers, survivors of the raid of 405/6 (Ch. 6). The Ostrogoths, similarly, were produced by an amalgamation of the forces of the two Theoderics in the 480s (Ch. 9).

The nature of our source material tends to highlight the part played in this process by dynastic ambition. Graeco-Roman sources rarely mention individual Goths other than overall leaders. More particularly, Jordanes' *Getica* brings one Gothic royal family, the Amals, firmly before our gaze, and, following Cassiodorus, consistently overstates the extent (both temporal and geographical) of its pre-eminence. Even the *Getica* cannot completely hide the existence of Theoderic Strabo, although the threat he posed to the Amals is minimized and backdated (Ch. 7). But Malchus of Philadelphia describes the intense struggle (to plagiarize the Duke of Wellington, a damned close-run thing) which preceded Theoderic the Amal's eventual triumph. Likewise, a passage in the *Getica* describes how, at an earlier stage in the family's rise to prominence, his uncle Valamer had overcome Gothic leaders from other families to create the force which provided Theoderic with his initial power-base (ibid.). The kingdom-forming Ostrogoths were thus created around the rising Amal dynasty, and Alaric had earlier played a similar role in uniting the Visigoths. The sources provide us with fewer details in this case, but a Darwinian process of competition had eliminated numerous potential rivals since 376, and, in his own lifetime, Alaric faced the challenge of at least one alternative line: the brothers Sarus and Sergeric (Ch. 6).

As they increased the size of the groups they led, the nature of the rule exercised by these dynasties changed. The kind of changes this involved can be nicely illustrated from the Amal family, who held power, as it were, before, during, and after the creation of the Ostrogoths. Above all, it increasingly became the norm that the eldest son alone had rights to succeed to an undivided inheritance. At the start of the period, after the elimination of non-Amal rivals, Valamer and his two brothers (Thiudimer and Vidimer) each wielded power. They acknowledged Valamer's pre-eminence, but lived in separate areas of Pannonia, and often waged war individually (Ch. 7). In part this changed by accident; the rule of Valamer was extinguished by his death in battle. It was also the product, however, of dynastic ambition. Thiudimer inherited overall pre-eminence on Valamer's death, and used the move into the eastern Empire in 473 as the occasion for a showdown with the third brother Vidimer, ending the pattern of fraternal succession (ibid.). Thiudimer then carried this aggressive dynastic policy further by designating Theoderic alone of his sons king in front of the whole group just before he died, ignoring the claims of at least one other son, Theodimund.[3] It is striking that similar changes affected the rulers of the Thracian Goths at the same time.[4] Refusing to share power with close relatives is a clear sign that Gothic leaders were regarding themselves in a new light.[5]

Dynastic ambition is also apparent in ceremonial and propaganda. Titulature took on an added dignity. For the Pannonian Goths, Valamer took the title 'King of the Goths' (Anon. Val. 12. 58), and there is every reason to suppose that he was the first Amal so to style himself. This dignity passed from Thiudimer to Theoderic, whose elevation (*Getica* 56. 288) provides documentation of the ceremonial that was developing to designate a Gothic king. It continued to increase in complexity, eventually incorporating use of the purple, presumably copied from the Empire.[6] The line of Theoderic Strabo, similarly, sought to emphasize its legitimacy in the face of this assertive competition from the Amals. In 473, Strabo borrowed from imperial titulature when demanding recognition as 'sole ruler' of the Goths (Malchus fr. 2). The fragmented state of the Gothic people makes this claim very ambitious (although one cannot be sure that it had never been claimed previously), and a measure of the way in which dynastic ambitions were spurred on by rivalry. Pretensions had increased; warband-leaders had appropriated the forms of royalty.

It would be a mistake, however, to place too much emphasis on dynastic ambition as the main motive force behind the creation of larger Gothic political units. Compared with their leaders, the rank and file of the Goths appear rarely in our sources, and when

---

[3] *Getica* 56. 288; cf. Wolfram, 267–8. Theodimund appears in Malchus fr. 20.

[4] After the death of Theoderic Strabo, power passed both to his son Recitach and his two (unnamed) brothers. Recitach refused to accept this, and assassinated his uncles (John of Antioch fr. 211. 5).

[5] Similar designs caused even greater dynastic strife in the Merovingian kingdoms: Wallace-Hadrill, *Long-Haired Kings*, 148 ff.

[6] Procopius, *Wars* 6. 30. 17; Agathias 1. 20. 10; Wolfram, 286 ff., 328–9.

they do, the role given them is often less than convincing. The lower orders of the Ostrogoths are mentioned by Malchus only in the confrontation of 478 between the two Theoderics in the Haemus mountains. The details of this episode seem rather contrived (p. 237). In Jordanes, the mass of the Ostrogoths appear twice: demanding to migrate from Pannonia and then later from Thrace. In the latter case, they wish to move because they are weary of their easy life in the eastern Empire, but this is a device to hide the fact that relations between the Amal and Zeno had deteriorated beyond hope of repair, the real cause of the move (*Getica* 57. 290–2). Equally, while pressure from below must have been taken into account before the departure from Pannonia, Jordanes (or rather Cassiodorus) has probably introduced the rank and file's demands to hide the split between Thiudimer and Vidimer (ibid. 56. 283–7; cf. p. 250).

The pattern of evidence for the Visigoths is similar. Those below Alaric appear only in a picture, painted for us by the poet Claudian, of Gothic leaders assembled for a council of war (*Get.* 478 ff.). Here we find a wise old Goth standing up to declare that it is folly for Alaric to invade Italy and take on the might of Stilicho (Claudian's employer). Alaric's attack on Italy may well have led to differences of opinion among his followers, and Alaric is likely to have held formal meetings with important subordinates, but the bulk of this scene is surely poetic fabrication, bearing little, if any, resemblance to the real process of decision-making among the Goths.[7] Despite the masses' absence from our sources, it would be a mistake to underestimate the degree to which pressure exerted from below, even more than dynastic ambition, was responsible for the transformations we have observed in Gothic society.

Following Jordanes, who presents Gothic tribal subdivisions as rigid from at least the third century onwards, it is easy to think of the mass of the Goths as clearly defined groups whose leaders could always rely on their support. This is very misleading. As we have seen, the majority of the Tervingi abandoned Athanaric in *c*.375/6, having lost confidence that his measures to deal with the Huns would prove effective (AM 31. 3. 4–8; cf. Ch. 4). Fritigern had to struggle against other leaders to ensure that his policies would be followed (ibid.), and, when things went wrong, Alaric

---

[7] Wolfram, 144 (with refs.) seems inclined to take it literally. For kings and councils of largely an earlier period, see Thompson, *Early Germans*, 37 ff.

faced the problem of desertions.[8] During the second wave of Gothic occupation of the Balkans, similarly, desertions from one Theoderic to the other altered the balance of power in 477 (Ch. 8).

Against this background, it is hardly surprising that the first concern of Gothic leaders was to satisfy their followers' needs and expectations. In the two agreements between Theoderic Strabo and Constantinople recorded by Malchus of Philadelphia, for instance, the economic clauses, securing a large income for Strabo's loyal soldiers, were placed first. The economic needs of their followers were equally pressing for the Amals (p. 247), as they had been for a succession of Visigothic leaders some fifty years before (p. 221). Another basic requirement of the rank and file is apparent in the concern of Gothic leaders for imperial recognition of the Goths' right to exist as an autonomous entity on Roman soil. As we have seen, Alaric was willing to drop virtually all his other demands in return for a fully valid agreement (Ch. 6). At a later date, the Theoderics did not feel quite so pressed (another indication of how imperial power had in the meantime subsided), but were anxious for the recognition inherent in the post of *magister militum*. Whether in decline or not, the Roman state remained powerful, and, before economic benefits could be enjoyed, it was vital to ensure that any gains were secure.

These considerations prompt two separate observations on the transformation of the Goths in the migration period. First, the rank and file's willingness to exchange one leader for another actually pushed those leaders into competition. Without a large following, no leading Goth, whatever his family's standing, had any power, so that leaders were forced to outbid potential rivals. They had both to offer, and in the end deliver, larger benefits to their followers than any potential rival, in order to retain the people who were the basis of their power. Pressures from below prompted and extended dynastic rivalries. Secondly, the elimination of one dynast by another is not by itself enough to explain the emergence of the larger groups who established successor states. It is also necessary to explain why, for example, after the death of Recitach in 483, the bulk of his followers were willing to transfer

[8] Claudian, *VI cons. Hon.* 250 ff. But Claudian is here trying to make the most of Stilicho's only limited successes against the Goths, and we must beware the poet's tendency to exaggerate his employer's achievements; when Alaric is next encountered, he does not seem unduly handicapped (p. 209).

their support to Theoderic the Amal. There were alternatives, and it is not immediately obvious why they made the choice they did. Or again, why, on the death of Stilicho, were former followers of Radagaisus ready to attach themselves to the group led by Alaric?

A primary motivation here is likely to have been a desire for increased security. The history of the migration period and the end of the Roman Empire in the west is often written (largely following our sources' perspective) from the Roman point of view, concentrating on the damage inflicted upon the Romans and their civilization. This perspective is perfectly valid, but one does not have to read far in the sources to realize that the migrations were also a period of extreme danger for the tribal groups caught up in them. Competing for survival and prosperity with both the Roman Empire and one another, tribal groups had to fight many battles.

We have been concerned with two Gothic groups who survived to found kingdoms in western Europe, but many other Goths had fallen by the wayside. Before 376 numerous Goths (not just Ermenaric and Vithimer) had been killed in 'many engagements' against the Huns (AM 31. 3. 2–3; Eunapius fr. 42). Apart from incidental casualties in six years of war between 376 and 382 (including two major battles—Ad Salices and Hadrianople—and a costly siege of Hadrianople), whole Gothic subgroups had been destroyed by Frigeridus (AM 31. 9), Sebastianus (31. 11), and Modares (Zosimus 4. 25), and Gothic hostages had been massacred (p. 149). Many more Goths were killed in trying to cross the Danube in 386 under Odotheus (*PLRE* i. 639), and in the course of Radagaisus' defeat in 405/6. Similarly, the Hunnic empire of Attila and his sons caused innumerable Gothic fatalities, whether in fighting for it at the Catalaunian Plains and afterwards (*Getica* 36. 192 ff.; Priscus fr. 49), in attempting to establish independence from it (*Getica* 52. 268–9; 53. 272–3), or in trying to escape into the eastern Empire under Bigelis (Jordanes, *Romana* 336). And, as we have seen, more Goths were to die in the Balkans from the 460s until 489, and in defeating Odovacar in Italy. In western Europe, the Visigoths were to suffer heavily from the Franks at Vouillé, and in twenty years of grinding warfare the Ostrogoths were reduced to insignificance by Justinian's armies. The Goths' general experience in these years was thus an extremely violent one. It is also fair to say that the Goths are representative, not an exception, in this respect. For instance, one half of the Vandals (the Silings) were destroyed in Spain in the 420s, Belisarius completing the process of genocide in North Africa a century later. Likewise, the Burgundians were savaged by the Huns in the 430s,[9] and the Rugi by Odovacar (John of Antioch fr. 214. 7).

Against this background, the attraction for the Gothic rank and file of attaching themselves to larger political units is hardly mysterious; the larger the unit, the more likely it was to survive. This is more than an argument from general circumstances. We also have some specific evidence that Goths chose to operate in larger groups for purposes of self-defence. No details survive of the unification of the Tervingi and Greuthungi, but it was surely founded on six years of co-operation in warfare against the Roman state (p. 191). For the other major component of the Visigoths, survivors of Radagaisus' following incorporated into Stilicho's army, the evidence is precise: they joined Alaric on Stilicho's death, because their families, quartered in Italian cities, were massacred in a pogrom (Zosimus 5. 35. 5–6). Theirs was a straightforward response to Roman aggression. The confrontation between the two Theoderics at Mount Sondis in 478 suggests that the later unification of the Thracian and Pannonian Goths had a similar origin. As we have seen, there are real problems with Malchus' account of this incident, but the sentiments he puts into the mouth of Theoderic Strabo ring true. He tells his namesake that the Romans alone would gain from inter-Gothic conflict, and that they had deliberately arranged the confrontation with that aim in mind. The logical extension of this was that the Gothic groups stood a better chance of extracting what they wanted from the Roman state by cooperating with one another (Malchus fr. 18. 2). It is hardly an accident that the eventual means of uniting the Pannonian and Thracian Goths was assassination (Ch. 9). This meant that, in ousting one of the rival lines, the Goths as a whole did not suffer the kind of casualties which would have handed the advantage to the emperor Zeno.

Both general considerations and more specific evidence thus suggest that the need for greater security was a powerful motivation behind the creation of the Visigoths and Ostrogoths. Once these larger groups had been formed, of course, they also had the necessary power to press the Empire for greater concessions. Hence Alaric, as we have seen, fundamentally changed the nature

[9] Refs. conveniently collected by O'Flynn, *Generalissimos*, 89 n. 4.

of what was at stake between Goths and Romans in the years after 395, and Theoderic the Amal was able to create and maintain a kingdom in Italy, rewarding his followers from the kingdom's tax-revenues (see below). To a considerable extent, desires to avoid danger and for greater rewards could go hand in hand. Presumably, however, Goths, and indeed others, had always wanted greater benefits, and it would seem to be the extra insecurity of the migration period which is the really new factor. Armed conflict on a large scale between Gothic (and other) tribal groups of the migration period and the Roman state is a major feature of the years after 376, and necessary to a full understanding both of the transformation of the Goths and the end of the Roman Empire in western Europe.[10]

This account of the transformation of the Goths between *c*.350 and 500 puts the emphasis firmly on the mass of the Goths, associating the main forces at work with their needs and aspirations. It is only fair to note that such a view to a considerable extent contradicts some other recent reconstructions which concentrate on the role of royal dynasties. According to Wolfram in particular, the Amals and Balthi were the real binding forces in Gothic society. He would see them as exercising the Gothic military kingship, a highly flexible institution which allowed anyone, whatever his ethnic origin, to become a Goth by accepting the rule of a representative of one of these dynasties. It is thus their unique royal prestige which gave the kingdom-forming Visigoths and Ostrogoths a centre around which to unite, and it was their tradition of rule, stretching all the way back to Scandinavia, which actually gave the groups they led a Gothic identity. As we shall see, there is no doubt that Visigoths and Ostrogoths were not purely Gothic, and Wolfram sees them as made up of groups, in reality

---

[10] It is possible to maintain that the end of the Roman Empire was 'an ostensibly peaceful and smooth process' (Goffart, *Barbarians and Romans*, 3; cf. Geary, *Before France and Germany*, 3 ff.) only by concentrating on certain aspects of a series of related phenomena. The final disappearance of the western Empire in the second half of the 5th c. involved relatively little warfare (though more, I think, than Goffart tends to allow), but this was the second stage of a continuous process, in which the first—the establishment of numerous autonomous or semi-autonomous tribal groups, such as Alaric's Goths, on Roman soil—had seen very considerable violence. Goffart, ibid., ch. 1 justifies himself by distancing the end of the Empire from the dramatic tribal and imperial conflicts of the 4th and 5th cc., but the argument is unconvincing.

very disparate, which were termed Gothic primarily because of the traditions of these ruling clans.[11]

I would not deny that the position and powers of overall Gothic leaders were enhanced by the social transformations of this period. As we have seen, the increase in royal self-perception is clearly visible, and the claims encapsulated in these developments were not merely propaganda. The acquisition of large annual subsidies in the course of dealings with the Roman Empire dramatically increased the powers of patronage available to Gothic leaders. What evidence there is would suggest that the leaders did control the distribution of these funds (p. 268). And once Visigoths and Ostrogoths had created kingdoms, still further powers were available. The successor states lie beyond our compass, but the use of Roman-style law-codes enhanced Gothic kings' legal role,[12] for instance, and the Roman administration they inherited brought in its wake substantial tax-revenues. When converted into salaries, these allowed Theoderic the Amal to maintain a hierarchy of administrative posts that could be distributed to Goths who showed suitable loyalty.[13] Similar resources were available to Visigothic kings.[14] Leaders of the new political units were thus able to focus the loyalties of their followers upon themselves and upon royal service in ways that had been impossible for their predecessors, who had led much smaller and poorer groups on the fringes of the Roman Empire.

I would argue, however, that to make the unity and cohesion of the kingdom-forming groups dependent on the Amals and Balthi, is to place too much weight on later dynastic propaganda. Neither the Amals nor Balthi had anything like as long a history of pre-

[11] Wolfram, esp. 5–12 (cf. also 92 ff., 115 ff., 231 ff.). Wolfram has been echoed e.g. by Liebeschuetz, *Barbarians and Bishops*, ch. 5, who describes Alaric's Goths (p. 49) as 'a warband of Gothic tribal "ideology", but only partly Gothic origin'. See also Geary, *Before France and Germany*, 61 ff. A more guarded approach to the Burgundians, but along similar lines, is Wood, 'Ethnicity'. I am grateful to the author for an off-print and much regret that I have as yet been unable to consult the rest of the volume from which it comes: Wolfram and Pohl (edd.), *Typen der Ethnogenese*.

[12] Wormald, '*Lex scripta* and *Verbum Regis*'; cf. Wolfram, 193 ff.

[13] Heather, 'Theoderic as Tribal Leader'; Wolfram, 290 ff.

[14] Wolfram, 211 ff. In partial contrast, Thompson, 'Fritigern to Euric', would see increasing patronage as fundamental to the history of the Goths in migration; see further n. 38.

eminence as the *Getica* (following certainly Cassiodorus for the Amals, and Ablabius perhaps for the Balthi) would claim. The two dynasties arose only with the groups they led, and the better evidence makes it clear that their pre-eminence did not predate the arrival of the Huns in the south-western USSR (Ch. 1). It is entirely in accord with this evidence that when the dynasties failed to provide suitable leaders, they were quickly ousted by Gothic 'nobles' acting in concert. As we have seen, the Amals did not long survive Belisarius' invasion of Italy. Similarly, the hold of the Balthi on Visigothic loyalties was fatally loosened by Clovis's assault on their holdings in southern Gaul, and by Theoderic the Amal's direct rule in Spain from 511 until his death in 526.[15] In any case, the fact that the Balthi survived for most of the fifth century at the head of the Visigoths probably gives a slightly misleading impression of dynastic continuity. Theoderic I's sons succeeded to the throne by murdering one another, and Theoderic II was surely attempting to forestall such a fate by giving his brother Fredericus a recognized share of power. He might have been well advised to extend this constitutional experiment to his other brother, Euric, who eventually assassinated him.[16]

Who, then, were these nobles who ousted the Amals and Balthi, and what was the source of their evident power? From the Balkan period of both Visigoths and Ostrogoths we have no more than a few names. Anstat, Invila, and Soas, for instance, were military commanders subordinate to Theoderic the Amal (*Getica* 56. 285; Malchus fr. 20). This kind of evidence is not very helpful. However, Procopius' *Gothic War* and Cassiodorus' *Variae* provide us not only with many more names of men holding intermediate military and administrative posts, but also show, in the case of Ostrogothic Italy, that the power of these men was to a considerable extent independent of any king or overall leader.

One of the *Variae* gives us precious insight into how lower-level leaders emerged. The Goths of Reate and Nursia in central Italy decided, we are told, that their leader, known as a *prior*, was to be a certain Quidila son of Sibia. Their choice was then accepted and confirmed by Theoderic, who died almost immediately, so that they felt it necessary to write again to his successor Athalaric to make sure that the choice would stand (*Variae* 8. 26). This

---

[15] Cf. Collins, *Early Medieval Spain*, 32 ff.
[16] Heather, 'Visigothic Kingdom'.

suggests something of a balance of power. Goths of this subgroup, at least, seem to have chosen their own leader (how is not specified), so that the *prior* owed his authority in part to his local position, rather than to the king's favour. Nevertheless, the king was consulted and his approval obtained, demonstrating that he had certain formal rights of intervening in his followers' affairs. How these would have worked in practice is unclear. He could perhaps not impose a total outsider as *prior* on a given locality, but it is likely that he could at least veto any candidate whose loyalty he had reason to doubt.

The evidence suggests that a similar balance of power operated throughout Gothic society in the Italian kingdom. We hear of a number of important Goths who had a local basis of support, which was clearly not under the close control of the king. Early in the Gothic war, a certain Pitzas rejected Wittigis' leadership and surrendered to Belisarius, along with half the Goths of Samnium (*Wars* 5. 15. 1–2). These men seem to have been loyal to Pitzas first and the monarchy second. This example is slightly compli- cated by the fact that Wittigis had just replaced the murdered Theodahad, and it could be argued that what we see here is a supporter of Theodahad rejecting Wittigis. Even so, we still have to account for Pitzas' ability to influence so many of the Goths of Samnium, so that the point can stand. Other examples, indeed, show that it was by no means abnormal for rank-and-file Goths to be more closely tied to local leaders than to the central monarchy. After Wittigis' surrender, which encompassed most of the Goths, for instance, one group in Venetia, under the leadership of Ildebad, refused to give in (*Wars* 6. 29. 41; cf. 30. 16 ff.; 7. 1. 25 ff.). And in the absence of a monarch, Goths of different localities tended to formulate policy individually. Thus, after the defeat of Teias, Goths north of the River Po were quick to negotiate an alliance with the Franks, while those south of it were much more cautious (Agathias 1. 5. 1–2). The common denomina- tor here is a local cohesion that went beyond more general allegiance to the Ostrogoths as a whole.

In some cases, the ties binding these locally distinct groups were older than their allegiance to the overall Amal kingship. Of this, the Rugi provide a striking illustration. Under Fredericus, son of King Feletheus, they had joined Theoderic and the Ostrogoths after being defeated by Odovacar in 487.[17] They then followed Theoderic to Italy, where Fredericus played an independent game, joining Odovacar's general Tufa before submitting a second time to Theoderic (Ennodius, *Pan.* 55). In 541, these Rugi still maintained their independent identity and had their own under-leader, Eraric, even though they had been part of the Ostrogoths for over fifty years. As Procopius tells us, they had refused intermarriage, keeping their name and purity of blood (*Wars* 7. 2. 1 ff.). Eraric may or may not have been related to the royal clan from which Fredericus came, but this does not affect the argu-ment. Within the different Gothic groups who came together under Valamer and Theoderic to form the Ostrogoths, there was presumably more of a tendency towards intermarriage than was the case with the Rugi, but they demonstrate that not all pre-existing identities and leaderships were destroyed when Goths and others joined the Amal bandwagon. The case of Gensemund confirms the point. Even after resigning his claim to royalty in the Amals' favour, he continued to lead an at least semi-independent military force in wars on Valamer's behalf (*Variae* 8. 9; *Getica* 48. 246; Ch. 7). Old bonds were not necessarily dissolved when groups joined the Ostrogoths.[18]

This evidence for the social and political structure of the Ostrogoths complements very well the rather more limited role for the Amal family that we have reconstructed. Warband-leaders recently turned kings had to accept intermediate leaders who were powerful in their own right. We have no comparable evidence for the Visigoths either in the Balkans or southern Gaul, but the situation is likely to have been similar. A series of Gothic nobles held important positions in the fifth century, and they probably also fuelled the inter-dynastic strife between Theoderic I's sons.[19] At least, a fractious nobility composed of men powerful in their own right is certainly visible from the early sixth century, and it is most unlikely that it had only then come into existence.[20]

The existing social order was not washed away, therefore, in the transformation that has been our central concern. Gothic political units increased in size during the migration period largely through

[17] Eugippius *V. Sev.* 44. 3–4; Procopius, *Wars* 7. 2. 1–2; cf. *PLRE* ii. 484–5.
[18] See further Heather, 'Theoderic as Tribal Leader'.
[19] See further Heather, 'Visigothic Kingdom'.
[20] Cf. Claude, *Adel, Kirche und Königtum*, 47 ff.

an aggregation of pre-existing units. Their leaders, the Gothic nobility of the Italian and Hispano-Gallic kingdoms, continued to wield real power even after accepting the overall leadership of a royal line (whether Amal, Balth, Triarius, or one of the probably many other dynasties whose names have not survived). This power remained rooted in their ties to these groups. The kingdom-forming Visigoths and Ostrogoths were larger than the fourth-century Tervingi, the only pre-Hunnic group for which we have good evidence, but not totally dissimilar. The kings of post-Hunnic groups could draw on larger financial resources and more sophisticated ideologies of kingship, but still stood astride a hierarchy of lower-level leaders, many of whom had an independent power-base. The later hierarchies were more complicated. Roman money and tax revenue funded increasing social differentiation, but, just as the *iudex* of the Tervingi had to work with his subordinate but still powerful *reiks* (Ch. 3), so an Ostrogothic or Visigothic king had to work with all his *comites*.[21]

One last issue demands our attention. It is simply a fact that the Visigoths and Ostrogoths, who established the Gothic successor states to the Roman Empire, were not composed just of Goths. As well as Goths, for instance, Athaulf had Huns under his command, who may well have been descended from a group settled, like the Tervingi, under the peace of 382 (cf. p. 157). Radagaisus, called a Gothic king, is said to have led a force composed of a number of different tribal groups, so that the survivors from his attack who later joined Alaric were presumably not all Goths. Paulinus of Pella also mentions a (seemingly small) force of Alans which moved in and out of the Visigoths in the 410s (*Euch.* 372 ff.). As we have seen, the Ostrogoths counted Rugi among their number, some Bittigur Huns are found in Italy in the course of the Byzantine war of reconquest,[22] and a number of other

[21] Cf. Wolfram, 144–5; there may well have been a difference of degree in the royal power exercised by Alaric compared with that of Fritigern, but the evidence Wolfram cites is Claudian's picture of Alaric's council of war, whose relationship to the real thing is likely to be minimal (see above). Similarly, the fact that Roman sources often call Alaric *rex* in the Latin sense of monarch does not show that the gradations in Gothic society had disappeared. As we have seen, the Visigothic nobles, descendants of the 4th-c. *reiks*, are alive and kicking in the 5th and 6th cc.

[22] Agathias 2. 13. 1 ff.; Jordanes, *Getica* 53. 272; cf. Burns, *History of the Ostrogoths*, 54.

groups were included within the Ostrogothic kingdom.[23] From this follows a simple question. Given that these other ethnic groups can be found among the Visigoths and Ostrogoths, what is it that made them Gothic?

The view of Gothic history advanced particularly by Wolfram allows of an easy answer. The Ostrogoths and Visigoths, like the Greuthungi and Tervingi who preceded them, were (it is said) polyethnic confederations that were called Gothic essentially because their ruling clans, the Amals and Balthi, preserved authentic Gothic traditions stretching back into the distant past; Gothic identity is thus primarily located in these ruling families (see above). But such a view of the essence of Gothic identity cannot stand once it is realized that the claims to unique preeminence advanced for these lines, essentially by Jordanes' *Getica*, are nothing more than dynastic propaganda. The Amals and Balthi were not ancient ruling lines; neither had a long enough history to supply the groups they led with their Gothic identity. In addition, much of the real power within these groups, as we have seen, was concentrated lower down the social hierarchy, making it implausible that these somewhat transitory royal houses should have dictated the identity of the mass of Ostrogoths and Visigoths.

We know, for example, that Goths who formed a subordinate part of a Hun-led force in the 460s retained a strong notion of their identity, which had been quite unshaken by the fact that they had had Hunnic leaders presumably for some time. These Goths had reinforced their sense of identity by a common oath (cf. p. 139), and it was so strong that Byzantine military commanders were able to split the mixed force apart by working on the Goths' feelings of resentment towards their Hunnic masters.[24] As this kind of evidence suggests, the answer to our question must lie, I would argue, in a more old-fashioned view of what 'Gothic' groups such as Ostrogoths and Visigoths actually were. Not all of the followers

[23] Wolfram, 300 ff.

[24] Priscus fr. 49. In a similar way, subject peoples of the Avar Empire retained their separate identity. Slavs, Gepids, and Bulgars all remained distinct, with some managing (like the Goths in the case of the Huns) to reassert their independence as the power of their masters declined. See, for instance, Whitby, *The Emperor Maurice*, 184 ff. with refs. Cf. Theophylact Simocatta 8. 3. 11–13: the Gepids maintained distinct settlement areas.

of Alaric or Theoderic the Amal shared a common, Gothic, ethnic origin, but the likelihood is surely that the majority of them did.[25] It is worth stressing from the outset that the presence of some non-Gothic elements does not make the Ostrogoths and Visigoths fundamentally multiracial. The central issue here is how numerous these elements actually were.

Some migration-period groups clearly were multiracial. The followers of Odovacar were so multiracial, indeed, that the sources record a bewildering variety of ethnic affiliations for both them and their leader.[26] It is also true, as Wallace-Hadrill put it, that 'warbands are tribes in the making'[27] and some warbands of very mixed origin do seem to have fused together to create new peoples. This has recently been suggested, for instance, of the Normans and the Ottoman Turks, both of whom, it has been argued, later generated historical myths to prove that their origins were more coherent than they actually had been.[28] But the fact that some groups were of such mixed origin does not prove that all were, and there are good reasons why this kind of model should not be applied to the Ostrogoths and Visigoths.

To start with, when dealing with these groups, the sources betray none of the confusion apparent in their treatment of Odovacar's following. No source considers the Visigoths and Ostrogoths as anything other than Gothic. It is worth reflecting, indeed, on the range of well-informed contemporary sources who insist on their Gothic ethnic identity. For the Ostrogoths, Malchus of Philadelphia, Cassiodorus' *Variae* (much of it the official correspondence of Italian Gothic kings), Procopius, and Agathias attest this basic fact. A similar range of evidence can be cited

---

[25] Wolfram, 300 at one point seems to adopt this kind of position, stating that 'Theoderic led to Italy not the entire Ostrogothic people but a federate army composed mainly of Ostrogoths.' He also refers on the same page, however, to the 'fundamental polyethnic character of the Gothic army' and elsewhere stresses 'polyethnicity' (e.g. 7 ff., 92 ff., 301).

[26] Cf. *PLRE* ii. 791: he is styled variously as a Hun, Scirian, Thuringian, Goth, and Rugian.

[27] *Early Germanic Kingship*, 11.

[28] Loud, '*Gens Normannorum*', 112 ff.; Lindner, *Ottomans*, esp. ch. 1; cf. Liebeschuetz, *Barbarians and Bishops*, 76 ff. Note now, however, Searle, *Predatory Kinship*, ps. II and III, suggesting very strongly that the Norman myth had potency because it was strongly rooted in reality.

making the same point about the Visigoths.[29] It thus seems quite clear that the kingdom-forming Visigoths and Ostrogoths considered themselves primarily Gothic, and were regarded as such both by their Roman subjects and the east Roman state. It is also worth noting that where no single ethnic group was dominant in political units thrown up by the migration period, official titulature was flexible enough to express this fact. Thus the Asding rulers of North Africa were *reges Vandalorum et Alannorum*.[30]

Equally important, while Ostrogoths and Visigoths are new political units—demonstrating this has been a central concern of this study—'Gothic' as an ethnic identity is not at all new. Unlike Normans and Ottomans, we have very good evidence that Goths as such did exist before the migration period (even if their political order then bore no resemblance to the later division into Visigoth and Ostrogoth). As we have seen, Gothic political units had quite well-developed institutions of central government even before the Huns, and acted on occasion with great ambition. Defining themselves consistently against the Roman Empire, the leadership of the Tervingi attempted to enforce ideological conformity in their lands (Ch. 3). Goths as such had had a lengthy history before the convulsions of the migration period; we are not dealing with an ethnic group that can be plausibly argued to have emerged only from the chaos engendered by the Huns. This, it seems to me, is the central point. A new political order was created among the Goths between *c*.350 and 500, but not a new ethnic identity.

The new political units were certainly not completely Gothic, but I would argue that the extent to which Visigoths and Ostrogoths were multiracial has been considerably overstated. The idea that the Greuthungi who crossed the Danube in 376 under Alatheus and Saphrax were a 'polyethnic' confederation, composed in virtually equal measure of Goths, Huns, and Alans, must be rejected (p. 145). The Greuthungi who contributed much manpower to the Visigoths were, as Ammianus confirms, essentially Gothic. Similarly, Alaric's revolt after 395 cannot really be equated with the growth of a multiracial warband such as the Ottoman Turks. From the outset it encompassed a very large

[29] e.g. Olympiodorus (via Zosimus, Sozomen, and Philostorgius), the titulature of the kingdom (Wolfram, *Intitulatio*, 77–8), Sidonius Apollinaris, and 5th-c. chroniclers.

[30] See Wolfram, *Intitulatio*, 79 ff.

group, and two contemporaries, Synesius and Claudian, clearly saw it as a general revolt of those, mostly Goths, who had been settled under the 382 treaty. As we have seen, this makes good sense both of the causes of revolt, and of Alaric's concerns as they appear in the sources (Ch. 6). The largest non-Gothic element among the Visigoths is likely to have come from the followers of Radagaisus, who joined Alaric after Stilicho's death. But the sources indicate that Radagaisus was a Gothic king, so that many Goths are likely to have been among his following. Most of the 'Roman slaves' said to have joined Alaric surely came from this source as well (p. 214), so that the Gothic element among the Visigoths is likely to have been very substantial. Alaric's force grew over time, and setbacks probably caused desertions (although our only source to say so is Claudian, who had a particular axe to grind: see above). Nevertheless, Alaric first mobilized the Goths settled under the 382 treaty, and many, perhaps the majority, of those added to his command were again Gothic. The Visigoths were a new political unit, but a Gothic one, in the sense that the majority of them had an ethnic identity which had been established before they gave their allegiance to Alaric.

Theoderic the Amal's Ostrogoths have attracted less attention from those wishing to stress 'polyethnicity', but similar points could be made. One example will suffice. On the basis of Jordanes, Ermenaric has been credited with a huge multiracial empire, but, as we have seen, this is a figment of Cassiodorus' imagination. The Pannonian and Thracian groups were both essentially Gothic (according, that is, to our sources), so that a similar conclusion to that reached over the Visigoths can stand. The Ostrogoths were Gothic because they were composed mainly of people who considered themselves Goths. The lack of confusion over the ethnic identity of Ostrogoths and Visigoths in the sources, the fact that this identity was already established before the Hunnic invasions, and the fact that narrative reconstruction tends to confirm that both were composed mainly of Goths, suggest very strongly that the kind of model applicable perhaps to Normans, Ottomans, and the followers of Odovacar should not be used here. Numerous non-Goths were included among Visigoths and Ostrogoths, but the unanimous insistence of very well-informed sources must surely mean that Goths really were dominant.

This, of course, is perfectly compatible with the presence of even quite large numbers of non-Goths. Apart from groups such as Rugi who joined *en masse*, outsiders, as Liebeschuetz has recently observed, would have been especially likely to have been incorporated via the bodies of armed retainers kept by prominent 'nobles'.[31] As we have seen, however, both kingdom-forming Gothic groups probably numbered at least *c* 100,000 people (pp. 214, 302), so that 10,000 and even 20,000 foreigners could have been accommodated without altering the fundamental Gothic character of the group. Over time, indeed, the predominance of 'true Goths', which, as we have seen, is the likeliest explanation for our sources' insistence that these forces were Gothic, is likely to have brought about the 'Gothicization' of even non-Gothic elements within the groups. Intermarriage, and the need to adapt to the language, customs, and perhaps the religion of the majority, would, given enough generations, blur distinctions, unless, like the Rugi, groups took positive steps to maintain their separate identities. Such a process of assimilation must have generated an evolution in identity as the groups adapted to one another, but we are dealing with no sudden break, and the ideas and attitudes of the Gothic majority are likely to have had much the stronger influence on the end result.[32]

What precisely this Gothic identity of the majority of the population consisted of is harder to say, and really the subject for a separate study.[33] It is perhaps just worth mentioning some lines of thought suggested by the sources. A common language, given literary form by Ulfila, is an obvious bond. We know, for instance,

[31] *Barbarians and Bishops*, 76; although many retainers would no doubt also have been recruited from within the group.

[32] I note that the passage from Ibn Khaldun cited by Liebeschuetz, *Barbarians and Bishops*, 78 to illustrate the process of multiracial ethnogenesis in fact describes the attachment of a single individual to another ethnic group and the way in which such individuals took on the identity of the majority. This presupposes, as I would argue is applicable in the case of the Goths, that a large group with a set identity already existed for such an individual to join. Ibn Khaldun is really describing cases such as the Greek merchant turned Hun encountered by Priscus (fr. 11. 2), or the absorption by the Slavs of individual prisoners (Ch. 3 n. 28). In all these historical examples, the ways of the majority, as is only natural, largely prevail.

[33] I intend to address the question more fully in a more general study of the Goths to appear in the Blackwells 'People of Europe' series.

that the tradition of Gothic biblical scholarship was still very much alive in Ostrogothic Italy.[34] Ulfila's non-Nicene brand of Christianity is another likely element. It is the overall implication of the persecutions of Christianity among the Tervingi that, even in the fourth century, the leaders of Gothic political units saw shared religious belief as an important part of group identity. Although the Goths probably first accepted 'Arianism' because it was the religion of the emperor Valens, they later clung to it with such tenacity that it surely became a means of differentiating themselves from inhabitants of the Empire.[35]

Legal customs are likely to have played a critical role. This is no place for a full discussion of 'customary law' among the Goths, but outsiders would have had to adapt themselves to the methods of dispute settlement already in force. Amongst the Ostrogoths, at least, we hear of the *belagines*, supposedly a set of written laws.[36] Some shared traditions about the past probably also played their part. For this, Jordanes' *Getica* provides just a little evidence. *Getica* 4. 28–9 reports that both Gothic songs and tales and the historian Ablabius gave similar accounts of the Goths' migration to lands above the Black Sea under Filimer. If Ablabius is our mysterious Visigothic historian (Ch. 2), then this would imply that both Visigoths and either Ostrogoths in Italy or other Goths in Constantinople (depending on whether it was Cassiodorus or Jordanes who had heard the tales) told much the same stories about the move organized by Filimer. Obviously, there are too many unknowns here for the point to be conclusive, but shared traditions, reflecting associations in the distant past, are the kind of thing that is likely to have distinguished Goths from other peoples.[37]

---

[34] Friedrichsen, *Gothic Version of the Gospels*, 157 ff.

[35] Heather, 'Gothic Conversion', with Liebeschuetz, *Barbarians and Bishops*, 49–50. On the Tervingi, see Ch. 3.

[36] Jordanes, *Getica* 11. 69; cf. Wolfram, 193 ff. Ibn Khaldun (cf. n. 32) also makes specific mention of law.

[37] For instance, it is usually considered that Germanic-language speakers emerged as a group distinguishable from other Indo-Europeans when a subgroup developed in this particular direction in isolation from the group to which they had previously belonged (e.g. Schutz, *Germanic Europe*, 310 ff.). It seems likely that Goths, Gepids, Franks, etc., who were all Germanic-speakers, were differentiated from one another by equally distinctive experiences at some point in the distant past.

I should stress that, in arguing for a Gothic identity which was more firmly established among large groups of people than has recently been suggested, I should not want to present it as too rigid. It is very important here to steer a middle path. As we have seen, political changes created larger Gothic groups with ever stronger institutions of central leadership. This development was to have profound implications.[38] Archaeological research has also made it clear that different ethnic groups, both nomads and settled agriculturalists, affected one another deeply in the course of the population movements associated with the Huns. It is possible to trace, for instance, the increasing prevalence of mounted warfare among the Goths, which is likely to reflect the influence of nomad peoples.[39] But physical remains do not tell us what language their owners and users spoke, nor what stories of the past they told. Despite such changes, Goths clearly did retain their identity under Hunnic domination (Priscus fr. 49), and were quite capable of reasserting it as Attila's empire collapsed. The fact that non-Gothic groups joined political units dominated by Goths means that not all those who considered themselves Goths would have been of purely Gothic descent, from the presumably single group which, back in the mists of time, first called itself 'the Goths'.[40] Nevertheless, the widespread appearance of Goths in the migration period and the robustness of their identity bear witness that, although the Gothic identity may have widened in this period, and to some extent been redefined, it was not a product of it. The fact that other groups may have absorbed the Gothic identity of the Ostrogoths and Visigoths suggests that its essentials had already been well defined before the arrival of the Huns.

---

[38] I would take a similar view to Thompson (argued especially in 'Fritigern to Euric') that, as social differentiation increased, Gothic leaders came to have more in common with Roman aristocrats than their followers. I would see this, however, as a phenomenon which slowly appeared in the successor kingdoms (especially in the long-lived Visigothic state), rather than, with Thompson, as a relatively swift development in the course of the actual migrations.

[39] Cf. Wolfram, 167–8, 302 ff.

[40] The word probably meant 'the people' (Wolfram, 19 ff.). Wolfram, 12–13 would still see a single Gothic kingdom in the 3rd c. but, leaving Ostrogotha aside (p. 37), the raids of this period seem to have been conducted by a number of disparate groups. It seems likely that the point at which being a Goth gave someone both an ethnic and a political identity should be situated in the much deeper past, perhaps in the days of the kings known to Tacitus (*Germania* 44).

As is so often the case, it is much easier to say what something is not, rather than what it actually is. Gothic identity is too enduring a phenomenon in our source material to have been carried by a few ruling dynasties, the realities of whose pre-eminence were much less grand than they liked to pretend. Goths remained Goths without the Amals and Balthi. They had also been Goths long before the Huns, and their distinct identity survived even Hunnic domination. The Visigoths and Ostrogoths who were created out of the chaos of the migration period and founded successor states to the western Roman Empire were not purely Gothic, but they were surely dominated by groups sharing a common language, together with perhaps a common religion and common traditions about a deeper past. Just as much of the real power in these groups was wielded by under-leaders, whose position was rooted in ties to the Gothic rank and file, so the groups were given their overall identity by the ethnic groups dominant within them.

APPENDIX A

GOTHIC TRIBAL NAMES

In the secondary literature it has been traditional to talk of 'Visigoths' and 'Ostrogoths' (often taken to mean respectively 'West' and 'East Goths') from the third or at least the fourth century. As we have seen, however, the two groups who formed kingdoms in the fifth century are not the direct descendants of the Tervingi and Greuthungi of the fourth century, and the latter should not be called, as they commonly are, 'Visigoth' and Ostrogoth'. My concern here is simply to trace the evolution of nomenclature against the realignments we have already observed in Gothic social organization.

Fourth-century usages seem straightforward; Tervingi and Greuthungi were Gothic groups who occupied lands above the Black Sea. A group named Tervingi is first attested in 291 (*Pan. Lat.* 3(11). 17. 1) and last mentioned in the *Notitia Dignitatum* from the early 390s (Or. 6. 61). The Tervingi seem to have been those Goths who held lands closest to the imperial frontier before the Hun invasions. The larger part of this group fled south of the Danube in 376, and it is presumably to these (or their descendants) that the *Notitia Dignitatum* referred in the 390s (see further p. 163).[1] Greuthungi, similarly, was the name applied to one or more Gothic groups who, before the Hun invasions, lived east of the Tervingi (p. 88). The name is last attested in a poem of Claudian from 399.[2]

The evolution of 'Visigoth' also seems clear. Originally 'Vesi' or 'Visi', the term became 'Visigoth' while continuing to designate the same group: that mixure of Tervingi, Greuthungi, and others who founded a kingdom in southern Gaul and Spain. 'Visi'/'Vesi' is last attested on 1 January 456, when it was used by Sidonius Apollinaris (*Carm.* 7. 399); Visigoth (Οὐισίγοτθοι) appears in later sources, such as Procopius, referring to the same group.[3] Its origin, however, is problematic. It is first used by the *Notitia Dignitatum* (Or. 5. 61) of an auxiliary unit in one of the eastern

---

[1] Cf. Wolfram, 25: the name perhaps meant 'forest-dwellers'.

[2] Claudian, *Eutr.* 2. 153, 196, 399, 576; cf. Heather, 'The Anti-Scythian Tirade', 156–7. The name perhaps meant 'steppe-dweller' (Wolfram, 25) which could be a general term for more than one independent political unit.

[3] e.g. Procopius, *Wars* 3. 2. 7 ff., 8. 5. 5 ff.; cf. Wolfram, 25.

praesental field armies, which were clearly meant to be parallel.[4] In the other, an identical position was occupied by a unit named Tervingi (Or. 6. 61). This would suggest that Visi and Tervingi were units of an identical type, and surely guarantees that both were Goths.[5] But it is unclear exactly which Goths this term designated in the early 390s. Given the later usage, the Visi were presumably Goths who contributed to the kingdom-forming group and yet were seemingly not Tervingi, since the *Notitia Dignitatum* makes a distinction between them. Since no record exists of any group called Visi entering the Empire, it may have possibly been a new name for those Greuthungi who came south of the Danube in 376, but this is only a guess. The Visi of the *Notitia* must either be a new group or a previously known group under a new name.

The original usage of 'Ostrogoth', similarly, is unclear. It is used first by Claudian in 399, who writes 'Ostrogothis colitur mixtisque Gruthungis' (*Eutr.* 2. 153). At face value, Ostrogoths were thus distinct from Greuthungi in 399, but our source is an invective poem, and there is no guarantee that Claudian was even attempting to be precise. The name would seem to mean 'East Goth',[6] and could possibly be a general term for Goths in the eastern Empire at this date, rather than a technical term specifying a particular political unit.[7] Ostrogoth is next used by Sidonius in *c.*470 of the group led by Valamir in Pannonia.[8] By this date, then, the term does seem to have had a more specific meaning, and, as we have seen, the eponymous Ostrogotha appears in the Amal genealogy and is echoed in the naming of Theoderic the Amal's children (p. 22), so that our sources seem to be consistent. However, in Cassiodorus' *Variae*, official correspondence from Ostrogothic Italy, the Gothic conquerors of Italy are referred to simply as 'Goths'.[9] Likewise, 'Ostrogoths' never appear in Byzantine sources, who always refer to them simply as 'Goths' even when distinguishing them from Οὐισίγοτθοι.[10]

Visigoth and Ostrogoth cannot be applied to the Gothic people before the Hun invasions. The fourth-century Tervingi and Greuthungi must be discussed as such, since great discontinuities separate them from the

[4] Hoffmann, *Bewegungsheer*, 90 ff.

[5] Cf. Wolfram, 24 (and 25 for its possible meanings).

[6] Wolfram, 25.

[7] There is no record of Ostrogoths (as opposed to Greuthungi) entering the Empire and being settled in Phrygia, but our sources are fragmentary.

[8] *Carm.* 2. 377 (AD 468); *Ep.* 8. 9. 36 ff. (476); cf. p. 59.

[9] Cf. Wolfram, *Intitulatio*, i. 77: the Gothic kings of Italy did not use either 'Goth' or 'Ostrogoth' in their official titulature; the Visigoth Alaric II (484–507) simply styled himself *rex Gothorum* (ibid. 77 ff.), although *rex Visigotorum* was a title between 612 and 621.

[10] Procopius and Agathias, *passim*; in particular Procopius, *Wars* 3. 2. 7 ff. Agathias never mentions Visigoths.

later Visigoths and Ostrogoths. The evidence is insufficient fully to document the genesis and significance of the later terms, but their basic meaning is clear. As long as the problems are noted, Visigoth and Ostrogoth can be used of the two new groupings who established successor states to the Roman Empire in the fifth century; they do not, however, mean West and East Goth.[11]

---

[11] I do not take *Historia Augusta* 25. 6. 2 as admissible evidence. It refers to 'Grutungi, Austrogoti, Tervingi, (Vi)si', in the time of the emperor Claudius in *c*.275. Since this would predate all other mentions of these terms, and those of 'Visi' and 'Ostrogoth' by over a century, and given that the latter terms were applied to new groupings who appear after a social revolution which started in *c*.375, a simple explanation suggests itself. The names are another indication that the *Historia Augusta* was a concoction of the 390s. This is the date, of course, when the later Gothic names are otherwise first attested. See Dessau, 'Über Zeit und Persönlichkeit' and the more recent works of Syme: *Ammianus and the Historia Augusta; Emperors and Biography; The Historia Augusta*. A 5th-c. date has also been proposed, which would merely strengthen the suggestion: Birley, 'Fresh Thoughts', 99–105.

APPENDIX B

GOTHS IN PANNONIA $c.380-408$

It has become a commonplace of modern historical reconstruction that in 380 Gratian made a separate peace with the Greuthungi of Alatheus and Saphrax, settling them in Pannonia.[1] Passages from Zosimus and the *Getica* provide the primary evidence, and the subsequent history of these Goths has been traced down to 408 when Athaulf (considered the successor of Alatheus and Saphrax) led a force of Huns and Goths from Pannonia to join Alaric in Italy. But Jordanes and Zosimus do not prove that a settlement took place, the evidence for any subsequent history is quite inconclusive, and there is a good alternative explanation for Athaulf's presence in Pannonia in 408.

The Settlement

(a) Zosimus

Zosimus 4. 34. 2–5 reports that when Vitalianus became commander in Illyricum, Gaul was threatened by two Germanic groups from beyond the Rhine (*sic*): one led by Alatheus and Saphrax, the other by Fritigern. Gratian was forced to allow them, once they had left Gaul, to cross the Danube and occupy Pannonia and Upper Moesia. They were intending to go to Epirus and attack Greece, but first provided themselves with forage. They also deposed Athanaric, head of the 'Scythian' royal family, so that no one should interfere with their plans. Athanaric fled to the emperor Theodosius, who had just recovered from a dangerous illness and welcomed him warmly, giving him, when he died shortly afterwards, a lavish funeral. The 'Scythian barbarians' were so amazed that they returned home, ceasing to trouble the Romans. The followers of Athanaric guarded the river (Danube) to prevent further attacks.

There is genuine information here, but the problems are obvious:

---

[1] e.g. Seeck, *Geschichte*, v. 141 ff.; Schmidt, 259–60; Stein, i. 193; Piganiol, *L'Empire chrétien*, 232 ff.; Várady, *Das letzte Jahrhundert*, 19 ff.; Chrysos, 138–40; Wolfram, 132; Demougeot, ii. 148–9 and 'Modalités', 145 ff.; (more cautiously) Cesa, 'Romani e barbari', 77 ff.; Liebeschuetz, *Barbarians and Bishops*, 27 n. 12.

1. In the opening lines the threat posed by the Goths to the Danube has been confused with separate attacks across the Rhine. The Goths were confined to the Balkans; Alamanni made the incursions over the Rhine.[2]

2. Fritigern, Alatheus, and Saphrax crossed the Danube in 376, not winter 380/1, when Athanaric fled to Theodosius.[3]

3. Athanaric had led the Tervingi before 376, but a majority of the people then rejected his authority (AM 31. 3. 8). He fled to Theodosius in 380/1 when he was rejected even by those who had followed him after 376 (p. 337).

4. Zosimus has a bizarre chain of cause and effect, whereby the magnificence of Theodosius' funeral arrangements for Athanaric cause the rest of the 'Scythians' to go 'home'. These 'Scythians' seem to be the Goths mentioned earlier in the passage as planning to attack Epirus and Greece, namely those of Fritigern, Alatheus, and Saphrax. It cannot refer to Athanaric's Goths, who remain to guard the Danube.[4] Athanaric's funeral in January 381 is thus made the cause of a peace with different Goths, concluded some eighteen months later in October 382.[5]

5. The Goths of Athanaric did remain south of the Danube, but so did those of Fritigern, Alatheus, and Saphrax. Their return 'home' is fiction.[6]

The passage is obviously confused,[7] but simultaneous attacks on Rhine and Danube, Athanaric's flight to Theodosius and subsequent death, and a peace with Goths whereby they remained in the Empire are all genuine events; it is their combination here which has created fantasy.

Two confusions are obvious. Attacks over the Rhine have been conflated with those over the Danube, and Theodosius' reception of Athanaric in January 381 has been linked to the peace of 382. Less obviously, the Danube crossing of Fritigern, Alatheus, and Saphrax in 376 seems to have been confused with Athanaric's crossing in 380/1. The report here that Fritigern, Alatheus, and Saphrax crossed the Danube has been seen as the author's invention, a way of getting them from Gaul to their rightful place in the Balkans.[8] But the passage links their crossing

[2] AM 31. 10; Ausonius, *Grat. act.* 2; Socrates, *HE* 5. 6; Sozomen, *HE* 7. 2.

[3] Athanaric entered Constantinople on 11 Jan. 381 and died on 25 Jan.: *Cons. Const.*, s.a. 381 (*CM* i. 243).

[4] Cf. Schmidt, 418 n. 2; but see also Paschoud, ii. 2. 409 n. 168; cf. Cesa, 'Romani e barbari', 86–7.

[5] Cesa, 'Romani e barbari', 84–6. Orosius 7. 34. 6–7 makes a similar mistake; cf. Schmidt, 419 n. 3.

[6] Demougeot, ii. 149 ff., and 'Modalités', 152–3 believes that the Goths 'went home' in 380 before returning in 382 when another treaty was made. This places too much trust in a confused passage. See also p. 148.

[7] Cf. Paschoud, ii. 2. 406 n. 166.

[8] Ibid.

to a plot to oust Athanaric from his position as 'King of the Scythians'. This recalls very strongly the circumstances of 376, when Athanaric lost the confidence of his subjects, and they decided instead to follow Fritigern across the Danube (AM 31. 3. 4 ff.). Another genuine event has thus been misplaced.[9] In sum, the chapter summarizes many of the salient events of the Gothic war: attacks on the Rhine, the Danube crossing of 376, Athanaric's crossing in 381, and the final peace of 382. The events themselves are genuine enough, but their interaction has been misunderstood.

This perhaps allows us to say something about the information that Gratian allowed some Goths to occupy Pannonia. Part of the material to which it is attached (that Gratian allowed the Goths to leave the Rhine and cross the Danube) is confused. But since the occupation of Pannonia and Upper Moesia is neither contradicted by another source, nor inherently implausible, we can provisionally accept it; all the other information in this chapter seems genuine enough. Zosimus' wording, however, is ambiguous (4. 34. 2),

[The Goths] reduced the Emperor Gratian to the necessity of allowing them (ἐνδοῦναι σφίσιν) . . . to occupy [καταλαβεῖν] Pannonia and Upper Moesia.

Depending on the force of ἐνδίδωμι and καταλαμβάνω, this could describe either a formal concession sanctioned by treaty, or an event which Gratian was forced to allow in the sense that he could not prevent it. The latter would imply no formal arrangement. It should be noted, however, that Gratian's action affected Upper Moesia as much as Pannonia, and that Fritigern was involved along with Alatheus and Saphrax. There is little here to suggest a separate peace, even if Pannonia was occupied at some point during the war.

(b) Jordanes

Jordanes, *Getica* 27. 140–28. 142 has traditionally been used to clarify Zosimus. It reports that the Goths were at first anxious when Theodosius was appointed emperor, but, on his falling sick, took new heart. Alatheus and Saphrax attacked Pannonia, and Fritigern moved towards Thessaly, Epirus, and Achaea. Gratian, however, relieved the situation, conquering the Goths, not by arms but by friendship. When he recovered, Theodosius was pleased with this arrangement, and gave his consent, inviting Athanaric, Fritigern's successor as king of the Goths, to visit him in Constantinople.

---

[9] Paschoud does not make this connection, which undermines his suggestion (ii. 2. 408–9 n. 166; cf. Wolfram, 73, 123; Cesa, 'Romani e barbari', 83–4) that the *proximorum factio* who drove out Athanaric in 380 (AM 27. 5. 10) should be equated with the chiefs mentioned by Zosimus. These men were south of the Danube and had been since 376, Athanaric was north of it; cf. p. 137.

Jordanes' and Zosimus' accounts of the Gothic incursions seem to be complementary. Fritigern's group alone, it would appear, attacked south, while Alatheus and Saphrax raided Pannonia. We can also date them. Both Jordanes and Zosimus place them before Athanaric's reception in Constantinople, and associate them with Theodosius' illness. Athanaric fled to Constantinople in winter 380/1. Theodosius' illness cannot be precisely dated, but probably occurred while he was still at Thessalonica (Socrates, *HE* 5. 6; Sozomen, *HE* 7. 4), which would place it before mid-November 380.[10] The attacks thus occupied, in all likelihood, the campaigning season of 380.

Jordanes has also been used here to prove that Alatheus and Saphrax's occupation of Pannonia was formally recognized by Gratian. According to this scheme, the attack on Pannonia was followed by the treaty with Gratian described by Jordanes, which is in turn associated with the occupation of Pannonia in Zosimus.[11] This approach ignores serious problems:

1. The *Getica* is quite wrong in making Athanaric into Fritigern's successor. He did not make a goodwill visit to Constantinople, but fled there. Jordanes' late report cannot be preferred to Ammianus' contemporary account (AM 27. 5. 10), and there is no indication that Athanaric was accepted back by those who had rejected him for Fritigern in 376.

2. The passage contains Jordanes' entire account of the Gothic war from Theodosius' elevation (19 January 379) to October 382, when peace was made. For a period of over three and a half years, therefore, the *Getica* reports basically one event: the separate attacks of the two Gothic groups. So much has been omitted that the significance of what has been included is hard to judge.

3. This is particularly true of the peace treaty between Goths and Gratian. According to Jordanes' understanding, this treaty, made during Theodosius' illness, was between Gratian and all the Goths, not just Alatheus and Saphrax. Before the treaty, all the Goths are in rebellion, and afterwards all at peace. The *Getica* is describing a treaty which ended the entire Gothic war, and which it is thus natural to equate with the peace of 382.

To make the *Getica* support a separate peace between Gratian and some Goths, it must be supposed that Jordanes has confused such a treaty with the second that brought most of the Goths into line in 382. Two arguments might be advanced. The treaty mentioned by Jordanes is

---

[10] Socrates dates the illness shortly after Theodosius' arrival in Thessalonica (winter 379/80), Sozomen seems to put it later, and Zosimus associates it with Athanaric's flight (winter 380/1). See Stein, i. 193 n. 12; Paschoud, ii. 2. 399–400.

[11] Methodology explicit in Piganiol, *L'Empire chrétien*, 232 n. 3.

dated by Theodosius' illness to *c*.380, and Gratian is given the major role. Neither is conclusive.

As we have seen, the *Getica*'s account of the Gothic war is sparse, selective, and in part mistaken. The juxtaposition of Theodosius' illness in autumn 380 with a peace-treaty could easily represent another mistake, especially since the *Getica* views this as ending the whole war. Themistius' oration 15, of 19 January 381,[12] suggests that this is indeed the case. Much of it is devoted to non-military affairs, but the war receives some coverage. We hear of Theodosius and Gratian resting between campaigns (p. 269. 15 ff.), and preparing for a war which will expel the 'Scythians' (p. 283. 11 ff. esp. p. 285. 15 ff.). There is not the slightest hint here that a major development—such as a peace-treaty with one of the two Gothic groups—had yet occurred. Themistius was Theodosius' propagandist rather than Gratian's, and might not have mentioned an action of the western emperor, but this does not seem sufficient explanation. Early in his reign, Theodosius was dependent on Gratian's goodwill, a fact reflected in Theodosius' propaganda from this period, where Gratian receives significant coverage. Themistius' oration 15, for instance, builds an elaborate metaphor of Gratian and Theodosius as twin steersmen of the ship of state (p. 280. 27 ff.), and gives Gratian full credit for having identified Theodosius' imperial virtues (p. 273. 10 ff.). This changed when the Goths ceased to pose a mortal threat (p. 173), but in 381 Theodosius could not have afforded to alienate Gratian by publicly ignoring a major achievement. Jordanes' equation of a peace, any peace, with Theodosius' illness in autumn 380 thus seems mistaken.

Arguments from the role given to Gratian are also inconclusive. Our only substantial accounts of the 382 treaty come from the eastern Empire, which has led modern scholarship to view the peace as Theodosius' creation. This, however, is a distortion. Gratian spent part of every campaigning season in the Balkans between 378 and 382, and it was primarily his troops who forced the Goths to make peace (cf. p. 172).

More positive evidence, finally, that the *Getica* is describing the peace of 382 is provided by Cassiodorus' *Chronicle*. In Jordanes, peace with the Goths is immediately followed by Athanaric's visit to Constantinople (27. 141 ff.), a combination which has reinforced the idea that the *Getica*'s peace occurred before January 381. In common with at least one other western chronicler, however, Cassiodorus misdates Athanaric's visit to 382.[13] This is relevant because all our evidence suggests that Jordanes closely followed Cassiodorus' now lost *Gothic History* (Ch. 2). To judge by his *Chronicle*, Cassiodorus in his history (and Jordanes by imitation) conceived of Athanaric as entering Constantinople not in winter 380/1,

---

[12] Dagron, 'Thémistios', 23.
[13] *Chronicle* 1138 (*CM* ii. 153); cf. Prosper s.a. 382 (*CM* i. 461).

but in 382. The peace placed by the *Getica* (and presumably by Cassiodorus) immediately before the visit, therefore, is meant to be nothing other than the famous one of 382.

Jordanes and Zosimus can clarify our understanding of the separate attacks, and date them to 380, but they do not document a Gothic settlement in Pannonia. Without support from Jordanes, who is actually referring to the peace of 382, Zosimus' words can only remain ambiguous.

A passage in Ammianus may provide further evidence for the fate of Alatheus and Saphrax in Pannonia. At the start of his account of Hadrianople, Ammianus reports some ominous Greek verses discovered at Chalcedon,

> Then countless hordes of men spread far and wide
> With warlike arms shall cross clear Istrus' stream
> To ravage Scythia's field and Mysia's land,
> But mad with hope then they Pannonia raid,
> There battle and life's end their course shall check.[14]

> Παιονίης δ' ἐπιβάντα σὺν ἐλπίσι μαινομένῃσιν
> αὐτοῦ καὶ βιότοιο τέλος καὶ δῆρις ἐφέξει

Ammianus was writing well after the event (as late as the 390s) and would only have included 'correct' omens, so that this passage must be an accurate, if brief, characterization of the war. The verses might suggest that the tribes who crossed the Danube in 376, though successful elsewhere in the Balkans, were defeated in Pannonia, but the text is not secure. The MS reading is *ΔΗΡΕΙΝ*, so that many have read δῆριν for δῆρις, in which case the passage records merely that the raiders did further damage in Pannonia.[15] Socrates reports another version of the oracle where the last line certainly refers to the raiders' defeat, but uses a different form of words, and the place of defeat is Thrace and not Pannonia.[16] It is unclear, therefore, whether we should (with Rolfe) emend Ammianus on the basis of Socrates. People who entertain mad hopes do often come to grief, and the Goths were in Thrace when peace was made in 382, so that Socrates' and Ammianus' versions could both make sense, but the argument is obviously far from conclusive.

If, however, we choose the nominative δῆρις for Ammianus on the basis of Socrates, then Gratian may have substantially checked the raid of

---

[14] AM 31. 1. 5, the translation of J. C. Rolfe (Loeb).

[15] Cf. the text and German translation of Seyfarth and the Penguin translation of Hamilton, 'Next on Paeonia turn their mad careers / To spread there likewise nought but death and strife.'

[16] Socrates, *HE* 4. 8. 6: Θρηϊκίης δ'ἐπιβάντα σὺν ἐλπίσι μαινομένῃσιν, | Αὐτοῦ κεν βιότοιο τέλος, καὶ πότμον ἐπίσποι.

Alatheus and Saphrax, survivors perhaps being settled on Gratian's terms (cf. p. 153). They might also have fled to Fritigern, with whom they had previously operated. A substantial defeat might also explain why Alatheus and Saphrax disappear from our sources after 380, but this is just a guess. Whatever the case, a settlement of Greuthungi in Pannonia is nothing more than a possibility. That Alatheus and Saphrax attacked Pannonia seems clear enough, but we have no good evidence that the attack was followed by a treaty. We must look again, therefore, at evidence for the subsequent history of the group supposedly settled in Pannonia.

Subsequent History

(a) The 380s

In the early 380s, Alans played a major role in Gratian's army. According to the texts, the favour he showed them was a prime cause of the mutiny which brought Maximus to the throne.[17] We also hear of Huns and Alans as a major military component of the regime of Valentinian II.[18] Neither of these episodes concerns Goths, and none of the groups is linked to Pannonia in any way. They have nevertheless been cited as illustrating the subsequent activities of the Pannonian settlers, because Alatheus and Saphrax are thought to have led a mixed Goth–Hun–Alan confederation. But, as we have seen, the evidence for the existence of this mixed group as any kind of lasting political entity is unconvincing (p. 145). And since these episodes mention neither Goths nor Pannonia, they provide no evidence that Alatheus and Saphrax were settled there. It is much more tempting to associate at least the Alans with numerous *laeti* known to have been settled in Italy (*Not. Dig.*, Occ. 42).[19]

In the mid-380s, Goths are mentioned by Ambrose in his account of his conflict with the empress Justina over the Portian basilica in the city of Milan. The empress held non-Nicene beliefs, and, in denouncing her as an Arian, Ambrose refers to Arian Goths in the imperial bodyguard. These Goths have been cited as evidence for Gratian's settlement, but the Goths here are regular troops, which does not suggest that a large,

[17] Aur. Vict. *Epit.* 47. 6–7; Zosimus 4. 35. 2 ff.; cf. McLynn, 'Ambrose', 221 ff.

[18] Ambrose, *Ep.* 24; cf. McLynn, 'Ambrose', 228 ff.

[19] But the Huns and Alans may have come from beyond the frontier; Stilicho used the Huns of Uldin north of the Danube against Radagaisus (Orosius 7. 37. 12; cf. Sozomen, *HE* 9. 5). Demougeot, 'Modalités', 144 ff. cites the Alans of the 380s to show that Gratian simply made the followers of Alatheus and Saphrax part of the regular army, but since there is no evidence that they led a mixed tribal confederation, the argument has little force.

ethnically distinct Gothic force was a major component of Valentinian II's regime, in the way that Huns and Alans were (cf. the episodes cited above).[20] The Goths known to Ambrose could have been recruited individually from a group settled in Pannonia, but they are not linked specifically to Pannonia, and there are many other ways for them to have entered the imperial army.

(b) Pacatus

After Theodosius' success against Maximus, Pacatus delivered a pan-egyric which refers to Pannonia (*Pan. Lat.* 12(2). 32. 4: trans. Nixon, 42),

> There marched under Roman leaders and banners the onetime enemies of Rome, and they followed standards which they had once opposed, and filled with soldiers the cities of Pannonia which they had not long ago emptied by hostile plundering. The Goth, the Hun and the Alan responded to their names . . .

This has been taken to show that those who once attacked Pannonia (the Goths of Alatheus and Saphrax) had been settled there, and were now filling its cities peacefully.

Since the enemy is specified as 'Gothus ille et Hunus et Halanus', the reference is certainly to the Gothic war, a further confirmation that Pannonia was attacked in the course of it. In their full context, however, the words 'filled with soldiers (*miles impleverat*) the cities of Pannonia' do not refer to a permanent settlement. Pacatus is here describing the actual war against Maximus, making a double contrast between the actions of the foreigners in the past and their activities on campaign. They now follow the standards which they opposed, and now fill the cities which their hostility once emptied. This strongly suggests that the influx of barbarian troops into Pannonian cities was part of Theodosius' military moves against Maximus, and not a permanent arrangement. Theodosius' forces did indeed advance through Pannonia to attack Maximus, battle taking place on the River Sava.[21] The natural meaning of Pacatus' words, that the influx of barbarian troops was the direct result of the campaign's manœuvres, thus corresponds perfectly with what else is known of the action. They carry no implication that Pannonia was the normal station of these foreign troops.[22]

[20] Ambrose, *Ep.* 20, *Sermo contra Auxentium* 2. Ambrose does not suggest that a large block of Gothic allied troops was involved, and some Goths came over to his side (*Ep.* 20. 20 ff.). Other sources (Augustine, *Conf.* 9. 7. 15–16; Paulinus, *V. Amb.* 12 ff.; Rufinus, *HE* 11. 15 ff.) do not mention Goths.

[21] Zosimus 4. 45. 4; Orosius 7. 35; Ambrose, *Ep.* 40.

[22] As far as we know, only Alatheus and Saphrax attacked Pannonia (p. 152), but it is important not to be over-precise when analysing a text such as Pacatus' panegyric. It seems likely that Pacatus is signalling that all those involved in the Gothic war had fought against Maximus.

(c) Amantius (of Jovia?)

The funerary inscription of a bishop Amantius was found outside Aquileia in 1771:[23]

> † egregius fidei sanctus mitisq. | sacerdos,
>   dignus quem cuper|et ple(p)s aliena suum, |
> dign(u)s ita geminis ducibus | consortia sacra
>   parti|cipare fidei, consilio regere |
> hoc iacet in tumulo, proprium cui | nomen Amanti
>   venturi meriti | prescia causa dedit.
> bis denis | binis populis presedit in annis:|
>   si non migrasset, laus erat ista | minor.
> depos. sb d. VIII idus Aprilis | ind. XI.
>   dp. Ambrosius diac. kal. Decemb. | Mariano et Asclepiodoto
> uu. cc. conss. | ind. VII.

Ambrose the deacon was thus buried on 1 December 423, and Bishop Amantius on 6 April of an earlier eleventh indiction, the two previous being 413 and 398. Aspects of the bishop's career seem clear. An Aquileian who seems to have gone elsewhere, he presided over his diocese for twenty years—378–98, or 393–413—and during that period had close relations with a foreign people and its two leaders.[24]

In the 1920s, Egger argued that the two leaders (*geminis ducibus*) could only be Alatheus and Saphrax, suggesting that this in turn strengthened an earlier hypothesis that the Amantius mentioned here should be identified with a bishop of Jovia of the same name.[25] A city of Jovia existed beside the River Drava in Pannonia Superior, and its bishop Amantius took part in the Council of Aquileia in 381 (Ambrose, *Ep.* 10). Chronological and geographical coincidences thus set up a chain of identification. That the *gemini duces* were Alatheus and Saphrax made it probable that the Amantius in the inscription was Amantius of Jovia, and this in turn located where precisely in Pannonia Alatheus and Saphrax had been settled (around Jovia). But these identifications are dependent upon too many hypotheses to be convincing.

Egger identified Alatheus and Saphrax with the *gemini duces* because of two coincidences; in both cases, two leaders were mentioned, and the Goths maintained a permanent Pannonian settlement between the years 379/80 and 408, which more or less corresponds to the years of Amantius' activity (choosing, of course, the earlier set of possible dates). This chronological coincidence is unconvincing. First, the later dates (393–413) seem more likely to be correct. Amantius' associate, Ambrose,

---

[23] *ILCV* 1061 Diehl (= *CIL* v. 1623).

[24] Egger, 'Historisch-epigraphische Studien', 329 ff.; cf. Thompson, 'Northern Barbarians', 65 ff.

[25] Egger, 333 ff.; cf. Fiebiger, *Inschriftensammlung*, 25 n. 34.

was buried in 423, so that the earlier dating (378–98) would have Amantius die twenty-five years before him. This does not preclude a close association, but the later dates (having Ambrose buried ten years after Amantius) are much less problematic.[26] They of course would provide no chronological coincidence between Amantius' activity and a supposed Pannonian settlement.

Equally important, the dates for the Pannonian settlement, which Egger thought secure, are not. The 379/380 date for the original settlement is established from Jordanes and Zosimus, who, as we have seen, prove nothing of the sort. The 408 date refers to the moment when Athaulf led a mixed force of Goths and Huns from Pannonia, but Athaulf had probably not been in permanent occupation of Pannonia before then (see below), and nothing substantial fills in the intervening thirty years. Egger failed to notice a further problem. By 408 (if, as he does, we take Athaulf as the successor of Alatheus and Saphrax), the Pannonian Greuthungi did not have the kind of dual leadership mentioned in the inscription; only Athaulf led the move to Italy. It is striking that Amantius deals with two *duces*, the kind of leadership provided by Alatheus and Saphrax, but such dual leadership is a well-known phenomenon.[27] After c.375, many foreign groups, about whom often little is known, entered the Empire.[28] The middle Danube region saw more than one settlement of barbarians in the period of Amantius' activity, and dual leadership is not so unusual a feature as to make the identification with Alatheus and Saphrax compelling.

Athaulf

Athaulf commanded a force of Huns and Goths in Pannonia in 408. How long he had been there is not specified; we are told only that he was Alaric's brother-in-law, and that his force was substantial. Athaulf thus springs into the narrative fully formed, and we are left to draw our own conclusions about his origins.[29] As the established view would argue, this makes it possible that Athaulf had in some way succeeded Alatheus and Saphrax as the leader of Greuthungi settled in Pannonia in 380. But when we first encounter him, Athaulf's command already seems to be an integral part of Alaric's force. He was Alaric's brother-in-law, Alaric

---

[26] Cf. Nagy, 'Last Century of Pannonia', 331.

[27] Cf. Thompson, 'Northern Barbarians', 66 n. 3.

[28] The *Notitia Dignitatum* records Marcomanni in Pannonia I (Occ. 34. 24), unspecified foreigners in Raetia (Occ. 35. 31–2) and Alans and Sarmatians under the *magister peditum* (Occ. 42).

[29] Zosimus 5. 37. 1 ff. This again probably reflects Zosimus' unsatisfactory editing of Olympiodorus; cf. p. 78.

'sent for' him ($\mu\epsilon\tau\alpha\pi\epsilon\mu\pi\epsilon\tau\alpha\iota$), as though there could be no doubt that he would come to Italy, and, in Italy, he was Alaric's second in command, an indication that he was already Alaric's designated successor.[30] Just before entering Italy, moreover, Alaric had himself occupied Noricum, in the north-west Balkans next to Pannonia. He had previously been encamped around Epirus and stopped in Noricum while attempting to force Ravenna to pay his troops (Zosimus 5. 29 ff.). It is more in tune with this evidence to suggest that Athaulf's occupation of Pannonia had taken place at the same time as Alaric's move into Noricum. Both would then have led parts of an integrated force moving north from Epirus into lands bordering Italy, Alaric carrying on over the Alps while Athaulf remained behind. In the aftermath of Stilicho's fall, Alaric clearly envisaged, at one point, settling his followers in the north-west Balkans (id. 5. 50. 3). Thus Athaulf perhaps stayed behind to secure the area on which the Goths had designs, until it became apparent that more ambitious enterprises could be attempted. If not absolutely conclusive, this argument certainly takes more account of the available evidence than the traditional view.

It is difficult at this distance, and with fragmentary texts, to prove categorically that something did not happen. But the texts held to document Gratian's settlement of Goths in Pannonia do not generate a convincing picture of its establishment and subsequent history.[31] Jordanes and Zosimus document no settlement, and nothing fills in the intervening thirty years before we find Athaulf's Goths in Pannonia. Since Athaulf would already seem to have been fully integrated into Alaric's command, and Alaric himself had recently been in the area, there is little reason to suppose that Athaulf's Goths had been in Pannonia for more than a few months, let alone three decades. It remains possible that Gratian settled Goths in Pannonia, but it is much more likely that he did not.

---

[30] When Alaric became *magister militum*, Athaulf became *comes domesticorum*: Sozomen, *HE* 9. 8.

[31] Várady, *Das letzte Jahrhundert* added extra episodes to the history of the Pannonian settlement, which have been rightly rejected even by those who accept that there was a settlement: Nagy, 'Last Century of Pannonia', *passim*; Harmatta, 'Last Century of Pannonia', 361–9; Mócsy, review of Várady, 347–60. Várady suggested that: (i) the Greuthungi first entered Pannonia in 376 (cf. Nagy, 300, 308 ff.); (ii) a first *foedus* was made early in 379 (Nagy, 319–20); (iii) there were Pannonian revolts in 392 and 395 (Nagy, 323 ff.); (iv) in 399 a new *foedus* split up the 'Drei Völker' confederation; the Huns remained in Pannonia, the Alans moved to Valeria, and the Goths to Italy (Nagy, 330 ff; Mócsy, 354–5).

BIBLIOGRAPHY

ACHELIS, H., 'Der älteste deutsche Kalender', *Zeitschrift für die neutesta-mentliche Wissenschaft*, 1 (1900), 308–35.

ALBERT, G., *Goten in Konstantinopel: Untersuchungen zur oströmischen Geschichte um das Jahr 400 n. Chr.* (Paderborn, 1984).

ALFÖLDI, A., *Der Untergang der Römerherrschaft in Pannonien*, ii (Berlin 1926).

ALFÖLDY, G., *Noricum* (London, 1974).

ALLEN, P., *Evagrius Scholasticus the Church Historian*, Spicilegium Sacrum Lovaniense, 41 (Louvain, 1981).

ANDERSON, A. R., *Alexander's Gate, Gog and Magog, and the Inclosed Nations* (Cambridge, 1932).

ANDERSON, T. M., review of Hachmann, *Die Goten und Skandinavien: Speculum*, 46 (1971), 373–5.

ANOKHIN, V. A., *The Coinage of Chersonesus*, BAR, IS 69 (Oxford, 1980).

AUSTIN, N. J. E., 'Ammianus' Account of the Adrianople Campaign: Some Strategic Observations', *Acta Classica*, 15 (1972), 77–83.

BAGNALL, R. S., *et al.*, *Consuls of the Later Roman Empire* (Atlanta, 1987).

BALDWIN, B., 'Malchus of Philadelphia', *DOP* 31 (1977), 91–107.

—— 'The Purpose of the Getica', *Hermes*, 107 (1979), 489–92.

BARNES, T. D., 'Imperial Campaigns 285–311', *Phoenix*, 30 (1976), 174–93.

—— 'The Victories of Constantine', *ZPE* 20 (1976), 149–55.

—— 'The Historical Setting of Prudentius' *contra Symmachum*', *AJP* 97 (1976), 373–86.

—— *The Sources of the Historia Augusta*, Coll. Latomus, 155 (Brussels, 1978).

—— *The New Empire of Diocletian and Constantine* (Cambridge, 1981).

—— 'Synesius in Constantinople', *GRBS* 27 (1986), 93–112.

BARNISH, S. J. B., 'The Genesis and Completion of Cassiodorus' *Gothic History*', *Latomus*, 43 (1984), 336–61.

—— 'Taxation, Land and Barbarian Settlement in the Western Empire', *PBSR* 54 (1986), 170–95.

—— 'Maximian, Cassiodorus, Boethius, Theodahad: Literature, Philosophy and Politics in Ostrogothic Italy', *Nottingham Medieval Studies*, 34 (1990), 16–32.

BAYLESS, W. N., 'The Political Unity of the Roman Empire during the Disintegration of the West, *AD* 395–457' (Diss. Brown University, Providence, RI, 1972).

—— 'Anti-Germanism in the Age of Stilicho', *Byzantine Studies*, 3 (1976), 70–6.

—— 'The Visigothic Invasion of Italy in 401', *CJ* 72 (1976), 65–7.

—— 'The Praetorian Prefect Anthemius: Position and Policies', *Byzantine Studies*, 4 (1977), 38–51.

BERGER, I., 'Deities, Dynasties, and Oral Tradition: 'The History and Legends of the Abacwezi', in Miller (ed.), *The African Past Speaks*, 61–81.

BERNHARDT, M., *Handbuch zur Münzkunde der römischen Kaiserzeit* (Halle, 1926).

BICHIR, Gh., 'Les Sarmates au bas Danube', *Dacia*, NS 21 (1971), 167–98.

—— *Archaeology and History of the Carpi*, BAR, IS 16 (Oxford, 1976).

—— *Geto-Dacii din Muntenia în epoca romană* (Bucharest, 1984).

BIDEZ, J., 'L'historien Philostorge', in *Mélanges d'histoire offerts à Henri Pirenne* (Paris, 1926), 23–30.

BIERBRAUER,, V., 'Zur chronologischen, soziologischen und regionalen Gliederung des ostgermanischen Fundstoffs des 5. Jahrhunderts in Südosteuropa', in Wolfram and Daim (edd.), *Die Völker*, 131–42.

BIRLEY, E., 'Fresh Thoughts on the Dating of the Historia Augusta', *Bonner Historia-Augusta Colloquium, 1975/6* (Bonn, 1978), 99–105.

BLOCKLEY, R. C., *Ammianus Marcellinus: A Study of His Historiography and Political Thought*, Coll. Latomus, 141 (Brussels, 1975).

—— 'Was the First Book of Zosimus' New History Based on More than Two Sources?', *Byzantion*, 50 (1980), 393–402.

—— *The Fragmentary Classicising Historians of the Later Roman Empire: Eunapius, Olympiodorus, Priscus and Malchus*, 2 vols. (Liverpool, 1981, 1983).

—— 'On the Ordering of the Fragments of Malchus' History', *Liverpool Classical Monthly*, 9/10 (December 1984), 152–3.

BLOȘIU, C., 'La nécropole de Letçani (dép. de Jassy) datant du IVe siècle de n.è', *Arheologia Moldovei*, 8 (1975), 203–80.

BOHANNAN, L., 'A Genealogical Charter', *Africa*, 22 (1952), 301–15.

BOSTON, J. S., 'Oral Tradition and the History of the Igala', *JAH* 10 (1969), 29–43.

BRADLEY, D. R., 'The Composition of the Getica', *Eranos*, 64 (1966), 67–79.

BRAUND, D. C., *Rome and the Friendly King: The Character of the Client Kingship* (London, 1984).

BROCKMEIER, B., 'Der große Friede 332 n. Chr. Zur Außenpolitik Konstantins des Großen', *Bonner Jahrbücher*, 187 (1987), 79–100.

BROOKS, E. R., 'The Emperor Zenon and the Isaurians', *EHR* 8 (1893), 209–38.

BURNS, T. S., 'The Battle of Adrianople: A Reconsideration', *Historia*, 22 (1973), 336–45.

—— 'Calculating Ostrogothic Population', *Acta Antiqua*, 26 (1978), 457–63.

—— 'Pursuing the Early Gothic Migrations', *Acta Archaeologia*, 31 (1979), 189–99.

—— *The Ostrogoths: Kingship and Society* (Historia-Einzelschriften, 36; Wiesbaden, 1980).

—— *A History of the Ostrogoths* (Bloomington, Ind., 1984).

—— 'The Settlement of 418', in Drinkwater and Elton (edd.), *Fifth-Century Gaul* (forthcoming).

BURY, J. B., 'Krumbacher's Byzantine Literature', *CR* 11 (1897), 207–11.

—— *History of the Later Roman Empire from the Death of Theodosius I to the Death of Justinian (AD 395 to AD 565)* (London, 1923).

CAMERON, A. D. E., 'Wandering Poets: A Literary Movement in Byzantine Egypt', *Historia*, 14 (1965), 470–509.

—— 'Theodosius the Great and the Regency of Stilicho', *Harvard Studies in Classical Philology*, 73 (1969), 247–80.

—— *Claudian: Poetry and Propaganda at the Court of Honorius* (Oxford, 1970).

—— *et al.*, *Barbarians and Politics at the Court of Arcadius* (Berkeley, forthcoming).

CAMERON, A. D. E. and A. M., 'Christianity and Tradition in the Historiography of the Later Empire', *CQ*, NS 14 (1964), 316–28.

CAMERON, A. M., 'Cassiodorus Deflated', *JRS* 71 (1981), 183–6.

—— *Procopius and the Sixth Century* (London, 1985).

CAZACU, M., 'Montes Serrorum (Ammianus Marcellinus XXVII. 5. 3) zur Siedlungsgeschichte der Westgoten in Rumänien', *Dacia*, NS 16 (1972), 299–302.

CESA, M., '376–382: Romani e barbari sul Danubio', *Studi Urbanati/B3*, 57 (1984), 63–99.

CHESNUT, G. F., *The First Christian Histories: Eusebius, Socrates, Sozomen, Theodoret and Evagrius*, Théologie historique, 46 (Paris, 1977).

CHEYETTE, F. L. (ed.), *Lordship and Community in Medieval Europe* (New York, 1968).

CHICHIKOVA, M., 'Fouilles du camp romain et de la ville paléobyzantine de Novae (Mésie Inférieure)', in Poulter (ed.), *Ancient Bulgaria*, 11–18.

CHRIST, K., *Antike Münzfunde Südwestdeutschlands: Münzfunde, Geldwirtschaft und Geschichte im Raume Baden-Württembergs von keltischer bis in alamannische Zeit* (Heidelberg, 1960).

CHRISTIANSEN, P. G., 'Claudian versus the Opposition', *TAPA* 97 (1966), 45–54.

CHRYSOS, E. K., Τὸ Βυζάντιον καὶ οἱ Γότθοι (Thessalonica, 1972).

—— 'Gothia Romana: Zur Rechtslage des Föderatenlandes der Westgoten im 4. Jahrhundert', *Daco-Romania*, 1 (1973), 52–64.

CLAUDE, D., *Adel, Kirche und Königtum im Westgotenriech* (Sigmaringen, 1971).

—— 'The Oath of the Allegiance and the Oath of the King in the Visigothic Kingdom', *Classical Folia*, 30 (1976), 3–26.

—— 'Zur Königserhebung Theoderichs des Großen', in *Festschrift für Heinz Löwe* (Cologne, 1978), 1–13.

—— 'Die ostgotischen Königserhebungen', in Wolfram and Daim (edd.), *Die Völker*, 149–86.

—— 'Zur Ansiedlung barbarischer Föderaten in der ersten Hälfte des fünften Jahrhunderts', in Wolfram and Schwarcz (edd.), *Anerkennung und Integration*, 13–16.

CONEA, I., 'Interprétations géographiques dans l'histoire du peuple roumain', in *Recueil d'études géographiques concernant le territoire de la République Roumaine publiées à l'occasion du XIXᵉ Congrès international de géographie* (Stockholm, 1960), 146–51.

CONSTANTINESCU, M., PASCU, S., and DIACONU, G. (edd.), *Relations between the Autochthonous Population and the Migratory Populations on the Territory of Romania* (Bucharest, 1975).

CRESCI, C. R., *Malco di Filadelfia, frammenti: Testo critico, introduzione, traduzione e commentario* (Naples, 1982).

CROKE, B., 'Jordanes' Understanding of the Usurpation of Eugenius', *Antichthon*, 9 (1975), 81–3.

—— 'Evidence for the Hun Invasion of Thrace in AD 422', *GRBS* 18 (1977), 347–67.

—— 'The Chronicle of Marcellinus Comes' (D.Phil. thesis, Oxford, 1978).

—— 'The Date of the "Anastasian Long Walls" in Thrace', *GRBS* 23 (1982), 59–78.

—— 'A.D. 476: The Manufacture of a Turning Point', *Chiron*, 13 (1983), 81–119.

—— 'Cassiodorus and the *Getica* of Jordanes', *CP* 82 (1987), 117–34.

CRUMP, G. A., *Ammianus Marcellinus as a Military Historian*, Historia-Einzelschriften, 27 (Wiesbaden, 1975).

DAGRON, D., 'L'Empire romain d'Orient au IVᵉ siècle et les traditions politiques de l'hellénisme—le témoignage de Thémistios', *Travaux et mémoires*, 3 (1968), 1–242.

—— *Naissance d'une capitale: Constantinople et ses institutions de 330 à 451* (Paris, 1974).

DAHLHEIM, W., *Struktur und Entwicklung des römischen Völkerrechts im dritten und zweiten Jahrhundert v. Chr.* (Munich, 1968).

DAICOVICIU, C., *Dacica* (Cluj, 1969).

DALY, L. J., 'The Mandarin and the Barbarian: The Response of Themistius to the Gothic Challenge', *Historia*, 21 (1972), 351–79.

DAUGE, Y. A., *Le Barbare: Recherches sur la conception romaine de la barbarie et de la civilisation*, Coll. Latomus, 176 (Brussels, 1981).

DEICHMANN, F. W., 'La corte dei re Goti a Ravenna', *XXVII Corso di cultura sull'arte ravennate e bizantina* (Ravenna, 1980), 41–53.

DELBRÜCK, H., *Geschichte der Kriegskunst im Rahmen der politischen Geschichte*, ii (Berlin, 1921).

DELEHAYE, H., 'Saints de Thrace et de Mésie', *AB* 31 (1912), 161–300.

DEMANDT, A., 'Magister militum', *RE* suppl. xii. 553–790.

DEMOUGEOT, E., *De l'unité à la division de l'Empire romain 395–410: Essai sur le gouvernement impérial* (Paris, 1951).

—— 'A propos des lètes gaulois du ive siècle', in *Festschrift für F. Altheim* (Berlin, 1970), ii. 101–13.

—— 'Modalités d'établissement des fédérés barbares de Gratien et de Théodose', in *Mélanges d'histoire ancienne offerts à William Seston* (Paris, 1974), 143–60.

—— *La Formation de l'Europe et les invasions barbares:* i. *Des origines germaniques à l'avènement de Dioclétien* (Paris, 1969); ii. *De l'avènement de Dioclétien (284) à l'occupation germanique de l'Empire romain d'Occident (début du VIe siècle)* (Paris, 1979).

—— 'Restrictions à l'expansion du droit de cité dans la seconde moitié du ive siècle', *Ktema*, 6 (1981), 381–93.

DESSAU, H., 'Über Zeit und Persönlichkeit der Scriptores Historiae Augustae', *Hermes*, 24 (1889), 337–92.

DIACONU, G., 'Archäologische Angaben über die Taifalen', *Dacia*, NS 7 (1963), 301–15.

—— *Tîrgşor* (Bucharest, 1965).

—— 'On the Socio-Economic Relations between Natives and Goths in Dacia', in Constantinescu, Pascu, and Diaconu (edd.), *Relations*, 67–75.

—— 'Zwei Gefäße aus dem 4. Jh. u. Z. von Pietroasele-Buzău', *Dacia*, NS 20 (1976), 269–71.

—— and ANGHELESCU, N., 'Despre necropola din sec. IV e.n. de la Radu Negru (r. Călăraşi)', *SCIV* 14 (1963), 167–74.

DRINKWATER, J., and ELTON, H. (edd.), *Fifth Century Gaul: A Crisis of Identity?* (forthcoming).

DUMVILLE, D. N., 'Kingship, Genealogies and Regnal Lists', in Sawyer and Wood (edd.), *Early Medieval Kingship*, 72–104.

DURLIAT, J., 'Le salaire de la paix sociale dans les royaumes barbares (v^e–vi^e siècles)', in Wolfram and Schwarcz (edd.), *Anerkennung und Integration*, 21–72.

ECKSTEIN, A. M., *Senate and General: Individual Decision-Making and Roman Foreign Relations, 264–194 BC* (Berkeley, 1987).

EGGER, R., 'Historisch-epigraphische Studien in Venezien', *Jahreshefte des Österreichischen Archäologischen Instituts in Wien*, 21–2 (1922–4), 309–44.

ENSSLIN, W., 'Die Ostgoten in Pannonien', *Byzantinisch-neugriechische Jahrbücher*, 6 (1928–9), 146–59.

—— *Theoderich der Große* (Munich, 1947).

—— *Des Symmachus Historia Romana als Quelle für Jordanes*, Sitzungsberichte der Bayerischen Akademie der Wissenschaften, phil.-hist. Kl. (Munich, 1949).

—— *Die Religionspolitik des Kaisers Theodosius d. Gr.*, Sitzungsberichte der Bayerischen Akademie der Wissenschaften, phil.-hist. Kl. (Munich, 1953).

ERRINGTON, M., 'Malchos von Philadelphia, Kaiser Zenon und die zwei Theoderiche', *MH* 40 (1983), 82–110.

FIEBIGER, O., *Inschriftensammlung zur Geschichte der Ostgermanen*, ii, Denkschriften der Kaiserlichen Akademie der Wissenschaften in Wien, phil.-hist. Kl. 70 (Vienna, 1939).

FINNEGAN, R., *Oral Literature in Africa* (Oxford, 1976).

FREEMAN, P. and KENNEDY, D. (edd.), *The Defence of the Roman and Byzantine East*, BAR, IS 297 (Oxford, 1986).

FRIEDRICHSEN, G. W. S., *The Gothic Version of the Gospels: A Study of its Style and Textual History* (Oxford, 1926).

—— *The Gothic Version of the Epistles* (Oxford, 1939).

FROLOVA, N. A., *The Coinage of the Kingdom of Bosporos AD 242–341/2*, BAR, IS 166 (Oxford, 1983).

GEARY, P., *Before France and Germany: The Creation and Transformation of the Merovingian World* (Oxford, 1988).

GEJ, O. A., 'The Cherniakhovo Culture Sites of the North Pontic Area', *SA* 1980/2, 45–51.

—— 'On the Date of the Chernyakhovo Culture in the Northern Black Sea Area', *SA* 1986/1, 77–86.

GOETZ, H.-W., *Die Geschichtstheologie des Orosius* (Darmstadt, 1980).

GOFFART, W., *Caput and Colonate: Towards a History of Late Roman Taxation* (Toronto, 1974).

—— '*Barbarians and Romans AD 418–584: The Techniques of Accommodation* (Princeton, NJ, 1980).

—— review of Wolfram, *Geschichte der Goten*: *Speculum*, 57 (1982), 446–7.

—— *The Narrators of Barbarian History (AD 550–800): Jordanes, Gregory of Tours, Bede, and Paul the Deacon* (Princeton, NJ, 1988).

GOODY, J. (ed.), *Literacy in Traditional Societies* (Cambridge, 1968).

GROSSE, R., *Römische Militärgeschichte von Gallienus bis zum Beginn der byzantinischen Themenverfassung* (Berlin, 1920).

GRUMEL, V., 'L'Illyricum de la mort de Valentinien Ier (375) à la mort de Stilicon (408)', *Revue des études byzantines*, 9 (1951), 5–46.

GSCHWANTLER, O., 'Ermanrich, sein Selbstmord und die Hamdirsage: Zur Darstellung von Ermanrichs Ende in Getica 24, 129f.', in Wolfram and Daim (edd.), *Die Völker*, 187–204.

HACHMANN, R., *Die Goten und Skandinavien* (Berlin, 1970).

HALDON, J. F., *Byzantine Praetorians: An Administrative, Institutional and Social Survey of the Opsikion and the Tagmata, c.580–900* (Bonn, 1984).

HALPHEN, L., *Les Barbares des grandes invasions aux conquêtes turques du XIe siècle*, 5th edn. (Paris, 1948).

HAMMOND, N. G. L., *A History of Macedonia*, i (Oxford, 1972).

HANNESTAD, K., 'Les forces militaires d'après la *Guerre Gothique* de Procope', *Classica et Mediaevalia*, 21 (1960), 136–83.

HARHOIU, R., *The Treasure from Pietroasa, Romania*, BAR, IS 24 (Oxford, 1977).

HARMATTA, J., *Studies on the History of the Sarmatians* (Budapest, 1950).

—— 'The Last Century of Pannonia', *Acta Antiqua*, 18 (1970), 361–9.

HEATHER, P. J., 'The Crossing of the Danube and the Gothic Conversion', *GRBS* 27 (1986), 289–318.

—— 'The Two Thousandth Year of Gothic History and Theoderic's Intervention in Visigothic Spain' (summary), *XXXIV Corso di cultura sull'arte ravennate e bizantina* (Ravenna, 1987), 171–8.

—— 'The Anti-Scythian Tirade of Synesius' *De Regno*', *Phoenix*, 42 (1988), 152–72.

—— 'Cassiodorus and the Rise of the Amals: Genealogy and the Goths under Hun Domination', *JRS* 79 (1989), 103–28.

—— 'The Emergence of the Visigothic Kingdom', in Drinkwater and Elton (edd.), *Fifth-Century Gaul* (forthcoming).

—— 'Theoderic as Tribal Leader' (forthcoming).

—— and MATTHEWS, J. F., *The Goths in the Fourth Century* (Liverpool, 1991).

HENIGE, D. P., 'Oral Tradition and Chronology', *JAH* 12 (1971), 371–89.

—— *The Chronology of Oral Tradition: Quest for a Chimera* (Oxford, 1974).

HODDINOTT, R. F., *Bulgaria in Antiquity* (London, 1975).

352 *Bibliography*

HOFFMANN, D., *Das spätrömische Bewegungsheer und die Notitia Dignitatum* (Düsseldorf, 1969).

HOREDT, K., 'Quelques problèmes concernant la diffusion de la civilisation de Sîntana de Mureş-Tchernéakhov en Roumanie', *SCIV* 18 (1967), 575–92.

—— 'Apahida II', *RgA* i, 336–7.

—— 'Wandervölker und Romanen im 5. bis 6. Jahrhundert in Siebenbürgen', in Wolfram and Daim (edd.), *Die Völker*, 117–21.

—— and PROTASE, D., 'Das zweite Fürstengrab von Apahida (Siebenbürgen)', *Germania*, 50 (1972), 174–220.

HORN, H., *Foederati: Untersuchungen zur Geschichte ihrer Rechtsstellung im Zeitalter der römischen Republik und des frühen Principats* (Frankfurt, 1930).

HUNT, E. D., 'Christians and Christianity in Ammianus Marcellinus', *CQ*, NS 35 (1985), 186–200.

IONIȚĂ, I., 'Contributions à la connaissance de la civilisation de Sîntana de Mureş-Tchernéakhov sur le territoire de la Roumanie', *Arheologia Moldovei*, 4 (1966), 189–260.

—— 'The Social-Economic Structure of Society during the Goths' Migration in the Carpatho-Danubean area', in Constantinescu, Pascu, and Diaconu (edd.), *Relations*, 77–89.

—— 'Die Römer-Daker und die Wandervölker im donauländischen Karpatenraum im 4. Jahrhundert', in Wolfram and Daim (edd.), *Die Völker*, 123–30.

JAMES, E., 'The Origins of Barbarian Kingdoms: The Continental Evidence', in S. Bassett (ed.), *The Origins of Anglo-Saxon Kingdoms* (Leicester, 1989), 40–52.

JEFFREYS, E., *et al.* (trans.), *The Chronicle of John Malalas* (Melbourne, 1986).

JIRECEK, J. K., *Die Heerstraße von Belgrad nach Constantinopel und die Balkanpässe; Eine historisch-geographische Studie* (Prague, 1877).

JOHNSON, A. C., and WEST, L. C., *Byzantine Egypt: Economic Studies* (Princeton, NJ, 1949).

JONES, A. H. M., 'The Constitutional Position of Odoacer and Theoderic', *JRS* 52 (1962), 126–30 = P. A. Brunt (ed.), *The Roman Economy* (Oxford, 1974), 365–74.

—— 'Collegiate Prefectures', *JRS* 54 (1964), 78–89.

—— *The Later Roman Empire: A Social Economic and Administrative Survey*, 3 vols. (Oxford, 1964).

—— *The Cities of the Eastern Roman Provinces*, 2nd edn. (Oxford, 1971).

KAUFMANN, G., 'Kritische Untersuchungen zu dem Kriege Theodosius des Großen mit den Gothen 378–382', *Forschungen zur deutschen Geschichte*, 12 (1872), 411–38.

KENNEDY, G. A., *Greek Rhetoric under Christian Emperors* (Princeton, NJ, 1983).

KISS, A., 'Ein Versuch die Funde und das Siedlungsgebiet der Ostgoten in Pannonien zwischen 456–471 zu bestimmen', *Acta Archaeologica*, 31 (1979), 329–39.

KLEIN, K. K., 'Frithigern, Athanarich und die Spaltung des Westgotenvolks am Vorabend des Hunneneinbruchs (375 n. Chr)', *Südost-Forschungen*, 19 (1960), 34–51.

KLOSE, J., *Roms Klientel-Randstaaten am Rhein und an der Donau: Beiträge zu ihrer Geschichte und rechtlichen Stellung im 1. und 2. Jhdt. n. Chr.* (Breslau, 1934).

KOPECEK, T. A., *A History of Neo-Arianism* (Philadelphia, 1979).

KÖPKE, R., *Die Anfänge des Königthums bei den Gothen* (Berlin, 1859).

KORKKANEN, I., *The Peoples of Hermenaric: Jordanes Getica 116*, Annales Academie Scientiarum Fennicae, Series B 187 (Helsinki, 1975).

KROPOTKIN, A. V., 'On the Centres of the Chernyakhovo Tribes', *SA* 1984/3, 35–47.

LAKATOS, P., *Quellenbuch zur Geschichte der Gepiden* (Szeged, 1973).

LAQUEUR, R., 'Malchos 2', *RE* xivA. 851–7.

LARSON, C. W. R., 'Theodosius and the Thessalonian Massacre Revisited—Yet Again', in F. L. Cross (ed.), *Studia Patristica*, 10, Texte und Untersuchungen 107 (Berlin, 1970), 297–301.

LATOUCHE, R., *Les Grandes Invasions et la crise de l'Occident au Ve siècle* (Paris, 1946).

LEWIS, I. M., 'Historical Aspects of Genealogies in Northern Somali Social Structure', *JAH* 3 (1962), 35–48.

LIEBESCHUETZ, J. H. W. G., 'Generals, Federates and Bucellarii in Roman Armies around AD 400', in Freeman and Kennedy (edd.), *The Defence*, 463–73.

—— *Barbarians and Bishops* (Oxford, 1990).

LINDNER, R. P., *Nomads and Ottomans in Medieval Anatolia* (Bloomington, Ind., 1983).

LOT, F., *Les Invasions germaniques: La pénétration mutuelle du monde barbare et du monde romain* (Paris, 1939).

LOUD, G. A., 'The "*Gens Normannorum*"—Myth or Reality?', *Proceedings of the Battle Conference*, 4, ed. R. Allen Brown (Woodbridge, 1982), 104–17.

MACARTNEY, C. A., 'The End of the Huns', *Byzantinisch-neugriechische Jahrbücher*, 10 (1934), 106–14.

MACCORMACK, S., *Art and Ceremony in Late Antiquity* (Berkeley, 1981).

McCORMICK, M., 'Odoacer, Emperor Zeno and the Rugian Victory Legation', *Byzantion*, 47 (1977), 212–22.

—— *Eternal Victory: Triumphal Rulership in Late Antiquity, Byzantium and the Early Medieval West* (Cambridge, 1986).

McLYNN, N. B., 'St Ambrose and Ecclesiastical Politics in Milan 374–397' (D.Phil. thesis, Oxford, 1988).

MAENCHEN-HELFEN, O. J., *The World of the Huns* (Berkeley, 1973).

MARTIN, K., *Theoderich der Große bis zur Eroberung Italiens* (Freiburg, 1888).

MATTHEWS, J. F., 'Olympiodorus of Thebes and the History of the West (AD 407–425)', *JRS* 60 (1970), 79–97.

—— *Western Aristocracies and Imperial Court AD 364–425* (Oxford, 1975).

—— *The Roman Empire of Ammianus* (London, 1989).

MAUSS, M., *The Gift: Forms and Functions of Exchange in Archaic Societies*, trans. I. Cunnison (London, 1966).

MILLAR, F., 'P. Herennius Dexippus: The Greek World and the Third-Century Invasions', *JRS* 59 (1969), 12–29.

—— 'Emperors, Frontiers and Foreign Relations, 31 B.C. to A.D. 378', *Britannia*, 13 (1982), 1–23.

—— 'Government and Diplomacy in the Roman Empire during the First Three Centuries', *The International History Review*, 10 (1988), 345–77.

MILLER, J. C., 'Listening for the African Past', in id. (ed.), *The African Past Speaks*, 1–59.

—— (ed.), *The African Past Speaks: Essays on Oral Tradition and History* (Folkestone, 1980).

MINNS, E. H., *Scythians and Greeks: A Survey of Ancient History and Archaeology of the North Coast of the Euxine from the Danube to the Caucasus* (Cambridge, 1913).

MIRKOVIĆ, M., 'Die Ostgoten in Pannonien nach dem Jahre 455', *Zbornik Filozofskog fakulteta* (Belgrade), 10/1 (1966), 127–8.

MITREA, B., and PREDA, C., *Necropole din secolul al IV-lea e.n. în Muntenia* (Bucharest, 1966).

MÓCSY, A., review of Várady, *Das letzte Jahrhundert Pannoniens*: *Acta Archaeologica*, 23 (1971), 347–60.

—— *Pannonia and Upper Moesia* (London, 1974).

MOISL, H., 'Anglo-Saxon Royal Genealogies and Germanic Oral Tradition', *JMH* 7 (1981), 215–48.

MOMIGLIANO, A., 'Cassiodorus and the Italian Culture of His Time', *Proc. BA* 41 (1955), 207–45.

—— 'Gli Anicii e la storiografia latina del VI sec. d.C.', in *Secondo contributo alla storia degli studi classici* (Rome, 1960), 231–54.

—— (ed.), *The Conflict between Paganism and Christianity in the Fourth Century* (Oxford, 1963).

MOMMSEN, Th., *Römisches Staatsrecht*, 3 vols. (Leipzig, 1871–88).

—— 'Stilicho und Alarich', in *Gesammelte Schriften*, iv (Berlin, 1906), 516–30 (= *Hermes*, 38 (1903), 101–15).

—— 'Das römische Militärwesen seit Diocletian', in *Gesammelte Schriften*, vi (Berlin, 1910), 206–83.

MONGAIT, A. L., *Archaeology in the USSR*, trans. M. W. Thompson (Baltimore, Md., 1961).

MOORE, J. M., *The Manuscript Tradition of Polybius* (Cambridge, 1965).

MOORHEAD, J., 'Theoderic, Zeno and Odovaker', *Byzantinische Zeitschrift*, 77 (1984), 261–6.

—— 'The Decii under Theoderic', *Historia*, 33 (1984), 107–15.

MUSSET, L., *The Germanic Invasions: The Making of Europe AD 400–600* (London, 1975).

NAGY, T., 'The Last Century of Pannonia in the Judgement of a New Monograph', *Acta Antiqua*, 19 (1971), 299–345.

NIXON, C. E. V., *Pacatus: Panegyric to the Emperor Theodosius* (Liverpool, 1987).

O'DONNELL, J. J., *Cassiodorus* (California, 1979).

—— 'The Aims of Jordanes', *Historia*, 31 (1982), 223–40.

O'FLYNN, J. M., *Generalissimos of the Western Roman Empire* (Edmonton, Alta., 1983).

PALADE, V., 'Eléments géto-daces dans le site Sîntana de Mureş de Bîrlad-Valea Seacă', *Dacia*, NS 24 (1980), 223–53.

PATSCH, C., *Beiträge zur Völkerkunde von Südosteuropa*, iii. *Die Völkerbewegung an der unteren Donau in der Zeit von Diokletian bis Heraklius* (Vienna, 1928).

PAVAN, M., *La politica gotica di Teodosio nella pubblicistica del suo tempo* (Rome, 1964).

PIGANIOL, A., *L'Empire chrétien, 325–395*, 2nd edn. rev. A. Chastagnol (Paris, 1972).

POHL, W., 'Die Gepiden und die *Gentes* an der mittleren Donau nach dem Zerfall des Attilareiches', in Wolfram and Daim (edd.), *Die Völker*, 239–305.

POULTER, A. G., 'Town and Country in Moesia Inferior', in id. (ed.), *Ancient Bulgaria*, 74–118.

—— (ed.), *Ancient Bulgaria*, 2 vols. (Nottingham, 1983).

PREISIGKE, F., *Wörterbuch der griechischen Papyruskunde* (Berlin, 1921–71).

Prosopography of the Later Roman Empire: i. *AD 260–395*, ed. A. H. M. Jones, J. R. Martindale, and J. Morris (Cambridge, 1971); ii. *AD 395–527*, ed. J. R. Martindale (Cambridge, 1980).

RADAN, G. T. B., and LENGYEL, A. (edd.), *The Archaeology of Roman Pannonia* (Lexington, Ky., and Budapest, 1980).

REUTER, T. (ed. and trans.), *The Medieval Nobility* (Amsterdam, 1979).

REYDELLET, M., *La Royauté dans la littérature latine de Sidoine Apollinaire à Isidore de Séville* (Rome, 1981).

RICHARDS, A. I., 'Social Mechanisms for the Transfer of Political Rights in Some African Tribes', *JRAI* 19 (1960), 175–90.

ROSENFELD, H., 'Ost- und Westgoten', *Die Welt als Geschichte*, 17 (1957), 245–68.

ROSTOVZEFF, M. I., *Iranians and Greeks in South Russia* (Oxford, 1922).

RUBIN, Z., 'The Mediterranean and the Dilemma of the Roman Empire in Late Antiquity', *Mediterranean Historical Review*, 1 (1986), 13–62.

RUNKEL, F., *Die Schlacht bei Adrianopel* (Berlin, 1903).

RYBAKOV, B. A. (ed.), *Černjachovskaja kul' tura*, Materialy i issledovanija po arkheologii SSSR, 82 (Moscow, 1960).

SABBAH, G., *La Méthode d'Ammien Marcellin: Recherches sur la construction du discours historique dans les Res Gestae* (Paris, 1978).

STE. CROIX, G. E. M. DE, *The Class Struggle in the Ancient Greek World* (London, 1981).

SAWYER, P. H., and WOOD, I. N. (edd.), *Early Medieval Kingship* (Leeds, 1977).

SCHENK VON STAUFFENBERG, A. GRAF, *Das Imperium und die Völkerwanderung* (Munich, 1947).

SCHIRREN, C., *De ratione quae inter Iordanem et Cassiodorum intercedat commentatio* (Diss., Dorpat, 1858).

SCHLESINGER, W., 'Lord and Follower in Germanic Institutional History', in Cheyette (ed.), *Lordship and Community*, 64–99.

SCHMID, K., 'The Structure of the nobility in the earlier Middle Ages', in Reuter (ed.), *The Medieval Nobility*, 37–59.

SCHMIDT, L., *Geschichte der deutschen Stämme bis zum Ausgang der Völkerwanderung: Die Ostgermanen*, 2nd edn. (Munich, 1933).

SCHÖNFELD, M., *Wörterbuch der altgermanischen Personen- und Völkernamen* (Heidelberg, 1911).

SCHUTZ, H., *The Prehistory of Germanic Europe* (New Haven, Conn., 1983).

SCORPAN, C., *Limes Scythiae*, BAR, IS 88 (Oxford, 1980).

SCOTT, L. R., 'Aspar and the Burden of Barbarian Heritage', *Byzantine Studies*, 3 (1976), 59–69.

ŠČUKIN, M. B., 'Das Problem der Černjachow-Kultur in der sowjetischen archäologischen Literatur', *Zeitschrift für Archäologie*, 9 (1975), 25–41.

—— 'Current aspects of the Gothic Problem and the Cherniakhovo Culture', *Archeologičeskij sbornik*, 18 (1977), 79–92 (English summary 129–30).

SEECK, O., *Geschichte des Untergangs der antiken Welt*, v (Berlin, 1913).

—— *Regesten der Kaiser und Päpste für die Jahre 311 bis 476 n. Chr.: Vorarbeit zu einer Prosopographie der christlichen Kaiserzeit* (Stuttgart, 1919).

SHERWIN-WHITE, A. N., *The Roman Citizenship*, 2nd edn. (Oxford, 1973).

STAAB, F., 'Ostrogothic Geographers at the Court of Theoderic the Great: A Study of Some Sources of the Anonymous Cosmographer of Ravenna', *Viator*, 7 (1976), 27–58.

STALLKNECHT, B., *Untersuchungen zur römischen Außenpolitik in der Spätantike* (Bonn, 1969).

STEIN, E., 'Untersuchungen zur spätrömischen Verwaltungsgeschichte', *RhM*, NF 74 (1925), 347–94.

—— *Histoire du Bas-Empire*, ed. and trans. J. R. Palanque, 2 vols. (Paris, 1949, 1959).

STREITBERG, W., *Die gotische Bibel*, 2 vols. (Heidelberg, 1908, 1910).

SULIMIRSKI, T., *The Sarmatians* (London, 1970).

SYME, R., review of Klose, *Klientel-Randstaaten*: *JRS* 25 (1935), 95–9.

—— *Ammianus and the Historia Augusta* (Oxford, 1968).

—— *Emperors and Biography: Studies in the Historia Augusta* (Oxford, 1971).

—— *The Historia Augusta: A Call for Clarity* (Bonn, 1971).

SYMONOVIČ, E. A., 'La verrerie des monuments de la culture de Tcherniakhovo dans les regions du Dniepr et la Mer Noire', *SA* 1977/1, 176–86.

—— 'Chernyakhovo Culture and Sites of the Kiev and Kolochin types', *SA* 1983/1, 91–102.

TÄUBLER, E., *Imperium Romanum: Studien zur Entwicklungsgeschichte des römischen Reichs* (Leipzig, 1913).

TEILLET, S., *Des Goths à la nation gothique: Les origines de l'idée de nation en Occident du Ve au VIIe siècle* (Paris, 1984).

TEODOR, D. G., *The East Carpathian Area of Romania V–XI Centuries A.D.*, BAR, is 81 (Oxford, 1980).

THOMPSON, E. A., 'Olympiodorus of Thebes', *CQ* 38 (1944), 43–52.

—— 'The Isaurians under Theodosius II', *Hermathena*, 48 (1946), 18–31.

—— *The Historical Work of Ammianus Marcellinus* (Cambridge, 1947).

—— *A History of Attila and the Huns* (Oxford, 1948).

—— 'Constantine, Constantius II, and the Lower Danube Frontier', *Hermes*, 84 (1956), 372–81.

—— 'The Settlement of the Barbarians in Southern Gaul', *JRS* 46 (1956), 65–75.

—— 'The Conversion of the Visigoths to Catholicism', *Nottingham Medieval Studies*, 4 (1960), 4–35.

—— 'Christianity and the Northern Barbarians', in Momigliano (ed.), *The Conflict*, 56–78.

—— 'The Visigoths from Fritigern to Euric', *Historia*, 12 (1963), 105–26.

—— *The Early Germans* (Oxford, 1965).

—— *The Visigoths in the Time of Ulfila* (Oxford, 1966).

TODD, M., *The Northern Barbarians, 100 BC–AD 300* (London, 1975).

TUDOR, D., *Sucidava: Une cité daco-romaine byzantine en Dacie*, Coll. Latomus, 80 (Brussels, 1965).

—— *Les Ponts romains du bas Danube* (Bucharest, 1974).

VÁRADY, L., *Das letzte Jahrhundert Pannoniens: 376–476* (Amsterdam, 1969).

—— 'Jordanes-Studien', *Chiron*, 6 (1976), 441–87.

VASILIEV, A. A., *The Goths in the Crimea* (Cambridge, 1936).

VERA, D., 'La carriera di Virius Nicomachus Flavianus e la prefettura dell'Illirico Orientale nel IV sec. d.C.', *Athenaeum*, NS 61 (1983), 390–426.

VICKERS, M., 'The Late Roman Walls of Thessalonika', *Roman Frontier Studies*, 1969, 249–55.

—— 'A Note on the Byzantine Palace at Thessalonika', *PBSA* 66 (1971), 369–71.

—— 'Observations on the Octagon at Thessalonika', *JRS* 63 (1973), 111–20.

WAGNER, N., *Getica: Untersuchungen zum Leben des Jordanes und zur frühen Geschichte der Goten* (Berlin, 1967).

—— 'Bemerkungen zur Amalergenealogie', *Beiträge zur Namenforschung*, NS 14 (1979), 26–43.

WALLACE-HADRILL, J. M., 'The Blood-Feud of the Franks', *Bulletin of the John Rylands Library, Manchester*, 41/3 (1959) = *The Long-Haired Kings*, 121–47.

—— 'Gothia and Romania', *Bulletin of the John Rylands Library, Manchester*, 44/1 (1961) = *The Long-Haired Kings*, 25–48.

—— 'The Long-Haired Kings', in *The Long-Haired Kings*, 148–248.

—— *The Long-Haired Kings and Other Studies in Frankish History* (London, 1962).

—— *Early Germanic Kingship in England and on the Continent* (Oxford, 1971).

—— *The Barbarian West, 400–1000*, 4th edn. (London, 1985).

WENSKUS, R., *Stammesbildung und Verfassung: Das Werden der frühmittelalterlichen Gentes* (Cologne, 1961).

—— 'Amaler', *RgA* i. 246–8.

—— 'Balthen', *RgA* ii. 13–14.

WERNER, J., 'Dančeny und Brangstrup', *Bonner Jahrbücher*, 188 (1988), 241–86.

WERNER, K. F., 'Important Noble Families in the Kingdom of Charlemagne', in Reuter (ed.), *The Medieval Nobility*, 137–202.

WES, M. A., *Das Ende des Kaisertums im Westen des römischen Reichs* (The Hague, 1967).

WHITBY, L. M., 'The Long Walls of Constantinople', *Byzantion*, 55 (1985), 560–83.

—— *The Emperor Maurice and His Historian: Theophylact Simocatta on Persian and Balkan Warfare* (Oxford, 1988).

WILKES, J. J., *Dalmatia* (London, 1969).

WILLIS, R. G., *A State in the Making: Myth, History and Social Transformation in Pre-Colonial Ufipa* (Bloomington, Ind., 1981).

WOLFRAM, H., *Intitulatio 1: Lateinische Königs- und Fürstentitel bis zum Ende des 8. Jahrhunderts*, Mitteilungen des Instituts für österreichische Geschichtsforschung, Ergänzungsband 21 (Vienna, 1967).

—— 'Athanaric the Visigoth: Monarchy or Judgeship? A Study in Comparative History', *JMH* 1 (1975), 259–78.

—— 'Gotische Studien I–III', *MIÖG* 83 (1975), 1–32, 289–324, *MIÖG* 84 (1976), 239–61.

—— 'Die Schlacht von Adrianopel', Anzeiger der Östereichischen Akademie der Wissenschaften, phil.-hist. Kl. 114 (1977), 228–45.

—— 'Einige Überlegungen zur gotischen *Origo Gentis*', in H. Birnbaum *et al.* (edd.), *Studia linguistica Alexandro Vasilii filio Issatschenko oblata* (Lisse, 1978), 487–99.

—— 'Theogonie, Ethnogenese und ein kompromittierter Großvater im Stammbaum Theoderichs des Großen', in E. K. Jäschke and R. Wenskus (edd.), *Festschrift für Helmut Beumann* (Sigmaringen, 1979), 80–97.

—— *History of the Goths* (Berkeley, 1988).

—— and DAIM, F. (edd.), *Die Völker an der mittleren und unteren Donau im fünften und sechsten Jahrhundert*, Denkschriften der Östereichischen Akademie der Wissenschaften, phil.-hist. Kl. 145 (Vienna, 1980).

—— and POHL, W. (edd.), *Typen der Ethnogenese unter besonderer Berücksichtigung der Bayern*, Denkschriften der Österreichischen Akademie der Wissenschaften, phil.-hist. Kl. 201 (Vienna, 1990).

—— and SCHWARCZ, A. (edd.), *Anerkennung und Integration: Zu den wirtschaftlichen Grundlagen der Völkerwanderungszeit (400–600)*, Denkschriften der Österreichischen Akademie der Wissenschaften, phil.-hist. Kl. 193 (Vienna, 1988).

WOOD, I. N., 'Ethnicity and the Ethnogenesis of the Burgundians', in Wolfram and Pohl (edd.), *Typen der Ethnogenese*, 53–69.

WORMALD, P., '*Lex Scripta* and *Verbum Regis*: Legislation and Germanic Kingship, from Euric to Cnut', in Sawyer and Wood (edd.), *Early Medieval Kingship*, 105–38.

ZAHARIA, E., 'Données sur l'archéologie des IVe–XIe siècles sur le territoire de la Roumanie: La culture Bratei et la culture Dridu', *Dacia*, NS 15 (1971), 269–88.

ZASETSKAJA, I. B., 'The Role of the Huns in the Formation of the South Russian Steppelands in the Late Fourth and Fifth Centuries', *Archeologičeskij sbornik*, 18 (1977), 92–100.

ZEILLER, J., *Les Origines chrétiennes dans les provinces danubiennes de l'Empire romain*, Bibliothèque des études françaises d'Athènes et de Rome (Paris, 1918).

INDEX

Ablabius, historian of the Goths 5,
  18
  and Jordanes 34, 35
  and Gothic oral history 61–2,
    63–4, 328
  a Visigothic historian(?) 38, 64–5,
    319
  see also Cassiodorus and Jordanes
Achiulf, Amal ancestor 57
Adamantius, official of Zeno 245,
  281, 291
  conversation with Theoderic the
    Amal 292–3
Ad Salices, battle of 73, 144, 157,
  179, 315
Aeneas 21
Agaragantes, Sarmatian people 129
Agathias, historian 324
agriculture, and Goths 122, 158–60,
  217–18, 221–2, 258, 266
Akatziri, nomadic tribe 242
Alamanni 149, 335
  and Roman subjugation 114
Alans, nomadic tribe 84, 169, 185,
  220
  and Visigoths 322
  and the western Empire 340–1
Alaric, Gothic leader 15, 60, 81, 175,
  183, 190 n., 220, 258, 263, 315
  achievement of 224, 316–17
  supposed relationship to
    Athanaric 30–1
  and Balthi 11, 31–2, 311
  and Eutropius 204–6
  first invasion of Italy 206–9;
    Jordanes on 35
  and followers 205–6, 213–14, 216,
    217–18, 222–3, 313, 314
  in Illyricum 210–11, 212, 213, 314
  and imperial military
    command 199–201, 205, 216,
    222–3, 309

offers to Honorius 215–17, 222–3
  and Olympiodorus 75–6
  revolt of (395–7) 193–5, 201–4,
    326
  rise to prominence 195–8
  second invasion of Italy 214–16
  and Theoderic I 32
  and Theodosius 184–6, 187, 195–6
Alaric II, Visigothic king 59
Alaricoi, alternative name for
  Visigoths 22, 27
Alathar, Goth(?) in Roman
  service 302
Alatheus and Saphrax, leaders of
  Greuthungi 13, 84, 88, 100,
    122, 136, 148, 180, 192, 335–6
  attack on Pannonia 153, 156, 336,
    337, 339; Ammianus on 339–40
  disappearance of 29–30, 157–8,
    173–4, 179, 224
  and funerary inscription of bishop
    Amantius 312–13
  and polyethnicity 144–5, 325, 340
  supposed settlement in Pannonia
    of 334, 336, 339, 340, 341, 344
  see also Greuthungi
Alavivus, leader of the Tervingi 13,
  122, 132–3, 137
alliteration, *see* naming practice
Amal, legendary Gothic king 21,
  22–3, 63
Amal family, Ostrogothic ruling
  dynasty 19, 52, 56–60, 229, 232,
    251 n., 311–12
  and Balthi 59–60
  and Cassiodorus 19
  and Ermaneric 23–5
  historical reality of 19–27, 319
  Jordanes' account of 10, 19, 58
  modern views of 10–12, 317, 323
  naming practices of 31
  and oral tradition 7, 251